IN THEIR OWN WORDS, THE PERSONAL STORIES
OF AMERICA'S WORLD WAR II VETERANS

BEYOND VALOR

World War II's Ranger and Airborne Veterans Reveal the Heart of Combat

Patrick K. O'Donnell

A TOUCHSTONE BOOK
PUBLISHED BY SIMON & SCHUSTER
New York • London • Toronto • Sydney • Singapore

TOUCHSTONE
Rockefeller Center
1230 Avenue of the Americas
New York, NY 10020

First Touchstone Edition 2002
TOUCHSTONE and colophon are trademarks of
Simon & Schuster, Inc.
For information about special discounts for bulk purchases,
please contact Simon & Schuster Special Sales:
1-800-456-6798 or business@simonandschuster.com
Designed by Lisa Chovnick
Manufactured in the United States of America

10 9 8 7 6 5 4 3 2 1

The Library of Congress has cataloged the Free Press edition as follows:

O'Donnell, Patrick K.
    Beyond valor : World War II's Rangers and Airborne
    veterans reveal the heart of combat / Patrick K. O'Donnell.
        p. cm
    Includes bibliographical references and index.
    1. United States. Army—Parachute troops—History—
20th century. 2. United States. Army—Airborne troops—
History—20th century. 3. World War, 1939–1945—Commando
operations—United States. 4. World War, 1939–1945—
Regimental histories—United States. 5. World War, 1939–1945—
Campaigns—Western Front. I. Title.

D769.347.O36 2000
940.54'21—dc21   00-061049

ISBN 0-684-87384-2
    0-684-87385-0 (Pbk)

*This book is dedicated to the World War II Veterans
whose personal sacrifices made possible
the freedom we enjoy today*

CONTENTS

MAPS

INTRODUCTION

They shall grow not old, as we that are left grow old;

Age shall not weary them, nor the years condemn.

At the going down of the sun and in the morning

We will remember them.

—Laurence Binyon, "For the Fallen"

In 1939, just twenty-one years after the end of a war more destructive than anything humanity had dreamed possible, Europe began a war that proved even more horrific and more widespread, bringing all the intervening technological advances to bear against civilians and soldiers alike. In December 1941, the United States joined a battle in which the stakes were enormous and the outcome by no means certain. But the story of war is familiar. Less familiar is the very personal and human side of war, a side often purposely hidden from easy view: war as seen, heard, smelled, and felt in the day-to-day front-line experience of the combat soldier. This book tells that hidden story, through the oral and e-mail histories of America's elite infantry troops who fought in World War II's European theater—paratroopers, glidermen, Rangers, and the 1st Special Service Force.

Throughout the war, America's elite troops often played a key role in the war's most important battles, leading the breakthrough off bloody Omaha Beach; fighting to help save the Sicily and Salerno beachheads; cracking the stalemate on Italy's Winter Line; spearheading the invasion of Holland; turning the tide in the Battle of the Bulge; and making the final plunge into Germany. On the home front, the little-known sacrifices of America's first African-American paratroopers were an important step toward integration of the United States armed forces.

Underlying these important victories are the countless individual experiences of the men who made them possible. Their stories go far beyond casualties taken, hills won or lost. In nine years and over six hundred interviews, I found that beneath the war of official documents and carefully composed memoirs lies a bottled-up, buried version shielded even from family members, because many of the memories are too painful to discuss.

The hidden war includes the love that these men had for one another. Friendships and bonds forged in the heat of battle are so strong that they survive today. These men were willing without hesitation to lay down their lives for the men next to them. Time and again, they describe submergence of self within the spirit and pride of these elite units. Wartime experiences, however horrific, were often the most complete and most memorable in these soldiers' lives. Not one of the six hundred men I interviewed ever complained about his war experience, though most of these men were only temporary citizen soldiers, not professional military men.

As these men delve into their recollections, three major themes emerge: their hidden war, the story of the elite units, and the broader story of World War II's Western Front, since their war is largely a reflection in miniature of the European Theater. A bit of background on these units shows how they fit into the picture of the war.

The great armies of history all had their elite units, including Rome's Praetorian Guard, Napoleon's Imperial Guard, and the Civil War's Iron Brigade. As one historian stated, "In battle they were the ultimate reserve if things went wrong, and the exploiting force if things went right."[1] Nevertheless, America's elite ground troops in Europe in World War II—the Rangers, airborne troops, and the 1st Special Service Force—were different and special compared to the elites of other eras as well as to the regular troops of their own.

THE AIRBORNE

The largest elite unit was the airborne. The first practical plans for employing parachute troops in combat were conceived in the waning months of World War I by a U.S. aviation pioneer, Brigadier General William "Billy" Mitchell. Mitchell proposed outfitting troops of the 1st Division with a large number of machine guns and parachuting them behind the lines on the German-held fortress city of Metz. A ground attack would be coordinated with the paratrooper assault, known as a "vertical envelopment." But the war ended before Mitchell's innovative plans could be tried.

After the war, the concept of vertical envelopment was neglected in the United States. The Soviet Union, on the other hand, pushed ahead with large-scale airborne exercises in the 1930s. Germany took notice of the Soviet exercises and began building its own airborne program, made up of paratroopers and infantry that would ride in gliders.

With the outbreak of war, the Germans successfully used paratroopers to seize critical military objectives in Norway, the Netherlands, and Belgium, where a small band of paratroopers and glidermen seized Fort Eben Emael, which many had considered impregnable.

These victories spurred the creation of the U.S. airborne program, and a fifty-man test platoon was formed on June 25, 1940. On August 16, Lieutenant William Ryder became the first member of the test platoon to make a parachute jump. In one demonstration jump, the famous airborne phrase "Geronimo!" was born when Private Aubrey Eberhardt yelled it after exiting the plane.[2]

Over the next few months, parachute tactics and techniques were developed and techniques borrowed from Germany and Russia. The fledgling program expanded as volunteers formed the 501st Parachute Infantry Battalion. A special élan was part of a program that stressed the role of the individual and the necessity that he be capable of fighting against any opposition. As the parachute program evolved, men were taught that they were the best, a lesson reinforced by rigorous training that had a high washout rate. Beyond the rhetoric, the troops began demonstrating their worth by smashing previous army training records.

Parachute training culminated with the individual completing five parachute jumps. The successful trooper earned the right to wear a pair of small silver jump wings designed by a young airborne officer, William Yarborough. Special leather jump boots and jump suits were also issued to paratroopers. An unofficial ceremony known as the Prop Blast, in which new paratrooper officers drank a secret concoction and toasted their success, marked the completion of airborne training. The recipe was then encoded into an old M-94 signal-encrypting device with "Geronimo" as the key word.[3] The Prop Blast survives today.

The U.S. airborne program remained relatively small until a pivotal German airborne operation in May 1941, when the Germans captured the British-held island of Crete in the largest German airborne operation ever. Losses were enormous and Hitler was persuaded never again to launch a major airborne operation. Not privy to the magnitude of German losses, however, the U.S. command looked at Crete as a success and began building up its airborne.

The buildup was led by General George C. Marshall, who foresaw large-scale American airborne operations. A Provisional Parachute Group was created along with three new battalions. After the attack on Pearl Harbor drew the United States into the war in December 1941, six new airborne regiments, consisting of roughly two thousand paratroopers, were authorized, and most of the men were handpicked.

The first division to be activated was the 82nd, at eight thousand men about half the size of a normal army division. A cadre of men from the 82nd later was set aside for the formation of the 101st Airborne Division. The army would create three other airborne divisions, the 11th, 13th, and 17th, plus several independent battalions and regiments, such as the 509th, 517th, 550th, and 551st. The units serving in Europe eventually became part of the First Allied Airborne Army, formed in the summer of 1944.

GLIDERS

Gliders gradually became part of the airborne program, the glider program slowly taking shape in 1942. Nicknamed "canvas coffins," the flimsy gliders had plywood floors and a steel tubing frame covered with a canvas skin. The standard Waco CG-4A Glider had a troop capacity of fifteen men and the capability to carry a jeep or small artillery piece. The engineless glider was towed by a C-47 transport plane until over its landing zone, when the tow plane would release a three-hundred-foot nylon towrope, and the glider made what amounted to a crash landing. Gliding was a dangerous and thankless job. In training alone, from May 1943 to February 1944, there were 162 injuries and seventeen deaths due to glider accidents.[4] Many more men would die when their gliders cracked up on the landing zones of Europe.

Looked down upon by the paratroopers, the "glider riders" were not issued jump boots or wings and did not receive hazardous-duty pay like the troopers; nor were they volunteers. A poster designed by the glider troops that began circulating around the barracks explained their plight: "Join the Glider Troops! No Jump Pay. No Flight Pay. But Never A Dull Moment." Eventually, glider regiments were formed and attached to the airborne divisions, proving their mettle on many occasions. Not until July 1944 would the glidermen receive their well-earned hazardous-duty pay and the right to wear glider wings.

THE RANGERS

The Rangers, based on the British Commandos, were born in the summer of 1942. They were created to conduct deep-penetration raids behind enemy lines and amphibious raids on enemy-held coasts. General George C. Marshall was again the primary figure behind their formation as a means to get more

Americans involved in the fighting in Europe, sending Colonel Lucian Truscott to Britain to implement the creation of a commando-type organization.

At the time, two U.S. divisions were training in Northern Ireland: the 1st Armored Division and the 34th, a National Guard division. Three thousand men from the units volunteered, and 520 were selected for Ranger training. Major William O. Darby, an aide to the commanding general of U.S. Army Northern Ireland, was given command of the new unit.

Major General Dwight Eisenhower, who then headed the War Plans Division of the War Department, stated that the term "Commando" belonged to the British and suggested that Truscott find another title. The title "Ranger" was selected, Truscott later writing that the legendary actions of the colonial frontiersmen Rogers's Rangers in the French and Indian War were his inspiration.[5]

The Rangers received their training at the Commando Training Depot at Achnacarry Castle in Scotland, where Commando recruits carried logs on their shoulders, learned hand-to-hand fighting, climbed cliffs, practiced amphibious assaults, had countless long-distance speed marches, and became skilled on a variety of weapons. Rangers followed a similar regimen, even using live ammunition to make the training close to real combat. One obstacle that each trainee had to overcome was the famous "death slide," for which men climbed a forty-foot tree, then slid down a single rope that was suspended over a raging river, all while under fire.

Under Darby's inspired leadership, Darby's Rangers grew to three battalions (the 1st, 3rd, and 4th), yet they would always remain a provisional outfit. Another battalion, the 29th Ranger Battalion, was formed in December 1942, but after conducting several small raids, it was disbanded in September 1943. After successfully spearheading amphibious assaults in North Africa, Sicily, and Italy and participating in numerous battle campaigns, Darby's Rangers were tragically destroyed in a doomed attack on Cisterna. Before D-Day, two more battalions, the 2nd and 5th, which had been training Stateside, arrived in England to play a significant role in the invasion and remained fighting in Europe through the end of the war.

THE FORCE

Of all of the elite units, the 1st Special Service Force had the most bizarre beginning. The Force was the brainchild of Englishman Geoffrey Pyke, an inventor, propagandist, statistician, financier, economist, and foreign correspondent. Pyke rarely bathed, shaved, or cut his hair, did not like to wear socks, and dressed in a badly stained, crumpled suit. Pyke's personality matched his appearance.

But for all his shortcomings, Pyke was a brilliant man, and many of his ideas became the basis for important advances in a variety of disparate fields. Most important, Pyke had the ear of several powerful people, including Winston Churchill and Lord Louis Mountbatten, who introduced Pyke to General George Marshall.

One of Pyke's schemes was built on snow—the simple realization that, for nearly half the year, much of Europe was covered in snow. Pyke theorized that whatever country mastered the snow would control Europe. He devised the Plough Project, which involved parachuting men and "snow tanks" into snow-covered areas. The men would ride the tanks across the snow and destroy strategic Axis targets such as hydroelectric plants in Norway and Italy. Just how they would get out remained a mystery. Nevertheless, the plan captured the imagination of Churchill and Mountbatten, who convinced a weary Eisenhower and Marshall to move forward on the idea. Lieutenant Colonel Robert Frederick was given the task of creating the specialized unit for the Plough Project, surely a surprise to Frederick, who had written a War Department report against its feasibility.

To form the unit, calls were put out for lumberjacks, prospectors, game wardens, and forest rangers, basically all men who felt at home in the outdoors. The Canadians also wanted to be involved in the Plough Project, and with Churchill's backing, Canadians were integrated into the Force, which became known as the North Americans. All together, three six-hundred-man regiments were created along with a service unit. The Force hovered around twenty-three hundred men and was staffed with roughly equal numbers of Canadians and Americans, with Americans slowly coming to outnumber Canadians as time went by.[6]

The skills needed to carry out the Plough Project demanded rigorous training in a wide variety of disciplines. Men learned every available weapon, becoming masters of demolition, qualified skiers, and paratroopers, and learned how to drive and repair the Weasel, the tracked "snow vehicle" developed for the project. Hand-to-hand fighting was taught as well as personal initiative. Thus one of the toughest fighting units of the war was born, and the modern U.S. Special Forces, considered by many the elite of the elite, trace their lineage to this group.

By September 1942, political interest in the project had waned and the bombers needed to transport the Force to Norway were not available, so the Plough Project was canceled. Pressure began to mount to disband the unit, but Marshall felt the unit could be deployed elsewhere. It was first shipped to the Aleutian Islands, where it made a bloodless landing at Kiska Island in August 1943. Shortly after the operation, the North Americans were transferred to Italy, where they would play a decisive role, and from there they went on to southern France, where the unit was finally deactivated.

All of these men and units can rightfully claim to be among World War II's best, and I am humbled by the men I've had the pleasure to interview and know. Sadly, it is a generation dying at a rate of at least a thousand a day. But this book is not really for romantics or war buffs. It is for those who are unaware of these stories and of a hidden history that is quietly slipping away. My work has been that of preservation, done in gratitude for a generation that sacrificed so much.

CHAPTER ONE

DIEPPE

The world will little note nor long remember what we say here, but it can never forget what they did here. . . . It is rather for us to be here dedicated to the great task remaining before us—that from these honored dead we take increased devotion to that cause for which they gave the last full measure of devotion.

—President Abraham Lincoln,
The Gettysburg Address

FOREVER YOUNG:
Howard Henry / Edwin Loustalot / Joseph Randall

The lives of these three American men, none older than twenty-three years, are frozen in time, etched into a bronze plaque that quietly marks the place where American ground soldiers first sacrificed their futures in Nazi-occupied Europe. They are not unlike countless other American lives that have been forgotten in a war that took place a little over half a century ago. But Henry, Loustalot, and Randall were part of a group of fifty Rangers who participated in Operation JUBILEE, better known as the Dieppe Raid.

On the moonlit night of August 18, 1942, a flotilla carrying 6,086 soldiers set sail from England for the French port and resort town of Dieppe. The raid had several objectives: to gather data on German coastal defenses to determine their strength for the eventual invasion of Europe; to give a large number of troops combat experience; and to force the Luftwaffe into an air battle under conditions favorable to the allied forces.[1]

In August, fifty Rangers—five officers and forty-five enlisted men—had been selected to take part in the raid.[2] The raid itself took place on a roughly ten-mile front near Dieppe, which is about 125 miles northeast of the Normandy landings. It involved three major attacks. The centerpiece of the raid was a frontal attack on Dieppe led by nearly five thousand troops from the Canadian 2nd Division and a handful of Rangers. Beforehand, a force of about one thousand British Commandos, a few French Commandos, and forty-four Rangers attacked the town's flanks.

The Commandos and Rangers had the mission of destroying the main German batteries located on each flank surrounding Dieppe; their destruction before the main assault on Dieppe took place was critical. Britain's No. 3 Commando and forty Rangers were given the task of destroying a German battery of 5.9-inch guns, called the Goebbels Battery by the British, on the eastern flank of Dieppe near the town of Berneval. On the western flank of Dieppe, four Rangers accompanied No. 4 Commando, assigned to land on the beaches near Varengeville and destroy several guns called the Hess Battery. The remaining six Rangers were integrated into the Canadian 2nd Division, which led the frontal assault on Dieppe.[3]

Paratroopers were also included in the original plan for the Dieppe operation. The only American airborne unit in Europe at the time was the 2nd Battalion of the 503rd Parachute Infantry Battalion. The unit was a natural candidate for the job.[4] After-action reports state that the airborne assault was scrapped because the moon and tide conditions were not favorable for both an amphibious and an airborne assault. At the time, with radar technology for guiding planes to a drop zone still under development, airborne assaults were significantly dependent on weather conditions.

At 6:30 P.M., the operation began as planned. The raiding flotilla crossed the seventy-mile stretch of the English Channel on its way to France. But by 3:46 A.M., German flares illuminated the night, blowing the flotilla's cover. A convoy of German torpedo boats escorting a German tanker inadvertently intercepted part of the assault force, sinking several Allied landing craft and alerting the German defenses around Dieppe.

After losing several landing craft to the German convoy, No. 3 Commando landed near Berneval, designated Yellow Beach 1. Only ninety-six Commandos and four Rangers made it ashore, where they were pinned down for the next three hours by machine gun and grenade fire. In the melee, it is likely that Lieutenant Edwin Loustalot was the first American in-

The Dieppe Raid—Aug. 19, 1942

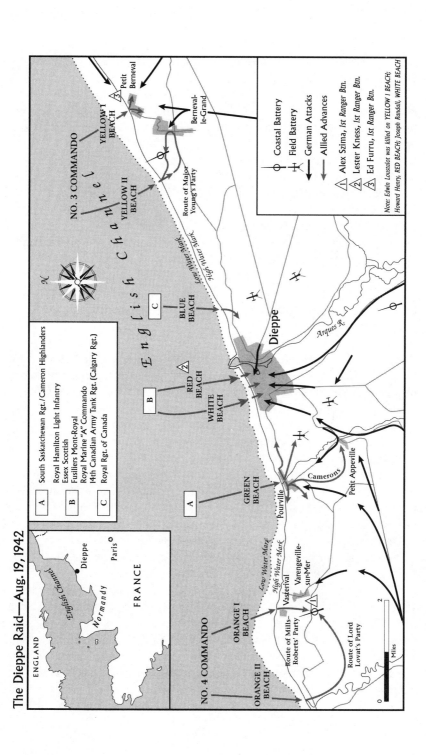

ENGLAND

English Channel

Normandy

Dieppe

Paris ✪

FRANCE

A	South Saskatchewan Rgt./Cameron Highlanders
	Royal Hamilton Light Infantry
B	Essex Scottish
	Fusiliers Mont-Royal
	Royal Marine "A" Commando
C	14th Canadian Army Tank Rgt. (Calgary Rgt.)
	Royal Rgt. of Canada

ORANGE II BEACH

NO. 4 COMMANDO

ORANGE I BEACH

Route of Mills-Roberts' Party

Route of Lord Lovat's Party

Vasterival

Varengeville-sur-Mer

Low Water Mark
High Water Mark

Pourville

GREEN BEACH

A

Camerons

Petit Appeville

Dieppe

Arques R.

WHITE BEACH

RED BEACH

B

2

BLUE BEACH

C

English Channel

Low Water Mark
High Water Mark

Route of Major Young's Party

YELLOW II BEACH

YELLOW I BEACH

NO. 3 COMMANDO

3

Petit Berneval

Berneval-le-Grand

N

Coastal Battery
Field Battery
German Attacks
Allied Advances

1 Alex Szima, 1st Ranger Btn.
2 Lester Kness, 1st Ranger Btn.
3 Ed Furru, 1st Ranger Btn.

Note: Edwin Loustalot was killed on YELLOW 1 BEACH;
Howard Henry, RED BEACH; Joseph Randall, WHITE BEACH

Miles
0   1   2

fantryman killed in the European Theater, as he led a charge to destroy a German machine gun nest.[5]

The only positive development on Yellow Beach came when eighteen No. 3 Commandos landed on Yellow Beach II, scaled a gully filled with barbed wire, and made their way to the Goebbels Battery's 5.9-inch guns. After taking up positions near the guns, the Commandos were able to pin down the German gunners with rifle fire, preventing the German guns from firing against the main Canadian force attacking Dieppe itself.

Meanwhile, on the right flank of Dieppe, No. 4 Commando was coming ashore on the beaches near Varengeville. The landing areas were designated Orange Beach I and II. No. 4 Commando was split into two groups. At 4:53 A.M., the first group, led by Commando Major Derek Mills-Roberts, landed on Orange Beach I. Fourteen hundred yards down shore, two Rangers and 178 Commandos landed on Orange Beach II. This group was led by Lieutenant Colonel Lord Shimi Lovat, a colorful character who occasionally wore tartan pants and carried a hunting rifle and horn. He and his group would hit the guns from the rear.

Two Rangers accompanied Mills-Roberts's Commandos as they traversed a gully filled with barbed wire. After cleaning out several villas that contained enemy troops, the Mills-Roberts group established a defense perimeter near the Hess Battery and proceeded to snipe at the Germans manning the guns. Soon Mills-Roberts's men were joined by Lord Lovat's group, which had fought its way to them from Orange Beach II. Along the way, two Rangers assigned to Lovat's group distinguished themselves by destroying a machine gun nest. Following a British Hurricane airstrike on the battery of 15-cm guns, both groups fixed bayonets and, on a signal from Lovat's hunting horn, assaulted the battery. With great courage they bayoneted, bombed, and shot the Germans who manned the guns. Only four German prisoners were taken.[6] After destroying the guns, both groups made their way back to the beach, where they were picked up by British navy landing craft at 7:30 A.M. To this day, the mission executed by No. 4 Commando is considered a model commando raid.

The frontal attack on Dieppe, on the other hand, was a disaster. Casualties in the Canadian units were enormous. The Royal Regiment of Canada took 97 percent casualties, and the other Canadian units did not fare much better. Of the six Rangers who were part of the Canadian force, Lieutenant Joseph Randall was killed by a hail of bullets at water's edge, and T-4 (Technician Fourth Grade) Howard Henry is believed to have met a similar fate along with his Canadian demolition team, which was cut down on Red Beach.[7] Ranger Lloyd Church suffered a head wound and was captured by the Germans. The three remaining Rangers assigned to the Canadians were fortunate to escape with their lives.

After what was left of the raiding force returned to England, the Allied spin machine highlighted the "lessons learned" from the raid while playing down the appalling losses and battlefield results. Two months later, with a core group of men having gained combat experience from the raid, the 1st Ranger Battalion was on ships bound for Operation TORCH, the Allied invasion of North Africa.

ROBERT SLAUGHTER

29th Ranger Battalion[8]

Rangers and airborne troops endured some of the most arduous training in the world. Although Robert Slaughter's training took place after the Dieppe Raid, it was the same regimen that all Rangers endured at the Commando School in Achnacarry, Scotland.

We were a proud group. We wanted to be the best, and we felt that we were. We wanted to show the British—they sort of challenged us. Most of our instructors were veterans of the Dieppe Raid and were from No. 4 Commando. We also had a captain from the Black Watch, and he was a son of a bitch. He was a very strict disciplinarian. He was an Empire soldier stationed in India or somewhere: well-educated fellow but tough as nails. He was the guy who either made or broke people, and he would send back people every day. The washout rate was high. We had hundreds of people volunteer, but less than two hundred made the first cut. Even the slightest slip-up and you were out.

I remember one day when we made a thirty-seven-mile speed march. We just got issued new paratrooper boots. After the march I had blisters all over my feet. My feet were just bloody and raw. But I wouldn't fall out. I was determined to finish up this thing. The next day we had to make another thirty-mile hike. At the time we were testing K rations. Every day they would weigh us before and after the march. We'd average about twenty-five miles, and we did this for ten days. I went from 205 down to about 176; it was the most grueling thing that I ever experienced in my life. When we finally got back to the base camp and finished training, my stomach had shrunk so much, they had this huge breakfast but I couldn't eat it. It took me two days to get adjusted.

The training toughened us. It made us proud. You'd rather die than let your buddy down. That's the way it affected me. It built physical and mental toughness.

[On a typical day] we'd get up really early in the morning, around five o'clock. Before breakfast we'd fall out. First we'd have reveille and roll call and then we'd strip down to the waist and we'd do a log exercise. It was supposed to build your muscles up and make you strong. We'd have several guys who would have a log the size of a telephone pole, and we'd throw it high up in the air and catch it. It gave you a little bit of weight training, something we didn't have in those days. It would make you real hungry for breakfast, but the food was horrible. After breakfast we'd do a speed march, hit the obstacle course or firing range. Every single day we did hand-to-hand combat drills.

One of our instructors was a British middleweight wrestling champion. This instructor weighed about 165 pounds or less, and we had this big Swede whose first name was Jake, he was from Minnesota, a big guy. [The instructor] was demonstrating how to parry a bayonet, how to take a rifle away from somebody. He said, "All right, one of you come out and I'll demonstrate it with you." So we pushed Jake out; he was our pride and joy. He was a huge monster. He went out there with his rifle and bayonet, and the sergeant said, "All right, come at me!" Jake kind of went in halfheartedly, and the sergeant said, "No, no. I want you to come at me like you're gonna kill me." Jake said, "Really?" And the sergeant said, "Yeah." Jake charged, and the next thing I know, Jake is on his back and the sergeant had the rifle in his hands and the bayonet pointed at his throat.

They had obstacle courses that you had to do double time all the way that had targets that would pop up and you had to shoot at the targets. You went in as squads, and the entire squad had to finish the course. If during the course of the drill one of the drill sergeants declared one of the men a casualty, we had to carry the man all the way around the course. We had to climb walls, cross rivers, and they would rate us. If the squad didn't make it in the prescribed time you'd have to run on Sunday, which was a day off.

We had all kinds of exercises, including living off the land without food or water. They dropped us off somewhere and they gave us a compass and a map. There were no buildings or anything, nothing to zero in on. We had to find our way back to a specific location. We also had amphibious training that included them firing live ammunition [near us] to make it realistic.

ALEX SZIMA

1st Ranger Battalion

On the western flank of Dieppe, No. 4 Commando along with Alex Szima and a handful of other Rangers were tasked with destroying artillery positions called the Hess Battery. The guns had to be destroyed for the main assault on Dieppe to have any chance of success. For the raid, No. 4 Commando was split into two groups. Group I, led by Commando Major Derek Mills-Roberts with seventy Commandos and two Rangers, included Sergeant Szima.

There were dead all up and down the trail. Every time a guy went up he had to bring down a body. I was told, "Sergeant Szima, police up the trail." By the time my war came to an end, it was sort of a relief. After taking the bodies down, I was given an opportunity to eat. I asked the cook if he could spare any coffee, and I put that tin cup to my lips. I couldn't drink it—I was shaking so bad. I couldn't put my lip to the canteen cup. I tried three or four times. I was just quivering. So I just did without it. At that point I was starting to crack up. If I wasn't careful I would have cracked up. I was in charge of tagging and transporting the bodies back to graves registration. There was so many of those dead bodies around, and at that point in time in Italy they said no more blankets for them. When we loaded them into trucks you've got to put the feet out and not have the heads near the tailgates, since you're going through towns. That was a whole different war from when I first started out at Dieppe.

[Szima recalls No. 4 Commando's actions at the Hess Battery.] Everybody stood up and started firing at the main guns. I fired a couple of clips at the flak tower and the ack-ack gun. Somebody said change positions, and rifle fire was coming down at us about one hundred yards to my right.

When a bullet goes by you, the air current will suck by, "whoosh, whoosh," like that. You hear the crack. You know the ones that are on you. I saw one of the Germans on top of the barn. I stood up and fired eight rounds and picked off every other slate shingle. Bang! Bang! Bang! Bang! Bang! Bang! Bang! Bang! The next thing I heard was Mr. Coulson saying, "Yank, don't fire that way. Lord Lovat will be coming down that way!" I saw at least four more Germans about 150 yards on the second-floor roof of one of the houses, and I put two clips into them. I found out later that they were knocked off.

Commando officers Webb and Coulson (in the foreground) and Lord Lovat (pointing), after returning from the Dieppe Raid. (Photo courtesy E. W. Jones)

This brings up a funny incident. Before we came to Dieppe, I was on the shooting range at Portland, England, and I had an unusual experience. While on the range, we were all ordered to fire five rounds into the nearest row of targets. I had an M-1 rifle and an eight-inch grouping of five rounds. Mills-Roberts and everybody else that was firing rushed down to inspect their own targets. [There was no phone communication with the pit area.] The target keeper said, "You got an eight-inch group, probably a record." When I returned to the line, I was greeted by Mills-Roberts, who said, "Are you a member of the U.S. Army Rifle Team?" I replied, "No, sir, I'm a bartender from Dayton, Ohio."

We all continued firing at the coastal gun position, and then heard this "whine, whine, ba ba dummm." It was a bagpiper. I'm not kidding [laughs]. So here comes this bagpiper, and Coulson told everybody to keep firing on the gun position. So you had to keep firing on the gun position while the bagpipes were going. Lovat's men came in and knocked out the guns. Lovat wore tartan pants, a sweater, and carried a deer rifle.

Several Commandos were killed or wounded around the barn, and I was looking for the other Ranger that I went in with, Frank Koons, because at this time I was really low on ammo, having fired my entire belt and four clips from the bandoliers. I waited in a rear-guard position as the Commandos

No. 4 Commando departs from Dieppe, France, on their return to England. Smoke (in the background) was used to screen their return trip. (Photo courtesy E. W. Jones)

started to withdraw as planned. Several Commandos were wounded, and we took the doors off houses and put the wounded men on the doors. Four German prisoners carried some of wounded men. They made the trek back [to the beach].

The wounded were helped slowly up the road. Our position was at a farmhouse gate which was connected to a high hedgerow. The Boyes Antitank Rifle gunner took a position on the left side of the road facing the demolished guns. We had our back to the withdrawing Commandos. I heard footsteps on the other side of the hedgerow. Logically I knew it had to be Germans. I took a position at the gate and out came Corporal Koons. I ordered him up the road to catch up with the slowly withdrawing Commandos. After several minutes, I ran over to the gun [antitank rifle] and picked up the front handle and we both ran to the first bend in the road. We were alone and the last men on the road. There were over a hundred dead all around us. As I looked around I was waiting for one of them to get up and start firing. We took up our second position and saw a truckload of German infantry come to the position we had just vacated. I told the gunner if they come past that point we fire. A man got out and went into the gate and returned to the truck. I said, "Fire!" He hit the truck and it turned into a pile of dust. I stood up and fired eight rounds. We took off and I grabbed the front end of the rifle again and we dashed to the next position, which was the next bend in the road. He passed me on the left side and we both went down. Rifle fire was zipping through the tree leaves. We reached the perimeter and the Commando gave the password, which I can honestly say I had forgotten.

LESTER KNESS

1st Ranger Battalion

Like most original members of Darby's Rangers, Lester Kness had a combat record that included spearheading four D-Day amphibious assaults and participation in six battle campaigns. He earned a Silver Star from a unit that did not believe in awards, where men were expected to perform above and beyond the call of duty. Lester Kness was a soldier's soldier who rose through the ranks as an enlisted man to eventually command a company and later became battalion operations officer. Here he recalls the scene on Dieppe's beaches.

I've got a lot of friends, a lot of loving among this group. There isn't any reason for it other than the truth that exists between us. There's a lot of truth in feeling.

There's a love called agape; it's something that is very similar. It's love because of sacrifice, because of the willingness to lay down your life for another. We feel it rather than know it. If you ask [Rangers] what they know, you get a lot of hogwash army stories and this and that, but if you ask them how they feel, you might get an inkling that they feel a love for one another. I just watched two of my old sergeants meet, and they stood there and hugged each other. It wasn't a good-fellowship hug, it was an "I love you" hug; there's a difference.

[During the Dieppe Raid] the shells went right through the ship. We were about five miles north of Dieppe on our way to a coastal battery. At the time I was a staff sergeant and was in second command of a British Commando squad. We were just moved up on deck and were all carrying mortar ammunition, bangalore torpedoes, and so forth. We were standing on deck, and the command craft was running alongside of us. I heard one of the navy men shout out colors—I forget what they were, blue, something, and such and such.

Meanwhile, shells that looked like little yellow balls were floating through the air, just beautiful, it was like the Fourth of July. I looked around and I was the only one standing there; everybody else had gone for cover. So I dropped the mortar ammo I was carrying and jumped into a gun turret on the ship. I was on the starboard side of the ship when the fire [ship's gunfire] was going out towards the left. The ship wasn't very wide because the gun covered both sides.

Several German boats attacked the ship, and we assumed it was a German E-boat [a high-speed motorboat with torpedoes similar to an American PT boat]. After a short gun battle, our little flagship sank the German E-boat.

I crawled out of the turret. About that time, up through the scuttle hole in front of me, which went down into the galley, came a bucket, and the British sergeant hollered, "Come on, Yank, help me put this fire out." So I got up, grabbed the bucket, handed it to him, and he threw it on the fire right off the left of the gun turret. He threw it on the fire and the bucket was full of fish, silver kippers. He said, "Blimey, look at these fooking kippers!" I passed the bucket back down and another bucket came up and we threw water on the fire until we got it out. That was salvation to me because I got busy doing something and got over my fright.

After we sank that E-boat, everybody got back and took their gear. The landing craft couldn't find us in the dark—it lost us. [The craft] had to get away, too. They didn't stand a chance. They didn't have anything to fight with, so they had to run. Consequently, we never had any landing craft to get to shore on. We rode around for about an hour until it started getting to daylight. Checking in and out, I'd try to find out what was going on.

We were headed in down to Dieppe. Our ship was down to Dieppe to pick up people off the beach. The German planes and American planes were just like flies on the milk house wall above us. There were bombs falling, artillery coming in from shore, the ships were firing, there was just something going on all the time. It was quite a picture. I'd never seen anything like it before or ever since.

It was daylight at this time. Several German planes went across the back of our ship. One in particular came across and was firing. He came across the back of our boat, and the British officer said he wouldn't stand up there like that. Two boys got hit, one shell and went through them both. They were killed instantly.

In the afternoon we moved the ship down by the shore. We picked up German pilots, British pilots, and American pilots. We must have had forty men on the ship. I could see the tanks on shore. I could see the men trying to get out. It was a disaster. The air was just full of flames, and the ships were firing. There were a lot of German aircraft. I couldn't see the German gun emplacements on shore or any machine gun fire or that nature. All I could see were the fellows running. I saw the litter bearers on the beach and the tanks and the people laying around them that had been killed. There wasn't any way they could escape. Many of the tanks were hit. Men were laying there, running, swimming. We lost a guy named Henry. He was killed there. It was just before dark when they started to move back across the Channel.

EDWIN FURRU

1ˢᵗ Ranger Battalion

Forty Rangers were integrated into No. 3 Commando assigned to Yellow Beach I and the four-gun group of 5.9-inch guns called the Goebbels Battery just east of Dieppe near Berneval. Before most of the task force could land, they encountered a German convoy seven miles offshore. Only five landing craft from the original task force landed on Yellow Beach I at Berneval, including Edwin Furru and three other Rangers.

It looked like the Fourth of July. Rockets and shells were going off everywhere, lighting up the entire sky. There were German planes flying overhead, and I saw part of a German E-boat go by. I almost took a shot at it but figured I would give our position away, and plus I didn't think I had much of a chance of hitting it anyway.

The E-boat attack caused many of the landing craft to disperse, but mine was on course toward the beach. We just pulled up on the beach. It was no sweat. So we went up towards this ravine that was covered with barbed wire. Somebody cut the wire with wire cutters and we went up the side of the ravine and kept walking. I remember passing a machine gun pillbox that wasn't occupied.

We walked through a garden behind a small cottage. So we cut across the garden and crossed a road. We came to a big building, a hotel or something. We waited there while a scout checked to see if the coast was clear. There was nobody up there, so we went up. We got up near the building and went along there for a ways and found a trail. We got in a firefight, and the fire was very heavy, and the Commandos that I was with, maybe a dozen men, decided that we should turn back.

I was the last man in our group. As we made our way back down toward the beach I came across two Commandos that were wounded and they said, "Yank, get out of here before you get shot!" I went a little further and I saw a body in a GI uniform. I went over to see who it was and it was Lieutenant Loustalot. He had been shot in the chest or gut. I noticed that the field glasses that he was wearing around his neck had the eyepiece shot off.

I continued to go down the ravine back to the beach. I felt something go by my neck and saw a black dot. The Germans were shooting what seemed to be a captured French 75. I thought it was a 75 because I was in an artillery unit prior to joining the Rangers and we were equipped with old French 75s when we were on maneuvers in Louisiana.

Anyhow, I went on down the ravine and met Sergeant Jacobson. I had a cigarette with him and we continued to make our way down towards the beach and went in a small cave that was on the side of the cliff. About half a dozen men were hiding in this shallow cave near the beach. We sat there for a while waiting for the boats to come back.

Meanwhile, we heard a lot of fire around us. We waited for a while and a squad of Germans came down to the beach. All they would have had to do was throw a few grenades into the cave and that would have been it. So we gave up.

I suppose we could have taken some of them out, but the Germans rounded us up and put us into trucks. We were in a convoy of trucks heading out of town. I heard a "brrrr" "brrrr" "brrrr" noise and I looked up and saw the telephone wires parting and coming down on the ground. I knew what was happening then. All of a sudden a Spitfire [British fighter] went zipping by. I didn't think a truck could burn that fast. So I hit the latch on the door and fell out. The guy beside me fell out and took off. I went over to the side of the road and took cover. When I thought it was over, I went back over to the burning truck and tried to pull one of the other men out. I went down to grab hold of him—I saw he didn't have any legs. I figured he was dead or would be dead pretty soon.

Anyway, Mother Nature called and I had to take a crap. As I was bending down I noticed there were several holes in my pants and shirt and I felt tingling in my knee. It felt like I hit my crazy bone. I looked down and there was a large piece of shrapnel in my knee. I figured that I didn't want to start crawling around with that, since the shrapnel could have chewed the hell out of it, so I just thought that I would wait for the Germans and hope to get to a hospital. Not long after that a group of German officers came by in a car and put me in the back seat and took me to a hospital. It's funny I can't remember anything from the time I was in the car with the German officers till I made it to the hospital.

CHAPTER TWO

TORCH: The Invasion of North Africa

It's the idea that we all have value, you and me,

We're worth something more than the dirt.

What we're fighting for, in the end, is each other.

—Joshua Lawrence Chamberlain[1]

Once the Allies had established the "Germany First" policy (as opposed to concentrating their resources against Japan), high-level planning discussions focused on how and when to liberate Europe. A direct assault across the English Channel into France was the inevitable path, and a plan code-named SLEDGEHAMMER was drawn up to put an invasion force on the Continent in 1942. SLEDGEHAMMER would then be followed up by an all-out assault known as ROUNDUP. The Americans favored an early cross-Channel attack, but the resources were not available for a full-scale invasion of Europe in 1942. The British instead persuaded the Americans to land forces in North Africa to relieve the British Eighth Army, which had been battling the Italians and Rommel's Afrika Korps.[2]

Code-named TORCH, the invasion of North Africa was a trident-shaped attack that landed three large amphibious task forces along the sprawling French North African coast. Both the Rangers and paratroopers would spearhead the center prong of the trident at Oran in Algeria.

By November 1942, however, America's airborne, which included paratroopers and glidermen, was barely two years old, and the force's structure and concept were still evolving.[3] The only American parachute unit in England that could take part in TORCH was the 2nd Battalion of the 503rd Parachute Infantry Regiment, or 2/503; just before TORCH, it was renamed the 509th Parachute Infantry Battalion.[4]

On the evening of November 7, 1942, the 509th left England in thirty-nine C-47s and began the fifteen-hundred-mile journey to seize airfields outside Oran, Algeria. French North Africa was still controlled by the Vichy French, and at the time of the invasion it was not known whether the French would fight or surrender. To cover either contingency, two airborne plans were devised: Plan Peace and Plan War. If the French decided to resist the Allies, Plan War would be implemented and the Tafaraoui and La Sénia airfields would be seized in a parachute night jump. If the French cooperated with the landings, Plan Peace would be exercised and the 509th would air land at La Sénia airfield with the assistance of the French.

Just before the long flight to North Africa, the paratroopers were informed that Plan Peace was in effect and a peaceful landing at La Sénia airfield was anticipated. During the flight over Spain, strong headwinds began scattering the planes from their formations and the planes did not pick up homing signals from a British ship that was to guide them to North Africa. By dawn on November 8, the thirty-nine C-47s were scattered from Spanish Morocco to points east of Oran, and instead of a peaceful reception, the French were resisting the landings. As some of the lead planes began their descent on La Sénia airfield, they came under intense antiaircraft fire. The pilots were able to avoid the airfield and land the planes on a dry lake bed west of Oran.[5]

Meanwhile, six planes, including the one that was carrying the 509th's commander, Lieutenant Colonel Edson Raff, were heading toward the Tafaraoui airfield drop zone. As they approached the airfield, Raff noticed a column of tanks and ordered his men to jump and attack the column. Upon reaching the ground, the soldiers quickly realized that the vehicles were American tanks moving inland from the invasion beaches.

Eventually, Raff's men reached the other planes that had landed at the dry lake bed of Sebkra, it was decided to load as many men as possible into three planes that had enough fuel to make it to Tafaraoui airfield. While en route to Tafaraoui, the planes were attacked by French Dewoitine fighter planes and forced to make an emergency landing; several men were killed by the fighters and fifteen were wounded. Eventually, the paratroopers reached both airfields and were greeted by American ground troops who had secured them earlier in the day.

The 1st Ranger Battalion's mission to seize forts outside Oran at Arzew Harbor, on the other hand, went off without a hitch. The Rangers were commanded by Lieutenant Colonel William O. Darby and were part of the

Central Task Force that landed at Oran, consisting of the 1st Infantry Division and the combat command for the 1st Armored Division and the Rangers. The Central Task Force had to contend with approximately sixteen thousand Vichy French troops and a city defended by several forts bristling with more than fifty guns.[6] The Rangers were to spearhead the Central Task Force's attack, seizing the main coastal guns on the high ground above Arzew, capturing Fort de la Pointe at the northeast corner of the harbor, and capturing part of Arzew and another fort above the town.

Moving ashore around 1:00 A.M. November 8, the first group of Rangers disembarked from a landing craft and seized its objectives. Surprise was complete; Fort de la Pointe fell with little firing, and men were dispatched to secure the harbor.

Meanwhile, the rest of the Central Task Force began entering Arzew and the beaches east of the city, heading inland to Oran. Over the next few days the Rangers helped to mop up resistance in the towns around Arzew. It would not be the last time that the Rangers were misused as regular ground troops rather than for their designated role of spearheading invasions or launching penetration raids deep behind enemy lines.

By November 12, 1942, the fighting west of Algeria had ended, and the Allies began moving to the Axis stronghold of Tunisia. Only eight days after its first airborne operation, the 509th was called upon again to make another jump and capture the Youks-les-Bains airfield on the Tunisian border.

Remarkably, the battalion was able to assemble most of its personnel from scattered positions all over the Oran and Algiers area. Without photographs or terrain models, the paratroopers boarded C-47 transports and flew to the French airfield. At approximately 10:30 A.M. November 15, the battalion jumped on Youks-les-Bains and landed on top of the French 3rd Zouave Regiment, which was dug in around the field with machine guns. Fortunately, neither side fired a shot, and after a conference with Colonel Raff, the French commander, Colonel Albert Berges, agreed to cooperate, and the vital airfield was in Allied hands.

Over the next two months, the paratroopers were at the edge of Allied lines in Tunisia. Colonel Raff, with the help of a tank destroyer unit and the French, organized the Tunisian Task Force, which essentially operated like the Confederate "foot cavalry" during Stonewall Jackson's legendary Shenandoah Valley campaign. Raff's force commandeered buses and anything else that was motorized and moved into the Algerian border town of Tebessa and then audaciously into Gafsa. The unit's first major engagement was at Faïd Pass, where the force captured the pass and more than 130 Germans and Italians.[7] Raff's presence energized the French and even caught the eye of General

Eisenhower, who wrote to General Marshall to praise a "small mixed detachment of Americans commanded by Colonel Raff, who has done a magnificent piece of work. . . . He has vastly raised the morale of French troops and we have derived untold benefit from the coverage we have thus secured."[8]

Then, on December 26, 1942, the 509th was handed an impossible mission. Thirty-one men were to jump and blow up a railroad bridge at El Djem that was crucial to the Axis supply lines. After several failed attempts to bomb the bridge, the Allied Force Headquarters determined it was best taken out by a small group of paratroopers—who would have little chance of returning alive. Raff caught wind of the mission and tried to get it canceled, but on the night of December 26, the thirty-one men took off in three C-47s for their hopeless goal. The mission failed, as Raff predicted, and only seven men returned to the Allied lines.[9]

Several weeks after El Djem, the members of the Tunisian Task Force melted back into their original units, which were now coming up into Tunisia. The 509th was taken off the line and moved to Oujda, French Morocco, where it was placed in a reserve position for the rest of the North African campaign and was eventually joined by America's first airborne division, the 82nd Airborne, which arrived in May 1943.

The Germans reacted to the Allied invasion by pouring troops into Tunisia, and the desert war in Tunisia became fluid, with the forces of both sides spread out over large distances. On the Axis side, the Italians manned most of the outposts while the Germans acted as a mobile reserve force that emerged in hot spots. Raids were the way to keep the Axis off balance, so on February 3, 1943, the Rangers were loaded into C-47 transports in Oran and flown to Youks-les-Bains for a raid on a remote Italian outpost at Sened Station.

Seven days after arriving at Youks-les-Bains, A, E, and F companies were put on trucks and dropped off twelve miles from the Italian outpost. That night the Rangers crept into position about four miles from the outpost, where they concealed themselves with shelter-halves and brush and waited to attack on the night of February 11–12. At 11:00 P.M., with bayonets fixed, the Rangers struck, killing all but eleven men from the ninety-man garrison and earning the nickname "Black Death" from the Italians.[10]

North Africa was a patchwork of American, French, and British units spread all over the desert landscape; they were slowly pushing the Germans into Tunis, the main port in Tunisia. General Montgomery's Eighth Army was squeezing the Germans from the east while the forces that landed in TORCH were closing in from the west. But Hitler was determined to hold on and was building up his forces for a major counteroffensive. The first blow fell when the Germans routed the French at Faïd Pass on January 30, 1943. Then on February 14, 1943, covered by an umbrella of fighters and

Ranger and Airborne Operations in North Africa

TORCH
Fredendall
(Nov. 8, 1942)
Central Task Force

TORCH
Ryder
(Nov. 8, 1942)
Eastern Task Force

S P A I N

Mediterranean Sea

A L G E R I A

T U N I S I A

LIBYA

Arzew Harbor

Oran
Arzew
Tafaraoui
Lourmel
Maison Blanche
Algiers
Bône
Tébessa
Youks-les-Bains
Teboura
Bizerte
Djedeida
Tunis
Gulf of Hammamet
Sousse
El Djem
Faïd Pass
Sened Station
Gulf of Gabès
Gabès
El Guettar
Gafsa
Sidi Bou Zid
Kasserine

Allied Advances
Parachute Drop

Operation TORCH Airborne and Ranger Activity Nov. 8, 1942

1st Ranger Btn.
Arzew Harbor
Arzew
St. Cloud
Oran
La Sénia
Tafaraoui
Lourmel
Sebkra D'Oran (Dry Salt Lake)

1	Bing Evans, 1st Ranger Btn.
2	Edson Raff, 509th PIB
3	William Yarborough, 509th PIB
4	William Yarborough, 509th PIB
5	Roland Rondeau, 509th PIB
6	Robert Reed, 1st Ranger Btn.
1	Lester Kness, 1st Ranger Btn.

0   Miles   100

Stuka dive-bombers, the 10th Panzer Division smashed through Faïd Pass and hammered the American II Corps at Sidi-Bou-Zid. This forced the Americans to withdraw to Kasserine Pass, where the Germans were finally halted. The Rangers were brought up to act as a rear guard for the withdrawing units and held key positions at Dernaia Pass.

During March, the II Corps was under a new commander, Lieutenant General George S. Patton, who resumed the famous offensive in which the 1st Ranger Battalion would play a key role. First, the Rangers led the 1st Infantry Division's attack on the crucial town of El Guettar. After moving through El Guettar, the Rangers had the important task of supporting the 1st Division's attack on the key mountain pass at Djebal el Ank. The pass was protected by a large force of Italian soldiers, dug in with machine guns and artillery that guarded the main approach, making a frontal assault impossible. The Rangers found a footpath that twisted through what was considered impassable mountain terrain, allowing them and a mortar company to come in behind the Italian positions, and at dawn on March 21, the Rangers struck the startled Italians and took more than two hundred prisoners while clearing the pass. The Rangers then linked with the 26th Infantry Regiment, which made a frontal assault on the Italian positions.

With the pass in American hands, the German 10th Panzer Division counterattacked on March 23 with sixty tanks and an infantry battalion, but were thrown back by artillery.[11]

At the end of March 1943, the battalion returned to Algeria for rest and additional training. During the rest period, Colonel Darby petitioned for and received approval to raise two additional Ranger battalions. The 3rd and 4th Ranger battalions were born from volunteers and a cadre of troops from the 1st Ranger Battalion.

On May 13, 1943, the Axis forces in North Africa capitulated, and about 275,000 prisoners were taken.[12]

WARREN "BING" EVANS

1st and 3rd Ranger Battalions

After a successful landing at 1:00 A.M. November 8, 1942, the Rangers captured Arzew Harbor, the main port outside Oran, Algeria, in textbook fashion. The port was bristling with coastal artillery and had to be subdued before the Allies' Central Task Force could land the bulk of its men. The Rangers quickly seized the main coastal guns on the high ground above Arzew and captured Fort de la Pointe at the northeast corner of the harbor. Bing Evans was the 1st Ranger Battalion's sergeant major, and after the operation became a commissioned officer.

It took a lot of guts and a lot of blood to be a Ranger. When I came back from overseas, I went in a skinny 225 pounds and came out weighing 140. I was an ugly-looking sight. When I got back, my wife—my girl—was waiting, and we got married within two weeks of me hitting the States. My father-in-law thought as much of me as he did his own kids, and he asked me to speak in front of the Chamber of Commerce. They had a bosses' night or recognition night of some kind. I agreed to do it. After I talked for a little while, they started asking questions. When it was all over, the local banker said to my father-in-law, "You know, Charlie, that was a very interesting talk, but only

Rangers outside Arzew Harbor, November 1943. (Photo courtesy U.S. Army)

about half of it was true, wasn't it?" So for fifty years I never opened my mouth because I realized it was impossible to get across to someone who had never experienced what it was like.

[The landing at Arzew] was very successful and very simple. I went on that with a certain anticipation, quite a bit of it. We were trained to do this. I wondered what it was going to be like, but I would say anticipation was my major emotion.

The landing itself was very uneventful. We were not discovered, to our surprise. We followed a coastal road to what we would recognize from a buoy off the coast and a gully. We took off at that gully and came up behind the gun batteries that overlooked Arzew and controlled the harbor of Arzew. We assaulted the batteries. We attacked them, got completely amongst them almost before they knew what had happened. I don't think there were any casualties on our side; there were a few on the other side, and prisoners. The battery was [taken] in just a short while: It took about a half-hour from the time we hit the battery itself, which was on quite an overlook.

We went through the town after that along with A, B, and C companies, which landed on the dockside and took the fort that served as barracks and headquarters for the troops. They surrendered right away; they didn't really have much of a choice because by the time we got in amongst them they didn't even have time to be armed. They were just in their barracks and quarters, and there we were.

[Other Allied troops] came in and landed without incident because we had the harbor under control. In fact, Colonel Darby was running it from City Hall. The troops, as they advanced on Oran, got into trouble. Our casualties started then when they started using us as infantry. The infantry got into trouble and they asked the Rangers to come in and help them out. The people who called on our help didn't realize that they were calling on companies of sixty men. Nevertheless, we bailed them out, got them out of their problem. We were misused, we were used as an infantry assault outfit in the front lines, but nevertheless we accomplished that objective also.

Shortly after acting as infantry assault, I was commissioned to second lieutenant. I got it because Gordon Klefman gave his life. He was one of those men that the infantry called up and said that they were stymied, they couldn't advance, so they called on a company of Rangers, probably fifty by that time. The one company went up there and did the job for the troops that had been stopped. He, in leading that, gave his life. It was quite an honor that I got the first battlefield commission, but when you stop to think about it, that somebody had to die for it to happen, then it becomes something else. Of course, that happened often in our outfit.

EDSON RAFF

509th Parachute Infantry Battalion

At ninety-one, Edson Raff can pass for a gentleman in his late fifties. In November 1942, he commanded the 509th Parachute Infantry Battalion and led America's first combat airborne jump. He would later command the 507th Parachute Infantry Regiment and lead the last combat jump in the European Theater. Raff's first combat jump into Vichy-held North Africa began on the evening of November 7, 1942, when the 509th left England in thirty-nine C-47s to seize the airfields outside Oran.

We finally got all collected down in Land's End [England], a couple of airstrips, and I was a little worried about going around the tip of the Brittany peninsula at night because of German fighters. I went down to a friend of mine who just happened to be a commander of a group of British fighters that were used for antisubmarine patrol, and I asked him whether he would assist us around the tip of the Brittany peninsula, and he agreed to do it. I did this because we had requested Jimmy Doolittle, who was in command of the American air forces, and his assistant to get us fighters and they refused to do it; they sort of washed their hands of the whole operation as if it were going to fail and they didn't want any part of it. I knew we would get there eventually and I never thought of failure. We went ahead with our training and finally got into our C-47s and we were going to fly by the Brittany peninsula and over Spain when we got there to get to our landing places in Africa.

As it turned out, there were thirty-nine planes, all flown by pilots, some of whom had three hundred hours of flying, and they had never participated in anything this long before, about fifteen hundred miles.

We were flying under Plan Peace [the French were not expected to fight] and took off at night from the fields around Land's End in England and headed south. Sure enough the [Allied] fighters came out and laid a raid on the Brittany peninsula, which discouraged the Germans from coming up at all, so we never had any trouble in that regard, and that was the only thing that had worried me. We flew straight south over Spain, and some people said they saw antiaircraft fire as we passed over Spain.

Then we turned left over the Mediterranean, over the coast, to the place where we were going to land. Somebody noticed a column of armored cars and tanks coming toward where we were, which was a place called Lourmel. I decided the tanks were enemy and we were going to drop to oppose them. We jumped, and that was the first jump, and I unfortunately had some K rations [a box of combat rations] in my pocket, and the K ration corner of them stuck in my ribs and I got a couple of cracked ribs. I eventually got a Purple Heart for the accident, which I refused, but General [George] Marshall back in Washington insisted that I take it. There I was, partly wounded, and we found out the column coming up the road was our own people in the armor division, and we were glad to welcome them. In the meantime, Bentley and his planes and a few others had landed on the salt lake, and I put up the American flag and gathered around, and they took off again.

The rest of the battalion was scattered from hell to breakfast. Some of the planes thought they were running out of gas, and they landed at Gibraltar, the British airfield there. One plane landed at a place [in] Spanish Morocco. Other planes landed in other places. We eventually made it to both airfields.

WILLIAM YARBOROUGH

509th Parachute Infantry Battalion

William Yarborough was one of the pioneers of the American airborne and designed the airborne qualification badge or jump wings, the paratrooper jump suit, and more important, numerous airborne tactics and strategies. He went on to command the Special Forces and retired as a three-star general. Here he recalls America's second North African jump, at the strategically located Youks-les-Bains airfield on November 15.

Part of the operation was to get the French on our side again; they had been divided by all that political crap that was taking place. They were unsure about who they were supposed to shoot at, and our arrival there congealed that in the proper direction.

It was about 350 miles to the east of Maison Blanche airport that we took off from. We had one fighter airplane as an escort. There was a minimal amount of briefing; we didn't know an awful lot about what we were going to get into or anything else. We arrived over the Youks-les-Bains airfield. You could see, all around the airfield, the French dug in to fighting positions. We weren't sure when we jumped whether they were going to be friends or foes, so it was a little bit ticklish. It was the 3rd Zouave Regiment that was dug in.

When we hit the ground, instead of fighting when they came out of the foxholes, they embraced us. This made us exceedingly happy. The commander took off his 3rd Zouave badge and pinned it on Ed Raff, our battalion commander. The other Zouaves did the same thing with the rest of us. It was a gesture that I figured ought to be part of the history of the 509th. I put in a request to the North African Theater of Operations that this gesture be made a permanent affair to the degree that the 509th would wear that badge in perpetuity, future generations would, and they would know what it was all about. Actually it marked the turning point in that area: The French were no longer sympathetic to the Germans and the Italians.

Part of us being there was to safeguard the gasoline supply which was there. Our air force was going to move in a little later to occupy it and they needed that petrol. After we landed, the Zouaves picked up our chutes and got all signs of our having been there erased. A German airplane came over to find out what the hell had happened and he was taken under fire by rifles and pistols and everything and he crashed on ahead. At least we saw pillars of smoke coming up, and we figured that's what happened to it.

It's not what you would call a big operation, but it had significance—psychological, political, and moral point of view.

When I first got any inkling that paratroopers were going to be part of the army, I felt I had to get into that new development. I volunteered so many times they kicked me out. They said, "When we want you we'll let you know. Now get the hell out of here!" I really, really wanted it because it represented a new dimension of warfare and it represented a challenge. Airplanes were new in those days, and even the smell of them was alien. I wanted part of that action.

I was happy then to be given a job that involved research and development. Packing new chutes and equipment, developing new harnesses and the hardware and all of the tactics and techniques that went along with that sort of thing.

There was an emotional, spiritual, and intangible side to the whole thing. That meant that the boots and the uniform and the insignia were part of the incentive, and we just felt that it was a new departure, and we were so enthused to be on the ground floor of the whole thing and see it develop. In those days, damn few people rode in airplanes, let alone jumping out of them. We felt, "Boy, we are in the forward edge of something that is really something big and important." I still have that feeling towards the airborne.

They're a little bit removed. Each one of them has tested himself in a way he knows that under certain circumstances he's going to produce, and maybe some of his other colleagues in other pursuits aren't quite sure until they're faced with the combat.

Only you can tell whether or not when you look down fifteen hundred feet and know that your arrival in good shape and in one piece depends a lot on what you do. You get some sort of an understanding of yourself.

After the capture of Youks-les-Bains Airfield, Colonel Raff, with the help of an American tank destroyer unit and the French, organized the Tunisian Task Force to make forays into Axis positions in Tunisia and keep the Germans and Italians off balance. The unit's first major engagement was at the strategic Faïd Pass in the center of Tunisia where, starting on December 2, 1942, Raff's force attacked. William Yarborough remembers the next day.

The first real tough encounter we faced was at a place called Faïd Pass. We had come across a number of the advance elements of this heterogeneous force of Germans and Italians, and the intelligence reports we had suggested that they had a defensive position at Faïd Pass. Faïd Pass is on the way to the Tunisian east coast. The terrain features of the pass dominated that road.

It was the first time I had ever really been in combat in this sense. A French officer alongside of me was telling me when I should dodge bullets and when I should get up and walk, and giving me sort of a feel of how you operated in combat. That served me in good stead later on.

Lieutenant Colonel Ed Raff, a scrappy, cocky guy who was full of dynamite, decided we were going to attack Faïd Pass and get around in back of it because their defenses were pointed in the other direction. We had a little bit of air support by the way of P-38s [Lightning fighters]. We also had three or four half-tracks that were open on top and had .50-caliber machine guns on top. It was a seedy and heterogeneous little force taking on a battalion-strength enemy made up of Germans and Italians.

We came up to Faïd during the night and deployed around the southern flank of the hill mass and began the attack at dawn, with the P-38s going in first and firing on the defenses. Then the open half-tracks began to move in, and then the enemy began to react and we found ourselves pinned down.

We worked our way around the southern flank and up into the high ground that overlooked the pass. We took the enemy under fire from there,

Major William Yarborough stands next to an ambulance that was strafed by German fighters. German POWs whom Yarborough helped rescue removed the wounded. (Photo courtesy William Yarborough)

and the son-of-a-gun was not going to move. Here we were across his line of communications, and he was across ours. As I recall, we were in a stalemate, and the French finally came up with a battery of artillery and began to bombard the pass from the forward side.

By late afternoon, we saw a white flag and they came out—the Italians sat in one place and the Germans sat in another. They had surrendered, but there was now the problem of taking care of prisoners. We were not prepared for that.

We decided to evacuate some of them to the rear in an ambulance with red and white markings on it when a German aircraft came over and began to strafe all of us, and he hit the ambulance. The ambulance driver got out and was trying to get the wounded Germans out of the ambulance. As he was fumbling with the rear door, there was another burst of machine gun fire from the plane, and he was cut in half.

Jack Thompson of the *Chicago Tribune* had jumped in with us and had willed me a French vehicle. It was a Peugeot; I'll always remember that because it only ran when it wanted to and I had a driver that spent most of his time under the hood trying to find out what was wrong. Anyway, I was walking along the road because my vehicle had been knocked out by enemy air. When I came up to the ambulance I could hear these guys yelling inside the rear compartment. So I got into the front seat and shot the lock off the door with my carbine and finally got the German prisoners out. The krauts strafed us again and then went away.

This was the nature of these "exercises" in that area, and it showed that the Germans were not worried if you had a red cross on you or whatever. People who have not operated under enemy air power have no idea as to the terror it can put into your heart. Every time we took to the roads we had to watch in all directions because they were there looking for us.

ROLAND RONDEAU

509th Parachute Infantry Battalion

In an attempt to disrupt German supply lines in Tunisia, the U.S. Twelfth Air Force concentrated its attacks on Rommel's shipping and bridges. But one essential bridge, six miles from the Tunisian town of El Djem, defied three bombing attempts to remain a significant artery in the Axis supply line.[13] On a request from the Eighth Army, Allied Force Headquarters ordered a small force of paratroopers to jump near the bridge and destroy it, with no provision made for their return. Roland Rondeau, one of seven survivors, remembers the doomed mission.

About a week before Christmas in 1942, we first got information that they wanted to send so many men out on a mission to demolish a bridge. Initially we didn't get much information, but as the days dwindled we got a briefing. We knew where our objective was. We were to jump and proceed towards the railroad bridge and destroy it. Once we accomplished our mission, we would head west and come back towards our lines. The next day after the jump we were to proceed west after the mission had been accomplished and a plane was going to come in and pick us up because it was all open area, part of the Sahara. The day before the mission was scheduled, they canceled the last part of it so we were left with the objective of reaching the lines on our own as a unit; we had to walk back. Initially they thought it would be ninety miles. We just had one canteen of water; it was up to us to provide for ourselves. We had K rations and chocolate bars for three or four days, which was all we could carry.

It was a night mission. We took off at 10:00 P.M., we flew towards our objective, we were close to it and getting ready to exit when we were fired upon and hit our plane. There was some antiaircraft firing done and it wasn't close, but we could see the streaks in the darkness. That didn't last very long. We dropped and we assembled minus a couple of men, and one of the main supply canisters that we had we couldn't find. So that left us with a little less ammunition, a little less supplies and most of the explosives to blow up the bridge.

We assembled around Lieutenant Dan DeLeo and proceeded in the direction that we had been briefed on; there was a little discussion about where to go. The two French enlisted men that were with us discussed it among themselves. They were supposed to know the area somewhat; they had pulled some duty in that section of Africa earlier. But at night you can get confused. They came to a conclusion on which direction we should follow, and Lieutenant DeLeo agreed with them. So we headed off in a certain direction.

When we got towards the railroad, we heard in the distance a train coming up. I don't remember what direction it was going. The line ran north to south, straight up and down. We waited for it to go by. It was blacked out completely. Once it had gone by, we marched up towards the tracks, and then from there we took the directions that we were supposed to initially take, that we were briefed on, and as far as I remember, we were to reach the railroad tracks and head south downward and turn right. So that's what [we thought we were] doing and followed that for several hours, and that's when we started to wonder if it was further away than we had been told or if we were heading in the wrong direction. We kept on going, and that's when we found out we were going in the wrong direction. We couldn't go back; by then, daylight was coming up, it was too late to turn around in the other direction because by then we would be out in the open and we would be able to be seen easily enough by any Arab running around in the area. We decided to blow up some sections of the track to delay any movement on the tracks.

Initially when we reached the railroad track, Dan DeLeo sent some men out to be advanced detail to work down the line for any things that would interfere with it. That was the last we saw of them. They were captured further down the line.

That left us in daylight, no objective in sight. There was little we could do. I can truthfully say we did not panic. There were no troops in the area. We decided to blow up what sections of the railroad that we could do with the amount of explosives we had and then head back west towards our lines. The demolitions men set the charges along the line, and in the meantime, we . . . provided security on both sides of the tracks, and then when we got the order that the explosion was going to be blown up, we took cover as best we could. Once they blew it up, we reassembled and we moved out as a unit heading west towards our line.

It didn't take too long after we moved out that we saw some troops coming up behind us from the east. How long before these troops caught up to us I don't know; it may have been an hour or two. Initially they were on foot; we did see a few vehicles after that. It was all flatland and that's what made it wide open and we could see in all directions. They spread out, some to the left and some to the right. After a while we came to an oasis (there were a few palm trees that we could lay behind and it gave us some protection) and set up a defense because they were coming closer. We had them in three directions now, from the north, south, and east. The only thing open was the west, but they were catching up with us pretty fast, so it was just a matter of stopping where we had a little defense because there were some embankments there. We stopped there and put up a defense. One man was in favor of each man taking off for himself. He voiced his opinion and others agreed. They wanted to take off on their own rather than stay and fight it out. We would take out on our own. Everyone agreed, so DeLeo gave each man [an] initial order to take off on their own if they wanted to. We all headed west, the only route that was open.

I stayed with Dan DeLeo and another good friend of mine, Frank Romero. He said, "If you stay, I am going to stay with you." And John Betters decided to stay. There were the four of us, and then we had the Frenchmen, they wouldn't leave, they wanted to stay as a little group. We took off heading west, as a group, six of us. We moved out very fast, almost on a run. We came to a road, and not long after we saw a truck coming down the road. We commandeered the truck and we decided to use it. We got right in the middle of the road and stopped them. I don't know if they realized right then and there that we were Americans, but he didn't hesitate in stopping because he had weapons pointing right at the truck.

The only thing left after that was to proceed. Dan DeLeo got in the front seat with the driver and put a sheet around him to make him look like an Arab. The rest of us were in the back of the truck laying down, and we had the top over us so we weren't seen. That's how we were able to drive right through a column of soldiers marching down the road: one column on the left and one column on the right, and we drove right through them. We could see them when we peeked through the tarp. They paid no attention to us. I don't know why, since they must have known by then that there were some Americans loose in the area, because later that evening when we got as far as we wanted to go with the truck, we left the truck and took off and came to an Arab settlement and we heard that same night that most of them [the 509th men on the jump] had been captured. That was the rumors that the Arabs had heard, but there was no verification of that.

We stayed there for a while and then we decided to keep moving on. For a couple of days we moved in only at night. We were on foot. We stayed under some sort of concealment during the day, as much as we could. After a couple of days we gave it up. I guess we got a little cocky, and we hiked all the way in day and night until we got to our lines.

The first sign of troops that we met up with were some soldiers in the distance. We had crossed one section of hills and little mountains, and we came up to an open section on the other side, and in the distance we could see some installations and guns set up, so we knew it was an outpost of some type, but what unit it was we didn't know for sure. We started to head in that direction and it was then that we saw them. They were waving their hands and telling us not to move and not to come in there . . . we were in the middle of a minefield! They came around and brought us in. They (a French outpost, French troops) sent out some men to lead us through it.

They had heard that there were some American paratroopers that had been dropped and they were going to be coming through: The different outposts had been warned to watch out for us. That was where it ended there. They took us back and they were glad to see us, and they notified our units, and that same evening some troops from the paratroopers came to get us.

ROBERT REED

1st Ranger Battalion

After the U.S. II Corps took a beating from the Germans for most of February 1943, General Eisenhower replaced its commander, Major General Lloyd Fredendall, with newly promoted Lieutenant General George Patton. Patton resumed the offensive with the 1st Ranger spearheading the 1st Infantry Division's attack on El Guettar and on March 20 cracking the Italian defenses at the crucial Djebel el Ank

Pass. In this e-history, Robert Reed, a medic, describes how by moving at night, along a serpentine mountainous trail, the Rangers were able to move in behind the Italians guarding the pass. For the battle that followed, the 1st Ranger Battalion received the Presidential Unit Citation.

The Axis had this one pass in front of El Guettar. The Italians had fortified the place with mines, artillery, and machine gun nests. It was just a narrow pass. The estimate was that it would take about three thousand casualties to take this pass because it was such a well-defended position. Meanwhile, one of our guys had done a reconnaissance and found that there was a sheep trail that passed behind the Italian positions. Darby figured that he could move his whole battalion through the mountains and come in behind all these Italian defenses. They were all looking west, and we would be to their east. So that's what we did.

Members of the 1st Ranger Battalion in Tunisia. (Photo courtesy U.S. Army)

We started out about dusk and we scrambled through these mountains, and we are slipping and sliding through these little goat trails. Having all your gear on made it even harder. At the time I was carrying an M-1 even though I was a medic. When we landed at Arzew, I was heavily armed. I had an M-1, a .45, three bandoliers of ammunition, and several grenades.

At dawn, we came upon a mesa-sort-of-looking thing. We were behind the Italian artillery, and Darby led the assault. Our company, B Company, stayed up on top. The other companies were moving infantry style down the bank of this mesa, overrunning the Italian positions. You could see them hopping from one position to another until they cleared the pass. We had about two hundred prisoners.

Then the German air force came. There was a flight of planes, maybe six or so. You could see them tipping their wings as each fighter pilot looked down on the ground, and then the one behind him would tip his wings. I guess it was part of their maneuvers. I looked up and I saw this German plane coming straight down at me. In the desert, there are these crevices in the ground where the water washed down, and I scrambled into one of those. I looked up and there were little bombs coming out of the belly of the plane, and it looked like they were aimed right for my nose; it was the most scared I'd ever been. The bomb hit a couple yards away. We had quite a few casualties, mostly Americans.

So then we lined up all the Italian prisoners, and I tried to get the Italians that weren't wounded to carry the litters of their wounded comrades. They didn't want to do it. So I had to grab them and push them to pick up the litters to carry their fellow Italians who were wounded.

LESTER KNESS

1st and 4th Ranger Battalions

On February 10, 1943, A, E, and F companies of the 1st Ranger Battalion were trucked to a position twelve miles away from the Italian outpost of Sened Station, which was garrisoned by the troops from the elite Italian Centauro Division and 10th Bersaglieri Regiment. After concealing themselves under shelter-halves and brush during the day to avoid detection, on the night of February 10–11, the Rangers fixed bayonets and attacked, killing all but eleven men from the garrison and earning the nickname "Black Death" from the Italians. The Rangers' orders stated that there would be no delaying or waiting after the attack on the outpost. Anyone who could not make the trip back to the base camp would be sacrificed. This order applied to Rangers and prisoners. It was an order that Lester Kness, a first sergeant, had no choice but to obey.

We were supposed to assault for thirty minutes. We had tape on our backs—XYZ for identification. We had Y on E Company, F was X, and A was Z. We didn't wear helmets; we wore little knit caps without any brims. Our orders were to kill anyone who didn't have tape on his back, or if they had a brim.

Everybody started running, except the second platoon didn't move. We had two new officers who were strange. The first platoon was under a sergeant I knew who was a very brave man, and when he hollered, his men knew him. Well, the second platoon stood—it didn't move. I ran over because I had been their sergeant and I hollered at them, and they started running, and I ran with them over the hill.

There was a battery there that was primarily firing into F Company. F Company was making an assault by squads and the [Rangers] threw a lot of hand grenades in front of them. They were moving pretty good; I could see them on both sides. I could see the flash of the field piece and I would shoot into it. I don't know if it did any good. One man had his head blown off by the gun. A Company men ran right into their [Italian soldiers'] tents. They were in their tents, coming out, putting on their clothes.

Then we had to pull out. I stayed at the base of this little knob that we assaulted, counting the men and checking to make sure that all the guys got out. I picked up Sergeant Joe Dye and a fellow from F Company. They both had been severely wounded; they couldn't walk. I shot them both with morphine and I had five men and myself to start back. Everybody had pulled out, and we had these two wounded. I had an Italian prisoner; he had been wounded in the shoulder. Our orders were to leave no prisoners, to leave nobody alive because we didn't want them to know what direction we were going. This prisoner couldn't keep up. We went probably a mile and he kept dragging back. One of my men could speak Italian and I told him to tell the prisoner that "he has to keep up or we have to kill him." One of my men ordered him up and he didn't come forward. I told him we had to kill him. I told [one of the men],

"You're going to have to kill him." He said, "I can't." I said, "Why?" And he said, "Because I know everything he's saying!" Which is an awful hard thing to do. For most of these guys it was their first time of drawing blood. It's hard. And one of the men took care of it.[*] [After enduring a harrowing night march that included avoiding enemy planes, the next day Kness's small group made it back to their lines.]

---

[*] I was ordered to do that. I did what I was ordered to do. I think one of the worst things a soldier can do is kill without justification, to kill a man just because he's there. I've threatened them but I didn't kill them. That was a long time ago. I get a little nervous sometimes when I start telling about some of it.

CHAPTER THREE

SICILY

In their rememberings are their truths

—Studs Terkel

After the defeat of Axis forces in North Africa, the Allies were divided on where to strike next. The Americans favored a cross-Channel attack in 1943, while the British sought to buy time before invading France and build on the Allied momentum gained in North Africa. To the British, the Mediterranean Theater was the most promising area to attack. Accordingly, Sardinia, Corsica, and the Balkans were all candidates for Allied invasion. The British and American Joint Chiefs aired their arguments at the Casablanca Conference, and by January 18, 1943, a compromise was reached: Invade Sicily to secure the Mediterranean Sea lanes, divert pressure from the Russian Front, and intensify pressure on Italy. In exchange, the British signed up to renew planning for a cross-Channel attack and committed themselves to a large buildup of U.S. forces in the British Isles.[1]

The invasion of Sicily was set for July 10, 1943, with the code name HUSKY. Allied landings would take place on the southern portion of the island. British and Canadian forces would make an amphibious landing on the southeast coast while the Americans would land in the southwest on the Gela, Licata, and Scoglitti beaches.

Because of their success in North Africa, Darby's Rangers had the mission of spearheading the American landings at the Gela and Licata beaches. The 1st and 4th Ranger battalions would land at Gela and the 3rd Battalion would hit Licata Beach. To guard against an Axis counterattack on the fragile Gela beachhead, the 82nd Airborne Division would parachute behind the beach.

The Axis troops on Sicily were powerful. The Italian forces numbered about two hundred thousand men, but their morale and willingness to fight were low. The Germans, on the other hand, were still eager to fight and had two divisions in Sicily: the elite Hermann Göring Parachute Panzer Division and the well-trained 15th Panzer Grenadier Division. They would later reinforce with two more crack divisions.[2]

Around 8:40 P.M. on July 9, 226 C-47s of the U.S. 52nd Troop Carrier Wing took off with 3,400 paratroopers from the 505th Parachute Regimental Combat Team. Attached was the 3rd Battalion of the 504th Parachute Infantry Regiment. The parachute drop was a disaster; paratroopers were scattered all over southern Sicily. Only the 505th's 2nd Battalion came down in a concentrated area, yet it was several miles off course from its designated drop zone. Several factors contributed to the poor drop: a lack of training on the part of the 52nd Troop Carrier Wing, no pathfinders to guide the planes to the drop zones by radar, and a gale that blew the planes off course.

Despite these difficulties, the small bands of paratroopers caused a tremendous amount of confusion to the Axis defenders by cutting communication lines and capturing Italian outposts. Ultimately, these small groups would accomplish missions that were earmarked for more than 3,000 men.

Not long after the start of the airborne operation, Allied troops were landing on Sicily's beaches. At 2:55 A.M., the 3rd Ranger Battalion encountered minimal resistance on Licata Beach and quickly destroyed or captured the Italian positions. By the morning of July 11, the 3rd Battalion was placed in division reserve.[3]

Gela Beach was a different story. The 1st and 4th Ranger Battalions hit the beach at 3:00 A.M. and antipersonnel mines and rifle fire took a heavy toll. D Company of the 4th Battalion, for example, lost all of its officers. After moving off the beach and destroying several pillboxes, the Rangers entered Gela. Fighting was house-to-house, but by midmorning the Rangers had the town.[4]

Their victory was interrupted around 10:30 A.M., when the seasoned Italian Livorno Division counterattacked and nine Italian light tanks broke the Rangers' outer defensive positions. Playing a deadly game of hide-and-seek, the Rangers destroyed the tanks using hand grenades, bazookas, and captured Italian antitank guns. After a brief respite, the tanks and supporting infantry from the Livorno Division attacked Gela again but were once again repelled by the Rangers.[5]

The Germans reacted quickly to the landings and nearly destroyed the Gela beachhead. The powerful Hermann Göring Parachute Panzer Division split into an eastern and western *kampfgruppe* (a battle group equipped with tanks and hundreds of troops). On July 10, mixed and scattered groups of paratroopers stopped the Hermann Göring western battle group from coming through Niscemi at the critical crossroads near Piano Lupo. Using only small arms and bazookas, the paratroopers engaged tanks at point-blank range and halted the column. Remarkably, these small groups of paratroopers accomplished all of the missions of a 3,300-man regimental combat team. Colonel James Gavin, commander of the 505th Parachute Infantry Regiment, later commented, "It was a remarkable performance, and I know nothing like it that occurred at any time later in the war."[6]

The next morning, after a strong rebuke from his superiors for his July 10 performance, General Paul Conrath, commander of the Hermann Göring Division, launched a vigorous attack with both his western and eastern battle groups. Tanks from the panzer division were able to skirt paratroopers and 1st Infantry Division's positions and approached Gela. Fortunately, they were stopped by naval guns, ground artillery, and tanks before they could reach the town.

Meanwhile, outside of the small town of Biscari on a place that has become known as Biazza Ridge, about 250 paratroopers faced the Germans' eastern battle group, consisting of seven hundred infantry, a Tiger tank company, and a supporting artillery battalion.[7] The beleaguered paratroopers led by Colonel Gavin, the 505th regimental commander, vowed that they would hold the ridge no matter what. Using little more than bazookas and a pack howitzer that was manned by the 456th Parachute Field Artillery Battalion, the Americans did exactly that. Later, with a supporting company of Sherman tanks and naval artillery fire, the paratroopers even counterattacked and the Hermann Göring Division's eastern battle group began to withdrew inland.

Before the Allies were able to savor their hard-fought victory at Gela, one of worst Allied friendly-fire incidents of the war occurred on the night of July 11, 1943. In an attempt to reinforce the beachhead, Colonel Reuben Tucker's two remaining battalions of the 504th Parachute Infantry Regiment were sent in to parachute behind Gela. On their way to the drop zone, despite warnings of their approach, the transports were peppered with friendly fire from the Allied invasion fleet and ground units. Twenty-three C-47 transports loaded with paratroopers were blown out of the sky, and three hundred paratroopers and airmen were casualties.[8]

But by July 12, the Allied beachhead was secure and the Allies were poised to move inland. Both the paratroopers and Rangers helped spearhead the Seventh Army's advance up the western side of Sicily.

While casualties were incurred, the remainder of the 82nd Airborne Division's campaign in Sicily consisted of long road marches against generally

Ranger and Airborne Operations in Sicily—July 10-12, 1943

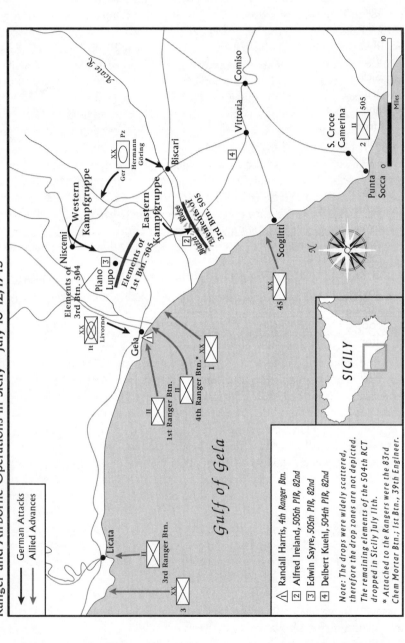

Legend:
- German Attacks
- Allied Advances

Licata
3rd Ranger Btn.

Gulf of Gela

Gela

Livorno

Piano Lupo

Elements of Niscemi 3rd Btn. 504

Elements of 1st Btn. 505

Western Kampfgruppe

Eastern Kampfgruppe

Hermann Göring Pz Ger

Biazza Ridge Elements of 505 3rd Btn.

Biscari

Vittoria

Comiso

Scoglitti

45

S. Croce Camerina

Punta Socca

2 505

1st Ranger Btn.

4th Ranger Btn.*

SICILY

Miles 0 10

△ Randall Harris, 4th Ranger Btn.
2 Alfred Ireland, 505th PIR, 82nd
3 Edwin Sayre, 505th PIR, 82nd
4 Delbert Kuehl, 504th PIR, 82nd

Note: The drops were widely scattered, therefore the drop zones are not depicted. The remaining elements of the 504th RCT dropped in Sicily July 11th.

* Attached to the Rangers were the 83rd Chem Mortar Btn.; 1st Btn., 39th Engineer.

minimal resistance. Notably, the unit was involved in the capture of the strategic cities of Palermo and Trapani. The Rangers, on the other hand, had more difficult combat objectives and were used as Patton's lead unit for the rest of the campaign.

After the Germans failed to destroy the Allied beachheads, Hitler realized Sicily was lost. Nevertheless, the Axis forces were able to execute a masterful rear-guard delaying action that tied the Allies down for thirty-eight days and at the end of the campaign withdrew most of their men and equipment from the island safely.

Sicily prompted American commanders to reconsider the way they were using their airborne forces. After the poor drops and disastrous friendly-fire incident, General Eisenhower and others questioned whether it was viable to continue to organize airborne troops into large division-sized units.[9] After an intense debate and a large airborne training exercise executed with precision by the 11th Airborne Division (which later fought in the Pacific Theater), the airborne units remained organized in divisions. Later Field Marshal Albert Kesselring, the German commander in the Mediterranean, said "The American paratroopers effected an extraordinary delay in the movement of our own troops and caused large losses." General Paul Conrath, commander of the Hermann Göring Division, also credited the paratroopers with halting his advance to the beach.

After the Sicilian campaign, both the Rangers and the airborne prepared to fight in Italy, where they would encounter many of the same units they had fought in Sicily.

RANDALL HARRIS

1st and 4th Ranger Battalions

On the night of July 10, 1943, the 1st and 4th Ranger battalions spearheaded the Allied landing at Gela Beach. Randall Harris, one of only two members of Darby's Rangers[10] to receive the Distinguished Service Cross, describes that night.

When we got into the landing craft, the water calmed down considerably. Prior to this, when we first got into the mother ship, we had waves that were two stories high. But when we got into the landing craft, the water was almost mirrorlike; it was kind of eerie. As we started to get closer to the beach, there was a lot of light in the sky from flares and rockets that illuminated everything.

Meanwhile, the landing craft next to us took a direct hit by an artillery shell, snapping a cable that held up the landing craft ramp, flooding the boat instantly. The men were packed in there like sardines, and they all went down with the boat. Only the coxswain survived; I helped pull him out. For many years, I suppressed this memory, thinking it was a dream—a lot happened that day.

I remember when I got off the boat. I had been loaded down with my regular gear as well as fifty to sixty pounds of ammunition and supplies that we had to carry to the beach. [The water] was about knee high when I got out, but I stepped into a shell hole and I went down about ten feet. I finally was able to get my head above water and got out. We started to move onto the beach.

About a hundred yards on the beach, the mines started going off; we were right in the middle of a minefield. Men were being hit all around me. I was a first sergeant at the time, and the company commander, Walter Wojcik, was in front of me. He got hit in the chest, and he turned around, looked at me, and said, "Harry, I've had it." (He called me Harry.) I could see his heart hanging outside of his shirt as he crumpled to the ground.

A couple seconds later, I got hit. My stomach opened up. It felt like I got hit with a baseball bat. I didn't feel much pain of any kind; I must have been in some form of shock. A handful of my intestines actually came out. I just picked up my web belt and used it to put everything back inside and I kept on going. I could see another one of my friends get hit.

I managed to get through the minefield and get up on a dike that ran along the edge of the shore. It was probably about fifteen feet high and flat on the top. When we got up on the dike, Andre saw a row of pillboxes and said, "Let's get 'em, Harry." The pillboxes were situated facing the ocean, and as soon as we got up on top of the dike we started to attack the pillboxes. Howard Andre and I took turns cleaning out the pillboxes. We were a team through the war. When I was a sergeant he was a corporal, and when I was commissioned and became a CO [commanding officer], he was also commissioned and become my XO [executive officer]. He was later killed in Anzio. When we started cleaning out the pillboxes, I would kick open the door and he would throw in a grenade. We would alternate and he would kick open the door and I would throw a grenade. We leapfrogged in this fashion and got about seven in a row. Then down around the last pillbox one of my men, Corporal Peter Deeb, came up and said, "Has this pillbox been emptied?" And I said, "No, you'd better look." Without knowing it at the time, I had been sitting in front of the slit of the pillbox with a machine gun aimed at my back.

The next thing I heard was the explosion of Deeb's grenade going off and him saying, "There were a whole lot of Italians inside the pillbox with their hands up."

ALFRED IRELAND

505th Regimental Combat Team, 82nd Airborne Division

On the gusty moonlit night of July 9, 1943, the 505th Regimental Combat Team with the attached 3rd Battalion of the 504th took off for Sicily. The paratroopers were to drop behind the beaches north and northwest of Gela. The drop was a disaster, and paratroopers were scattered all over the southern portion of the island. Alfred Ireland banded together with other men who made their mark at Biazza Ridge. Here about 250 paratroopers led by then–Colonel James Gavin faced the Hermann Göring Division's eastern battle group and stopped it before it reached the Gela beachhead.

Back in '42 we received word that the Japanese would trick our guys by calling out names of the different individuals, major this, colonel that, and captain this. So headquarters wanted nicknames put on every officer in the whole regiment. At that time Gavin said, "Al, I want you to nickname every field officer and all the key people." So I had to sit down and come up with names for everyone. That's how Slim Jim [Colonel Gavin] got his nickname. I nicknamed him Slim Jim because at the time there was a pretzel called Slim Jim Pretzels and he was a tall slim guy and I said, "I hope you don't mind, but I'm nicknaming you 'Slim Jim.'" He laughed and said, "That's fine." I nicknamed Gorham "Hard Nose" because that's just exactly as I saw him. He was a tough, hard-nosed soldier. He was the kind of guy who would do it all himself.

For the flight to Sicily, we left the Kairouan Airdrome on time. As I remember, we departed there probably around 8:30 or 8:45 in the evening of the ninth and flew across the Mediterranean. Our point of reference to get there was to pick up the little island of Linosa and fly over Malta. We didn't fly over either one, and this confused us. All we got as a reference point was a convoy, a navy convoy with the troops that were going to be landing on the beaches. We were warned not to fly over them because they were going to think we were Germans and they were going to shoot us down. I can remember lying on my belly looking out the door and seeing all this. I told Gavin, "Colonel, we may be in trouble!" He looked out and said, "I believe you are right." We went by the convoy without incident, and this at least gave us an indication that at least we were on the right track to Sicily. Shortly after that we picked up land just around midnight.

The crew chief kind of gave us the word to get ready. We were supposed to go over and land somewhere just northeast of Gela, but the way that it worked out we didn't land there, we landed more down between Scoglitti and Vittoria, maybe a little below that. I was standing at the door with Jim [Gavin], and the flak was starting to come up all around us. One C-47 got hit, crashed, and blew up near us. The pilot asked us if we needed to make another pass. I said, "If we go around again we may not make it." He said, "I think you are right." We got the green light and we got out.

As we came down we were being buffeted by wind. I oscillated [turned] into it, and when I landed, I hit a stone wall and fractured my left kneecap; it was minor at the time. You don't feel that much when you got that excitement

Colonel James Gavin, then commander of the 505th, speaks with his troops before their jump in Sicily. (Photo courtesy Leslie Cruise, Jr.)

going on. The adrenaline was flowing, and when I hit the wall I didn't even think that I hurt myself bad until I tried to walk and it gave way.

I looked around, and there wasn't anybody around, and I took a few steps and ran into Benjamin Vandervoort [Van]. I said, "Have you seen anybody?" He said, "No." And I said, "Have you seen the old man?" At that time Gavin showed up, and there was the three of us, and we picked up a couple more troopers, so at that point it was Gavin and the S-1 [personnel officer] (that was me), S-3 [plans and operations officer] (Van), and four troopers.

We began to move in the direction of the compass to what we thought was toward Gela. I don't know how far we got when we saw an Italian guy who was walking down the road. He was whistling along, singing a song, and we grabbed him. He was so scared he didn't know what was going on. He was a soldier. We couldn't get much out of him until we finally got him to tell us about where we were. He said that we were not far from Scoglitti. It turns out we were at least twenty to twenty-five miles off of our regimental drop zone.

We had the prisoner under a shelter-half with lights so no one could see us from the outside or above. Gavin and I were trying to hold the shelter-half, and Van was trying to work the guy over to get more information. We did get out of him enough to know about where we were; that was the only clue we had to our location. We were quite a ways from our objective. The objective we had was to hit the areas just northeast of Gela. Van said, "I know how to handle a POW case like this," and he pulled out his trench knife. He next removed the prisoner's belt and reached down with his trench knife to snip buttons off the prisoner's pants so he would have to use both hands to keep his pants on. The prisoner thought that Van was going to kill him. He was so scared that he was more trouble than he was worth, and we told him to "get out of here" and he was gone.

As we went through the night, we got into a couple of altercations. There were seven of us. Gavin was the kind of person . . . he had one thing on his mind and that was to get to his objective. Anything that was going on was done to try and get to that point. He wanted to speed it up, so we took off and we cut communications wherever we could find them; we were all working on it.

About daylight, we were shot at by a patrol of Germans. It was a pretty brisk firefight at close quarters. One of our troopers was killed and another was wounded, and we lost him later as we moved out.

After the firefight, we continued to head for Gela. About 0230 we picked up some more troopers, and by around 5:00 A.M. we passed through Vittoria and picked up more men from the 3rd Battalion and we got moving in a good manner.

We soon made contact with the enemy where Biazza Ridge crosses Gela and Vittoria road. When we got on that road to Gela we encountered some troops from the 45th Division, and they said not to proceed because the Germans held the road ahead. So Gavin in his own style said, "Well this seems like a pretty good opportunity for us to go ahead." We had a fair number of troops with us, so we figured we had a good chance. Along the way we captured a German officer who was coming along on a motorcycle, and he spilled his guts. He told us what was up on the ridge. The Germans occupied the ridge. He told us we would be coming in contact with a sizable German force.

With the troops we had along with the engineer company [B Company of the 307th] reinforcing us, we took the ridge; we drove the Germans off the ridge. We surprised them by coming after them. We sent our scouts out to find out their strengths and developed a strategy from that point. We worked our way up on the flanks and we gave the Germans a fair amount of fire right on the ridge because we were coming up on the lower side. We were all firing our weapons. The more we could fire the better off because it gives the impression of a unit in strength coming at them. I helped secure the right flank on the ridge.

Then we established a little CP [command post] up there. I don't remember exactly what position we were on the ridge as far as the CP. We were on the reverse slope just below the top of the ridge. The Germans were in the valley below the ridge.

Shortly after we had captured the ridge, we started digging slit trenches and foxholes. Everybody was trying to dig their foxholes deep enough so that the tanks would roll over us. Everybody was scraping with their helmets and trenching tools, but it was hard ground. We hardly had time to dig holes when they attacked and hit us hard. They drove up five or six tanks and infantry; they were coming at us. They looked like they were the biggest tanks ever invented. I thought we had it when the Germans got up within fifty or sixty yards of the CP, but we held them off with a lot of heavy firing, and we used pack 75-mm howitzers to kind of slow them down.

During the attack, they were pounding us with a lot of mortars. They had these Russian mortars that were like screaming meemies [German rocket-propelled artillery], and when they came in and hit the ground, you shook, [they] just bounced you out of the foxhole. I remember praying, "Don't let one drop on me." They were hitting all around.

After [we] pushed off one of their counterattacks [Gavin] and I were talking, and [he] said, "We are staying on this goddamned ridge—no matter what happens!" My hole was right next to his, and I said, "You know, if they do this again too many times, I don't know whether we can hold this position. Maybe we should have somebody go and see if we can get some help from the beach." Gavin said, "You know, if we stay here without help, we'll be here forever." He said, "You know, you're right." I said, "We oughtta get some help from the division or corps or somebody by the beaches." He said, "Well, you go and get it." So I said, "Why don't we send somebody?" I did not want to leave him at the point. He said, "That's a good idea." He said, "You go because maybe you can convince them about what's going on and we need help." I said, "OK, hold the fort."

I took off and went across the lower part of the ridge to this little gatehouse and then started down the road. I got a hold of this guy, a Sicilian with a bicycle, and I borrowed it from him—liberated it—and I drove the bicycle down the road. I didn't really have a good fix on just where the 45th Division and the II Corps headquarters was until I crossed the railroad track down about just southwest of Vittoria. I ran into a patrol of the 45th Division and I asked them where the headquarters was, and they directed me down this trail, and I took it and went on down to the headquarters of the 45th, and at the same time it was the headquarters of the II Corps, which was under Bradley's command.

When I got in there I wanted to see the G-3 [planning and operations officer] so I could get the situation and give it to them of what we were up

Alfred Ireland (white tank top) and fellow 505th troopers on their way to Oujda, North Africa. (Photo courtesy Alfred Ireland)

against. They took me to the G-3 tent, and there was General Bradley and Middleton, who was commander of the division, and Bradley was commander of the corps. When I walked in I introduced myself. I said, "I'm Captain Ireland of the 505th Regimental Combat Team and we're in one hell of a battle up on Biazza Ridge." I pointed out on the situation map and I said, "We're trying to hold off a very strong German force from coming in to divide the invasion force." [Bradley] turned to Middleton and said, "Give him what he wants." I'll never forget it as long as I live, the words he used. He said, "What do you want?" I said, "Everything you got! First we'd like some heavy artillery. If we could lay it in on these guys on front of the ridge we might be able to hold them off for a while." And then I said, "Can we have a company of tanks?" I didn't think I was going to get it. He said, "Absolutely." He told the G-3 to get going on it. Then he said, "Besides that we'll give you a liaison with a 155-mm howitzer battalion." He also gave me a navy artillery support party.

An observer went along, and we got up there, and that's when we started laying in some of the heavy stuff in front of the ridge. He turned to me and said, "What targets?" After the navy fire came in, it quieted the Germans down. Later on in the evening the company of tanks showed up [six tanks].

When the [American] tanks came up, it was strange because the guys had been shot at and beat up all day. We had a lot of casualties; we had a good forty or fifty men that were killed and about a hundred wounded. When those tanks showed up, I was up with the artillery observer; we were right on the ridge. You could hear the clanking of the tanks coming up from the rear, and at first the guys were moaning, "More tanks." When they saw they were Sherman tanks, the guys started cheering.

When the tanks arrived, Gavin said, "We are going to counterattack." I said, "You're going to counterattack the Hermann Göring Division?" [Laughs.] And he said, "Yes." But that's the way he thought, and we got everything organized. We got everybody we could get our hands on: cooks, clerks, and medics, anyone that could carry a rifle. We lost a lot of men and only had about a hundred left. Anybody that was there that could shoot, we got a gun in their hands. We just got everybody together.

I can't remember if anybody blew a whistle or what. We surged forward. It didn't last very long because many of the Germans took off.

EDWIN SAYRE

505th Parachute Infantry Regiment, 82nd Airborne Division

Before the war, Edwin Sayre was a rancher from Texas. During it he rose from private to captain. Sayre later served in Korea and Vietnam, finally retiring at the rank of colonel. During the invasion of Sicily, his small band of paratroopers captured several of his regiment's critical objectives near Piano Lupo and helped to blunt German tank attacks aimed at the Gela beachhead.

We landed in a vineyard right near an Italian and German outpost. It was a mile or so from where we were supposed to be. The outpost was actually an old winery that was on a rocky hill. I first took a shot at taking the outpost at two in the morning, and then we waited until dawn and started shooting at them. We ran into intense machine gun fire. There was an awful amount of fire. Plus I didn't have all my people at that time. I was short one platoon. The Germans and Italians pinned us down. I tossed the grenade on the center machine gun. We then threw a few hand grenades in a few apertures in the outpost—that was it—and captured about seven Germans and twenty Italians.

After the attack, I met Lieutenant Colonel Gorham, and he complimented me on capturing the outpost: "Good show," but then he said, "Let's not forget what the main objective is." He then pointed to a map and said, "Back down about a mile or so, the amphibious forces are coming in." And he then pointed to a road junction, and in the middle of the road junction [was] a large concrete emplacement with walls that were ten feet thick. It had apertures all around it with machine guns, barbed wire all around. The outpost controlled this roadway.

He said, "The mission of this regiment was to capture that pillbox so when the amphibious forces landed they could ride right through that junction." Well, anyway, my company captured this pillbox. I'd like to say it was through a brave act and all that, but it wasn't anything like that at all. I was coming down the road with my prisoners trying to contact the 1st Infantry Division and I saw the objective, the pillbox. At the time we had a battleship offshore that was firing 16-inch shells. But unfortunately the pillbox was in a low spot and they couldn't hit it with the shells. The shells were landing about a hundred yards to the outside.

I had a very good interpreter, a man named Calanreno. His family had been from Sicily. He could speak Italian better than they could. [Laughs.] I then told one of the Italian prisoners to go down to the outpost. The prisoner was very reluctant to go down there because he was afraid he was going to get shot. But I gave him an opportunity he couldn't refuse. I told him he would be shot if he didn't go down there. Before he left I said: "You tell those people, if they don't come out with their hands up in ten minutes, that we are going to bring all that fire down from the guns out there and just blow them to hell." And by golly the whole damn bunch of them walked out with their hands up. [Laughs.] So we immediately went down and occupied the pillbox. We took about forty prisoners. It wasn't an hour later when the 16th Infantry [Regiment] of the 1st Division arrived and I told them that we took the objective.

Meanwhile, I got on their telephone system and contacted General Ridgway, who was in the 1st Division's headquarters, and I told him that we captured the [505th's] regimental objective. We were then attached to the 16th Infantry because no other paratrooper units had gotten anywhere near us.

[Later] I then met up with the battalion commander, who said, "Since you've already been up on that ridge, I'll let you lead the attack." By that time it was getting a little dark. I had about fifty men. So the 1st Battalion commander of the 16th Infantry put me and my men up front and the commander said that I was to lead the attack. I said to him, "How am I going to find my way up that ridge?" It was so dark you couldn't see your hand in front of your face. He said, "That's no problem. Here's a German communication wire, and I'm sure it leads right up to where the Germans are." [Laughs.] So he just put it in my hand and said, "Just follow this," and laughed.

I took the thing and we started out. It was a very steep ridge. Well anyway, the Germans were up in this high position and we were climbing up on this ridge, and the rest of the battalion of the 16th Infantry was behind us. Soon the Germans heard us and opened up with machine guns. The machine gun fire missed us and went right in the middle of the 1st Battalion of the 16th Infantry and they had a lot of casualties, including the battalion commander. He was seriously wounded and was barely alive.

In the meantime, we crawled right on up and started to assault their defenses. They were in trenches that were two to three feet wide and about six feet deep. They were cut into solid rock. They were damn good defenses as far as organization was concerned. But there weren't many Germans in the trenches. We were successful in driving them out. I would say there were about twenty-five to thirty Germans in the trenches. We drove them back and occupied their positions.

They made a determined counterattack at daylight. Then we were up on the ridgeline. It started to become daylight and German tanks were coming down the road. A few of my men attacked with bazookas. I also inherited the forward field artillery observer of the 16th Regiment. They were about fifty yards in front of us and it looked like we were about to get overrun. We called for artillery fire and we got good artillery fire. They hit the lead tank right in front of us; they hit the turret. It didn't knock the tank out but it jammed the turret and the tank caught on fire. The poor Germans inside the tank couldn't get out. You could hear them screaming inside the tank from half a mile away. I had a few nightmares hearing the screams of Germans. The shells then started going off that were in the turret of the tank and that kind of discouraged the other tanks from attacking. There were about four or five tanks. The tanks were from the Hermann Göring Division.

As they were coming up on the ridge, the 1st Division had a tank destroyer company; the tank destroyers were half-tracks with 105s mounted on them. They had a lot of firepower. They pulled up on the ridge and fired about two rounds. The Tiger tank then swung its turret around and fired a few times. They almost looked like rag dolls when the men inside the tank destroyers went up in the air when a shell from the Tiger tank hit the tank destroyers. They knocked three of them out as fast as they could drive up on the ridge. They blew them to pieces before they could get a round off.

My orders at the time were just to hold the position or die. [Laughs.] The lieutenant next to me then said, "Do you think we are going to get out of this thing alive?" I said, "Of course we are," and then I said, "They are not going to come up in here at daylight, and when it gets dark we'll crawl out of here." But I really thought the tanks were going to come right up on our position, and if they did we didn't have the means to stop them.

Thankfully, the artillery was able to stop the tank attack. The artillery fire was close; we weren't more than fifty yards from the tanks, but we were in six-foot rock trenches so we were relatively safe. The Germans then fired on us with large mortars. The only way they could hit us was to drop one right in the trench, and they did do that. I almost died of pure fear because it hit the trench and it bounced around. And you could see it bouncing around, and I thought, "Wow, I have bought the farm!" I thought in the next bounce that thing is going off, but it didn't. It finally came to a rest and never went off.

The tanks withdrew and we led another attack. We then attacked another town and took it, and then they put the company in reserve.

DELBERT KUEHL

504th Parachute Infantry Regiment, 82nd Airborne Division

Chaplain Delbert Kuehl takes us to the night of July 11, 1943, when
his unit was making a parachute jump to reinforce the Gela beachhead, surviving one of the worst friendly-fire incidents of the war.

I never carried a gun in combat. I was in one of the first regiment organized,
the 504th. When I was in chaplain school, the commandant came out and said,
"We have an unusual request. We need a Catholic and Protestant chaplain for
the paratroopers." I volunteered right away, and a few others did, too. I got selected and went off to parachute training.

I got quite a bit of flak when I first got there. They said, "We don't need a
chaplain. We need someone who can carry a gun." I was called "Holy Joe"
and "Jumping Jesus" and a few things like that. To show you how bad it was,
we had eighteen hundred men in the regiment, and I arranged for a chapel
service, and I advertised it wide in the regimental newspaper. When the service came I only had two men show up. One man was drunk. He got into the
chapel by mistake. So I had one man that could understand what I was saying. It was pretty discouraging risking my neck jumping out of airplanes to
be chaplain, but I didn't say anything and I prayed much.

Things changed in combat. I made it a point to be on the front lines almost continually, and the men appreciated that. I also carried a medical bag
and cared for the wounded. I began to see a difference, and we had one hundred or two hundred men at the services. I would get the men together, and
many of their lives changed—some radically. One of the worst fellows that
we had became a chaplain and went to the Korean War as a chaplain. It was
very rewarding.

Let me tell you about Sicily. We were in the African desert, and I suppose
eight-thirty or nine o'clock, when the colonel [Reuben Tucker, commander
of the 504th] spoke to our group, he said, "I want you now to be the kind of
soldiers you were trained to be, and I know you will be." Prior to that we had
gone through the sand table exercises in preparation for the drop. We expected that we would receive opposition, but we didn't expect to have any unusual opposition. Before we went, I had a service around a large cactus, and
we boarded the planes.

Now something that I realized, this doesn't mean much to most people, is
that we jumped a T-5 parachute in our training, and just before we loaded up

the planes that evening they said, "We're sorry, but we don't have enough T-5s," and they asked us if anybody wanted to volunteer to jump a B-7. So I volunteered to jump a B-7. I wouldn't be talking to you today if I didn't have the B-7.

So we took off around nine-thirty heading across the Mediterranean. There was a slight moon shining, but not much. We flew quite low. We had a checkpoint, I don't remember which island it was, but I saw that. They told us that we would be coming over Sicily and that we would drop amber flares for recognition to the navy and other units signaling that we would be dropping in.

I was the only paratrooper officer in our plane and was standing in the door with First Sergeant Lee. We were flying very low. I saw the amber flares drop. Shortly after the amber flares dropped, somebody got trigger-happy in the navy, and it looked like a mammoth Fourth of July celebration. The sky was full of tracers, and between the tracers there is more bullets. It was just full of tracers. I saw plane after plane go down in flames. Some exploded in the air; others crash-landed in the sea. Tragically, some that were on planes that crashed in the sea, a few of them were alive and they [the navy] shot them in the water. One of our medics, who later survived, was shot in the water.

Our plane was hit many times. The pilot was hit, and the crew chief was killed. Several of our men were also killed.

Interestingly, when we were in Africa, one of the fellows in the stick [planeload of paratroopers] had a friend that was one of the ground maintenance men that serviced our plane. They were both from Wisconsin. It seemed kind of unbelievable at the time, but they were from the same town. He was saying how he hated to see his friend take off that night. When the plane returned from the jump, he counted 546 bullet holes in the plane. After we were done fighting in Sicily, we returned to Africa and maintenance men showed us the plane and how many holes were in it.

When I stood in that door, I couldn't believe what I saw. I don't think any of our fellows could. Seeing plane after plane being shot down, I was surrounded by peace that I have never experienced before. It was unbelievable— almost like there was an angel standing at your side. This happened just before this holocaust began. It was tremendous peace.

We were flying over a rocky mountain range or group of hills; I don't know how high they were. The red light went on above the door and shortly after that the green light went on. Sergeant Lee was the first out the door. I soon followed him and I heard someone saying, "No!" "No!" "No!" The next fellow behind me saw a ridge coming up. I landed on the ridge. I had a B-7 parachute. If I had a T-5 I would have been splattered all over the rocks. The B-7 had a pilot chute, which pulls the main chute out much faster.

I landed on the rocks and I think I must have been knocked out, because I don't remember what happened. I was bleeding in several places and my jump suit was torn. There was a rock wall in front of me. So I made my way down the rock wall and met the fellow who jumped behind me and he had two broken legs. The next fellow I encountered had one broken leg.

I heard a machine gun firing and said to myself, "That sounds like our machine gun." In our training they taught us how to distinguish between German and American weapons. I could see two fellows approaching the wall. I heard them speaking English. As they got closer to the wall, I yelled "Halt!" Our password was "George Marshall." So I yelled "George." There was no answer. At midnight the password had been changed, but I didn't know it at the time. I figured the next thing they would do was throw a grenade over the wall. So I said, "Hold your fire; I'm an American. Don't shoot! I'm coming over the wall." I stood up, and one of them fired. To this day I don't know how he missed. They came forward and shoved a rifle in my back and told me to march forward. If there was only one of them I would have spun round and knocked his rifle away. But there were two of them, so I couldn't do that. I said, "Can't you see this American flag on my uniform and the cross on my helmet?" I said, "I'm an American paratrooper chaplain."

They marched me forward, and five rifles were pointed at me. I yelled, "Put those rifles down. I'm an American!" I was angry—even chaplains get angry. I said, "Do you have an officer here?" Finally, an officer from the 45th Division came forward and I told what happened. I said, "Look, I told these fellows that I was an American and they even saw the American flag on my uniform but still fired." I said, "Give me one of your men so I could round up my paratroopers so we aren't killing each other." They didn't give me anybody. So on my own in the dark I hollered for Sergeant Lee. They were scattered. Finally I got a few of them together. Eventually we linked up with the 45th Division men without shooting each other and got medical attention to our men that needed it.

At the time I didn't realize it, but even with the B-7 parachute I had both kidneys dislodged from the jump. I was in a tremendous amount of pain. I went through the whole war with pain from time to time. But fortunately, I was able to make it through the war and come home with the troops. When I came back to the States I was in army hospitals for fifteen months. I was in one hospital after another, and they had to operate on both kidneys several times.

For the rest of Sicily we did have some men killed, but most Italians surrendered. I'll give you an interesting example of what happened. I was with the medics one day, and we had a captured half-track. Most half-tracks had rubber on the track wheels, but on this half-track the rubber was worn off and it made a lot of noise when it went down a cobblestone road. I don't think we even had a gun on the half-track. Somehow we got left behind by our troops. So we were going up a road, making enough noise to wake the dead. Finally, the road split into a Y. So we asked ourselves, "Which way did our troops go?" We went right. The next thing you know white flags were sticking out. We asked ourselves, "What's going on here?" The chaplain and the medics took that town. It was one of the funnier things that happened during the war. [Laughs.] They could have shot us all to pieces since we didn't even have a gun on the half-track.

CHAPTER FOUR

TOUGH OLD BOOT: Southern Italy

Italy is like a boot. You must, like Hannibal,

enter it from the top.

—Napoleon Bonaparte

Throughout the invasion of Sicily, the Allies debated where to strike next. The positions taken were the same, the Americans still favoring a cross-Channel invasion of France in 1943, then known as operation ROUNDUP, later renamed OVERLORD, the British still for operations in the Mediterranean. Winston Churchill argued that Italy was the "soft underbelly" of Europe and that an invasion would knock Italy out of the Axis. The British also considered using Italy as a springboard to invade the Balkans and fight their way up into Central Europe. More important, a lack of Allied landing craft for the cross-Channel attack made continued operations in the Mediterranean tactically more realistic, as did the concentration of troops in the area as a result of the invasion of Sicily. At the end of July 1943, a decision was reached that Italy would be invaded, with the understanding that the invasion would be conducted on a shoestring and the bulk of Allied forces would be channeled to OVERLORD, which was tentatively set for May 1944.[1]

Even before the fall of Sicily, the Italian government was looking for a way to end Italy's involvement in the war. Behind-the-scenes political discussions among King Emmanuel III, the cabinet, and the high command brought about the collapse of the Mussolini government, and tentative offers for a separate peace with the Allies were secretly being extended.

But before a peace plan could be hammered out, the Germans, anxious about an Italian collapse, rushed additional German divisions into Italy. Naturally, the Italians wanted some assurances from the Allies that they would be protected from the wrath of the Germans. The Italians insisted that several divisions be landed near Rome. Unable to move that many troops on Rome, the Allies devised a plan code-named GIANT II to drop the 82nd Airborne Division five miles northwest of Rome.

Meanwhile, as the secret peace negotiations dragged on, the Allies were moving forward with their formal plans for an invasion. The range of Allied tactical fighter aircraft to provide air cover for the invasion dictated that the invasion take place south of Rome. Two landings would take place. The first was a diversion called BAYTOWN, in which the British Eighth Army would cross the strait of Messina and land on the toe of Italy on September 3. One week later and 150 miles to the north, the main Allied landing, code-named AVALANCHE, would hit Salerno.[2] A secondary attack by the British 1st Airborne Division would hit the heel of Italy near Taranto.

After being briefed about the proposed drop on Rome, Matthew Ridgway, then commander of the 82nd Airborne Division, petitioned most of the Allied high command to consider the risks involved. Finally, Ridgway convinced Generals Alexander and Eisenhower to allow Brigadier General Maxwell Taylor, then the deputy commander of the 82nd Airborne Division, and Colonel William Gardiner, of the 51st Troop Carrier Wing, to make a secret mission into Rome to investigate the feasibility of the drop.

Once in Rome, Taylor and Gardiner found that a large discrepancy existed between what the Italians thought could be done and what the Allies thought they could do with GIANT II. The operation depended on four Italian divisions first securing the paratroopers' drop zones and aiding the 82nd's fight into Rome against the area's forty thousand German troops backed by about two hundred tanks.[3] Taylor correctly sized up the situation and radioed Eisenhower that it was a suicide mission and that it was unlikely that the Italians could or even would fight the Germans.

As Taylor was communicating the message to Eisenhower on the afternoon of September 8, 1943, C-47s crammed with paratroopers were on the runway preparing the take off for Rome. The message to cancel the jump was delivered to Ridgway on the airfield as the planes started taking off, averting what would have been a monumental military blunder.

On the night of September 8, as General Mark Clark's Fifth Army was preparing to assault Salerno, the troops were surprised to learn that the Italians had surrendered. Anticipating the element of surprise and an easy battle, the Allies began landing in the early-morning hours of September 9. Spearheading the operation was a Ranger task force made up of the 1st, 3rd, and 4th Ranger battalions. Their task was to secure the rugged Amalfi Coast area, on the left flank of the beachhead at Maiori. If held by the Germans, the high ground over the Amalfi Coast could be used to fire artillery at the beachhead. Two battalions of British Commandos also spearheaded the landing.

As the Allies hit the beach, the Germans were waiting. Two days earlier, the German 16th Panzer Division had dug in around the Salerno area. When the troops landed, they were greeted by withering machine gun and artillery fire and German loudspeakers blaring: "Come on in and give up. You're covered."

Surprisingly, Darby's Rangers encountered minimal resistance as they moved ashore at Maiori. Moving inland, the Rangers quickly took up positions on high ground overlooking the plain of Naples, dominated by the Chiunzi Pass, on the extreme left flank of the invasion area. Once on top, Colonel Darby radioed General Clark: "We have taken up positions in the enemy's rear and we'll be here until hell freezes over."[4] From Chiunzi, the Rangers controlled the high ground overlooking the German main line of communication from Naples to Salerno.

The Germans reacted swiftly and violently to the Ranger capture of the pass and launched numerous large-scale attacks to unseat the Rangers. The Rangers never yielded. Though outnumbered by an estimated nine to one, the Rangers repelled each attack and followed up with a counterattack of their own, earning themselves two more Presidential Unit Citations.[5]

Over the next two days, fresh Germans units from all over Italy began pouring into Salerno. Starting September 12, the 29th and 16th panzer divisions began a large attack on the north flank of the VI Corps, while the Hermann Göring Division and 15th Panzer hit the British X Corps. With disaster looming, Mark Clark began making plans to abandon the beachhead.[6]

September 13 was the critical day for the shrinking Salerno beachhead. Shortly after midday, German troops launched an all-out effort to drive the Allies into the sea. By the end of the day, the Germans were less than five miles from the beach. German propaganda broadcasts claimed it was another Dunkirk.

The only hope for quick assistance lay with the 82nd Airborne Division, which after the canceled Rome drop was in Sicily and available for commitment. On the morning of September 13, Clark sent a letter to Ridgway to make plans to drop the 82nd behind Allied lines on the beachhead. Ridgway's response was brief: "Can do."

Never had an airborne operation been put together in such a short time. Maps were thrown up against the sides of planes and read by flashlight as thirteen hundred paratroopers of Colonel Reuben Tucker's 504th Parachute

Infantry Regiment boarded the planes. A half-mile-long "T" made up of lighted jerry cans filled with gas and sand marked the drop zone as the paratroopers started dropping on target to the cheers of Salerno's beleaguered defenders.[7]

Following up on the success of Tucker's jump, Clark decided to drop Colonel James Gavin's 505th Parachute Infantry Regiment on the beachhead, giving the defenders another twenty-one hundred men.[8] Later, the 82nd's 325th Glider Infantry Regiment would arrive on the beachhead by boat.

Another jump took place the night of September 14–15 with the hope of stemming the flow of German men and materiel to the beachhead by securing the crucial road hub of Avellino, far behind the German lines. That night, everything that could go wrong did. Radio equipment designed to lead the planes into Avellino failed, and the 509th was misdropped over a wide area, nearly leading to the annihilation of the battalion. For the next several weeks, small bands of 509ers fought a guerrilla war against the Germans—cutting communication wires, laying mines, and sabotaging German convoys. Remarkably, 80 percent of the 598 men who jumped eventually filtered back to Allied lines.[9]

The arrival of Allied reinforcements led to a stabilization of the beachhead and precipitated the German decision to withdraw north. After a final doomed attack on September 16, the German Tenth Army began pulling back. Blowing up bridges, felling trees, and mining roads, the Germans employed a scorched-earth policy that would come to characterize the entire Italian campaign.

Pushing through the Chiunzi Pass, the Allies captured Naples on October 1, 1943, and turned their attention north toward Rome. Between Naples and Rome, the Germans were turning Italy's nearly impassable mountainous terrain into killing fields, first making a fighting withdrawal to fortified positions behind the Volturno River and then pulling back to a series of fortified defenses called the Winter Line.[10]

After assisting the British X Corps crossing at the Volturno River, the bulk of the 82nd Airborne Division was on its way back to England for the invasion of Normandy. But the manpower shortage in Italy was so severe that one regiment of the 82nd Airborne Division, the 504th Regimental Combat Team,[11] would stay behind and slog it out in the mountains and mud. The 504th was joined by Darby's Rangers and the 509th Parachute Infantry Battalion.

Cold weather, mud, and the mountainous terrain that the Germans fortified made fighting in Italy a nightmare. By November 1943, the Fifth Army was being bled white before the Winter Line. Mines, barbed wire, and concrete pillboxes with interlocking fields of fire took a steady toll on the Allies as they slowly pushed forward.

In the mountaintop villages such as Venafro and San Pietro battle raged for control of the Winter Line. The Allies took 188,000 casualties as they inched their way up the spine of Italy.[12] As the manpower shortage in Italy worsened, Allied commanders used lightly armed Rangers and paratroopers as heavy infantry instead of holding them back for special operations, and they were shot to pieces in the process.

In November 1943, another elite unit, the 1st Special Service Force, arrived in Italy, and it managed to crack the Winter Line. Known as the "North Americans," since the unit was staffed in roughly equal numbers by Americans and Canadians, this all-volunteer group had trained in the cold weather of Fort Harrison, Montana, where members mastered a variety of skills including demolitions, sabotage, hand-to-hand combat, and ski combat, and most were trained parachutists.

The Force had trained for long-range sabotage missions,[13] but its first action, in August 1943, was a bloodless landing at Kiska Island, in the Aleutians, which had recently been abandoned by the Japanese. The Combined Chiefs of Staff then directed them to Italy.

Shortly after arriving in Italy, the Force was given the formidable task of assaulting the heart of the Winter Line: the twin peaks of Monte La Difensa and Monte Rementanea. Entrenched on top of the three-thousand-foot mountains were elements of the 15th Panzer Grenadier Division that had hurled back several earlier attempts to take the peaks.

In one of the most daring missions of the war, the Force moved around the base of the mountain undetected thanks to a heavy artillery barrage and diversionary attacks by the British and the United States 36th Infantry Division. Waiting until they had the cover of darkness on December 2, the Force proceeded to scale the northwest side of Difensa, which, starting at the two-thousand-foot level, is a seventy-degree cliff. Because the Germans considered the north side of the mountain impassable, especially at night, they left it largely undefended. Undaunted, the North Americans worked their way up to the top.[14] Once there, the Force overwhelmed the stunned German defenders, and after two hours of intense combat gained control of the saucer-shaped crest.

After the fall of Difensa, the Germans plastered the mountaintop with artillery fire. Hunkered down in captured German pillboxes and foxholes, the Force endured until a few days later, when the North Americans crossed over a saddleback ridge connecting the two mountains, taking Rementanea after a fierce struggle.

With the capture of the two mountains, the Winter Line was cracked, opening the way for the Allied advance on the next German defenses: several additional mountaintops around the tiny village of San Pietro and a line of

Ranger and Airborne Operations in Southern Italy—1943–1944

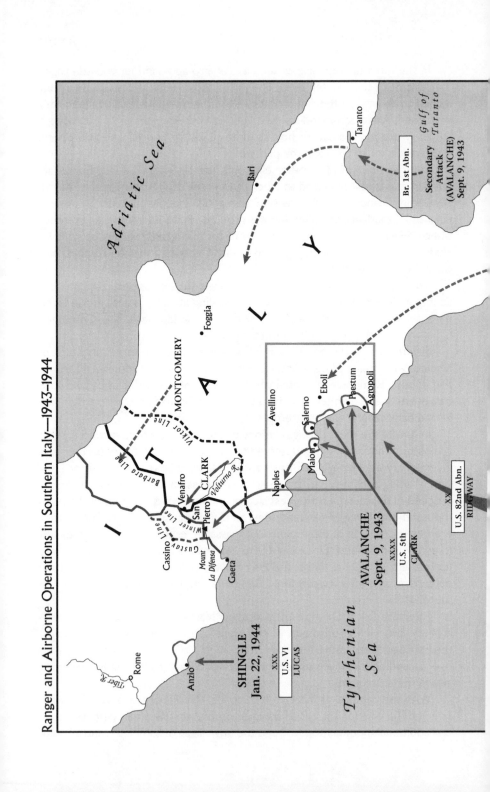

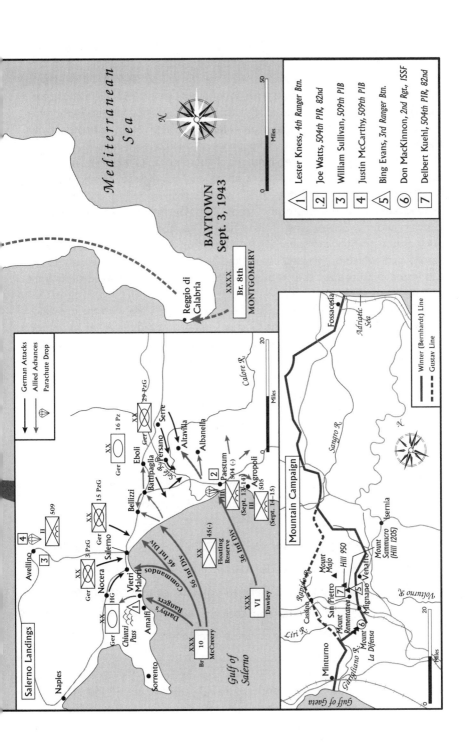

Salerno Landings

Naples

Sorrento

Amalfi

Chiunzi Pass

Darby's Rangers

Maiori

Vietri

Salerno

Nocera

Avellino

3 [4]

509 [3]

Ger — 3 PzG

Ger — HG

Ger — 15 PzG

Ger — XX

Ger — 16 Pz

Bellizzi

Battipaglia

S. Persano

Serre

Eboli

Ger — 29 PzG

Altavilla

Albanella

Calore R.

Br. — 10 — McCreery

Commandos

56 Inf Div

46 Inf Div

Paestum

304 (-)

Agropoli

505

Floating Reserve 36 Inf Div

45(-) (Sept. 13–14)

(Sept. 14–15)

VI — Dawley

Gulf of Salerno

Miles 20

German Attacks
Allied Advances
Parachute Drop

Mediterranean Sea

N

Miles 0 50

Reggio di Calabria

XXXX
Br. 8th
MONTGOMERY

BAYTOWN
Sept. 3, 1943

1 — Lester Kness, 4th Ranger Btn.

2 — Joe Watts, 504th PIR, 82nd

3 — William Sullivan, 509th PIB

4 — Justin McCarthy, 509th PIB

5 — Bing Evans, 3rd Ranger Btn.

6 — Don MacKinnon, 2nd Rgt., 1SSF

7 — Delbert Kuehl, 504th PIR, 82nd

Mountain Campaign

Volturno R.

Gulf of Gaeta

Minturno

Garigliano R.

Mount La Difensa

Mount Remetanea

Mount Lungo

San Pietro

Rapido R.

Cassino

Liri R.

Mount Maio

Hill 950

Mignano Venafro

Mount Sammucro (Hill 1205)

Isernia

Sangro R.

Fossacesia

Adriatic Sea

N

Winter (Bernhardt) Line
Gustav Line

Miles 20

Miles 0 20

German fortifications known as the Gustav Line. The fall of Difensa gave the 1st Special Service Force and its commander, Robert Frederick, legendary status. Winston Churchill commented after the fall of Difensa, "If we had a dozen men like him, we would have smashed Hitler in 1942. He's the greatest fighting general of all time."[15] But the price tag for taking the mountains was high. The six days of action on Difensa and Rementanea had cost the North Americans 511 casualties, roughly one-third of their men.[16]

After piercing the Winter Line, all of the elite units would continue to play a major role in the Fifth Army's northward advance toward Rome. The 3rd Ranger Battalion and the 504th were heavily involved in operations around San Pietro, which stood in front of the German stronghold of Monte Cassino and the Gustav Line. The 1st Special Service Force continued operating as line infantry and spearheaded attacks on the western spur of Monte Sammucro, which dominated the skyline behind San Pietro. In January 1944, the Force captured another mountain, Monte Majo, in much the same way as it had taken Difensa.

The slow pace and bloody cost of the advance up Italy, with the prospect of more of the same ahead at the Gustav Line, prompted the Allies to opt for an end-around amphibious landing at Anzio (in addition to the continuing push up the boot) to break the bitter stalemate and capture Rome.

LESTER KNESS

1st and 4th Ranger Battalions

In the early-morning hours of September 9, 1943, the Ranger force hit the left flank of the Salerno beachhead at Maiori. Encountering minimal resistance, they moved six miles inland and took up positions on the high ground in the Sorrentine Mountains, holding the crucial Chiunzi Pass. From there they guarded the far-left flank of the beachhead, mortaring German columns as they rolled down Highway 18, on their way to attack the Allied toehold at Salerno. Company Commander Lester Kness remembers one of the thirteen days of fighting at the pass.

There's a certain amount of pride of having the respect of the guys that you're serving with. They have a demand that's unwritten that is put on you:

that you'll do your utmost. You'll be there regardless of what happens or you'll lay your life down. You might be scared to death. If you're not scared, you're a damn fool. But you might be scared to the point that you can't function and you shake all over.

We were up on the Chiunzi Pass after we got into Italy. I believe it was the 3rd Battalion, I knew the company commander, he came up to me and said they were going to move down the mountain off to the left and approach the German positions down there. I had outposts out there, so I said, "Guys, you got to keep low. Have your men keep low and they can get down past the rocks and the brush so the Germans can't spot them." So he told his men to follow the man ahead of them. As the column moved down the mountain they started standing up. The Germans opened up on them point-blank with 88s and just splattered that side of the mountain. I don't know how many were killed or wounded, but I was right back over the ridge, and the medic from this company ran up and I stopped him. He dropped down on his hands and grabbed me around my feet, just shaking and scared to death.

I said to one of my men, "Get this man off of me." He reached down and pulled the fellow up, and I said, "You take him up on that ridge and order him down to patch up his men, and if he doesn't go, you slap the daylights out of him and order him again, and if he doesn't go, you take out your .45 and order him once more. If he doesn't go, you kill him." So he took the kid up there and took him near the edge where he had to go over and he said, "Now you heard what he said. I don't want to hurt you. I don't want to shoot you, but I will. You better get down there and patch up your men." He went right over the ridge.

About two months later we were up in Venafro, and the 3rd Battalion got close to us, and one of my men came up and said, "There's a guy here from the 3rd Battalion who wants to see you." They wouldn't let anybody get close to me, I don't know why; maybe they thought they were going to shoot me. Anyways, this kid came up and said, "You don't remember me, Lieutenant Kness?" I said, "No." He said, "Well, I remember you. You ordered me shot up on that Chiunzi Pass. I want to thank you for what you did. If you hadn't done that, I would have been a psycho case back in the United States 'cause I was clear out of my head. I was just scared to death, but you scared me worse. I went down that hill. I've been in some close fights since and have never been bothered like that one." I said, "Well, let me tell you something: I was the same way, and you have to have somebody to help you through that first initial phase of fear. When you get over that, then you can function." He thanked me profusely.

JOE WATTS

504th Parachute Infantry Regiment, 82nd Airborne Division

Joe Watts remembers the 82nd's canceled jump on Rome.

[About 1700 hours on September 8, at Trapani, Sicily.] After officers' call to regiment, we assembled and were briefed. Two or three airfields around Rome, Italy, were pointed out. We were to parachute on an airfield north of Rome, deploy, dig in, and hold until reinforcements arrived, within three days. We began scurrying around, rerolling bundles and packing up. C-47s began circling the airfield for landing as trucks arrived in the company area. The aircraft flew in a steady line circling the field, then flying toward the tall, conical mountain north of the city of Trapani, atop which a town was referred to as Rudyard Kipling's "City in the Sky." As the aircraft seemed to be about to collide with the mountain, they banked to the west, flew parallel to the airfield, then out over the sea, banked again, and again, to land from west to east. They looked so tiny, so vulnerable, when flying with the mountain as a backdrop. Those C-47s were coming in from all over Sicily and Africa. Soon after they landed, the trucks arrived in our company area and took us toward the refueling aircraft as an officer in a jeep shouted tail numbers for each unit. At our assigned aircraft, we laid out equipment and bundles and a truck manned by riggers drove from plane to plane issuing parachutes. We mounted our bundles on the para-racks under the belly of the plane, six racks per plane. Extra bundles were designated door-bundles. Once the labor was complete, we chuted up and loaded.

Our 1st Battalion aircraft were in the air and forming up to fly to Italy when jeeps came screaming onto the tarmac among the 2nd Battalion taxiing aircraft. Badoglio had renounced the armistice terms—he needed more time. The Rome operation was canceled. A sigh of relief was felt but the bravado talk began: "I was ready for that jump!" "Too bad, I'd've really been hell on wheels!" "Let's go anyway! I'm ready, really ready!" And so forth. But while chuting up and taxiing there wasn't a word. Just each man tending to his equipment keeping his thoughts to himself. The noise was unbearable. The aircraft already airborne returned to the airfield and everyone went back to their bivouacs. The next morning we learned the Germans didn't trust Badoglio so several panzer units had [been] ordered in and were manning our proposed drop zone.

By the end of the day on September 13, 1943, the German attacks were less than five miles from the Salerno beach, and General Mark

Clark was considering evacuation. The only hope for quick assistance lay with the 82nd Airborne Division, which was in Sicily and available for commitment. An airborne drop was quickly drawn up, and thirteen hundred paratroopers from Colonel Reuben Tucker's 504th Parachute Infantry began landing in the Paestum sector of the beachhead that evening. Joe Watts remembers the jump and subsequent move to positions around the towns of Albanellia and Altavilla in this e-history.

A day or two passed, and to stay in shape, F Company 504th Parachute Infantry Regiment went on a road march. From our bivouac on the airfield, we hiked across town and up the mountain road above Trapani. We had just arrived at the top of the hill, it must have been about noon, and were looking forward to melons and rest, maybe beer and wine when a jeep screamed up the road with an officer from our battalion . . . standing and holding on to the windshield frame, shouting for us to return to the airfield immediately. We were to load for a drop that night. The jeep picked up the company commanding officer and another man, his runner for the day, to return to the battalion for briefing. The remainder of the company jogged most of the way down that hill in one-third the time it took to climb, arriving in our bivouac at about four o'clock. C-47s were circling to land like buzzards around roadkill. We were briefed on the run: Jump to relieve the pressure on U.S. Fifth Army at Salerno.

Most of us slept for an hour and hoped there would not be a recurrence of our first combat jump [when they encountered friendly fire over Sicily]. But well before we neared the Italian coast, we were ordered to stand and hook up. We were ready in the event our plane was hit by enemy fire. We started jumping from six hundred to eight hundred feet. There weren't any antiaircraft or enemy planes to greet us. As I exited the door, there was a large "T" beginning to light up below me on the DZ. I later learned it was our old battalion commander from Sicily, Bill Yarborough, that arranged the gasoline drums and lighted the "T." We assembled but had lost about six or eight troopers from 1st Platoon with broken bones as they hit some rock walls just to the south of the DZ.

The company was now down to less than 110 men for duty. At the end of the DZ we boarded trucks and moved east and north. We drove past the ruins of an ancient temple at Paestum. There was a towed 37-mm antitank gun pointing down the road from the direction from which we had come, manned by GIs. It seemed silly, incongruous, for this tiny gun and twentieth-century soldiers to be standing in front of these very ancient ruins, ruins that resembled pictures of the Parthenon in Greece. We arrived at the CP of 1st Platoon, just below the crest of a ridge looking north with the rooftops and church tower of the town of Altavilla. The Germans of the 26th Panzer Division were down the forward slope preparing for a counterattack.

During one German breakthrough on our right, enemy soldiers tried to return to their lines again by circling behind us and moving up the draw between us and Altavilla. But we killed two and captured three that night. The next morning one of the U.S. Navy ships in the gulf fired its big guns—12-inch or bigger—at the enemy, but one or two rounds fell short. They landed behind our battalion.

Regiment moved their CP into one of the craters, the other was designated a repository for friendly and enemy dead until the battle was over and proper Graves Registration Unit (GRU) personnel could clean up the battlefield. And since company runners do everything, our company first sergeant sent me to work on the battalion GRU team. Dogs and cats were all the dead I had ever seen until I joined the army and arrived in North Africa. But here I was undergoing training in the mortician's trade. The battalion surgeon directed us to gather the dead, friendly and enemy, or their remains, by smelling them out, placing them on very odoriferous litters, and moving them to the crater for temporary burial.

Since the trees on the slopes had been pruned by artillery fire and since most of the dead I worked through were in the draw behind F Company, the First Sergeant could keep an eye on me so I couldn't cut out of the detail, I had to work. At first I tried to just neaten the battlefield by picking up weapons, ammunition, and equipment. But that didn't work; the noncommissioned officers in charge of the detail took over that job, fast. I was relegated to bodies and parts.

These were the days before body-bags. We always tried to roll the body onto a poncho or shelter-half. Some guys had gloves, most of us didn't. The first day or so we handled bodies and parts with shovels. Later we just reached down and picked it up and put it on the litter. I spent most of two days retching, the odors and sights were so terrible. I covered my mouth and nose with a piece of parachute silk to keep from breathing the odors. And I began looking at the dead as machines that had ceased to function. This helped. But in the evenings when I returned to the company no one would have anything to do with me because my clothes retained the smell of the dead and my own puke. I couldn't draw rations like everyone else. Even today I conjure up those scenes of the GRU detail when the sweet, nauseating odor of putrefied flesh accosts my olfactory senses as I stumble across the carcass of a dead deer or other animal in the woods.

WILLIAM SULLIVAN

509th Parachute Infantry Battalion

On the night of September 14–15, the 509th Parachute Infantry Battalion dropped into the crucial crossroads town of Avellino, twenty miles behind the German lines. The situation at the Salerno beachhead was still precarious, and the drop was made to disrupt German reinforcements and stabilize the British sector of the beachhead.[17] Navigational errors and faulty radar equipment, known as Aldis lamps, carried by the 509th's pathfinders (paratroopers who had dropped earlier to guide the main body of paratroopers to the drop zone) caused the battalion to be scattered over a wide area. Holding Avellino was impossible, but the men, as Staff Sergeant William Sullivan relates, managed to at least avoid the enemy.

The jump itself was an event because we didn't jump when we were supposed to. I was the jumpmaster of the plane. That remained quite an experience for me because when we came over to the drop zone this wise pilot could see something we couldn't see even though it was night, and he aborted the jump. In other words, he turned the light off; he didn't turn on the green light. He sent a man back to tell me. Hell, I was in the door and I had the men up. The red light comes on and you get the men to stand up, hook up, and get in the door and watch for the green light and go out the door. You don't tell them, "Follow me," they just go out the door; they're trained to follow you. So here I am sweating it out, the red light comes on and I've got the men up, we're all crowding in the door and I'm in the door. The damn light doesn't come on. We pulled back from the door. The pilot went down, he wasn't going over the city of Avellino. He made a complete one-eighty and he came racing back up the line passing the other C-47s dropping our guys.

Now I'm looking out the door. I'm facing troops coming in behind us and they're jumping; I could see them coming out the door. So he [the pilot] goes down and picks up the whole tail of it and goes back and then dropped us, gave us the light. It probably saved my ass because many of those men were captured. We landed in the drop zone, which was south of Avellino.

Members of the 509th Parachute Infantry
Battalion preparing to board C-47s before
the jump at Avellino. (Author's photo)

Not long after the jump, Christ, it seemed the whole German army moved into the area and they were hunting for us—they were hunting for us like rabbits. That scared the hell out of me. They were going up and down the rows of corn and shooting anything that moved. It reminded me of when I was a kid, in the fall. We used to hunt rabbits that way. The idea of being captured or the idea of someone hunting you scares the shit out of you. The idea of fighting back is one thing—you take a rifle and here comes the enemy and bang, bang. But the idea you were being hunted, there's nothing you can do, you have to hide.

JUSTIN McCARTHY

509th Parachute Infantry Battalion

After eluding German patrols, small bands of paratroopers sought refuge in the hills surrounding Avellino. Living off the land, the paratroopers mounted raids on German convoys and positions, tying up German soldiers and relieving some of the pressure on Salerno. Lieutenant Justin McCarthy recalls one of the many operations conducted to hamper the Germans' ability to reinforce around Salerno.[18]

There was a German bridge down this road, and a lot of German trucks were going down this road. [Major Dudley, the ranking officer] said, "It's not a big bridge, but it would delay them for a while if we could knock it out." I said, "Okay, so that's what we'll do."

Corporal Jeanes was a demolitionist. He had his demolition kit, and we had a few antitank mines. So we got everything that we could use together, and then we had a couple of Italian guides, two brothers, and another Italian named Fernando. Fernando was good. I was leery of the two brothers. They were going to guide us to the bridge. I told one of the men in our group—he spoke enough Italian to know what was going on—I said, "Don't let them know you can speak Italian; listen to what they're saying. If we walk into an ambush, he's the first one you're going to shoot." They'd lead us and then they'd tell us to "wait here, wait here." And then they'd go on, the brothers, they'd disappear and then they'd come back. I thought they'd lead us someplace where the Germans were waiting, then they'd get the hell out of there and then they [Germans] would open up on us from both sides of the trail. They turned out to be all right, except they told us they'd give us plenty of advance notice and all of the sudden we were at the bridge.

Major Dudley sent a runner down and said, "Do a reconnaissance and wait for my order." I went down with Weber and a couple others, and we were down the road when all of a sudden we heard a motorcycle coming. We just flattened in the rocks right beside the road and the motorcycle went by. I could have almost stuck my foot out, it was so close. The Germans didn't have any idea that we were there. So we checked back with the major, and he said, "Take your guys, and you go down with Corporal Jeanes. Take whatever you think you'll need. Sergeant Weber will have a couple of guys on the other end of the bridge."

When we got to the bridge, Jeanes went under the bridge to set the charge. Jeanes said, "Christ, we don't have enough here to blow up that bridge. I can blow a hole in it, probably, but that's all." We turned around and we got out from under the bridge. We saw a half-track go by. At the bridge there was a building beside it, and it [the half-track] stopped there and went into the building and we could hear voices; we couldn't hear what they were saying. We were trying to see if they left anybody on that damn half-track, because if they did and they had a 20-mm on it, they could give us a real hot time. Shortly afterward, what do you know, firing breaks out and the next thing you know it seems like everybody in the world is firing. There was rifle fire coming from all sides.

We were up on the bridge, and I had two men below, and we were handing them bags of earth to tamp the explosive. They were handing it up to me and I was handing it to Jeanes. Jeanes was laying up under the bridge. In the

509ers dug in on the side of a mountain in southern Italy. (Author's photo)

meantime, the firing was getting worse and it was coming right down into the bridge. All the sudden Jeanes jumped, and I thought he got hit. I stayed there a minute, and with that somebody let go a blast and it went right into the wall right beside me, and I said, "Let's go!" and over the side I went. The four of us were down in the water running through the creek. We started back towards the hill where we left the guys on the hill. I'm down in the water and wham! everything blew. We went up the hill and looked down and saw the hole. We put a hole in the bridge. I said, "Jeez, that ain't a hell of a big hole." A German truck came down the road and hit the hole in the bridge and we opened up on it with everything we had and we then proceeded up the hill.

WARREN "BING" EVANS

3rd Ranger Battalion

After a bloody crossing at the Volturno River, the Allies faced a German defensive line across Italy known as the Winter Line. The focal points of the line were mountains around the towns of Venafro and San Pietro. Venafro held an important road junction and was called by the BBC the "hottest spot on earth." The lightly armed elite units were being used in the place of heavy line infantry while playing a major role in the Fifth Army's operations. Bing Evans reports on a mission to take a mountain in the Venafro–San Pietro area.

Colonel Darby asked me, "I want you to go up, take a patrol on top of that mountain, and see what they have and see what we can do." I took a patrol on top of that mountain and found what they had there. It wasn't very much; I was kind of surprised. When I came down and reported this, he said, "Can you take that with your company tomorrow night?" I said, "Yes, I can." We infiltrated up the side of that mountain and we took what we thought was the top of that mountain. It had two tops! We sat on one, and the Germans sat on the other, and there we sat looking at each other.

There was a very sharp drop on both sides. They couldn't get at us and we couldn't get at them for the same reason. On the top of the mountain, voices would carry; we could hear them moving around over there like they were in the next room.

Finally I yelled over there, "Can anyone over there speak English?" The answer came back, "Yes, I can." I said, "Look, we're in kind of a bind here. Neither one of us can do anything about this, really. Why don't you stand up over there and I'll stand up over here and we'll talk this situation over?" I said, "I'll give you a few minutes to clear it with your men. I don't want anyone getting killed over this." He said, "Okay, just give me a few minutes."

I yelled, "Are you ready?" He said, "Yeah, but you stand up first." So I stood up on my side of the mountain, and he stood up on his. I tried to talk him into coming over to get a date with a Red Cross girl (I hadn't seen them, but I heard we had them). We were probably a football field away, but it seemed less, maybe seventy-five yards instead of one hundred yards. Then I tried to talk him into coming over for a steak dinner. Can you imagine that? I hadn't seen one in I don't know how many years! He was pretty set.

I had a couple of patrols and learned where they had most of their stuff, their command post, they had a couple of machine guns, the snipers and where the men were, how they were laid out. I reported this to the colonel for when it came time to take the other side of the mountain.

In the meantime, every afternoon around about three we'd have a truce, and I'm going to say it was more like fifty yards because we got to standing up on both sides and throwing souvenirs back and forth. Then the truce would be over and it would be deadly serious war. Well, I found out his name was Hans, and Hans had been in this country at Michigan State training in hotel management. His folks owned the biggest hotel in Leipzig, Germany,

A rifle squad of D Company, 3rd Ranger Battalion, in a mountain village in southern Italy. (Photo courtesy U.S. Army)

and they were elderly, and he was going to take over that hotel. They sent him over to our country to get educated. When he went back to visit his folks, Hitler got him into the army. He would have come over, come to our side, except if he had, then his folks would have had to pay the price. That night we infiltrated into their lines and gave the order to try and capture Hans, but he was killed in action that night; I saw his body.

[Around San Pietro] we advanced in broad daylight now on another hill. The lead platoon was led by a man who had been the first sergeant of A Company when I was first commissioned and went in as a second platoon leader as a second lieutenant; his name was Earl Parish. We got close, and they started dropping hand grenades at us, and one of them hit Earl Parish in the back and rear, in the buttocks, and blew him up pretty badly, and we had to get him down that mountain; we knew he was going to die.

We fought a rear-guard action getting Earl Parish down that mountainside to that first-aid station. They gave me a Silver Star for that action, and Earl Parish gave his life.

It never leaves you. My wife is very patient. She knows exactly how to handle it when I start having one of my nightmares. She says I give her a little warning. The first time, we were first married, I had a nightmare and she laid her hands on me and I accidentally knocked her clear across the room under a sewing table; she learned never to touch me. She'll say my name and will keep repeating it and I'll come to. We've learned how to live with it.

DON MacKINNON

2nd Regiment, 1st Special Service Force

Arriving in Italy in late November, the 1st Special Service Force was given the formidable task of assaulting the heart of the Winter Line: the twin peaks of Monte La Difensa and Monte Rementanea. On the night of December 2, about six hundred men from the Force's 2nd Regiment[19] began to scale the northwest side of Difensa. Because the Germans thought it impassable, it had been left largely undefended. Once on top, the Force overwhelmed the stunned German defenders in a brisk firefight. A few days later, the North Americans crossed a saddleback ridge, capturing the second peak, Monte Rementanea, and cracking the Winter Line.

On December 1 we were loaded into six-by-six trucks, it was raining like hell, and we started off for the front. It was a dark night, and you could see the flashes of artillery even from Santa Maria. As we got closer, of course the noise got louder and louder, and the flashes were reflected off the low clouds; it was a very threatening atmosphere. The people who were driving our trucks were not part of our unit; they were service guys who were sent up to transport us to the front. They just went like hell-bent for election on the slippery roads with the pouring rain. I thought we were going to go into a ditch several times. Eventually we got to a place called Presenzano, which is about ten miles from La Difensa. We had to then get off the trucks and do a forced march across country to the bottom of La Difensa. This meant following creek beds and going through farmers' fields and through small hamlets and past artillery positions. The artillery was just fantastic: You couldn't hear yourself think.

We finally got there and bivouacked that night at the bottom of La Difensa in the pouring rain; we were sopping wet. We tried to get some sleep, but it was very difficult because of the noise and the rain. We didn't have tents; we just had ponchos. We tried to string them up. We were in sort of low shrub area where you could string your ponchos up on the shrubs and try and get some protection from the rain. It was a bad night, and I don't know how many hours of sleep we got, probably two or three. In the morning the sun came up and they decided to take us up through the 36th Division positions on the side of the hill to a bivouac area further up in the tree line. That's where we started to clean our weapons and get dried out and find some dry socks and get ready for the attack.

In the meantime, the scouts had been sent ahead to find a path up to the summit. Ropes were set up to aid in climbing the cliffs. We started out, late in the afternoon, and we worked our way around the mountain to the base of the cliffs. The 3rd Platoon started up first. We got to the top and there was just this narrow path along the ridge. There was enough room for the whole platoon to get up there, and then we moved along a little bit and the 2nd Platoon came up, and so on. I don't remember the climb being difficult. I think you are so tensed up at that point. You've got only one thing in mind and that is to get up there, and you know you've got to do it. I think all those scrapes and all those minor things that happened on the way up, we were all in such good shape anyway that we could handle it without too much trouble.

We did pass by, as we were coming over there, some of the dead from 36th Division from earlier unsuccessful attacks, bodies that had never been recovered. This was kind of shocking when you are first going into action—you are wondering, "Who's going to be next?" I was just eighteen at the time. It was the first killed in action that I had seen. The bodies were bloated up and smelly; it wasn't a pretty sight. Nobody had been able to get up there and get them out because there was so much sniper fire and machine gun fire in daylight. The conditions were so difficult that they just didn't do it.

We started out, and the artillery was just absolutely fantastic. They called it the million-dollar hill in some stories, there was so much artillery spent on it. As we got to the top, the guns, the 105s and maybe even some 155s, were firing, lifted their fire over the top so it wouldn't hit us. It just sounded like freight trains, one after the other going in both directions over the top; I've never forgotten the noise.

As we approached their positions, we were challenged by the Germans, and my section, which was in the lead, managed to jump behind a row of quite large rocks for protection. 6th Section went to our left, but it was a more exposed section and they had three guys killed right away. We just kept firing over the rocks, keeping our heads down.

There was a saucerlike area at the top of it [Difensa] and quite large, maybe one hundred yards across, and the German positions were all around the rim of this saucer and in the center of it. At the very top of the saucer, at the other side of it from the side we approached on, was a cavelike position. I think that was their command post. We used it afterwards ourselves.

How long the firing lasted, I have no idea. The guy who was next to me behind the rocks, a fellow named Sid Gath, he fell back on me. I thought it was just him moving around, and I said, "Come on, Sid, you're leaning on me." He fell back, and the whole other side of his head was gone. He'd taken machine gun fire down the side of his head. That was my first real close experience; he was a good friend of mine. I was a bit stunned for a while. I had a cigarette and resumed firing.

In total, the company lost nine men in the first two days, mainly to machine gun fire. The problem was that as the Germans started moving out, they moved across kind of a saddle to the next hill, which was called Rementanea, another sort of peak in the area. As they moved out they had the perfect range back to us for their mortars. Over the next two or three days as we took over their positions, boy, they just let us have it with mortars, particularly with screaming meemies. We stayed up there a little bit too long. I think one of the problems was the British were attacking to our left on another hill, and I think they were waiting for radio contact to sort of coordinate the attack properly. Our commanding officer came up to the top of La Difensa and he was running the show.

The prisoners started to come in; I think we had thirty or thirty-five prisoners in the center, and they were all gathered around in the depression with guards around them. Two of us were ordered to take a couple of our wounded guys and several prisoners who could walk down. There were three or four Germans; I can't remember exactly how many. Two of them looked like Boy Scouts. They had a mixed bag of troops, it was the Hermann Göring Panzer Division that we were fighting, but I think they had a lot of raw young recruits with them.

We took these prisoners down the mountain with Folsom, who had been wounded by shale. (The Germans were firing into the rocks, and shale was flying all over the place, and there were four or five guys who got shale embedded into their bodies. One guy was blinded in one eye, and Folsom got hit in the arm—a lot of the shale was embedded in his arm.) I got him and the prisoners down and turned them in, and I had to come back up the hill again. By this time I was really bushed. I fell in behind Colonel [Robert] Frederick, the commanding officer, and he had his translator with him. I had slung my rifle behind to get back up the hill, and he said, "Get that rifle off your shoulder, soldier, there are snipers around here!" I took it off but as soon as their attention was taken by something else I reslung it.

I went back up and found my platoon, and they were all sheltering in the old German positions. These positions were very shored up; they had all sorts of time to move in things like railway ties. Some of the positions were almost impregnable. The Germans often did that; it was part of the Winter Line they set up.

They were moving new weapons up to us. We didn't take our 60-mm mortars in the beginning, so they brought those up, and they brought up rifle grenades, which we used, and more light machine guns—we used the Johnson machine guns. As we got near the top, one of these stretcher gangs was coming down; the Germans were carrying their own guys with guards. The Germans were walking, and one of them was complaining like hell because according to the Geneva convention, he was apparently saying, he should have a stretcher.

I was relieved because my feet were so swelled up from being wet for several days. I couldn't get my boots on, and I was ordered back down the hill, and I got to a field hospital and got a night's sleep; boy, that was great! I got dry clothing, and the next morning I was told that my company had been relieved and that they were heading back to the barracks in Santa Maria.

I don't think there's any other unit that had the esprit de corps that we had. I'm saying that; I don't know for sure. It was just phenomenal because we had so much intensive training, commando training of all types, including parachute qualifying, demolition, mountain climbing, amphibious training on Chesapeake Bay, all that stuff. The fact that Canadians and Americans were integrated in the same platoon, there was a need for each guy to not look stupid for his own country. I think there was such a bond established there, it made one hell of a fighting unit.

There is a love between the men, and you still see it at the reunions. You may not have a lot in common any more with the guys you served with, but you've got that bond; either you were carried out in a stretcher or you lived in a foxhole with guys for days on end or whatever, and that just gives you that special feeling about each other.

DELBERT KUEHL

504th Parachute Infantry Regiment, 82nd Airborne Division

During December 1943, the 3rd Ranger Battalion, 1st Special Service Force, and 504th Regimental Combat Team (RCT) were still battling in the mountains around the tiny village of San Pietro, which dominated the main approach the Fifth Army would take to Cassino, the heart of a belt of fortifications after the Winter Line known as the Gustav Line. The mountain fighting was miserable. After one all-night attack on a mountain near San Pietro, several wounded men were left in no-man's-land in front of the German lines, and as described here, Protestant chaplain Delbert Kuehl organized a rescue party to retrieve the men.

I didn't have to be up there on the front line, but I thought, if the chaplain is going to help these men, he better be where they are wounded and dying, too. So I spent almost all my time continually on the front lines in Italy up there in the mountains. It was tough, but I was a hunter and fisherman before I went in and I knew how to take care of myself.

We went over one night—we were up on the 1205 mountain area. One night, we went over our mountainside to the German side and attacked all night. We pulled back before dawn, and we got back on the other side and somebody said to me, "Chaplain, we've got some wounded men over there." I said, "We've got wounded men over the German side? We can't let them

Paratroopers of the 504th pass by German vehicles riddled with shrapnel and machine gun fire near San Pietro, December 1943. (Photo courtesy U.S. Army)

die." So I got hold of medics, and we said, "We don't know what's going to happen, but let's get over there."

We got a tattered Red Cross flag, put it on a stick. We got a couple of those litters. Maybe there was about eight or ten of us. We knew that if they were radical, fanatical Germans, we weren't coming back. It was a wide-open stony slope down to the German side, plus there was a lot of mortar and machine gun fire.

We got up to the top and started down single file, and they opened up with the machine guns, and they were right alongside of us. I got splattered with little pieces of rock that were broken up by the machine gun fire, and I thought, "Well, this must be it." We just kept going. We went down and they stopped. The mortar fire and machine gun fire stopped. They were regular German troops, not the fanatical ones, otherwise I would not be talking to you. We picked up several wounded, and then I remember the last one, I draped the fellow over the back of my shoulders and he put his arms around my neck and I dragged him up the mountain.

We got over on our side and we were able to save the lives of several of these wounded men. Somehow United Press got a hold of this activity, I don't know how they got my picture, but it went out all over the United States that the chaplain also went over into the German lines and he gave out cigarettes to the wounded men. They're dying there and I'm giving out cigarettes to the men! I never gave out a cigarette in my entire life. That's their conception: Men are dying, and what's the chaplain doing? He's giving out cigarettes to them instead of stopping their bleeding and saving their lives.

CHAPTER FIVE

ANZIO

Theirs not to make reply,
Theirs but to do or die.

—Alfred, Lord Tennyson, "The Charge
of the Light Brigade"

The winter of 1943–44 brought the Allies a bloody stalemate in Italy. After the Allied breakout from Salerno, the Germans proved that they were masters of the southern Italian topography. Mountains, mud, rivers, narrow roads, and even snow became the natural obstacles around which the Germans built elaborate defensive positions. Beginning in December 1943, the Allies were being gored on the forward defenses of another elaborate belt of German fortifications: the Gustav Line. A decision, driven primarily by Winston Churchill, eager to capture Rome, was made to try an amphibious landing to break the stalemate. But Churchill eyed the political points to be gained while largely ignoring the military risks.[1]

The plan hatched to break the stalemate was code-named SHINGLE. From the start, it lacked sufficient resources for success. Several Allied generals were appalled by the plan. Major General John Lucas, whose VI Corps was leading the assault, wrote in his diary, "I felt like a lamb being led to the slaughter. . . . This whole affair had the strong odor of Gallipoli and apparently the same amateur [Churchill] was still on the coaches' bench."

Operation SHINGLE began on January 22, 1944. The plan called for only thirty-six thousand men to land behind the Gustav Line at Anzio. Unlike the mountainous terrain that helped to stall the Allied advance, the area around Anzio was relatively flat, featuring farmlands that were cultivated at the encouragement of Benito Mussolini's fascist state in the 1930s. Simultaneously, the Allies would strike the Gustav Line, breaking through it, linking up with the Anzio forces and eventually taking Rome.

Spearheading the landings on Anzio were Darby's Rangers, now designated 6615 Ranger Force, the independent 509th Parachute Infantry Battalion, 83rd Chemical Mortar Battalion, and H Company of the 36th Engineer Regiment. Flanking the Rangers and paratroopers were the 1st British Infantry Division, which landed on beaches north of Anzio, and the 3rd Division, which landed to the south of the beachhead. All of the landings were uneventful, the Germans caught completely off-guard.

While the seaborne forces took Anzio, the 504th was scheduled to make an airborne drop at the base of the Alban Hills to set up blocking positions to prevent German reinforcements from reaching the beach. At the last minute the drop was called off and the 504th went in by landing craft.

Fearing another Salerno, the Allies cautiously built up the beachhead rather than striking quickly toward Rome. While the mistakes made at Anzio were both political and military, even Lucas's harshest critics tend to agree that advancing on Rome or seizing the Alban Hills immediately after the landings would have been a disaster. 1st British Division commander Major General W. R. C. Penny wrote, "We could have had one night in Rome and 18 months in P.W. Camps."[2] The Germans quickly responded to the landings, implementing contingency plans for a landing behind their lines, and began ringing the Anzio beachhead with battle-hardened troops. Within weeks, the entire German Fourteenth Army, commanded by General Eberhard von Mackensen, was in front of Anzio. Mackensen's marching orders from Hitler and his commanding officer, one of the greatest commanders of the war, Field Marshal Albert Kesselring, were first to hold Anzio and then to "lance the abscess south of Rome."

On January 30, 1944, Lucas decided to launch an all-out attack to break out of the beachhead and capture the town of Cisterna, synchronized with Mark Clark's attack on the Gustav Line at Cassino on February 1. But von Mackensen was planning his own attack and massed 36 battalions of infantry in the Campoleone–Cisterna salient, supported by a substantial force of tanks and artillery.[3]

Spearheading the attack on Cisterna were Darby's Rangers. On the night of January 29–30, the Rangers began to infiltrate behind the enemy lines to capture and hold Cisterna, which was at the junction of several roads and Highway 7 leading to Rome. The 504th provided a diversionary attack to the right while the 7th Infantry Regiment hit the Germans to the left of the

Ranger attack. The 4th Rangers would follow up the attack an hour later, clearing the road to Cisterna for additional reinforcements.

The Rangers crept in single file along an irrigation ditch known as the Pantano Ditch, dispatching several German sentries with knives along the way. Shortly before dawn, the 1st Rangers emerged from the end of the ditch and were about eight hundred yards from Cisterna. As the Rangers emerged from the ditch they found themselves in the middle of a bivouac area for well-trained German Fallschirmjägers (paratroopers). The German paratroopers were alerted and began opening fire with machine guns and mortars. Initially, German tanks and infantry attacked but were stopped by the Rangers.

Several miles behind the 1st and 3rd Ranger battalions, the 4th Rangers were up against a solid wall of German resistance. Even with the help of the Ranger Cannon Company (a group of half-tracks with mounted 75-mm guns), they could not break through the German defenses; casualties began to mount. The flank attacks by the 504th Parachute Infantry Regiment and the 7th Infantry Regiment also stalled.

The melee around Cisterna continued through the morning. With the stranded Rangers running low on ammunition, the battle deteriorated to a hand-to-hand struggle. More enemy tanks and flak wagons (German half-tracks generally armed with four 20-mm cannons) hit the Rangers. Using sticky bombs and bazookas, and even climbing on board the tanks, opening the hatches, and spraying them with machine gun fire, the Rangers knocked out seventeen tanks and half-tracks even though outnumbered at least ten to one.[4]

Rescue attempts failed: The 4th Ranger Battalion desperately tried to break through but was halted outside the small community of Isola Bella, about two miles southwest of Cisterna. With their superior numbers, the Germans had an iron grip around the Ranger positions, pouring in additional tanks and self-propelled guns from the Hermann Göring Panzer Division.

The Rangers could stop the German assault no longer. The Germans positioned captured Rangers in front of several German fighting vehicles and slowly marched them into the shrinking Ranger pocket, presenting the Rangers with a surrender ultimatum, stating in English over loudspeakers that the prisoners would be summarily shot if they did not surrender. Several Rangers were machine-gunned and bayoneted to drive home the message. This grisly scene compelled many of the remaining Rangers to surrender.[5] Others fought on, the battle raging all afternoon and reaching its nadir when the sergeant major of the 3rd Battalion reported to Colonel Darby that he was destroying the battalion radio.[6] Approximately eight hundred men from the 1st and 3rd Ranger battalions were either killed or captured at Cisterna. Only six Rangers from the doomed battalions returned to the Allied lines.

According to Hermann Göring Division records, 680 Rangers were taken prisoner. This number seems overstated, however, and based on eyewitness accounts, it is likely that only 450 prisoners were captured and that between 250 and 300 Rangers perished in the attack.[7]

The disaster at Cisterna marked the end of Darby's Rangers, one of the Army's best combat units of World War II. Faulty intelligence doomed the attack, allowing the Rangers to be overwhelmed by sheer numbers of German infantry and armor. Today, one of the streets in Isola Bella is appropriately named "Via dei Rangers," and a marble memorial marks the site of the bloody battle.

On February 10, 1944, what was left of the 4th Battalion was attached to the 504th Parachute Infantry Regiment. In late March, the 4th Battalion was attached to the 1st Special Service Force and the unit was finally disbanded. Men designated as veterans were shipped back to the United States, while the remaining Rangers were integrated into the Force.

The Rangers' defeat at Cisterna was only part of a larger debacle for the Allies. The Germans stopped the rest of Lucas's VI Corps offensive, and Clark's army was unable to break through the Gustav Line. Anzio, designed as a knife in the back of the German lines, instead became a huge liability for the Allies. To stave off total disaster, Clark pumped an enormous number of troops into the beachhead.

As the Germans continued to build up their forces, the struggle at the beachhead came to resemble the fixed lines of a World War I battlefield. Soldiers lived a molelike, miserable existence in the flat Anzio plain with few places to take cover and seek protection. Buried most of the day in foxholes and water-filled trenches, men beat off continual German attacks and tried to survive round-the-clock shelling. No place on the beachhead was safe from the shelling, including field hospitals.

On February 2, the 1st Special Service Force arrived on the beachhead. Depleted from its actions against the Winter and Gustav lines, the Force was down to 1,233 men from 2,300. Nevertheless, the unit was given the division-sized task of holding Anzio's extreme right flank, an area covering one-fourth of the beachhead.[8]

After seizing the critical bridges over the Mussolini Canal, the 504th also manned a large five-thousand-yard front along the Mussolini Canal between the 3rd Infantry Division and the 1st SSF. The unit was worn down from constant German attacks yet did not allow a single penetration of its lines. Additionally, the 504th's 3rd Battalion served with the British at the Carroceto sector, where the fighting was so intense that after sixteen days the 3rd Battalion was reduced to 35 percent of its effective strength.[9]

The Anzio Beachhead

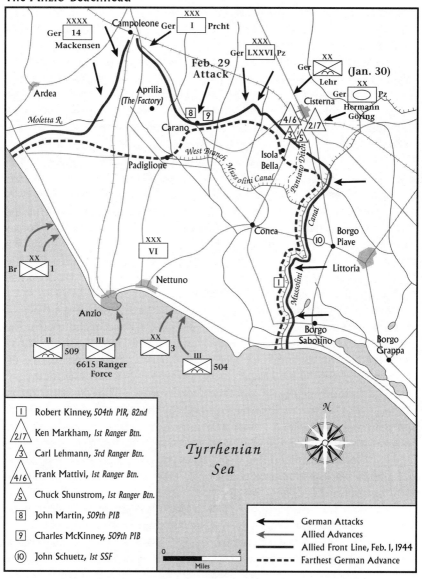

Ger XXXX 14 Mackensen
Campoleone
Ger XXX I Prcht
Ger XXX LXXVI Pz
Ger XX Lehr (Jan. 30)
Ardea
Aprilia (The Factory)
Feb. 29 Attack
Ger XX Pz Hermann Göring
Cisterna
Moletta R.
Carano
8 9
4/6
2/7
3 5
West Branch
Isola Bella
Padiglione
Mussolini Canal
Pantano Ditch
Conca
Mussolini Canal
10
Borgo Piave
XXX VI
Littoria
Br XX 1
Nettuno
Anzio
Mussolini
II 509 III
XX 3
III 504
Borgo Sabotino
Borgo Grappa
6615 Ranger Force

1 Robert Kinney, 504th PIR, 82nd

2/7 Ken Markham, 1st Ranger Btn.

3 Carl Lehmann, 3rd Ranger Btn.

4/6 Frank Mattivi, 1st Ranger Btn.

5 Chuck Shunstrom, 1st Ranger Btn.

8 John Martin, 509th PIB

9 Charles McKinney, 509th PIB

10 John Schuetz, 1st SSF

N

Tyrrhenian Sea

German Attacks
Allied Advances
Allied Front Line, Feb. 1, 1944
Farthest German Advance

0   4
Miles

The independent 509th Parachute Infantry Battalion also controlled valuable real estate on the left flank of the 3rd Division. Like nearly every unit on the beach, it threw back countless German attacks and aggressively patrolled the German defenses at night.

The Germans continued to attack as they built up their forces, and on February 16 they made an all-out effort to wipe out the beachhead. The weight of the attack fell on the 45th Division. After making some initial gains, the German advance was halted by Allied artillery and reserves. Losses on both sides were staggering as the Germans continued their attempts to annihilate the beachhead. The final major German attack occurred on February 29, the bulk of three German divisions hitting a seam between the 45th Division and the 3rd Division lines defended by the 509th.[10] Starting in the early morning, German engineers blew holes in the barbed wire and thousands of screaming Germans descended on B Company's position dug into a hill and behind a creek. After overrunning B Company, the Germans were halted by A Company of the 509th and one of the largest artillery concentrations of the war. An estimated 66,500 rounds of artillery hit the Germans—and B Company's positions—stopping the attack.[11] Halting the German attack earned the 509th its first Presidential Unit Citation.

March brought a general stalemate at Anzio; both sides were exhausted from the fighting, the battlefield as barren as the surface of the moon. The masters of the Anzio beachhead patrols were the 1st Special Service Force, which terrified the Germans with large two-hundred-man raiding parties infiltrating deep behind their lines. Stickers with the distinctive Force arrowhead patch adorned with a statement in German, "The Worst Is Yet to Come," were left as calling cards after raids by the North Americans.[12] This aggressive patrolling allowed the Force to carve out a unique one-mile buffer between the lines, and the Germans gave the force the nickname "Black Devils." The end of March also brought an end to fighting for the depleted 504th, which was shipped back to England, where it was initially scheduled to participate in the Normandy buildup.

The battle for Anzio lingered on until May 23, when nearly every gun on the beachhead fired on the ruins of Cisterna, softening up the German defenses for the Allied breakout. Spearheading the breakout was the 1st Special Service Force. The day before, the Gustav Line was breached at Cassino, and Allied troops went pouring through the holes, moving north to link up with the beachhead forces. The twin Allied thrusts linked up on May 25. The advance on Rome was painful, but on June 4, the Eternal City was in Allied hands, only two days before what would be the greatest amphibious invasion in history—D-Day.

ROBERT KINNEY

504th Parachute Infantry Regiment, 82nd Airborne Division

The Allied landings at Anzio were largely uneventful, but the Germans responded quickly to the landings and began ringing Anzio with troops. The Allies dug in as each side probed the other's defenses. Robert Kinney describes one such German attack.

After the landing, we started right on in, walked several miles into the Mussolini Canal. They told us to dig in, and we dummy dogfaces figured, "Why don't we go to Rome? We're on the damn track." There wasn't much fire, but we dug in there.

On the night of the twenty-fourth [of January], our platoon sergeant sought me out. I was dug in somewhere, probably sleeping, and he said,

Paratroopers from the 504th in the Mussolini Canal, January 1944. (Photo courtesy U.S. Army)

"Kinney, I want you to take a machine gun, take one of the older boys and a couple of these new recruits, and report to C Company." I reported to C Company and an officer told me to go dig in on the left; we were expecting a boomer in the morning. So we dug in and got right up at dawn. The fog was lifting and those mortars started; we got a bunch.

That morning the Germans attacked our position and destroyed my squad. I was acting corporal that day and had two brand-new guys right from the States; they had just come in, and one was killed and one lost both legs that night. I was hit in the backside; I didn't dig that hole deep enough, that's all. But I dug that machine gun in. There must have been a German out there, very much aware of us, and that mortar was intended for me, I know it was, but it hit to the right and it killed that boy.

Before the mortar hit, he said, "Where do you want me to dig in?" I said, "Over to my right there, and keep that box of ammo handy—if I need it I'm going to yell at you." I said, "Don't get to where I can't reach you." He was that close, and that mortar killed him—it landed right on him. The other man was hit, and it took both of his legs. It hit me, tore my fanny open, took a big chunk of meat out of there—I could afford that. So I carried the boy who got hit in the legs back to the medics and stood there and watched as they trimmed his legs off. He was a young fellow, about nineteen years of age.

We were taken off the beachhead and sent to a hospital in Naples and got sewed up. Several weeks later we were all down the hospital—lots of us down there in Naples. One of the officers of the 504th came down and said, "Anyone from the 504th who can stand up, can walk, meet me down here at the end of the hall." We all went down, about forty of us in casts, bandages, arms in slings and everything. He said, "Your buddies up there are catching hell and we've got to go back if we can. You don't have to, we're not going to order you, but we're looking for volunteers." We said, "Hell, we'll go."

We just had the best-spirited bunch of scrappers you ever saw. I was wearing a kind of diaper, and the nurse gave me a bottle of boric acid soap to keep it [my wound] clean with. We went; only one guy didn't go.

KEN MARKHAM

1st Ranger Battalion

At 1:00 A.M. on January 30, the 1st and 3rd Ranger battalions began infiltrating behind German lines to capture and hold the town of Cisterna as the centerpiece of General Lucas's all-out attack to expand the Anzio beachhead. Intelligence incorrectly indicated that the Germans did not have significant forces in the area. Moving in single file along a drainage ditch, the Rangers moved through the German lines undetected, the 4th Ranger Battalion trailing the two lead battalions. Just before dawn, the 1st Ranger Battalion, out in front, emerged from the cover of the Pantano Ditch and hit a German bivouac area that became a hornet's nest of activity. Ken Markham, the 1st Ranger Battalion's lead scout, remembers the Rangers' doomed mission.

I was the scout of the company. Major [Jack] Dobson [commander of the 1st Battalion] was second in line as we went down a drainage ditch. Frank Mattivi was next to me as we went on up to Cisterna. After moving about three thousand yards, we heard some artillery fire off to the right of us; it was a battery of 88s. Major Dobson halted the column and got on the radio and tried to call Colonel Darby to see if we could try and knock out the battery of 88s. He couldn't get Darby; he was an old soldier, knew his mission, so we went ahead.

We got to the roadway that was going parallel to Cisterna. I got across the road; I was the first man across the road. There was an olive orchard over there. It was a bivouac area for what seemed to be a whole division that pulled into that area for a counterattack. Major Dobson and I and Frank Mattivi got in there and we started to open up [fire on the Germans] because that was all we could do. He told me to cross the road and try to get back to Major Miller, who was the battalion commander of the 3rd Ranger Battalion. I got back there and you just couldn't believe how much firefighting was going on. Everybody was all confused. I finally got across the roadway going back towards Major Miller. I jumped across a hedgerow there; I jumped right into a bunch of Germans. Everybody was so confused. I started shooting and firing my way out of there, and I crawled over to a bunch of bushes. I finally got to Major Miller, where I thought he would be. So I found a 3rd Battalion sergeant and I said, "Sergeant, where's Major Miller?" He said, "He was hit just a few minutes ago. A mortar shell just got him. It hit his head and blew him all to pieces."

I told him what Major Dobson told me to tell Miller. I wanted to get back to my company. I told him to get in touch with the commanding officer and that we were in an olive orchard. I started working my way back to the line. Tanks were firing into Cisterna; there was just a mass of fire, you couldn't even crawl across the road, so I crawled into a ditch right there, and I bet you there was about a dozen dead Rangers in the ditch. Captain Chuck Shunstrom and another fellow by the name of Captain Saam, they were laying in the ditch with me.

CARL LEHMANN

1st and 3rd Ranger Battalions

Sergeant Carl Lehmann's e-history describes the chaos as the 1st and 3rd Rangers emerged from the Pantano Ditch into a German bivouac area.

I was near the head of C Company on the left and, though a sergeant, I had no squad at the time and was carrying a load of TNT (for precisely what I cannot remember). Shortly after the start we could hear faint fire commands coming from a Kraut battery. As we progressed the commands got louder till it appeared we were quite near it; the order became fainter as we passed on. Close to dawn the mortar shell which killed Major Miller exploded forward in the ditch and caused me and, I guess, almost everyone in my file to leap out of the ditch to the left into what's best described as chaos compounded. We leapt into and sped through a Kraut bivouac (a hasty one for sure, because there were no tents or foxholes—just men asleep in their blankets) as the Germans, startled awake by the shells, were rolling out of their blankets and running away hands up with us shooting them back and front. (I reject the assertions of half a dozen historians—most who were in swaddling when our ramps went down—that it was an ambush. That Kraut yelling fire orders surely did not know we were there, nor did those we killed rolling out of their blankets.) I expended one clip and ran on till I was through the camp and coming to a shallow hedgerow running in the same direction as the ditch. I ran up the hedgerow until I was exhausted and flopped down, shortly coming to realize that a whole string of men had followed me up the hedgerow. Paralleling the hedgerow to the left was a shallow crest, on which, against the lightening sky, there first appeared a flak wagon, then individual soldiers. All were easy targets and we drove the flak wagon off before it could get its guns into action. We then engaged the soldiers milling about with the apparent advantage of their not knowing our position. I emptied my M-1 [rifle] so much and so fast that the wood was smoking.

I was summoned by a shout from Perry Bills (I don't know how he knew where I was) that the battalion was assembling "over here." I ran towards him, and the string of men with me did the same in a line towards the Pantano. Exhausted again, I flopped down into a crowd scattered over a field and under fire from the crest. I was of a notion to lay some smoke to get out of the field and tried to do so with a British phosphorus contact grenade. It fizzled, and an officer, seeing what I did, tossed me an American phosphorus grenade. The only open space to explode it was quite close, and after I threw it, I sprinted out from under the tendrils and got lost.

I spent the next couple of hours with a group of the 1st Battalion, and then, learning that Bills was toward the right flank, started to make my way there. On the way, I came to a barn and got the notion to climb to the loft to have a look about. When I got to the loft, I saw another ladder going up to the peak, and I was halfway up it when I heard a clatter outside. I came off the ladder and saw it was a self-propelled gun. I tossed a grenade into it and got to the ground on the other side in one jump. I lit running and was under way when I heard the grenade go off. I don't know what happened to the gun, although it was not in place several hours later, when I could observe the place where it was.

I finally found Bills and most of his platoon and dug in with them on the right flank. We could see, at extreme range, German vehicles using the Cisterna road. While there our platoon leader, Clarence Meltesen, came into our position with a bullet hole in his chest and I clearly remember giving him up for dead because he was spraying blood with every breath. I had dug a hole near Bills, and during a quiet time I dozed, then waked to a shout from Bills: "Them bastards is giving up!" "Them bastards" were our guys being marched towards us, hands up. As one, we decided to get the hell out of there and head toward the beach. We got about a mile before we were pinned down. "We" included Scotty Munro, Larry Hurst, C. J. Hodal, and perhaps twenty others.

When it became inevitable that I was going to be captured, I managed to bury my Luger, fighting knife, and (stupid!) wristwatch! Hurst got shot through the shoulder and I bandaged him with my wool scarf. We were herded into a farmyard and searched. The one who searched me was about sixteen years of age and, when he got to the contents of my shirt pocket, he went ballistic! I had about twenty German epaulets from German tunics that I found in a bunker. He directed me away from the others and repeatedly asked permission of the Feldwebel to shoot me, but the Feldwebel, as I blessed the sainted Frau who birthed him, repeatedly shook his head and said, "Nein."

FRANK MATTIVI

1ˢᵗ Ranger Battalion

After a bloody melee in the German bivouac area that left at least one hundred Germans dead, the Rangers found themselves eight hundred yards short of Cisterna, on flat, open ground with little cover and surrounded by an area infested by Germans. Forming roughly a three-hundred-yard perimeter, the Rangers held off the German attacks while two companies of Rangers attempted to take Cisterna, but the Germans slowly gained the upper hand. Frank Mattivi recalls the battle.

We walked all night; we started that evening about dusk. We got up in that area, and we crossed one little road. We heard these Jerries; you could hear them talking. We kind of scooted by them. We got up there, probably another one hundred yards, and all hell broke loose. One of the Jerries spotted one of the point people and everybody started firing, shooting, grabbing people and screaming and knifing people.

Well, they had several tanks, self-propelled. I was on one side, Gabriel was on the other side, and I can't remember the sergeant, he had the bazooka on the opposite side. I had one of the sticky bombs. I crawled up on the side of one of the tanks. I opened the hatch and dropped the sticky bomb in there, and that bazooka hit on that opposite side on a turret, and I went flying. Well, after that, for about an hour, hell, I didn't know what happened. I couldn't hear. I finally came to my senses later on. We got the tank knocked out; there were two more of them burning. At that point it was hard to explain, it was chaos.

One of the men had the radio, he was in the house, and at that time that was probably around ten, eleven o'clock. Hell, everybody was running out of ammo. We were getting desperate because they were all around us. Probably about the second hour they started firing big artillery in there. All the officers were killed, every one of them, so I had the company. We had about thirty men at that time; we had lost a lot of men.

CHUCK SHUNSTROM

1st Ranger Battalion

The breaking point of the battle occurred when the Germans began using captured Rangers as human shields.[13] The Germans moved the column of Rangers into the shrinking perimeter while a loudspeaker blared a surrender ultimatum in English: "Surrender or we shall shoot the prisoner!" Several prisoners were bayoneted to drive home the message. Captain Chuck Shunstrom, a winner of the Silver Star and then acting commander of the 1st Battalion, describes the battle in this hitherto unpublished after-action report for Colonel Darby, written shortly after Shunstrom's 1944 escape from a German POW camp.

Our casualties were becoming very heavy. There was a great deal of enemy automatic firing coming into our positions. When the enemy had pinned us down with automatic fire, we would hear single shots as they sniped at men in our position. So far both battalions occupied an area of about three hundred yards in diameter. At this time, Captain Saam, executive officer of the 1st Ranger Battalion, came back from a patrol. He was on our left flank. He immediately took command of both battalions. Captain Larkin, the executive officer of the 3rd Ranger Battalion, had assumed command immediately after the death of his battalion commander, Major Miller. Captain Saam immediately took two companies of the 3rd Ranger Battalion and sent them to a position about three hundred yards in our rear with a mission of closing the gap in the circle that we had formed and to dig in and hold at all costs. He informed [me] that C and D Companies had been unsuccessful in their enveloping movement to the right flank, and that he had ordered them to dig in and hold the ground that they had. This left four companies of the 3rd Ranger Battalion in the immediate vicinity of the command post in reserve. He then gave orders that the radio operator call back for reinforcements on the radio. A battalion aid station was set up in a building where the radio was kept about 25 yards from the command post's position. During the fighting which took place for several hours, both battalions had many losses from enemy small arms fire. Meanwhile a report would come back asking for more ammunition as the men were running out. Finally the order was given for all four companies remaining in reserve to give one-half of the ammunition they were carrying to be sent out to companies on the line. All this time help was being asked for on the radio. Our plan now was to hold what we had until help came. To advance any farther than where we were now would be suicide. We were completely surrounded by the enemy, who had superiority in fire-power and who was generally occupying commanding positions over the area that we were in.

At about 1330 hours, a report came back that some prisoners were seen with their hands in the air at a position about two hundred yards to our rear. The report stated that these prisoners looked to be Americans. Captain Saam and [I] immediately left their positions to investigate. An investigation showed that the report was correct. [We] saw about twelve American soldiers with their hands in the air being quickly surrounded by what appeared to be German paratroop infantry supported by two armed personnel carriers. Sporadic small arms fire was heard all during this operation. Two of the German guards were seen to fall. Immediately two more German soldiers bayoneted two American soldiers, who were then prisoners with their hands in the air, in the back, killing them. The Germans formed their ten men into ranks and marched them towards another position that Lieutenant Evans, company commander of the 3rd Ranger Battalion, occupied. Lieutenant Evans's Company refused to surrender. Instead his company ambushed the guards killing two more. The Germans retaliated once again by bayoneting two more of our men in the back. Lieutenant Evans's company was very low on ammunition and eventually ran out, being captured. The Germans by now had about 80 American prisoners and formed them into a column of fours and immediately started to march them towards the center of our position, where our command post was. Captain Saam immediately dispersed the four remaining companies that were in reserve and planned an ambush for the oncoming German soldiers who were guarding the American prisoners. Lieutenant Evans was made to lead this column up the road. The Germans kept shouting, "Surrender or we shall shoot the prisoner!" All the time small arms fire was coming into our positions from the enemy to our front and flanks keeping us well pinned down. The oncoming column came to a position about one hundred fifty yards from the command post and halted. The orders for our ambush were not to fire until given the order, but someone fired a shot into the oncoming column and killed one of our own men. This one shot started everybody else in the ambush firing, and the result was that two or three of our own men were killed in the column plus one or two Germans guards. The Germans immediately backed off and took cover and started to spray our column of prisoners with automatic fire from submachine guns. The men that had set up in ambush immediately ceased firing, and a few of them who were evidently new in combat immediately got hysterical and started to leave their positions and surrender. All attempts to stop this disobedience of orders failed. Even an attempt to stop them by shooting them failed. Eventually, all men surrendered and were taken prisoners by the Germans.

FRANK MATTIVI

1st Ranger Battalion

Outnumbered at least ten to one and with no ammunition, the Rangers were unable to hold their perimeter. After the battle, those Rangers who survived were rounded up and forced to march through the streets of Rome, as remembered by Frank Mattivi.

At that time everything was over with. We had run out of ammo and the Jerries had us surrounded; it was about noon. They would come out and roust people out of where they were. We were lying in ditches kind of waiting for them. Maybe they'd go by. They got everybody who was in the area. In fact, they formed a half-circle around there and rousted everybody up on their feet. They rounded us up, and the guys who were wounded, they couldn't get up, and the Jerries went around and killed them. They just went up and shot them with rifles and some of them had Lugers. I remember one guy, I still had my .45 in my holster, it didn't have any ammo, he grabbed it and he looked at it and took his 9-mm and shot it up in the air and he took my .45 and threw it in the brush. I thought right then and there that I was going to die. You didn't have time to get mad; you were disgusted because there wasn't anything you could do.

We walked around with our hands in the air for an hour or so. They marched us down in a ravine. There were guards in front of us and guards behind us. When we got down there we noticed the guards behind us got out in front. The guy next to me said, "Well, I think maybe we've had it." We thought maybe they were going to take us down there [into the ravine] and shoot us. About that time there were two motorcycles coming down, and these officers came down there, and I heard one of them say, "Nix, nix." They were talking there for maybe fifteen, ten minutes, and so I think maybe they had something to do with us not getting killed.

We stood around for quite a while and they ran a bunch of trucks in, and from there we went to a holding area. It was just a temporary stockade. They kept us there for a day or so and then from there they loaded us into trucks

Rangers being publicly marched past the Roman Colosseum and through the streets of Rome. Such a march of POWs was in violation of the Geneva Convention rules regarding the treatment of POWs. (Photo courtesy National Archives)

and we went to a castle up in the line. They kept us there all night, and we were bombed by our own aircraft. You could hear them coming over, the bombs kind of hit on the outside; it shook the castle a little bit, nobody got killed, but they destroyed some buildings.

After we left the castle, the next day was when they took us and marched us around the Colosseum in Rome. They just unloaded us and marched us through the damn streets there. They [Italians] were spitting at us. There were ones up in the balconies jeering at us, cussing in Italian.

KEN MARKHAM

1ˢᵗ Ranger Battalion

After the march through the Holy City, the Rangers were placed in boxcars for the long trip to POW camps in Germany. Ken Markham describes the march, his brief escape, and his subsequent trip.

They [Germans] got us up on the road. There must have been 250 of us. They got us up on that roadway and marched us in the dark. They got us down in a gully and set up machine guns, and I thought they were gonna waste us all right there. They then backed trucks up in there and they moved us down to a little church right outside of Rome. They told us that we were going to sleep there for the night. They just piled us into that thing. Didn't get much sleep that night. They got us into the trucks again and to the Colosseum in Rome. Outside the Colosseum, German photographers were taking propaganda pictures and movies of us. It was humiliating, and they were saying the elite American troops were finished, and so forth and so on.

They had us in a temporary prison camp for four to five days and then put us in boxcars and moved us up to Florence. We got up towards Florence and they gave us some bread; that was our rations.

Maybe about ten miles past Florence I was able to escape from the train. They had two little portals on each side of the boxcar. In between that there was a partition and barbed wire around the window. I was able to work the partition and the bars loose and I worked the barbed wire loose. I took a blanket and pushed the barbed wire back and was able to crawl through the window headfirst. I guess the train was going thirty-five to forty miles an hour, so I pushed out the window and then I just rolled and rolled and rolled. I must have rolled a hundred yards. I was banged up pretty good. There was another guy who followed me out. The Germans were shooting at us.

He was going to meet me at a little bridge that we saw as we passed, so I worked my way back down there, waiting for him, and I heard more fire. I met him at the place. The next thing I remember is that we ran into a guy who was riding a bicycle. It was four in the morning. I thought to myself, "Maybe this guy was with the Underground or something." I asked him for something to eat because we were really hungry. Luckily, he took us into his apartment and the next day got in touch with the Underground. We stayed with the Underground in an apartment in Florence for nearly a month.

We were there with some other Allied prisoners, including a British soldier who went out one night and the Gestapo followed him back to our apartment. They surrounded the place. They put a machine gun on each side of the house. I saw what was taking place, so I crawled up on top of the roof. The civilians that were in the house went up on the roof also. The Gestapo got up there and shot the civilians.

They put me in a civilian prison in Florence, and I was there for about thirty days. I was in almost a kind of dungeon, and I didn't see daylight for almost thirty days. They had about five of us in a cell. It was just big enough for us to lie flat on our backs. They had one little wooden bucket in the corner for a latrine, and they gave us one cup of soup a day—that was it. One boy got really sick, and I somehow got the guard to get in touch with the Red Cross because he was going to die if he didn't get medical attention. The Red Cross got us into a regular POW camp, Stalag 7A.

I'm just a survivor. I did what I had to do just to survive. That's all you can ever do in life anyway. I've got a lot of friends that are buried over there.

JOHN MARTIN

509th Parachute Infantry Regiment

Undeterred by the failure on February 16 of Operation *Fischfang*, the largest German counteroffensive against the beachhead, the Germans drew up plans for another large-scale attack. On February 29, 1944, the bulk of a three-division attack hit a section of the line held by the 509th Parachute Infantry Battalion. The outpost farthest forward on the 509th's line was occupied by John Martin's B Company, which was dug in behind a hill northwest of the village of Carano. B Company's position was overrun before dawn, but the valiant company slowed the German attack long enough for A Company and a massive artillery barrage to stop it cold. Only a single officer and twenty-two men from B Company were able to withdraw to the main defensive line, as John Martin, B Company's commander, remembers.

We walked up there, and McKinney and I were staying in the same hole, and another one of my men and the two radio operators were in a hole nearby. Shortly after that a German barrage began. We had a warning that the Germans would attack that night. One of the men in the S-2 Section [battalion intelligence section] sat down by the hole and talked to me for some time, and he told me that the Germans were going to attack early in the morning because he heard them digging in. Shortly after he left, the Germans began their attack, and it was preceded by heavy artillery.

There were lots of Germans. It was before dawn when they broke through. They came through the left flank, along the creek. It was a massive wall of gray bodies. It began to crumble our left side. Then the Germans overran the whole position. There was a lot of shooting up there. Several men jumped out of their holes, and the two radio operators got killed. I remember that McKinney said something about, "Let's go," and he jumped out of the creek and took off and the first sergeant followed him. I jumped out of the creek because there were Germans all over the place.

That's when I got hit. It was one of the most frightening moments of my life. I was down in the creek, and a German with a machine pistol was throwing grenades, lots of grenades, at me, I guess, and I got hit and it knocked me out. That's all I remember until I heard a voice say, "Lieutenant." I woke up and I thought my left leg was gone, but he [the man who woke me] said, "It looks all right to me." Then we went down the creek a short way and we found a German. I think it was the same one that fired the grenades at me. I couldn't tell for sure, but I think it was the same one, and he was wounded.

The American barrage got heavy. We went into a hole, the German first, and then I got in following him, and then the two men [who saw me in the creek] got in. Then we heard some Kraut say "Hands up" in German. We came out, and he saw that we had a German prisoner of war, and I told the German before that, "You speak quick," and he said something to the guy outside. We got out, and that's when I was taken prisoner. They took the two men and told them that they would have to do something and that's the last I saw them. I found out later that they had helped evacuate the German dead and wounded.

I went back up the creek as a prisoner and passed the German lieutenant who was in charge of the German company [one of the companies that overran this area]. There were bodies all over the place, Germans and Americans. I got back to the railroad track, which was five to six hundred meters from where we were, and they put me behind it. It was the aid station. They were treating various Germans who were injured. There was one guy who had a piece of shrapnel sticking out of his arm, and they took his arm off right there. Then I got hauled back to the rear and saw hundreds of dead Germans along the way from our artillery fire.

CHARLES McKINNEY

509th Parachute Infantry Battalion

As the attack began to unfold, Allied artillery fired 66,500 rounds against the German attack, most of it concentrated, by necessity, onto B Company's position. Charles McKinney, B Company's exec-

utive officer and the only officer to make it back to friendly lines that
night, describes the carnage.

We had replacements that evening about eleven o'clock, as I remember, before moving out on this outpost line. We took out about a hundred people, I
believe. We relieved the rifle company that was out there. This is out about
several hundred yards out in front of the main line of resistance. We were told
when we got out there by this commander that we were relieving another
company. I remember telling the company commander, I said, "Well, you
guys are going to get a shower tomorrow because I heard they're moving up
a shower unit here to Anzio and you'll get a chance to have a bath." By then
we had been up there about five weeks and not one had their clothing off. I
was there over seventy days and I never had my clothes off in those seventy
days. He said, "No, we'll never get to take a bath tomorrow because you guys
are going to get hit tomorrow morning and we'll be in a counterattack." "So
how did you know this?" He said, "We've heard them [Germans] moving up
and digging in out there for the last two or three days and it sounds like
they're close enough now that they're going to hit you probably tomorrow
morning." This was about midnight.

Sometime after that we got a call from battalion headquarters, I don't remember who it was from, they told us the same thing: "They captured some
prisoners. You're going to be hit tomorrow morning." He told us when and
the artillery will be coming in and that we were going to counterattack with
artillery and expect the Krauts at daylight.

You know it's going to be coming, but you figure, okay, it will be a small
attack. We held a vital spot between the 3rd Division and the 45th Division.

Right on schedule, about 4:30, here comes the artillery, and then just before daybreak—here they come. I have framed in my office an AP, Associated
Press, article . . . I'll read you the headline: "Nazi tanks and dead litter Anzio
beachhead." The small headline under that says, "Mass of 45,000 Nazis on
Front of 1,000 Yards." That pretty much describes it. There were so many
people, and it was all in a haze; it's not light, but you can see.

Really, honestly, from that point on I really don't know that much about
what happened. After the war I ran into John Roy Martin down in Texas, and
we hugged and kissed, and I said, "John, what the hell happened that morning, because I really couldn't put it together." And he said, "Well, did you remember that grenade going off right between you and I?" I said, "No, I do
not." He said, "Well, a grenade went off between you and I, knocked me
down." (I think it injured his legs.) The next thing I know, I'm in this big ditch
behind us and going down the ditch and being shot at up on the bank. I ran
into our forward artillery adviser and I said, "Bring in this artillery." He said,

"What about all of our people?" I said, "Hell with our people, we've got to bring this stuff in there because this is a major attack." He started bringing in the artillery. This was probably the most concentrated barrage ever. I think there was twenty-two battalions of artillery that came in on that one spot; all the artillery I guess on the Anzio beachhead.

It just blew the damn place up. You could walk on body to body of the dead. It was really something. My best figures are that we lost all officers except myself. I was the only officer that came out of it; I wasn't captured. I think out of the hundred, we lost all but twenty-two were either captured or killed, gone, all but twenty-two. It was just a real fiasco . . . we shouldn't have been out there.

Three divisions of people, forty-five thousand, were coming at us. When the fight was over that morning, you've never seen so many bodies in your life lying on that field dead.

When you look at it—and hindsight, of course, they always say is twenty-twenty—as you look back at it you think, "What in the world were we doing out there?" We were the trip wires out there, and I guess it was just our misfortune to be out there that week. We used to keep that place one week and you'd rotate it. You'd go back to reserve or back to the main line of resistance and it just happened that it was our week out there.

JOHN SCHUETZ

3rd Regiment, 1st Special Service Force

The World War II Monument Association recently stated that America's World War II veterans are dying at the rate of more than one thousand per day. Countless obituaries contain the words, "He served in World War II." Most of the deaths are little noticed. John Schuetz, an enlisted man, is one such veteran who quietly slipped away. A few months before his death, this interview captured some of his thoughts about the war and the pride he felt serving in the 1st Special Service Force at Anzio.

In Anzio, we went on a lot of patrols at night to find out where the Germans were and how far back they were. I was a young man, twenty years old. We did a lot of patrolling. I remember getting in the damn minefields. Somehow the Germans would sneak in there and put mines out and it would fix us; we had to be awful careful.

We were going towards our objective, and somehow or another the Germans had a listening post out and they heard us coming. We were always awful quiet, and we had very good discipline and fire control. Anyway, they heard us coming and opened up on us with a MG-42 machine gun. I can still hear the sound of that gun. You were more or less in awe; you really didn't know the consequence, what would happen to you.

We had an awful lot of courage; that was the main thing on the Force. It cost a lot of people their lives because they were overactive, overcouraged. Men would rush in where they should have thrown a few grenades first. There was a real close comradeship, and I think any man would throw his life on the line for another one. You never thought about that, you'd just do it; you were trained to do it, and that was it.

[After the war] I went to Detroit; my mother lived there. I worked for my uncle a little while, and then I went to Omaha and worked with my dad on construction. I was going through post-traumatic crap. I was itching and scratching my face all over; I didn't know what was wrong with me. I know now, but I didn't know then; nobody else did, either. Of course I got to drinking quite heavily. I found out that wasn't gonna cure nothing; I was always sick, so I quit that crap. Eventually, I finally adjusted to civilian life. It took about two years. I didn't like it. I didn't like it when the Force broke up. I thought, "Now what the hell am I gonna do?" I wanted more combat. I know that sounds crazy, but that's how you felt. You wanted out; at the same time you didn't. It took me two years to adjust, but it's still on my mind all the time. My medals are hanging on the wall here; my plaque [a wooden 1st SSF plaque created by his son] is hanging on the wall over there. I look at it and I think, "Hell, how did I do that?" I reminisce a lot. I never gave it up. It is the highest point in your life; you are never going to do something like that again.

CHAPTER SIX

THE WAR FROM WITHIN: The Triple Nickles

We make no ordinary sacrifice, but we

Make it gladly and willingly with

our eyes lifted to the hills.

—W. E. B. Du Bois, "Close Ranks"

This is the story of the 555th Parachute Infantry Battalion—the Triple Nickles. In a segregated U.S. Army, in a segregated United States, blacks usually were relegated to menial jobs such as mess hall waiters, janitors, and ammunition handlers. Few were given the chance to see combat. Black soldiers in the South sat in the back of the bus, drank from separate water fountains, and were barred from officers' and NCO clubs. But beginning in the winter of 1943, what was to become the 555th Parachute Infantry Battalion helped change this racist standard.

America's first black paratroopers can trace their unit's beginnings to the War Department's Advisory Committee on Special Troops Policies (Special Troops referred to African-Americans), which was created in late 1942. One of the advisory committee's recommendations was the creation of a battalion of black paratroopers. Acting on the committee's recommendation, General George Marshall ordered the activation of the 555th Parachute Infantry Company. Nearly a year would pass before an "experimental" black test platoon was formed, on December 30, 1943.

A few months later, the test platoon grew into a company of handpicked men, including former college students and seasoned noncommissioned officers. The 555th was distinctive for its all-black officer corps; nearly all black units at the time were staffed by blacks but led by whites.

From their first day of training, the Nickles had to overcome racial barriers. Even after they received their jump wings, officers and noncoms were not permitted to enter the officers' or NCO clubs on base. The Nickles sat in the back of the bus when they traveled from Fort Benning to nearby Columbus. Confrontations with police had to be avoided at all costs, since the slightest provocation could lead to jail time and stiff fines. Black pride, long before the term became popular, and the conviction that they were the best airborne unit in the army saw the men through.

By July 1944, the 555th Parachute Infantry Company was moved to Camp Mackall, North Carolina. At Mackall, the unit was redesignated Company A, 555th Parachute Infantry Battalion. In official orders, the unit number was followed by an asterisk and the words "Negro Personnel."[1]

Mackall was not that much different from Benning. The camp theater was divided along racial lines, but blacks did have access to post facilities such as the NCO and officers' clubs. While in North Carolina, the unit went through intensive training and took on more personnel, growing to more than four hundred men. While at Mackall, the Nickles also formed a football team and played against nearby college teams.

Meanwhile, the war was raging in Europe and the Pacific, and the Nickles were eager to serve their country overseas. At the time, in the months after D-Day, U.S. divisions overseas were starved for replacements, but the 555th was not called. Instead, in late April 1945, it received orders to report to Pendleton Air Base, Oregon, for a "highly classified mission."

Unbeknownst to the Nickles and the American public, the Japanese were secretly launching balloons made of paper and silk that carried incendiary bombs. Aimed at industry in the Pacific Northwest, the balloons were carried from Japan to the United States by the high-altitude jet stream that crosses the Pacific. The balloon-borne incendiary bombs ignited several forest fires across Oregon, Idaho, Washington, and California.

The U.S. government kept quiet on the true cause of the fires, both to prevent panic among the American public and to keep valuable intelligence from Japan. The government also devised Operation FIREFLY to deal with the balloons. FIREFLY called for the 555th to become "smoke jumpers," parachuting into the conflagrations caused by the balloons and by natural causes such as lightning.[2] The Nickles also had the hazardous duty of disabling the Japanese incendiary devices.

Throughout the scorching summer of 1945 and into late autumn, the Nickles put their lives on the line, helping to prevent the Pacific Northwest from going up in flames. The Nickles conducted more than twelve hundred individual jumps, every one of which was risky since the drop zones were in very rugged terrain, resulting in many broken bones and even a crushed chest.

By the end of autumn, Operation FIREFLY was winding down and the Nickles were transferred to Fort Bragg, North Carolina, where they were reassigned to the 13th Airborne Division. After a brief training period, the 555th was administratively attached to the 82nd Airborne Division, commanded by General James Gavin.

On January 14, 1946, the 82nd Airborne Division was given the honor of marching in the victory parade up New York's Fifth Avenue. Even though the Nickles never set foot in Europe or contributed to the division's battlefield success, General Gavin insisted that the 555th be given the same battlefield decorations that other men of the 82nd wore on their uniforms and that they march with the rest of the division in the parade. It was a proud day for the unit. That day, America saw a glimpse of the future as the Nickles marched smartly up Fifth Avenue. Two years later, even before President Harry S. Truman issued the order to integrate the armed forces, the 555th would become one of the first units in the army to be fully integrated.

WALTER MORRIS

555th Parachute Infantry Battalion

For most African-Americans in the army, World War II was a constant battle against segregation and racism. In this war, Walter Morris was America's first black paratrooper. Morris recalls the beginning of the 555th in the first few weeks of 1944.

I was the first one selected. At the time, I was a first sergeant in the service company in Fort Benning, Georgia. I had 150 men in the service company, and our sole duty was doing guard duty for the parachute school. We patrolled the airfield, we patrolled a packing shed and the various jump towers they had there and the calisthenics field. Our tour of duty was from four in the afternoon until eight the next morning. At four, the white parachute students would complete their training, and then we would take over and start guarding the various installations.

It was doing that guard duty, the monotony of every day walking around airfields and empty calisthenics fields, I noticed the morale of my men was so low. As first sergeant, I had to do something about it. It occurred to me that maybe if we imitated the white paratrooper students, it would give our men some added incentives to act like soldiers rather than servants, which is what I always called that duty. So it was one day at four when the white students left the field, I got our men, those who were not on guard duty, and I formed them and double-timed them to the calisthenics field, which was close to where our barracks were, and we began to go through the same routine that the students went through on the five-foot platform: that you jump down into a sort of sawdust pit and you practice how to do what was called the fluid roll, which was a method of falling and distributing the shock throughout the body so it wasn't concentrated on any one spot, the ankles or the knees. We learned how to do the fluid roll.

Then we went to the C-47 fuselages that they had there, and that was to train the student how to jump from a plane. There were certain routines you went through, you hook up and you checked your equipment, and you stood in the door, and you exited the door by counting thousands: one-one-thousand, two-one-thousand, three-one-thousand was equivalent to three seconds. If the chute doesn't open in three seconds, you knew you had to pull your emergency chute. The students practiced jumping out of that fuselage down into a sawdust pit that was five feet below.

We did that for a couple of weeks, and I noticed first that our men became very efficient in the exercises and, number two, their conduct had improved, their morale had improved, their dress was neater and their response, when you talked to them, they looked you straight in the eye. It was working, that imitating the student idea.

We thought no one knew until one day General Ridgley Gaither, who was the commanding general of the parachute school, was on his way back to his office around five in the afternoon, and he looked across the calisthenics field, which was supposed to have been empty at five, and here he saw seventy-five black soldiers going through calisthenics, push-ups, and jumping out of the plane counting one-thousand-one, and he didn't know what in the world was going on out there.

He called me to come to his office the next morning. When I got the order to go to General Gaither's office I couldn't imagine what I had done wrong . . . but it must be a very important affair.

The next morning I got on my bicycle and I rode to his office and was introduced to him, and he asked me to explain what he saw. I did and told him why. He was very impressed and said, "Well, that's good. Now I'm going to tell you a secret, Morris. I'm going to let you in on a top secret. In the next few weeks, we're going to have an order from Washington activating the 555th Parachute Infantry Company. It will be all-colored company, separate company. You'll have black officers and black men." This was the first time, to my knowledge, in history that the army designated a unit having black officers and black men.

He asked me if I would like to be the first sergeant of that unit, and of course I was thrilled! I often tell the story that I know how I got to General Gaither's office because I had my bicycle, but after I learned about the black parachute company being formed, I left that office and I don't have any idea how I got to my office. I don't know whether I rode my bicycle or flew!

I was given a furlough and went back to New York and gave my mother the news. I showed off my boots—I had no business wearing them, but I had them. I had the paratrooper pants and the jump jacket. I don't remember if I had wings or not, but I had everything else I shouldn't have had. I was home for a few days in December and I got the call to report back to Fort Benning because the cadre that had been selected were seventeen men from the 92nd Infantry Division. I met the train, we came back to Fort Benning, and along with the seventeen I had two men from the service company apply for parachute duty, and being a segregated army there was no place for them, so they put those two men in my company. That made a total of twenty of us, and we started training in January.

The first week, of course, was hell. It was from daylight to dark, running, jumping, doing push-ups, getting our body in physical shape for the other three weeks of training. We completed the course, and seventeen of the twenty graduated. Sixteen at one time; the seventeenth man, Carstell Stewart, had to leave at the third week to go to a funeral, his mother had died, and when he got back he had to finish his week with the white students. Technically he was the first man to integrate the army!

Once we got our wings, the army then sent six black officers to Fort Benning to get their training. When they completed their four weeks, then the army opened the gates, so to speak, to all colored volunteers who wanted to be paratroopers. Some of the men from my old service company applied and were accepted. We went on from there.

We were so excited to have been given the opportunity to prove we could do more than guard duty or driving trucks or loading ships or loading ammunition, serving tables, or cooking. We were now given the opportunity to be paratroopers, and it was a very wonderful feeling. There were obstacles put before us, but we overcame them.

The soldiers in Fort Benning were betting that the black soldiers wouldn't have the nerve or the guts to jump out of a plane. There were actual bets made throughout Fort Benning, Georgia! That hurt us. There wasn't much taunting; they were just ignoring us as soldiers. It hurt to the extent that when we were on the post and saw German and Italian prisoners of war picking up cigarette

butts and candy wrappers with the POW stenciled on the back of their cover-
alls, those men, those prisoners who killed American soldiers, were given the
opportunity to walk into the post exchange and buy cigarettes or whatever
they wanted to, but we, as black soldiers in uniform, couldn't go into the post
exchange. That was off-limits to us. We couldn't go into the main theater;
rather, the army built a theater and post exchange in the area where we had
our barracks.

At first we had to sit in the back of the bus. As the war progressed and
more colored soldiers came to Fort Benning, they decided to have a colored
bus. They had a white bus and a colored bus. We had our own bus, but the
problem was if you were in Columbus, Georgia, after twelve, after curfew
hour, and your colored bus had gone, if there was a white bus sitting there
waiting, you couldn't get on it.

BRADLEY BIGGS

555ᵗʰ Parachute Infantry Battalion

Bradley Biggs, the first black officer accepted for parachute duty, dis-

cusses the Nickles' sense of pride.

I went to Fort Benning with the idea that it was not a case where we had to
prove that the Negro soldier could jump out of an airplane but prove that we
should have been there all along.

The unit started because the McCloy Report made its recommendation to
President Roosevelt to start a battalion of black paratroopers. General
[George C.] Marshall, then the chief of staff, he took his own pencil and
wrote in: "Start a company."[3] When it got down to the parachute school it became an experimental test platoon. That was degrading. That was insulting. It
was demeaning. We swore to ourselves as men that we would not fail and
wouldn't disgrace ourselves.

When I got off that train at Fort Benning, you could see the signs, colored
and white. When we got our wings, we went off to the main post and I asked
for membership in the officers' club. They said, "No, we are going to give you
your own club." What they did was convert a service area and make it into a
makeshift officers' club. They gave us a cook and called it an officers' club. It
was insulting. After we obtained our wings, we were part of the army's elite
troops. We completed some of the army's most intense and demanding training. Prior to that I was a professional football player, went through OCS,

trained with several other units, so why should we be treated as second-class citizens?

There are many thoughts we have now that we don't remember in such detail that our emotions get in the way. That's what we had lived through. We fought segregation and discrimination and intolerance. They tried to burn us out. They did burn us out, but it made us stronger. It made us angry. It made us persevere. We were determined that all that came in front of us didn't have to relive what we went through. We helped carry integration on our backs. We helped make it possible. It makes me feel like we accomplished something. I feel that we lived for something that was worthwhile.

We wanted to be the finest military organization in the U.S. Army. We had a lot of firsts. But we were not trying to socialize the army. We wanted to do it for ourselves, and we realized if we did it for ourselves, the rest would follow. We didn't just observe, we participated, and we didn't await change, we forced it.

Eventually, after the war, we got word that we would be integrated as the 3rd Battalion of the 505th Parachute Infantry Regiment of the 82nd Airborne Division. The civilian population got to see that their white sons would be led by a black soldier. We trained our men that they were going to be leaders in an integrated army. So these white soldiers would go home and say, "Mom, Dad, my squad leader is a black soldier. He's my friend; I respect and admire him." That is our success. That's where the civil-rights attitude come from, and that's where we as black servicemen helped remove a cancer that was part of American society that was born in segregation and discrimination.

I remember one incident that almost destroyed the 555th. The men had just gotten their wings; they were very, very proud. Corporal Adolph Crisp: When I was a platoon sergeant in 1942, he was my runner; he was also my friend. The men were gathered in a service club. The men were noisy, and someone called a military policeman. . . . The MP told the men to quiet down. Our boys were kind of arrogant, exchanged some words. Eventually, he was backed into a corner.

He [the MP] then did something he should never have done: He pulled his .45 and put a round in the chamber. The boys kept moving forward and tried to disarm him. The MP fired and put a bullet in Crisp's stomach.

When that happened, our men got riled, and the following night about forty of them got together and were about to turn out the MP barracks.

When I heard about it, Lieutenant Cal Cornelius and I went out in front of a big tree in front of the orderly room that they were using as a meeting point. The men were carrying their jump knives and sticks. We tried logic at first. We told the men, "Don't do this." "We will take care of this."

Bradley Biggs, first African-American paratrooper officer (center), seated with fellow Triple Nickle paratroopers. (Photo courtesy Bradley Biggs)

"If you do, you'll set back the cause that we will never, ever recover from." We said, "If you do this, the unit would be disbanded."

One of the men yelled, "If Crisp dies, that will be murder and there'll be hell to pay!"

Then Cal said, "If Crisp dies, we'll handle it. And the first one of you men to set foot on that sidewalk will get his jaw broken." At that, Cal stepped on the sidewalk, and I joined him.

They could have bowled us over, but they didn't; they had too much respect for us. That was the night that we didn't know which way the ball was going to bounce.

The next morning, everything was quiet and calm. . . . The commanding general came down and addressed the men and said, "Gentlemen, you are still on probation and can be disbanded. All it takes is the cutting of an order and you will go back to where you started from."

CARSTELL STEWART

555th Parachute Infantry Battalion

Carstell Stewart, an original member of the test platoon, describes
an incident that occurred during the early days of the unit.

I was trained in basic infantry in Texas, and I was placed in the 92nd Division
and in the heavy weapons company. We trained mostly in marching and that
sort of thing. We didn't do much training in military tactics.

An order came down that they wanted a cadre for the parachute test platoon and they needed about twenty soldiers. I volunteered, and I was lucky to
be picked because there was a tremendous number of people who volunteered. From there we went to Fort Benning, Georgia.

The first day at Fort Benning, everybody was uptight a little bit because we
didn't really know what we were going into. Our cadre, the people who were
going to train us, were very athletic and were strong young paratroopers who
were going to train us and show us how to become paratroopers. There was a
little apprehension, but after a couple of days of exercising and talking, we got
to know them better, and then we went on to accomplish what we set out to do.

They had intended to really work us over. They ran us until they became
exhausted, but most of us were in pretty good shape. You had to be in excellent condition to compete as far as remaining in the platoon, remaining in the
team. You had to do push-ups; everything was on the double. If you made a
mistake you were punished by push-ups—"Give me fifty"—"Give me a hundred"—"Drop down, give me two hundred push-ups." That was a carryover
from the way they were taught; that was the protocol in treating basic people
who wanted to become paratroopers. They were trying to break us—that was
a normal thing in that position. We tried to break guys when we trained guys.
It was a type of hazing situation: Are you tough enough? Can you compete?
Can you be one of us? We wanted to be the best! That's the way they looked
at us. It wasn't that they were white and we were black. It was just a one-on-
one, man-to-man thing.

We were segregated. We had our own places. We had our own mess hall.
We were located in a segregated area. If you went to the show, you had to sit
in a separate place, and when you rode on the bus, you had to sit on the back
of the bus. Those things were routine: It was the law of the land, it was the
South. It had been that way for two hundred, three hundred years, and it
wasn't going to change in this short period of time.

A lot of the fellows from the North didn't understand what was really going on because they had never come in contact with that situation. In order for them to survive, they had to commit themselves to doing what the law required at that particular time.

The protocol was (this was before Martin Luther King and before Jackie Robinson, and this was before the nonviolence that came later on) we were told that we had to contain our feelings and we had to contain our anger in order to become a member of the paratroopers. We had to put up with this southern situation if we wanted to accomplish our goal. This is the type of self-restraint and self-determination in order to reach our goal of being a paratrooper. If we got out of this mode we would be dismissed. We had to learn self-control, discipline, in order to reach our goal.

I was a very angry young man. This is not a natural thing for a young man to come into contact in this situation. I was born in the South but was taken to the North when I was four or five years old, and then I was taken back and went to a southern school in Baltimore, Maryland, but the segregation and discrimination was not as acute.

The young lady that I have been married to for fifty years lived in Columbus, Georgia, and I used to visit her on occasion. She lived not too far from a country type of store where the local gentry used to hang out there, whittling sticks and chewing snuff and spitting tobacco and really pooling their own ignorance. They used to sit on benches in front of the store—it was actually a shack.

I went into the shack and I ordered a grape pop. Where I was from at that time, they called a soda drink a pop. This guy who was the proprietor of the store, he reached under the counter and takes out a bottle of Coca-Cola and he puts it on the counter and said, "Hey, nigger, this is grape pop! This is the home of Coca-Cola; we don't sell pop here." Then he reached down on the other side of the counter and put a .45 right on top of the counter. He said, "Nigger, drink that grape pop!" I drank the pop. I was thinking, "Contain yourself, maintain your balance, and you know what you got to do and you know what you are down here to do. Be cool and get through it and move on. It will be another day to continue what you need to do."

So I drank the pop and swallowed my pride because I knew what I was there for. They thought we were going to be failures. In order for us to be successful, I had to control what this man was trying to provoke me to do. I was able to make my decision and walk out and not cause any problems. That's what they wanted to do, to cause problems, to make us not be able to bring about a successful conclusion, being a black parachute group. They—many of the white population, the military, the soldiers, and some of the other paratroopers. We had boots and they figured we shouldn't be wearing boots. We were invading their private domain.

TED "TIGER" LOWRY

555th Parachute Infantry Battalion

Typical of many of those who volunteered for the Nickles was Ted "Tiger" Lowry, a professional boxer, one of many professional athletes in the unit. Tiger Lowry, who still has a boxer's build, discusses his background and entry into the 555th.

My first fight, I was a little leery about fighting because when the guy came in, on the back of his robe it said Rhode Island Champion. I said, "Holy Moly, they're matching me with the champion of Rhode Island for my first fight?!" So instead of me really fighting I just kind of hanged back a little and he wanted to fight, so my trainer told me, "You're going to fight him again." All that week, I lived in a house with a bunch of fighters, and they gave me the silent treatment, they turned my plate over and under the plate was a note on there saying, "You're chicken, you can't fight, go back home to Maine." They wouldn't talk to me the whole week. That night we went to fight I said I know what I'm going to do, I'm going to jump right off the stool and I'm going to throw all my punches and get knocked out and then I'm going to go home. And that's just what I did, I jumped off the stool, got him in his corner, and knocked him out. From then on I did that for four straight weeks and that's where I got the name Tiger.

I played football in high school, and there was a man there, and his son played football also with me. The man used to be a boxer, and he was trying to teach his son how to box . . . and I picked up what he was teaching his son and I found that I liked it. I used to say that one day I plan to be a boxer, never thinking for a minute I'd be one. When the teachers used to ask you what you wanted to be, I would always say a boxer. Sure enough, I became a boxer.

What happened was an amateur show came up, and one of the boys dared me to go into the amateurs. I always took a dare, so I did it. I fought three times that night. I knocked everybody out. I was supposed to fight a fourth fight, but the fellow refused to fight me.

Before I went into the service, I had seventy-five pro fights, and then I was drafted. My biggest fight was when I won the light-heavyweight championship of New England. After I got into the service, I left my boxing equipment at home.

I was in an outfit in Alabama in a field artillery unit, and the outfit I was in had a bunch of illiterates, no education at all; they must have took them right off the streets. The officers didn't respect us at all. I had a lot of pride, so I didn't like the outfit! We read in the paper that they were trying to get together this black paratrooper outfit and that they had priority, so I decided that I wanted to get out of this outfit, so five of us signed up. We had to take a test. Out of the five, I was the only one that passed the test, so I went away to the paratroopers.

I didn't think that I was going to make the paratroopers because I didn't think I could ride in a plane. I couldn't even ride in an elevator; I was uncomfortable in an elevator! But I took the training and I passed and I got my wings and everything. I really liked it.

The spirit in the outfit was terrific. No one in there had an IQ under 110. It was a buddy-buddy system. I was very proud. I felt like I had something to fight for. My family was living good; I was living good.

I was from New England. I had never been discriminated against; I knew of it, but it never affected me in any way. I really felt like I had something to fight for; that's why I was gung-ho.

Everyone in the outfit had pride; we were cocky. We were the elite and we were well trained. We jumped an eighteen-man stick [a stick refers to the number of paratroopers in a plane] in nine seconds flat. You couldn't even brush up against a paratrooper without another one taking offense. We had each other's back. We had to, because we didn't get any respect from the civilians. The other paratroopers, they had to respect us because we were doing the very same thing they were doing and doing it as well, if not better.

I had a civilian call me "boy." I tell you, that really got to me. He was unkempt, tobacco juice coming out the side of his mouth. I was at the railway station, going home on furlough. He said, "Boy." I looked around to see who he was talking to and he said, "You, you boy, I'm talking to you!"

"Me?"

"Yeah."

"What do you want?"

He said, "Where're you going?"

I said, "I'm going on furlough."

He said, "How many days you got?"

I said, "Fifteen."

"Ain't no sense your going home. Stay here with me, pick some cotton, and I'll pay ya."

I had never seen cotton! I said, "You've got to be out of your mind."

He said, "What'd you say, boy?"

Just then the train came. I was just about to get in trouble, I'm sure I was. I got on the train—that was the only thing that saved me.

The one experience that hurt me the most was that I had on a United States uniform, I had just qualified as a paratrooper, we got a pass to go to town, we got on the bus, and the city buses that came to post, we had to go to the back of the bus. It so happened that I took the army bus to the town [Columbus, Georgia], and when I got out of there I was going to Phenix City, Alabama, and I had to get on the city bus. As I got on the city bus, on the front of the bus was a bunch of soldiers, and they laughed at us and pointed at us when we got on because we had to go to the back of the bus. We didn't pay it no mind; we were used to it. We knew what was expected of us and how to keep out of trouble. We did what we were supposed to do. We were advised, "Don't upset the apple cart."

We got in the back and we were sitting down and the soldiers were laughing and carrying on both sides of the aisle, the two front seats. We looked on their backs and saw POW. Each of them had a jacket with POW on it, and that meant prisoners of war. They were Germans. That meant that they had been captured on the firing line and they had probably killed some American soldiers, and they were allowed to sit on the front of the bus and we had to go to the back! I never lived that down.

Joe Louis came to town, and it was in Camp Walters, Texas, where I was. They boxed him in Camp Polk, Louisiana, and they needed someone to box him; they asked me to box him. I said, "You got to be crazy, he's the champion of the world! I'm not in his class." The company commander, the colonel of the post, came down and said, "I understand that you refuse to box Joe Louis." I said, "Sure." He said, "Well I'll tell you, there's boys here that will never get a chance to see him. They're going overseas and may never get back. I'm going to give you a direct order." A direct order is very bad; you don't have a choice! I told them, "Joe's got to tell me that he's not going to hurt me!"

. . . We boxed, and the man that was in my corner was Sugar Ray Robinson. So I went into the room and they said, "This young man is going to box you." Joe looked at me and said, "That little kid? Naw, I'll hurt him!" That rubbed me the wrong way. So I said, "You what? I fought this fellow (I can't remember his name) and beat him." Joe Louis said, "Put your gloves on." He figured I knew something about boxing. We boxed.

We got in the ring, and when they mentioned his name, the whole place went crazy—Joe Louis, world champion. And then Tiger Lowry, New England—you could have heard a pin drop!

WALTER MORRIS

555th Parachute Infantry Battalion

The Triple Nickles eagerly awaited an opportunity to enter combat, but the men's courage was not matched by that of the army brass, which couldn't bring itself to integrate the 555th into combat units that were starved for replacement troops. Instead, the 555th was transferred to the Pacific Northwest to fight forest fires caused by Japanese incendiary balloons and natural causes.

They didn't know what to do with all these black paratroopers, but we got lucky because at that time the Japanese were sending over aerial balloons across on the trade winds, and the balloons were calibrated to fall on the western shore from Canada to California. The Forest Service's smoke jumpers were not enough to handle the amount of fires that were caused by the balloons, and the campers, and the lightning. So the Forest Service, whose responsibility was to fight forest fires, called on the army to help and asked the army if they could spare any paratroopers. The Army was happy to do that because they had the 555th, and they assigned us to that mission.

Smoke jumper exiting a C-47. The Nickles were fitted with field-expedient smoke-jumping gear that was a combination of civilian and military equipment. The overalls are United States Army Air Force sheepskin flight clothing, and Riddell football helmets were fitted with face shields. (Photo courtesy Melvin Lester)

We thought, when we were ordered to go west, that we were actually going to the Pacific; we were so happy. As it turned out, Operation FIREFLY, which was the code name, was not the Pacific; it was to fight forest fires.

We were trained in Oregon for two weeks to jump into trees (which was counter to what we had learned as paratroopers, to miss trees) and to learn how to jump with a new chute that was devised for the Forest Service men.

We were taught to jump into trees because the clearings you would find in those mountains were mostly rocks and boulders. It was safer to land in the trees. They gave us a fifty-foot letdown rope.

My jump was in Mount Baker in Washington State. We had several injured men. It was really something, because it took the one officer and the twenty men to get that one man down from the mountain. We found out how tough it was to come down a mountain.

We did thirty to thirty-five fires for the 1945 season. The fires that we fought were caused by lightning or careless campers. A few by the Japanese balloons. There are still many of those balloons lying in the mountains.

Our assignment was, once we located the area where we wanted to jump, we gathered our equipment, and we only had two pieces of firefighting equipment, a shovel and a pick. You had to build fire lanes. The method to retaining a fire up in those mountains, you had no water or fire retardants, we had to clear a lane around the fire in order to contain it. What happened in this particular fire that I'm talking about up at Mount Baker, we worked very hard to get a fire lane to contain this fire, and fortunately the wind at night dies down and the fire dies down and everything is quiet. In the morning everything starts up, and the fire started up, and what happened, the fire jumped the fire lane from one treetop to another, and when that happened you have to go through the process of creating another lane. We were very fortunate with this particular fire because it started raining. It rained all day and all night and it helped us contain this fire. For three days we were up there, and the Forest Service came to relieve us.

We completed the fire season in 1945 and we were commended by the commanding general of that area, and we returned to Camp Mackall and later to Fort Bragg.

MELVIN LESTER

555th Parachute Infantry Battalion

On January 14, 1946, the 82nd Airborne Division along with the 555th was given the honor of marching in the victory parade up New York's Fifth Avenue, as described here by Melvin Lester.

We did not want a parade. Everybody was so sloppy when we were doing the drills for the parade, and when some colonel came over he said to us, "I don't believe this is the same outfit I saw at Fort Benning, Georgia. Down there, everything you guys did was perfect. I've never seen an organization as sloppy as this one!" We really didn't care because so many of us wanted to get out of the service, and we didn't ask for a victory parade.

So the day for the victory parade came. We got dressed for it. The 82nd had been overseas and won many citations that were on their uniforms. They let us wear the same uniform that the 82nd wore.

We got on the train taking us to the Pier 58 in New York. On the train, everybody's pride had come back, and we said we weren't going to be outdone. We marched off the train just like you were supposed to.

They put us on the end of the parade, and as we marched down Fifth Avenue people were like, "Are those black boys?" Black people in the crowd went crazy and were coming out to greet us.

Walter Winchell was broadcasting the parade, and when we went past the reviewing stand, as we passed he announced: "stony-faced, eyes to the right, surpassed by none." They had that clip in the paper the next day, and I kept that picture until it turned brown and just crumbled up!

I felt pretty good about the parade, but I was feeling better about going home because I was offered a tech sergeant three, nine days' furlough—they were doing everything to get guys to reenlist. I said, "No, I'm going home." I didn't reenlist, but a lot of them did. I guess the majority reenlisted. I had had my fill of the army, and I came home. On the way home I had an interesting experience.

I was on the train going to Cincinnati to visit my wife when the porter called, "Last call for dinner," in the dining car. [I] got up and started toward the dining room, and the MP stopped me to ask where I was going. I said, "-I'm going to the dining car." They said, "We'll call you when we get ready to feed you." I said, "I'm not eating on a GI meal ticket, I'm paying for my meal, and this is the last call," so they stepped aside.

I went on into the dining room, and the [host] seated me at the first table on the right side of the train. And then he called the porter and whispered to the porter, and the porter came over and pulled the black curtain across the seat, separating me from the white people in the dining car.

I blew my top! I pushed it back. . . . [The host] looked back and saw that it was open [and called the porter to shut the curtain again]. When he came over, I said, "If you came over to pull that curtain, I would advise you not to do it, because if you pull that curtain, I'm going to whup your ass! I'm risking my life jumping out of airplanes for this country, and I would just as soon die here than to die out there [fighting] or anywhere else."

They didn't pull that curtain.

CHAPTER SEVEN

INVASION: Normandy

Tonight is the night of nights.

Tomorrow throughout the whole of our

homeland and the Allied world the bells

ring out the tidings that you have arrived,

and the invasion for liberation has begun.

—Robert Sink, Commander, 506th Parachute Infantry
Regiment, invasion prayer to his troops before D-Day

They stood shoulder to shoulder in the early morning hours of June 6, 1999, at the old Ste. Mère-Église cemetery. For many veterans, this was the first trip back to Normandy in fifty-five years. A darkened, weathered sandstone monument is the only reminder of Normandy's first U.S. cemetery, where most of America's fallen soldiers were buried by the truckload. Among the veterans, the bonds of brotherhood are still visibly present. Fifty-five years later, these men came back to remember those who did not return home with them. As young men they were participants in one of the great turning points of World War II—Normandy.

In June 1944, the German army was still a formidable foe. To defend against the invasion, the Germans were able to field fifty-eight divisions that included a mobile reserve of about two thousand tanks as part of their Atlantic Wall defenses.[1] The Germans had learned in Italy that if they concen-

World War II veterans return to the old cemetery at Ste. Mère-Église during the fifty-fifth anniversary of D-Day for a ceremony to honor fallen paratroopers. (Author's photo)

trated their forces and acted quickly, they might be able to repel an Allied invasion on the beaches.

America's Ranger and airborne troops were the ideal assault forces to pierce these defenses. Spearheading the amphibious portion of the invasion were the green yet exquisitely trained 2nd and 5th Ranger battalions, designated the Provisional Ranger Group. Making the airborne assault were the seasoned 82nd Airborne Division, the All-Americans, and the 101st Airborne Division, the Screaming Eagles. Among the Rangers' missions in support of the Normandy invasion during its first two months was also the attack on the heavily defended port city of Brest, in Brittany.

The 82nd Airborne's primary objectives on D-Day were to take the town of Ste. Mère-Église, which straddled the key N-13 highway, and to capture certain bridges that crossed the Merderet River, so that German reinforcements could be blocked from reaching the Utah Beach landing areas. Meanwhile, the 101st Airborne Division was assigned to secure four causeways or built-up roads that crossed a flooded area leading to Utah Beach. Control of this flooded area was critical. The 101st also was to take the locks that controlled the water levels behind Utah Beach and secure and destroy several bridges that crossed the Douve River,[2] all of which was necessary to prevent

German reinforcements from linking up with their beach defenses. Paratroopers were to secure the landing areas, followed by about 375 glidermen, mostly carrying antitank guns, who would reinforce them on D-Day. Additional glider reinforcements would land the evening of D-Day, with the main glider landing occurring the next morning. Glider units also landed by sea with the 4th Infantry Division at Utah.[3]

Then, at 0115 on June 6, 1944, about 13,100 American paratroopers started dropping from C-47s into Normandy.[4] The delivery operation was a disaster, and few units landed where they were supposed to. (In fact, only one regiment, the 505th, landed close to its target—Ste. Mère-Église.) American troop-carrier flight crews lacked the training they needed for an operation of this magnitude, and they encountered turbulent cloudbanks and flak that limited the pilots' ability to identify their positions.

Once on the ground, small groups of paratroopers from disparate units assembled and moved toward objectives designated for battalions. While the scattered drops made it difficult for paratroopers to seize their objectives, they caused a tremendous amount of confusion for the Germans. Paratroopers seemed to be everywhere. Cutting communications, ambushing reinforcements, and seizing towns, the airborne troops were wreaking havoc among the Germans, causing them to divide their forces and convincing them that the airborne invading force was much larger than it was.

In the early morning hours of June 6, the first reinforcements started to arrive by glider. Landing a World War II glider was a dangerous business—like making a dead-stick landing with an engineless airplane. These crash landings were made even more perilous by the presence of hundreds of stakes, dubbed "Rommel's asparagus," planted wherever the Germans suspected Allied gliders might land. Casualties were high, yet the gliders provided much-needed reinforcements to the beachhead.

By dawn, small groups of men from the 101st Airborne Division had captured four causeways that led to Utah Beach. These actions were critical to the invasion and made Utah far less bloody than Omaha Beach, which did not have a supporting airborne assault. Emblematic of the airborne's success was E Company of the 506th Parachute Infantry Regiment's destruction of an artillery battery at Brécourt Manor. The battery, defended by about fifty soldiers from the elite German 6th Fallschirmjäger (Parachute) Regiment, was capable of lobbing shells on Utah Beach from a position that would be difficult for the landing troops to attack. The German garrison that was dug in with supporting machine gun nests was routed by thirteen paratroopers.[5]

Several of the 101st's other objectives proved more challenging, but by noon on D-Day the Screaming Eagles had secured the locks along with the bridges at Brevands and Le Port. Once the bridges were secured, roadblocks were established, hampering the Germans' ability to feed reinforcements across the Douve and into Utah Beach. The Screaming Eagles' next objective was the capture of the crucial town of Carentan, which like Ste. Mère-Église straddled the important N-13 highway.

Like the 101st, pockets of the 82nd Airborne Division were strewn all over Normandy. Places like the town of Graignes became legendary as bands of paratroopers, surrounded and outnumbered, held off much larger German forces for days. Fortunately, enough men from the 82nd were concentrated in a triangular area around Ste. Mère-Église, between the town of Ste. Mère-Église and the causeways and bridges at Chef-du-Pont and La Fière. After securing Ste. Mère-Église, which was crucial to preventing German reinforcements from hitting the beach, groups of men from different airborne regiments fought to defend the Ste. Mère-Église triangle in one of the great victories of World War II.

On the morning of D-Day, members of the 5th and 2nd Ranger battalions were making their way through the choppy waters off Normandy to their D-Day objectives. The Rangers were divided into three elements designated Forces A, B, and C. The mission for Force A (consisting of D, E, and F companies of the 2nd Ranger Battalion) was the destruction of six large-caliber guns that were thought to be in hardened concrete bunkers on top the cliffs of Pointe-du-Hoc, which is located roughly between Omaha and Utah beaches. The guns could pose a significant threat to the Omaha and Utah beach landings. Force C (consisting of the 5th Ranger Battalion and A and B companies of the 2nd Ranger Battalion) was to wait offshore for thirty minutes for a prearranged signal to reinforce Force A on the cliffs. If Force A failed to take Pointe-du-Hoc, Force C was to land on Omaha Dog Green Beach, make an overland attack, and seize the gun emplacements on the cliffs. Finally, Force B (C Company of the 2nd Ranger Battalion) had the crucial mission of climbing the cliffs at Pointe-et-Raz-de-la-Percée on the extreme right flank of Omaha Beach, on top of which was a series of mortar emplacements that could send down flanking fire on the forces assaulting Omaha Beach.

At 0645 the landing craft ramps dropped and Force B stepped into hell. Artillery, mortar, and machine gun fire ripped through the bodies of the Rangers as they made their way across the Charlie sector of Omaha Beach to the ninety-foot cliffs of Pointe-et-Raz-de-la-Percée. Using bayonets and toggle ropes, the Rangers scaled the cliff and seized the German positions on top, denying the Germans the high ground.[6]

To this day, the assault on the cliffs of Pointe-du-Hoc captures the public's imagination. But the Rangers' heroics aside, the primary focus of the mission was to destroy the German guns on top of the cliff. The guns, however, had been moved, towed inland a mile or so from the cliffs for protection from Allied naval and aerial bombardment. Still, the Rangers beat the Germans to the punch. After securing their position on top of the cliffs, a small group of Rangers found the guns, mysteriously without their crews. They placed thermite grenades on the guns' breach mechanisms to save Utah from a devastating barrage of artillery fire.[7] The Rangers also cut the Grandcamp coastal road, preventing the Germans from moving reinforcements from one beach to another. For the next two days, outnumbered and forced to use captured German weapons as supplies ran low, the Rangers beat off several company-sized German counterattacks. For its actions at Pointe-du-Hoc, the battalion won its first Presidential Unit Citation.

Meanwhile, a seasick Force C was waiting in the choppy waters off the Normandy coast to execute its primary mission: reinforce the assault on Pointe-du-Hoc. The signal it received was garbled. So, unable to determine the status of Force A, the Rangers had to assume that the mission had failed. They proceeded to their secondary mission: Land on the Dog Green sector of Omaha Beach, make an overland attack, and seize Pointe-du-Hoc. This led to a fortunate chain of events that helped save Omaha Beach.

The Dog Green sector, like most of the rest of Omaha Beach, was a charnel house. The assault was bogged down, and men were trapped on the beaches. On the Dog Green sector alone, many of the men from the 116th Regiment of the 29th Infantry Division and A and B companies of the 2nd Ranger Battalion were gunned down the instant their landing craft ramps dropped. Observing this carnage, Lt. Colonel Max Schneider, the Force C commander, ordered the remainder of his force to Omaha Dog White, a relatively quiet sector of the beach. This decision helped turn the tide at Omaha and had a significant impact on the invasion. Once on Dog White, the 5th Rangers plus men from the 116th Infantry who were already on the beach moved inland, assaulting the bluffs near the seaside town of Vierville. They knocked out several machine gun nests and blew a hole in the Germans' barbed-wire beach defenses. That became the crucial exit from Omaha Beach.[8]

After breaking through the beach defenses, the Rangers moved toward Vierville. By noon on June 8, after intense fighting, they linked up with the Rangers at Pointe-du-Hoc. After their actions around the beachhead, the Rangers got a respite beginning June 9. They spent the next week in a non-leading role that included heavy patrolling, but by June 16, both units were placed in the First Army Reserve. In July and the first week of August, the Rangers spent their time training, guarding prisoners, and assimilating replacement personnel into the units.

On June 7, the Germans launched several relentless attacks on the beleaguered airborne troops in the rough triangle around Ste. Mère-Église and

Ranger and Airborne Operations in Normandy—1944

Legend:
- Allied Advances
- Causeways
- 82nd Planned DZs
- 101st Planned DZs
- Planned LZs
- Allied Beachheads at the End of D-Day

1. Albert Hassenzahl, *506 PIR, 101st*
2. Dutch Schultz, *505 PIR, 82nd*
3. Lynn Compton, *506 PIR, 101st*
4. Julian Ewell, *501 PIR, 101st*
5. Sid Salomon, *2nd Ranger Btn.*
6. Ray Alm, *2nd Ranger Btn.*
7. Frank South, *2nd Ranger Btn.*
8. Len Lomell, *2nd Ranger Btn.*
9. John Raaen, *5th Ranger Btn.*
10. Bill Reed, *5th Ranger Btn.*
11. Clinton Riddle, *325th GIR, 82nd*
12. Ed Jeziorski, *507 PIR, 82nd*
13. Francis Naughton, *507 PIR, 82nd*
14. Stanley Clever, *506 PIR, 101st*
15. Jack Isaacs, *505 PIR, 82nd*
16. Francis Lamoureux, *508 PIR, 82nd*
17. Louis Mendez, *508 PIR, 82nd*
18. Robert Edlin, *2nd Ranger Btn. (Brest)*

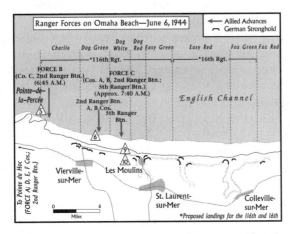

Ranger Forces on Omaha Beach—June 6, 1944

← Allied Advances
⌢ German Stronghold

Charlie Dog Green Dog White Dog Red Easy Green Easy Red Fox Green Fox Red

―――*116th Rgt.――― ―――*16th Rgt.―――

FORCE B
(Co. C, 2nd Ranger Btn.)
(6:45 A.M.)

FORCE C
(Cos. A, B, 2nd Ranger Btn.;
5th Ranger Btn.)
(Approx. 7:40 A.M.)

Pointe-de-la-Percée

2nd Ranger Btn.
A, B Cos.

5th Ranger Btn.

English Channel

To Pointe du Hoc
(FORCE A; D, E, F Cos.;
2nd Ranger Btn.)

Vierville-sur-Mer

Les Moulins

St. Laurent-sur-Mer

Colleville-sur-Mer

0   6
Miles

*Proposed landings for the 116th and 16th

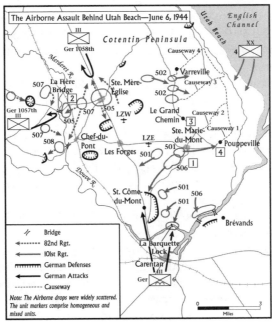

The Airborne Assault Behind Utah Beach—June 6, 1944

English Channel

Cotentin Peninsula

Utah Beach

III
Ger 1058th

Causeway 4

Merderet R.

507   La Hère Bridge

Ste. Mère-Église

502   Varreville

Causeway 3

Ger 1057th
III

507   505

507   505

LZW

502

Le Grand Chemin

Causeway 2

507

508

Chef-du-Pont

Les Forges

LZE

Ste. Marie-du-Mont

Causeway 1

Pouppeville

Douve R.

501

501   501

506

St. Côme-du-Mont

501

501   506

Brévands

La Barquette Lock

Carentan

Ger
III   6

Bridge
82nd Rgt.
101st Rgt.
German Defenses
German Attacks
Causeway

Note: The Airborne drops were widely scattered.
The unit markers comprise homogeneous and
mixed units.

0   3
Miles

La Fière. Some of the most intense fighting of the war occurred near La Fière Bridge as the German 1057th Regiment launched a savage infantry assault supported by tanks. A mixed force of several units, but primarily consisting of the 505th Parachute Infantry Regiment, held the causeway and Ste. Mère-Église. Over the next few days, the battle for La Fière—the key, for the Germans, to getting reinforcements to Utah Beach—raged on. Finally, after a bloody frontal assault, the 82nd secured the La Fière causeway.

The day after La Fière was secured by the 82nd, the 101st Airborne Division turned its attention to taking Carentan. At the time, Carentan was a seam in the American lines. The Allies' fear was that Hitler would pour armor through this gap and penetrate the still vulnerable beachhead. Holding it open was the German 6th Parachute Regiment, one of Germany's finest units in Normandy. The 101st's first attack against the German 6th failed to take the town but included a bayonet charge that broke down the German outer defenses. The Allied high command, recognizing the situation was critical, ordered a naval and artillery bombardment to pulverize the city.

When the barrage lifted, on the night of the eleventh and twelfth, the 101st attacked, forcing the German 6st Parachute Regiment to abandon the city. The next day the Germans counterattacked with a very powerful force consisting of the 6th Parachute Regiment and the 17th SS Panzer Division. But the 101st, with tankers from the 2nd Armored Division, stopped the attack and held the city.

After the capture of the critical Merderet River crossings, the 82nd Airborne Division continued to play an important role in the battle for Normandy. Plans called for the bulk of the 82nd Airborne to attack from two directions: the 508th Regiment, along with supporting units, north across the lower Douve to link up with 101st Airborne near Carentan, and the 507th, 505th, and 325th southwestward along the Douve River. (This southwestward attack led to the unplanned crossing at St. Sauveur-le-Vicomte.) After some intense fighting that included a German counterattack supported by tanks, St. Sauveur-le-Vicomte fell, cutting off the Cotentin Peninsula from German reinforcements.

The constant fighting in Normandy was decimating the airborne ranks. The earthen walls (the infamous hedgerows) created over the centuries by Normandy farmers to separate their fields provided nearly the perfect defense for German soldiers. Despite these natural barriers and stiff German resistance, the 82nd continued to push south over the Douve River, helping enlarge the Normandy beachhead. June 17 represented the last real fighting for the 101st Airborne Division, after which they assumed defensive positions around Cherbourg. By the second week of July they were on boats back to England.

The 82nd was not yet finished fighting. The first week of July was not a good one for the Allies. The Germans had bogged down the invasion; a stalemate loomed. Accordingly, an Allied breakout from the beachhead was ordered. General Omar Bradley, the American commander, wanted to use practically every unit at his disposal to break the deadlock. After fighting continuously for nearly a month, the chewed-up 82nd Airborne Division was selected to spearhead the breakout. The division was barely ready; many of its rifle companies were under strength by 40 percent[9] and two of its regimental commanders, seeing the condition of their men, protested against the need to launch another offensive. General Matthew Ridgway considered the protests and determined that the unit could make one last offensive.

On July 3, Bradley's breakout, led by VII Corps, had begun. The 82nd led the way and was the only U.S. unit that made any real progress, capturing all of its objectives. Despite the early success of and contributions of the 82nd, the offensive failed.

Eleven days later, on July 14, the battered division joined the 101st Airborne Division in England. Only then was it clear just how costly Normandy was for the airborne. The 101st Airborne Division suffered 4,670 casualties while the 82nd suffered 5,245 casualties out of an original force of about 13,500 men per division.[10] The divisions also accumulated an impressive array of Presidential Unit Citations among their regiments and battalions.

By August, the Rangers' respite was coming to an end. They were trucked south near St. Lô and were placed in a defensive position to support General George S. Patton's offensive that eventually led to the overall breakout from the beachhead. Shortly thereafter, the Rangers were deployed as the VIII Corps spearhead to crack the formidable German defenses at the port city of Brest, about two hundred kilometers down the French coast from Normandy in Brittany. Brest was the second-largest port in France. This made its facilities very appealing to the Allies, who were having difficulty delivering the vast supplies needed to feed their armies on the Continent.

Hitler recognized Brest's value and turned it into a fortress. Heavy artillery, self-propelled guns, minefields, and a series of fortifications and strong points manned by about fifty thousands troops, including the elite 2nd Parachute Division, ringed the city. An attacker typically wants a three-to-one advantage in forces to overwhelm a defender, but at Brest, the VIII Corps was practically evenly matched in manpower with the German defensive units. Nevertheless, the VIII Corps' savage campaign at Brest, begun August 25, forced a German capitulation by September 18. In the course of the struggle for Brest, the Rangers were used as assault troops to knock out German forts and strong points. Ironically, before Brest fell, the Germans destroyed its port facilities, rendering them unusable for months.

Normandy was the decisive battle of World War II in Western Europe. It represented the supreme effort of the Western Allies to defeat Hitler and the German army's last true opportunity to alter the course of the war. America's elite troops played a key role in the operation. Throughout the battle, the airborne and Rangers performed magnificently. The sacrifices of countless privates, corporals, sergeants, and officers from these units contributed directly to the success of the American landings.

ALBERT HASSENZAHL

506ᵗʰ Parachute Infantry Regiment, 101ˢᵗ Airborne Division

On the evening of June 5, General Dwight D. Eisenhower paid a visit to the paratroopers of the 101ˢᵗ Airborne Division before the Normandy drop. Casualties for the operation were predicted to be as high as 75 percent, the highest of any of the forces participating in the invasion. Albert Hassenzahl was one casualty who lived to tell about his Normandy experience—an experience that is intertwined with the life of another man.

For over fifty years I kept the war pretty close to my chest. I have some very close friends and family members who finally prevailed upon me to open up about the war. I also decided to talk about it for the son of my close buddy.

The evening before we went into Normandy we were visited by General Eisenhower, Winston Churchill, and a whole load of staff from both sides. We were in an airfield marshaling area preparing to head to Normandy that night. They just happened to hit our battalion. I was in the front row. I'll never forget one personal experience when Ike, General Eisenhower, just happened, for whatever reason, to stop in front of me. He came up to me and looked right into my eyes and in a very soft voice said, "Good luck, soldier." That always stayed with me. I guess it did bring me good luck, because I survived.

As we boarded the planes, we were weighted with the reserve parachute, weapons stuck everywhere, your pockets bulging with ammunition, knives, and whatever else. At the very last minute our battalion received a truckload of what they called "leg bags"; they were canvas bags that had straps with a short line that wrapped around your leg with a quick release. We never jumped with them before.

On top of that, my job when the green light went on . . . was to lead my people out of the airplane. As we were over Normandy, there was a lot of flak coming up at this point. We wanted to get out of the airplane. It was black, pitch black. Dark in the plane and dark outside except for the tracers which were coming up around us. Some of the planes were hit, of course.

We didn't jump very high; it seemed as though I had two oscillations and hit the ground. When I hit the ground: completely black outside, I saw nothing. The Germans hit a couple of my men within a few minutes of following me out the door.

Shortly after landing, all I can tell you is it was a running firefight between a couple of hedgerows. It was near either Ste. Mère-Église or Ste. Marie-du-Mont. That was the general area that I dropped into.

During the day we contacted some Krauts. I had this burning sensation in my right chest, and my legs went out from under me. I was out in the open along with the other fellows; the Krauts were retreating, they were running back to get under cover. I was conscious, and I remember my friend and my sergeant, Joseph Zettwich, known as Punchy, come out under risk of his own life, and he pulled me himself back behind a hedgerow under cover. My jacket was saturated with blood and I had a gaping chest wound. We all carried a large compress; each man had one. He took my compress; I still recall his comment, something to the effect: "Jesus Christ! I don't know what I can do, but I'll do the best I can." He did. He patched me up as best he could.

I was in and out of consciousness; I was losing a lot of blood. Shock sets in, too, when you get a wound like that—you just get numb. You get into a foggy mental state. Fortunately, I was getting hauled back (I don't remember how) to the aid station. The battalion aid station was close to the fighting. Krauts were around us and everything was scattered pretty well and we were all intermixed together, Krauts and Americans.

We had a regimental Catholic chaplain, who I knew quite well. He came up and took a look at me and started giving me Last Rites. That kind of snapped me out of it. I told him to "get lost, get the hell away from me!" I wasn't going to die. Then I remember Bill Pine, he was my platoon leader at the time, came up to me and said, "Oh, what happened, what's going on?" I tried to talk to him, and the words wouldn't come, and I could feel fluid coming out of my mouth—it was blood. He just patted me on the side of the head and told me to relax and he'd try and see me later. He told me years later that he never expected to see me alive again.

These battalion aid stations were really close to whatever lines we had at the time. This station was an old château that the Germans must have known was an aid station. They were throwing mortars at it. They would hit the tiles on the roof and the tiles would sail off and hit some of the guys that were ly-

Father Sampson, Catholic chaplain with the 101st Airborne Division, says a final prayer over the division's dead, who are wrapped in silk parachute shrouds. (Photo courtesy U.S. Army)

ing there. I remember saying to myself, I hope one of these tiles doesn't hit me in the eye.

The next thing I remember was taking a jeep ride down to the beach on a stretcher for evacuation to the LSTs [Landing Ship Tank] to go back to England or wherever they were going to take you. I was laying on this beach—this was off of Utah Beach—and all the time I had been given supplies of plasma, and if it hadn't been for the plasma I would have died. They ferried the wounded out to the LSTs that were anchored offshore. I'm lying on the beach and they started to evacuate a bunch of the guys, and then they stopped because the weather kind of closed in.

The wind was blowing across the beach. I had a blanket over me. The wind blew the blanket partially off of me and it was very cold, but I didn't have the strength to reach the blanket. Then a very odd thing happened to me. An arm reached across my body and pulled that blanket up and tenderly tucked it around me. The arm belonged to a German POW who had been wounded and was lying on the stretcher next to me. I didn't say a word to him, but I was able to move my head a little and looked over at him. I looked in his eyes, he looked at me, neither one of us said a word, but mentally I

Albert Hassenzahl says goodbye to Joseph "Punchy" Zettwich at Henri Chapelle American Cemetery, June 1994. (Photo courtesy Albert Hassenzahl)

might have said "thank you" with my eyes and he might have said "you're welcome" with his. I've often wondered what happened to that German soldier that was next to me—if he survived the war.

[Hassenzahl recalls how he tried to aid Zettwich at Bastogne in December 1944.] Our battalion and the battalion of the 10th Armored Division were completely surrounded at a town called Noville. We attacked up to the high ground, were driven back by tanks, and all we had were light machine guns and a few bazookas and not many rounds for the bazookas to fight these tanks. It was the one point in my life that I thought I had it, we'll never get out of this predicament.

We finally got orders to pull back. There was a little crossroads named Foy, and we hit a German strong point there. Punchy was hit at Foy during a firefight we had there. We carried Punchy across the road after the firefight went down a little bit and we loaded Punchy on a half-track, and I told him, "Punchy, you're going to be OK." He looked at me—I'll never forget him— he said, "No, Lieutenant, I don't think so." And he died in the half-track on the way back to the company. Punchy saved my life in Normandy and I tried to save his but I guess I wasn't successful. [Chokes up and cries.]

In 1994 I found Punchy's grave at the American cemetery in Europe. I went to the cemetery office with my comrades and we found several of our people, and I made it a point to find Punchy because I had heard he was never brought back to America by his family. That day I put my arm around his headstone and talked to him. I said some things that are personal.

ARTHUR "DUTCH" SCHULTZ

505th Parachute Infantry Regiment, 82nd Airborne Division

One of the characters portrayed in the 1962 film *The Longest Day* was based on the real-life experience of Dutch Schultz. He wasn't a stereotypical hero: The movie portrayed Schultz saying the rosary as the flak-riddled plane carrying him and other paratroopers flew over Normandy. After the drop, Schultz found himself near Ste. Mère-Église and one of Normandy's hottest spots—the La Fière Bridge.

Before we jumped, I really didn't realize what I was getting into. I still thought it was like playing soldier when I was a kid. I had a romantic vision of war.

We were supposed to take off on the fourth, but it was postponed due to weather. We had a lot of meetings briefing us about our objectives. We took off on the evening of the fifth. At the time, Great Britain was on double daylight savings time. It was light out even at 9:30 or 10:00. We had a lot of equipment, about a hundred extra pounds. One of the things that they gave us was a Teller mine, and Teller mines were used against tanks. They also gave us a gammon grenade. This is the first time that anybody in the platoon had seen a gammon grenade [a small beanbaglike grenade filled with high explosives for knocking out tanks]. They told us to keep the cap screwed on tight. Anyway, while we were loaded into the planes waiting to take off, there was a tremendous explosion. What happened, of course, was that a gammon grenade had gone off and had blown one of the planes sky-high, killing or injuring most of the people in the plane. There were only two people that came out of that unscathed. They got onto another plane and were both killed in Normandy. It was then that I started to realize, hey, this is for real.

When we started to take off, I took out my rosary and started to say the Hail Mary. I was saying one rosary after another promising the Blessed Mother that never, never, never would I violate the Seventh Commandment, thou shall not commit adultery and all the sex stuff that went with it, until I was married. I still say at least one every day. That was the promise that I had made. I kept saying it over and over. Some of the other guys were also praying. The old-timers were sleeping.

We hit the coast of Normandy around 1:00 A.M. As we hit the coast, I noticed that the plane was rocking and rolling a bit and I saw flames coming out of the engine. So at that point I turned to the guy next to me and pointed to the engine and said, "Look at the flames coming out of the engine." He said, "Those aren't flames, that's ack-ack" [German antiaircraft fire]. They were shooting at us! [Laughs.] I really got frightened, really frightened. When they told us to stand up and hook up and check each other out, the plane started to go down, it was hit. Fortunately the pilot was able to level it off, but we lost a lot of altitude. We couldn't get out of there fast enough. I mean we got up on our feet, checking the other, and we were ready to go.

When I jumped, I counted one-thousand-one, one-thousand-two, and on three the parachute opened. I oscillated once and twisted upward and the next moment I hit the ground. I didn't feel anything at the time. There was nobody in this area where I had landed. I was in a field surrounded by hedgerows. So the first thing I did was take my knife that I was so fond of and cut myself out of my harness. In the process of trying to find somebody, someone fired at me.

While I was walking around in the daylight I saw a paratrooper. He was in a prone position maybe 150 yards from where I was. I went up to him and I approached him from the rear and I said something like, "Hi, trooper" or something like that. There was no response. So I knelt down on my knee and I saw some white substance on his hand. His eyes were open and he had a hole in his forehead. There was no blood. This was the first dead person that ever I saw. You can't imagine what this felt like. It was becoming more apparent to myself that I wasn't prepared for this.

I wandered around until I met Jack Tallerday, who rounded up several paratroopers from other units. We started to move toward La Fière Bridge, an 82nd objective. None of us other than Jack had experience in combat. I started to feel more comfortable around the other men since they didn't have experience before; only Jack had been in combat. I could share my fears with their fears. I could identify them. There was some sense of comfort being with my people even though they weren't in the same unit. Jack was nearly killed and the group became separated. I spent the night dug in along some railroad tracks with some other men.

The following day we were ordered toward the bridge again. When I got down by the bridge some of our people were in an apple orchard. From this position we could look straight down on the bridge [La Fière]. We were there to stop any attack by the Germans to take the bridge. On June 6 the Germans made a major assault on the bridge. Several tanks tried to cross with a lot of infantry. But several of our bazooka men and Johnny Johnson, who was manning a 57-mm gun, stopped the attack.

Once I settled in with my buddies, some of my fear vanished because we had two guys that saw combat in Italy. Things were going well until the Germans started hitting our position with artillery and mortar fire. One of the combat veterans started saying how bad things were and was saying that we were all going to be killed or captured. Whatever sense of security I had went right out the window. I figured that he must know how bad things really were—he's a combat veteran. Finally, Garrison, the other combat veteran, had enough of what he was saying and told him if he didn't shut up he would kick his ass. It worked; he shut up. My morale was sinking fast. If it had gotten much lower I could have walked on it. I later learned that our resident doomsayer was commonly known as a sad sack.

We suffered a lot of casualties during these barrages—but there was one particular casualty that I will never forget. That night I went to the rear for some reason and I ran into Lieutenant Colonel Mark Alexander. A young paratrooper came up to us and said, "Colonel, I've been hit." We stopped and looked and we didn't see anything. Then he turned around and we saw a huge gaping shrapnel hole in his back. Alexander called for a medic and started to calm the man down and tell him he was going to be all right. I don't know if this man made it or not. What was so incongruous to me at that moment was how this trooper was able to walk, and the other was that this battle-tough commander showed us tender care in the middle of all that death and destruction. I was never able to comprehend a loss of life, or a moment of kindness, or an act of sacrifice in a way that I could evaluate it. At best, I only experienced the feeling and pushed these experiences deep inside me.

Later, when we were moving forward, a friend of mine ran across a German soldier lying on the ground crying for help, obviously in a great deal of pain. My friend went up to him and started prodding the man with his rifle asking for his pistol. The German was still crying when my friend put the muzzle of his rifle between the German's eyes and pulled the trigger. I watched him and there was no movement in my friend's face. I was both appalled and awed by what I saw. There was a part of me that wanted to be just like him. I wanted to be tough like they taught us in training but I couldn't. Fifty years later I saw him for the first time since the war at a reunion and brought up the incident—he broke down into tears.

I kept stuffing my fears inside. I buried them deep. I was presenting a false bravado. It caused me to cross the line and later in life start drinking. About ten years after the war I broke down completely. Finally, during the early 1960s, I stopped drinking and have been sober ever since. For me, World War II was a constant struggle with myself.

LYNN COMPTON

506th Parachute Infantry Regiment, 101st Airborne Division

On June 6, a squad of about a dozen men of E Company (reinforced later by a few other men from D Company) from the 506th Parachute Infantry Regiment took out a battery of German artillery that was pointed at Utah Beach, significantly affecting the success of the Utah landings. The attack is an excellent example of how a well-trained force could overwhelm a much larger force. Lynn Compton, an E Company second lieutenant, remembers the action.

I landed in an orchard near some hedgerows. It was very quiet right at that moment; there wasn't anybody around. For some reason the release thing on my chest harness didn't work, so I had to cut my way out. Pretty soon I could see one guy drifting down in a chute, and he landed about fifty yards away from me. I got up and ran over to him and he challenged me. We were from different outfits, but I had the password, so we got together.

We started stumbling around in the dark looking for guys to get some people together. By that time I could see other people coming in. The Germans were firing up at them, and I saw some of the guys getting hit.

We finally got on a road. I had no idea where we were. I ran across a guy from another company, he was from D Company, an officer. He had a broken leg and he was laying in a ditch alongside the road. He had one of those Thompson submachine guns with him, and I didn't have any weapons because my weapon was in the leg bag that broke off my leg when we jumped! So I talked him out of his submachine gun and I told him, "If you get picked up by the medics you won't need a gun, and if the Germans get you you'll be better off without the gun, they won't have an excuse to shoot you." He let me have the gun.

I wandered around on the roads, and more and more people began to gather; we got together maybe a dozen people. I hadn't fired a shot yet.

As we were walking along the road . . . we heard the sound of incoming artillery and we dropped down in this ditch. This was a huge shell, one of those big things fired offshore by the navy. This thing sounded like a boxcar; when it hit the ground it was a dud or we would have all been wiped out.

We cut some telephone wires and we took a few prisoners; they were Polish and Russians. They came out surrendering to us, and we didn't have any place to put them so we just sort of walked them along the road. We were try-ing to find our way back to this objective we had, which we never did find. The objective was the causeways—we never made it there. We were a few miles from where we were supposed to be.

We just sort of stumbled around in the dark and did any sort of damage we thought we could do. We captured a few people and we shot at a few peo-ple. I was coming up this road with a handful of guys. There was some shelling going on. They were hitting the roofs of buildings, farmhouses. That's when Lieutenant Dick Winters said, "Well, I think there's some ar-tillery out there someplace across this field." He said, "Why don't you go out there and take a look and see what you can find."

There was about a dozen of us at the time, and it was around nine at night. I stripped down except for this submachine gun, which I cradled in my arms, and on my belly I made my way across this field. The guys were shoot-ing from behind me kind of laying down, covering fire with machine gun fire. I made it about a hundred yards across this field, and there was a hedgerow there. I looked through it and I could see some Germans were dug in and I saw these two guys stoking this cannon. So I thought, "Oh, hell, I'll jump through here with this machine gun and take these guys out." I leaped through the damn brush into the trench with this machine gun. As I went to pull the trigger and it didn't go off! I pulled the hammer back and it ejects a live round—it's got a broken firing pin! So I'm standing there and these two guys look at me and they're wondering what the hell I'm doing. They take off running, so I threw a couple of hand grenades, and I hit one of them right in the head as it exploded.

By that time, a couple of guys came charging up and jumped through the hedgerow with me, and we got into these trenches and were running around shooting anything in sight. Bob Brewer was there with me, and one other guy, and I remember there was a wooden carton or case laying there in this thing, and on top of it was one of those German grenades they call "potato mashers." It was lying on top of this carton, and somebody kicked the box, and the thing rolled off into the middle of this trench and the pin fell out. We all just kind of pushed ourselves against the side of the trench and it went off. It didn't hurt anybody.

We worked our way down this trench line the rest of the night. More and more guys started showing up. We wanted to push out from there, but every time we started to move we'd get shot at, and a couple of guys would get killed in front of me as we tried to work our way down this trench system. It was the first time I saw a person killed in front of me.

I got out of the trenches and moved up onto some higher ground. I could see there were two trenches running laterally, and I was up there shooting down in this one direction where I thought the enemy was. These other guys were trying to make their way down into the trench, shooting Germans. Meanwhile, we were being raked by German machine gun fire from the hedgerows. There was just a lot of confusion, but suddenly somehow it all came to rest. We stopped and we were able to move out of there, and we moved up the road to what turned out to be Carentan. It was about 11:30 when we were finished. During the course of the attack our guys destroyed the guns.

Later a blustery, blowhard guy from headquarters came down. I didn't like him very well, he was a sergeant and he thought because he worked at headquarters he was a cut above everyone else. He was standing there, and we jumped this young German kid out of this hole, and he stood up and he was crying and he was putting his hands up over his head, crying and begging us not to do anything to him. He thought we were going to kill him. He was scared to death. I was saying to him, "Calm down," and this goddamn sergeant from the division comes up and he's got a World War I trench knife with a pair of brass knuckles and he hits this guy right in the mouth with those brass knuckles and split his teeth wide open—for absolutely no reason. He had to show how tough he was. It burned me up. I thought it was absolutely uncalled for. If it had been one of my guys I wouldn't have been as mad, but these guys [from headquarters] don't get closer to five miles of the action. He waits until things quiet down and then he busts some prisoner with his brass knuckles.

JULIAN EWELL

501st Parachute Infantry Regiment, 101st Airborne Division

By dawn on D-Day, small groups of men from the 101st Airborne Division had captured four causeways that led to Utah Beach, making it impossible for the Germans to reinforce their defenses. Lieutenant Colonel Julian Ewell describes how, with a hodgepodge of clerks, military policemen, and artillerymen, he took the town of Pouppeville, at the end of causeway number one.

I landed in a pasture between some hedgerows. It was a dark void: You couldn't see a thing; you could barely make out the fact that you were in a field. We then went about the usual drill of assembling. It took quite a while to round our men up. Even though we weren't under any immediate fire, it still took a while due to the darkness and hedgerows.

By dawn we only had a small portion of the battalion and division headquarters rounded up. My battalion was in division reserve, so we jumped with division headquarters. Not long after I landed, I ran into General Taylor, the commanding general, General McAuliffe, the artillery commander, and Jerry Higgins, the chief of staff. We eventually got organized.

The division signal company had jumped with us, but their radios were lost in the jump. As a result, we didn't have contact with the subordinate regiments which were to seize the exits of the causeways from the beach. Around dawn, General Taylor decided, since he wasn't aware of what the assault units were doing, to order my battalion to head toward the nearest causeway exit and secure it.

Behind Utah Beach, the Germans had flooded the entire area. As a result, the link from the Utah landing beaches were four causeways about a half-mile or a mile long.

We went for the exit of one of the causeways, the small village of Pouppeville. This group was led by General Taylor, General McAuliffe, the chief of staff, and myself. I don't think we had a company of infantry. Most of our group was staff types from division headquarters. This led General Taylor to say: "Never were so few led by so many."

As we were clearing the town, I was peeking around the corner of one of the buildings and a bullet grazed the top of my helmet. I had a camouflage net there, and the bullet cut one of the strands of that netting. I was lucky as hell. If it had been three or four inches lower I wouldn't be talking to you today.

After we had essentially cleared the town and were reorganizing, one of the cruisers offshore lobbed a few shells at one of the houses just about a hundred yards away. I thought, "Uh oh, we are now in deep trouble." We got on the radio [to the Allied cruiser] and were able to turn off the shelling.

As we cleaned out the town, we had about forty Germans surrender. Soon the 4th Division came cautiously up the causeway and then went about their business.

SID SALOMON

2nd Ranger Battalion

At 0645, the landing craft ramps dropped and Force B—C Company of the 2nd Ranger Battalion—became the first Rangers ashore on

June 6. Artillery, mortar, and machine gun fire was directed against the men as they made their way across Omaha Dog Green Beach to the top of the ninety-foot cliffs of Pointe-et-Raz-de-la-Percée. Under fire the Rangers scaled the cliff and attacked the Germans on top in an effort to deny them crucial high ground over the Charlie sector of Omaha Beach.

I was in C Company, 2nd Ranger Battalion, and we had our own separate mission. C Company went in alone at Pointe-et-Raz-de-la-Percée. We had two platoons, each in its own landing craft. I was in charge of one, and the other platoon leader was in charge of the other. Our goal was to cross the beach, climb the cliff, and neutralize the mortars and machine guns that were positioned on top of a beach that intelligence had indicated could threaten the landing at Omaha Beach in front of the town of Vierville. I had thirty-seven men in my landing craft. After we crossed the beach and climbed the cliff I only had nine men left—nine out of the thirty-seven.

It was dawn when we went in. At about 4:00 A.M. in the morning we left the HMS *Prince Charles* and boarded the landing craft. We were a good ten miles out in the Channel, and it took us over an hour to reach the beach. It was still dark at the time.

The trip was tough coming in. Keep in mind, it was postponed due to rough seas. The men started getting sick. We were issued paper bags, like you get in airplanes. The men filled them up and threw them over the side. Some men started using their helmets.

We could hear the ping of the machine gun bullets hitting the side of the landing craft, and mortar shells were landing near the landing craft. I could see the concentric circles formed by the shells hitting the water. It was quite something, of course. One of the men joked, "Hey, they're firing at us." It added a little humor to the situation.

In the dry runs that we had prior to the invasion, we had never had all the equipment that we had that day. We never had the rations or ammunition. We were issued three squares of something that looked like a Hershey bar. You could not finish one square since they were so packed with calories. What I'm getting at is that during the dry runs we never had the extra ammunition or rations, so when we boarded the landing craft, everybody was squeezed together. It was very cramped with thirty-seven men. There was a wooden bench on either side of the craft. The men sat on either side facing into the center. Then, in the center of the boat, there was also a bench that went from the bow to the stern. The men straddled it facing forward. When everyone got into the landing craft, there wasn't any room for me. That didn't bother me, so I stood near the bow next to the steel door and started talking to the British sublieutenant who was in charge of the landing craft. I stood up for most of the trip, but when we got close to the beach and started receiving machine gun fire, the sublieutenant and I crouched down behind the steel ramp. He had the rope in his hand that released the door on the landing craft.

[As] we rehearsed the landing, basically I would be the first man out and alternately each man would jump from right to left. Bear in mind, the tide was coming in; as each man jumped off, the boat was getting lighter and the boat moved ahead. When I jumped off, I held my tommy gun over my head. I jumped into not quite chest-high water, and it took a few seconds to get my feet on the ground. In the meantime, the second man, Sergeant Reed, jumped off to the left. I always figured that the first man out would be hit. Fortunately, the Germans didn't know when the ramp would lower. But they had us zeroed in with their machine guns, and the second man, Reed, was hit. He had fallen down, wounded, and had slid underneath the ramp. So I pulled him from under the ramp and dragged him to the water's edge. I said to him, "Sergeant, this is as far as I can take you, I have to get along." I pulled him up onto the shore and then started to run across.

A mortar shell landed right behind me and killed or wounded all of my mortar section. I got some of the shrapnel—it hit my back and I landed right on my face. I fell down in the sand and thought I was dead. I reached into the pocket of my field jacket looking for my maps. At that instant, I asked one of my men who was next to me if I was hit and he said yes. So I said, "You got to take my maps."

In that instant, the sand was being kicked in my face by a machine gun. Right then and there, I said to myself that I wasn't going to die. This was no place to be lying, so I took my maps, I got up, and ran toward the overhang of the cliff. An aid man came over to me and took my field jacket and shirt off and started digging shrapnel out of my back. These were the days before penicillin, and each man carried a sulfa pack, and he put it on my back. He said, "That's all I can do for you now." I said, "Take care of the rest of the guys." I started to climb up the cliff.

The cliff was approximately ninety to a hundred feet high. I've been back several times since the war. We didn't have grappling hooks like they did up at Pointe-du-Hoc. Each man had a six-foot piece of rope that had a noose at the end of it and, ideally, we were to link the ropes together and scale the cliff. We didn't bother with that since, of course, so many men had gotten killed and wounded. We had two men that in our practice runs were excellent climbers and always made it to the top first. As usual, they made it to the top. We went up on toeholds and by digging our fingernails and bayonets into the cliff.

When we got up on top we had only nine men left in my platoon. That wasn't an effective fighting force by any means. The other platoon leader, Bill Moody, joined me up top. We were laying up there in a shell hole. We decided to take a look at things to get a lay of the land. We were lying in this shell hole and peering ahead at a well-dug-in trench. We were there only a minute or two and all of a sudden Bill Moody, the 1st Platoon commander, fell over on my shoulder. He had been killed by a bullet hole through his eyes. I grabbed the man next to me and said, "Let's go!"

We ran ahead and jumped into the trench. The trench was perpendicular to the top of the cliff. We went along there and came to a dugout. I carried two white phosphorus grenades and I held my hand and said, "Stop!" I approached the dugout. Bear in mind, the Germans had years to build the trench and dugout part of their defenses. I threw a white phosphorous grenade through the entrance and waited a minute. We then sprayed the entrance. We saw an old wooden table and a steel locker that they used for their uniforms. We started moving down the trench. As we went down the trench, we saw another trench that went down to my right. I figured that this was going to be a little more difficult, since we could be surprised from behind. We went a little further around a curve and were face to face with a German soldier. We were both equally stunned, but I grabbed him and I figured this might be a good time to have a prisoner instead of killing him right then and there. I said, "Let's send him down to the company commander," who was down at the beach with dead and wounded men maintaining order.

I sent the prisoner down the cliff. I don't know if he got down on his own or if they pushed him down—that was immaterial to me. We figured it was silly to go any further inland since with so few men we wouldn't be an effective fighting force. We figured the best thing to do would be to hold that ground, and that's what we did. We proceeded to knock out a machine gun section and a mortar section.

Painted on the walls of the mortar area were targets for stakes that were in the ground for positions up around the beach at Vierville. Each position was numbered, so it was easy for the German 81-mm mortar crew to zero in on positions on the beach. We knocked out the German position and figured that we were doing our best by still holding our ground.

RAY ALM

2nd Ranger Battalion

At 7:40 A.M. on June 6, 1944, Companies A and B of the 2nd Rangers landed on Omaha's Dog Green Beach with horrific losses, as described here by Ray Alm of B Company of the 2nd Ranger Battalion.

The mother ship that I was on for the invasion of Normandy was the *Prince Charles*. We climbed down scramble nets from the *Prince Charles* into the landing craft and we made our way towards the beach. It was very rough, and lots of men got sick. We were all standing up in the landing craft as we made our way into the beach area. At the time, I was in B Company of the 2nd Ranger Battalion and was in charge of a mortar crew. I was staff sergeant at the time.

We were about two hundred feet from the beach when a shell blew off the front of our landing craft, destroying the ramp. My two best buddies were right in front of me, and they were both killed. When we went over the side of the landing craft (to avoid machine gun fire), the water was about twelve feet deep. After the shell hit, it was pretty much everyone for themselves.

I was holding a .45 pistol and carrying a bazooka with eight shells; it was so heavy that I just went right under the water, so I had to let everything go except the shells. Eventually when I got to the beach I picked up a German rifle that I used.

When we all got together on the beach, things were getting kind of bad. Fortunately, the colonel (Max Schneider) called the battleship *Texas* for support fire, and it made a direct hit on the pillbox that the Germans were in. We also had two destroyers, and they took turns all day long firing at targets. They saved us; they were terrific.

When we were on the beach, there were two other Rangers and myself running, and a German machine gun was firing at us. We hid behind an anti-tank obstacle. The three of us ducked behind it. We then headed towards the front again, towards the street. It was terrible; there were bodies all over the place. They wiped out almost the entire 116th Infantry Regiment; they just murdered them. They were floating all over the place, there was blood in the water—it was just dark.

FRANK SOUTH

2nd Ranger Battalion

After taking the German positions on top of Pointe-du-Hoc and destroying the guns that had been towed inland, the Rangers dug in. The Germans' counterattacking force outnumbered the Rangers and nearly broke through their weakened defenses. Frank South, a combat medic, offers his recollections in this e-history.

Early in the morning we had a breakfast of coffee and, as I recall, two pancakes. Then came the call of, "Rangers, man your boats!" The medics were spread among the LCAs [Landing Craft Assault] for obvious reasons. I had been assigned to one of the three F Company LCAs and would be one of the last men off, again for apparent cause.

Within a reasonable time our assault craft were in formation and headed in over rough seas. Several of the men became seasick, but the others spent their time checking their arms and equipment and in indulging in rather black humor. Frequently I have been asked about any fear I, or we, felt. I personally recall nothing but a sense of wonder that all this was finally taking place and being terrifically excited. I believe that all of us were particularly anxious that we would do our jobs and not be found wanting.

Before too long it became apparent that set and drift had its way with the formation and that we were headed for Pointe-et-Raz-de-la-Percée, C Company's objective, instead of Pointe-du-Hoc. Lieutenant Colonel Rudder picked up the error and had the RN officer correct our course. The mistake put us twenty to thirty minutes late, allowing more preparation on the part of the enemy, as well as considerable machine gun and rifle fire from shore.

As we closed the beach, the Royal Navy crewman (Tolhurst) used his Lewis gun for covering fire until he burned his hand severely. He died a few years before the fiftieth anniversary; his son has stayed in touch with the 2nd Rangers since the war.

F Company landed on the left flank of the landing area below the cliffs. The LCA I was on got our grapnel rockets off in good order. But high up on our left flank was a machine gun nest that was in a superb enfilading position. We could not find it until later. We were caught in its field of fire. The LCA to our left came in so close that their rockets would have hit the side of the cliff instead of on top. Sergeant Cripps dismounted the rockets from the boat and brought them in so they could be fired at a higher angle. This required that they be individually hand-fired using a "hot box." Since he was under almost constant machine gun fire, this took enormous self-control and concentration, but Cripps was able to successfully put the grapnel hooks up over the lip of the cliff.

As my LCA (884) landed, I still had the huge pack on my back to get ashore. I was aft in the landing craft—for good reason because we had to get the rockets fired, the lines up, and the climbers off first. We were under constant fire at this time, and my pack was so large it got in my way. As the others jumped off the ramp, the bow of the boat raised and the boat shifted slightly. When I jumped off I found myself in a shallow (at the time it felt very deep) shell hole, bent double so that my head was immersed. I realized that I well might be beamed by the ramp if it lifted in the swell and came down on me. I slipped the pack off and scrambled onto the beach. Reaching back I managed to grab the monster and drag it in after me. The next thing I know someone yelled "Medic!"—a guy off to my left had been hit in the chest. At this time, a number of people were getting hit by small arms, machine gun fire, and grenades.

Of the landing force at the Pointe, by D plus two we had about ninety men able to bear arms—many of them wounded. One of our difficulties was getting our wounded men to agree to be evacuated so that they could get proper treatment beyond what we could give them.

LEN LOMELL

2nd Ranger Battalion

After the 2nd Ranger Battalion secured the top of Pointe-du-Hoc, a platoon lead by First Sergeant Len Lomell was able to establish a critical roadblock cutting the coastal road between Utah and Omaha, thus blocking German reinforcements and communication between the beaches. The destruction of the guns had been the Rangers' primary mission. However, they had been towed inland for protection from Allied shore and aerial bombardment. Len Lomell recalls discovering the guns and the steps taken to render them inoperable.

We only had about twelve or thirteen men left, after getting to the coast road, ten men were either killed or wounded. After we set up the roadblock and destroyed all German communications, Jack Kuhn and I went down a farm road. This was our secondary objective, to establish a roadblock on the coastal highway to prevent German reinforcements from hitting the beaches. As we were about to go down the sunken farm road about forty or fifty Germans, heavily armed, in a combat patrol passed by us, twenty feet from us; they were headed to Utah Beach. They went by, we never took a shot at them; we didn't want to get involved in a firefight because it would only slow us down from our primary mission of finding and destroying the coastal guns of Pointe-du-Hoc.

This is all farm country, pastures, high hedgerows. We went down the sunken road heading inland. You could have hid a column of tanks in it, that's how wide and deep the road was. We saw heavy tracks on the road so we figured we ought to take a look, so we did. We were leapfrogging. What I mean by that is first Jack covered me and I went forward and then I covered Jack and he went forward. We went in about one hundred to two hundred yards. It came my time for me to go in front and I looked over the hedgerow into an apple orchard. Sticking out of this apple orchard were these long gun barrels with netting over the top with fake leaves on it. I said to myself, "God, here they are!" We were surprised to find the five guns were aimed at Utah Beach, not Omaha Beach [for unknown reasons the sixth gun was missing]. About one hundred yards west of that position were about seventy-five Germans who were in various states of undress because they were putting jackets and shirts on; they were being rallied. They were being talked to by some officer standing in his vehicle about a mile inland from the Pointe. This was now about eight in the morning.

There were twelve Rangers left in my platoon at this point. We only had one thermite grenade each. Each man carried one. We weren't heavily laden with field packs or other equipment. I only had my submachine gun and a sidearm, ammunition, and a thermite grenade. It made the climb up easier. We had this thermite grenade which was special for this particular type of action because we were going to lay them on the moving parts of the artillery to destroy the movable gears on the guns. There is no noise, it doesn't explode. Air hits it and the incendiary contents of the grenade turns to molten metal-like substance and runs all over the moving parts and it seeps down into the crevices and when it cools off it put the guns in a firm inoperable weldlike position. You don't hear a thing. The heavy-foliaged dip in the swale where the guns were positioned kept me out of the Germans' line of sight. I took my tommy gun, wrapped it in my field jacket, and smashed the sights on all five guns. I didn't know if I was going to get back so I wanted to do as much damage as possible. After that I said to Jack, "We gotta get more grenades." We only had two so we had to get back to the roadblock as quickly as we could

Rangers fighting on top of Pointe-du-Hoc, June 1944. (Photo Courtesy U.S. Army)

and get the ones from the guys there. We went back, it was only about a hundred plus yards, and they gave us all their grenades. We placed the grenades on the guns and destroyed all five, rendering them inoperable by 8:15 in the morning, and the Germans didn't see or hear a thing.

Staff Sergeant Kuhn was covering me, protecting me from the Germans, and in a hurry to get back, and Jack said, "Hurry up!" Hurry up!" We were making our way back to the other men, climbing up the nine-foot hedgerow, and an explosion of unknown origin blew us both off the hedgerow into the sunken road. It deafened us; we couldn't hear each other talk for a while. We notified Colonel Rudder by 9:00 A.M. that our mission had been accomplished.

We ran as fast as we could back to our roadblock and joined the guys. We held the roadblock for two and a half days until we were relieved. That night we had a tremendous battle with the Germans. In the late afternoon, we finally got eighty-five guys together to put up a defensive position for that night. We were still in position around midnight when the Germans first attacked. They came out screaming with tracer bullets going off, flares in the air, and it sounded like thousands of them; of course there was only a few hundred. But a few hundred against eighty-five is a lot as far as we were concerned.

JOHN RAAEN

5th Ranger Battalion

Observing the carnage on the Omaha Dog Green sector, Lt. Colonel Max Schneider, the Force C commander, ordered the remainder of his force to Omaha Dog White, a relatively quiet sector of the beach where the Ranger assault and men from C Company of the 116th Regiment established the crucial exit from Omaha Beach. John Raaen, a 5th Ranger officer, describes the landing in his e-history.

The beachmaster on Dog White stopped talking. We were about to find out why. We were still about a thousand yards out, and I had not seen the tragedy that struck A and B companies of the 2nd Rangers and did not realize that we would land well to the east of our target beach. As we approached the beach, one of my officers ordered the men to keep their heads down while he and occasionally I observed the developing situation. Schneider's wave landed to our left front.

For us in the second wave, still on the water and less than five minutes behind, the noise had now become deafening. An LCT [Landing Craft Tank] to our right front was hit by artillery fire and burst into flames. Other artillery shells were detonating all around us, with small arms adding to the inferno. The scene was one from hell. Smoke from the fires on the face of the bluff, fires from burning vessels and equipment, black ugly puffs from artillery bursting, dust and flying debris everywhere. A minute or so later, my LCA [Landing Craft Assault] began to maneuver through the obstacles. Another ship fifty to a hundred yards to our right, LCI 91, was hit by artillery.

We were almost to the beach when suddenly the coxswain gunned the engine and we hit the bottom with a jolt. The ramp dropped and Sullivan dashed out to the left. I was second and chose the right, and shouted, "Headquarters! Over here!" The water wasn't as high as my boots. Our coxswain had done well by us. Ten yards of shallow water amid the damnedest racket in the world. You could hear the bullets screaming by. Somewhere an Oerlikon or a Bofors was beating out sixty rounds a minute at us. Rifle fire was coming from our right, as was most of the machine gun fire. A DD tank to our right let a round fly.

And now I was on the beach. It wasn't sand, more like gravel or small rocks, sloping upward. Forty or fifty feet ahead I came to a funnel of water.

Machine gun bullets chewed the water up as I jumped into it. I remember thinking, "The Germans are trained like we are, bursts of three to five rounds, release and fire another burst. Jump in while the bullets are still splashing." I dashed into the splashes and yelled for the men behind me to keep moving. My runner, McCullough, was two behind me. I could feel him more than see him as he hesitated. The splashing stopped, he jumped ahead and was hit by the next burst. Then dry beach again.

Ahead another fifty feet was the seawall. It was packed with men two and three deep. They couldn't dig in because the rocks were six to eight inches in diameter, layered deeply. The seawall was made of logs, three or four feet high, with stone breakwaters running back toward the sea every hundred or so feet. These breakwaters would prevent good lateral communication on the beach, though they did give us good protection from the flanking fire that poured down the beach from our right.

As I dropped down into the shelter of the seawall, I looked back. My men were coming up, dropping to the right and left of me. Artillery was falling at the water's edge, but only small arms from our right front was hitting near the seawall. Bodies were strewn all over the beach from the water's edge to the seawall. Other men were hiding behind the obstacles and wreckage near the water's edge. Still others were making the dash from boats to the seawall.

I tried to get my lifebelts off. They wouldn't come, jammed from something or other. I rolled over; still no luck. I could not go on like that so I stood up, and still no luck. I looked around; it was my first look at men in combat. They were huddled against the seawall as I had been only moments earlier, cringing at every bullet that cracked past. Artillery fire was churning the water's edge. To our left I saw LCI 92 touch down. As I watched, men started down the side ramps. Wham! An artillery round caught the starboard ramp. They must have hit a flamethrower there, for the whole side of the ship burst into flames that spread to the deck.

I looked back at our LCA. Men were still coming down the ramp. There was Father Lacy, the last man coming out. He wasn't ten yards from the boat when wham, an artillery round hit the engine compartment of the LCA. Father Lacy was all right, but even though I couldn't see what happened to the crew, I knew. They had done their job well—too well, for the LCA was caught hard on the beach, too hard to back off. I looked away. My first dry landing—well, almost dry—and the coxswain and petty officer paid for it with their lives.

I didn't see Father Lacy again on D-Day, but others saw him and like minstrels sang his praises. Lacy didn't cross the beach like we heroes did. He stayed down there in the water's edge pulling the wounded forward ahead of the advancing tide. He comforted the dying. Calmly said prayers for the dead. He led terrified soldiers to relative safety behind debris and wreckage, half-carrying them, half-dragging them, binding up their wounds. Never once did he think of his own safety. Always helping those that needed his help to survive that awful inferno.

When the 5th Rangers left the beach a few minutes later, Father Lacy stayed behind at the water's edge, doing the work for which God had chosen him. True to his word, the padre caught up with us later. He was delayed, he said.

I also briefly encountered General Cota. When he asked where Colonel Schneider was, I pointed out the general area and offered to take him there. He more or less said, "No, you stay here with your troops." It was then that he turned to my Rangers, who were hanging on every word and gesture, and said to them, "You men are Rangers! I know you won't let me down!" Then he left and headed for Schneider.

When Sullivan passed me my orders from Colonel Schneider, he told me I was to shift left to Schneider's position where a hole in the wire would be blown. I was to follow C Company through the gap. After Cota left, I shifted my half of Headquarters Company fifty to a hundred yards to the left, over to the area of the gap, and waited some distance back from the seawall but still protected by the nearest breakwater. Here I was rejoined by the rest of my company, the half that landed in Schneider's LCA. When C Company's last machine gun squad came in from my right, I led the company through the gap in the wire.

ELLIS "BILL" REED

5th Ranger Battalion

Once on Omaha Dog White, the 5th Rangers moved inland, assaulting the bluffs that overlooked the beach, clearing a vital exit through the wire for most of the forces on the beach. The official motto "Rangers Lead the Way!" was also first spoken on bloody Omaha Beach by the commanding officer on the beach, General Cota. Bill Reed recalls his role as member of a platoon that knocked out a key German strongpoint to facilitate the breakout from the beach.

We could see the action from the landing craft as we came in. There was a tremendous amount of firepower coming from both flanks. Machine gun fire and artillery fire was pouring in. Before we landed on the beach, I could see a group of people behind the seawall. These men were mostly from the 29th Division. They were leveled out and not moving. The beach was at low tide. We had to run across about 150 yards of beach with my platoon leader, Lieutenant Dawson, who received the DSC [Distinguished Service Cross], and Woody Doorman, who was a bangalore torpedo man. Our job was to place the torpedo under the wire and detonate it, ripping a hole in the wire for the rest of the troops to move through.

Woody and I had three bangalore torpedoes; they were about five feet long and were strapped to our M-1s [rifles]. We carried two bandoliers of M-1 ammunition, a pistol on our side, and demolitions strapped to our back. On the top of our helmet we had a fuse lighter. This was about a five-second fuse that would set off the torpedo.

When we exited the landing craft many people had flotation belts, and if the water was over your neck you would turn upside down. When we got off the boat and into the wet sand we had to run for the seawall. Men were dying around us, lying in different positions, and tanks were burning.

Finally we got behind the seawall on the beach. At this time, General Cota, who was the assistant division commander of the 29th, made the statement "Rangers, lead the way" or "Rangers, let's get moving"—to us it meant "Let's get moving."

Woody and I had to assemble each piece of the torpedo, get up from behind the seawall, push the bangalore torpedo across the road on top of the bluff and put it under the concertina wire. Once we had the torpedo in place we took the fuse wire out, pulled the fuse, and yelled, "Fire in the hole!" and jumped back over the wall. The result, if it worked, was a hole in the concertina wire. The amazing thing was that both blasts were completely coordinated. We trained previous to this for two months.

They [the Germans] didn't stop firing while we were doing this, if you know what I mean. [Laughs.] They were firing down the line, and there was a lot of machine gun and mortar fire. I don't know if I was so scared or what, but I moved as fast as I could to get everything set. Once the explosion went off, Woody and I were supposed to have a spool of white tape on our back so we could lead the people through the minefield. Since the landing was so rough, that spool of white tape was gone. I made sure the fuse lighter went off, since we were told in our training that if it didn't go off we were to sacrifice our bodies and lay on the concertina wire as the men stepped on us. So I made damn sure that the torpedo detonated. [Laughs.]

Meanwhile, men started moving through the holes Woody and I created, and Lieutenant Dawson took command of my immediate group. Our platoon led headquarters and one company of the 29th through my hole.

We were the first on the top in that area. As the men moved through our holes in the wire, one of our scouts got cut in half by a machine gun. I was told to fire the rifle grenade at a machine gun nest, but like everything else in the U.S. Army, it was a big dud. So at that point Lieutenant Dawson got up and charged it with his submachine gun and kept blasting. When we got up close they put their hands up. I remember that one German had his arm dangling by only a piece of flesh. That was our first visual face-to-face contact with the enemy. Everything prior to that was at a distance.

CLINTON RIDDLE

325th Glider Infantry Regiment, 82nd Airborne Division

On June 7, the bulk of the 82nd Airborne's glider reinforcements began arriving in Normandy, many glidermen becoming instant casualties as a result of perilous landing. The 325th Glider Infantry Regiment, shaken but intact, moved up from its landing zone and joined the maelstrom at La Fière Bridge. In an attempt to flank German positions on the other side of the bridge, the 325th's 1st Battalion was sent downriver to ford the Merderet River in an encircling maneuver that would link up with pockets of airborne forces trapped on the German side of the bridge. But as Clinton Riddle describes, the Germans were waiting.

We made preparations for the invasion by studying sand table maps for a number of days. The weather was bad but eventually it cleared, and on June 7 we loaded into British Horsa gliders, which were made mostly of plywood and towed by a C-47.

After we were over the English Channel for some time, the plane began to sputter and bog down. The plane started to go down, and we were starting to overrun the plane. That created slack in the towrope connecting the glider to the plane. We were only about a hundred feet from the sea and could see the waves below.

We started throwing out anything that would lighten the load. We had jerry cans full of water and threw anything like that over. I was up front and I was able to look over the pilot's and copilot's shoulders. I could see what was going on. The plane's engines were failing. It was tense in the glider cockpit as the copilot had his hand on the release to cut the towrope that connected the plane and glider. The pilot said, "Just wait, just wait!" I could hear the engines in the plane keep cranking over and cranking over. Eventually I saw the blue smoke appear on one of the engines as it finally turned over!

As we came over Normandy, we encountered some flak. We weren't able to land where we were supposed to because of the Rommel's asparagus. So they released the towrope, and the pilot saw an open field and brought the glider down. As we came down, the glider's wing hit a few trees and we bounced a few times.

The landing area was littered with wrecked gliders. We had six gliders in our company, and every glider in the company was destroyed except for the one I was in. What happened so often was that the front wheel of the glider would come up through the floor and cut the men's legs off.

About the same time that we landed, two German fighters strafed our position. Not far from where we landed, I noticed a farmer milking his cow. We slowly moved up this road to our objective since we were worried about snipers. When we passed the farmer, I pulled my canteen cup out and asked him for some milk—so I had warm milk for breakfast.

We proceeded on that day until we assembled the battalion. That first day we didn't encounter that much combat. I was able to get some sleep that night in a briar patch, but after that we were engaged in heavy fighting every day and remained in combat for over thirty days without replacements.

At the time, we had just the regular combat shoes. In the beginning, glider troops were treated like second-class citizens by the airborne; we weren't allowed to wear jump boots. But after we rescued the paratroopers a few times they gave us the right to wear paratrooper boots. I have a pair here that I still wear even today for parades and stuff. They are still in pretty decent shape.

It was on June 8, shortly after midnight, that we began the attack. We kept trying to find a place to cross the Merderet River on a plank; a burning building provided light. After my company crossed the river, we ran into a trap set by the Germans. I was with the battalion, following the line companies in the attack. They had to cross an open meadow and walk into this apple orchard. Most of the men were lined up in a skirmish line to sweep the orchard of Germans. But the Germans were waiting and set up a deadly crossfire. So many of the men were killed when we ran into German machine guns.

My foxhole buddy from Ohio was killed in the ambush. While we were in Italy he got a letter from his wife about his newborn baby boy. She sent some pictures and I rejoiced with him; he was a very good friend. That particular day he was carrying out the job that I usually had as the company runner. They sent me to the battalion as the battalion runner. The next morning I went over and saw all of the dead bodies of the men, including his. I could have been there, and I always felt bad that he never had a chance to see his boy. I also remember this particular boy who was from New York. His folks sent him a pair of black leather gloves. He had these gloves on the day they walked into the trap. The next morning I went back up there and you could almost step from one to the other because they were lined up side by side. Nineteen of my men I knew and became friends with were dead. The soldier who had the black gloves on had his hand up in the air like he was reaching for someone. For a long time after that, I wouldn't wear gloves in combat or after the war—even during the Bulge, when it was so cold. I kept picturing the black gloves and the soldier reaching for someone in my mind.

ED JEZIORSKI

*507th Parachute Infantry Regiment, Attached
to the 82nd Airborne Division*

One of the most spectacular assaults of the war was the capture of La Fière Bridge on June 9. The bridge or causeway was several hundred yards long and had to be secured at all costs to prevent the Germans from sending reinforcements to Utah Beach. Several hundred Allied paratroopers were trapped on the German side of the bridge, and the 325th Glider Infantry Regiment spearheaded an attack across it that reached the other side but became bogged down. Finally, a single company of paratroopers fought its way across the bridge and broke through the German defenses on the other side, as Ed Jeziorski describes.

We had been told that we were to be ready; we were the reserve for the 325th. If something happened to them, we were going to do it. The exact words I don't recall, but I do know that there was not even a thought of anybody having some apprehension or second thoughts of going [across the open causeway].

The 325th were in columns, and they were spaced correctly, and they were doing things the way they were supposed to. They kept as low as they could so not to make too good targets, but as they were moving they were just being

knocked down left and right. There was no place to hide on the open causeway. A lot of men were getting killed. Their attack got bogged down.

At that point . . . a little second lieutenant, and he was a recent addition to
our company, he yelled, "Come on, you paratroopers, let's go!" That's when
we went! There was a file of us on one side of the road and a file of us on the
other side of the road; we were probably five yards apart, maybe even closer
or wider. We started going, and it was just an unbroken line. It was just pouring in that much, that heavy [German artillery, mortar shells, machine gun
fire]. This was the hottest day that I had ever been in.

As I crossed the bridge I had the machine gun on my right shoulder. After running several yards, the whole side of the road came up. It came up in a
heck of a mass of dirt and right on top of me and knocked me down. I had to
scramble to really get out from under the thing, but when I came out from under it, I looked and it looked like everybody was going the wrong way. I said,
"This way, guys." They said, "No, Jez, this way." It could have been a heck of
a round of artillery, but I don't know, it could have been a land mine. I didn't
hear any noise, just the entire side of the road came up and came down on top
of me.

Captain [Robert] Rae kept telling us to "keep moving, keep moving, keep
moving!" I was the only machine gunner of the ninety or so in the company
of us. The fire was very, very severe. It was a continuous hum, a buzz of the
rounds going by you. As we crossed the bridge, and it was narrow at that
point, the little lieutenant was dropped and I never saw him again. I'm pretty
sure he was nailed real well.

Guys were dropping, sure; how many of us got through, I don't know.
Stuff was coming in and things were really hot. Finally, we made it to the
other side. The stone wall at Le Manoir [a house and barn on the German side
of the bridge] had holes knocked out and punched in it. Automatic weapons
were in those holes, and they had them sandbagged and tied down so they
never had to expose themselves. All they did was pull the trigger and they
had everything covered. You tried to work through that as best you could.

Once on the other side of the bridge, Boys [an assistant machine gunner]
put the tripod down and I put the gun in the pod and we were working in the
open, I was firing in the open. That's when Boys got hit. I had another guy
come up, you had an ammo bearer always that was carrying a box of ammo,
his name was Hine, and he was killed on D plus six. Hine was working the
gun with me.

There was a 42 [MG-42 German machine gun], and he was throwing a
lot of lead, just like they can do! As it was going over my head. I just held [the
trigger] down on him until there was no more noise.

FRANCIS E. NAUGHTON

*507th Parachute Infantry Regiment, Attached
to the 82nd Airborne Division*

The small village of Graignes, south of Carentan and deep behind German lines, was the site of a fierce battle between a beleaguered force of about 160 American paratroopers and a vastly superior German force. After numerous assaults on the tiny village, the massive German force broke through the perimeter that the Americans, with the assistance of the French, had fought to hold, as remembered by Francis Naughton.

We had several small skirmishes, but the first real firefight was at the bridge [near Graignes]. This bridge was only about one-half mile to three-quarters of a mile from the town. The bridge was concrete and steel, and it was a pretty good-sized bridge. We had about eight or ten men from the regimental demolition platoon, and they all had their demolition kits. The men had TNT and composition C that they had carried with them. They also had demolitions that had been brought in by the French. The French were now very much involved in our operation. The mayor, Alphonse Voydie, was a man of remarkable vigor and personal charm. Under his leadership, many of the French citizens were searching the swamp for ammunitions and other supplies that had been dropped in A-5 and A-6 containers.

We had been able to recover very little ammunition and supplies on our own, but the French were recovering many ammunition containers. They were doing this at the direction of Mayor Voydie, who laid down the law on this matter of giving us assistance. He was a good leader—a great man. So they brought in machine guns, mortars, and mortar ammunition. We probably had less than a basic load. But we had more than we came in with. We probably had some of the 101st [Airborne Division] ammunition containers, no doubt about it. We had a lot of containers. As they were bringing in ammunition, I remember this young lady bringing in supplies under a load of hay. She did this at great personal risk. Her whole family, the Rigault family, was involved in helping us.

The French deserved a lot of credit for the defense of the town. We [Naughton and other survivors] covered all this in detail when we made our pitch for decorations for these French citizens—forty years later. By the way, we were successful—had all of our recommendations approved. There in this little town it was unique because the French, although they didn't, for the most part, fight in terms of carrying a weapon (although some did), they were providing us with food and ammunition and were going out and risking their lives to supply us with information.

All we had initially were K rations. One lady who ran the only café in town became, in effect, the mess sergeant. She also was decorated for her actions—forty years later. She was a remarkable woman. The priests had been very helpful too. They knew the lay of the land. They knew people and they knew Germans and they knew what would likely take place. Both of them were of course executed, as were their housekeepers. So due to the efforts of our French friends, we were in pretty good shape as far as weapons and ammunition. We had mortar ammunition, machine guns, grenades, and ammunition for the M-1s, and we had explosives: We had lots of composition C.

As I mentioned, our first real firefight was at the bridge that led into the town. Major Johnson ordered me to take the demolition section and a small platoon (twenty-five to thirty men) down to the bridge and blow it up, thus denying the Germans an easy way in our back door. I remember asking the sergeant, Sergeant Murray, how long it would take him to prepare for demolition of the bridge. He said he should have it ready to blow in about twenty minutes, so I had about twenty minutes to deploy the platoon. It so happened that he was accurate to the minute. Sergeant Murray was a fine NCO. He was killed a couple of days later.

I had placed men beyond the bridge and up around a turn in the road to give us early warning if the Germans started advancing. It seems that the major's timing and intuition was very good, or maybe it was Captain Brummitt's—or both of them—since the Germans chose this particular time (about 10:00 A.M.) to move toward Graignes by the back door.

The Germans were right at the bridge. [People] will say that I waited until some Germans were on the bridge and then ordered the bridge blown—that's only a story. I was closest to the bridge, and my vision was partially obscured. When the Germans were very close to rushing the bridge, Sergeant Costa gave me the word, and then I gave the signal to press the plunger and blow it. Anyway, it sure put a stop to their advance.

As soon as the bridge was blown, all the firing stopped. That was about it. After the explosion, the Germans scattered. It must have been quite a shock to them, I guess. You know, it scared me with all that steel and concrete stuff going up in the air. So I'm sure that if you're approaching that bridge and all of a sudden it goes up in smoke, it has to throw you off-balance.

The next day we did have a firefight down there, but again, not very much. We patrolled every night. We patrolled constantly, every direction we could, where there was dry ground, but you have to remember it was a patrol. We can't be accused of doing nothing. We were very active there during that time. I think I led a patrol every night in addition to everything else. I think most of the officers could say the same.

Sunday was the last day. Saturday night we'd had several patrols that were trying to penetrate our defense. Not severe—only patrol actions, but they were hitting on three sides. And I remember the major decided that he would go with me to inspect the perimeter. We had about a hundred men around the perimeter. We had the mortar platoon, machine gun platoon in place, and we had just about everybody who could hold a rifle on line.

Nothing happened early Sunday (June 11), and the major said that Catholics or anybody else who wanted to go to the church, which was located right next to the command post, could go to Mass. I went into the church just before 10:00 A.M. Shortly after 10:00 A.M., all hell broke loose. The firing was pretty close. It turned out to be nothing more than a sizable daylight patrol action, which quickly intensified. The attack was piecemeal, short-lived, and about ten minutes long. We inflicted heavy casualties. They hadn't been very smart, the way they attacked. But later on that day (or night), they smartened up.

About two hours later, they attacked again. Here again, early warning and good fields of fire served us well. We were doing great (defensively). Just about dusk, they attacked again, and by this time we knew that we were outnumbered enormously. We had good communications, and we had redistributed the ammunition. Lieutenant Reed did a great job with his machine guns, but he didn't have enough crews. When they threatened to break through in a particular area, he would move his guns about accordingly. I remember Sergeant Hinchcliff and Corporal Knesh especially. All crews were outstanding, though.

After the second major attack, we met in a little café across from the church taking stock of how much ammunition was on hand and reviewing our defense plan. This was, in effect, an officer's call. In addition to the major, I remember Captain Brummitt in particular as having a good grasp of the overall situation. As events were later to prove, he emerged as an authentic hero.

Of course we all realized the seriousness of the situation. There was a young waitress providing us with coffee, and she was singing as she went from table to table. I remember Major Johnson turning to us and saying, "I wish I could feel as good about all of this as she does." Anyway, the major decided to stay and fight. In retrospect, this may have been the time to leave. There are a lot of arguments pro and con.

Then, as I mentioned, about dusk the main attack began and our casualties started piling up in the aid station. About two hours later, the real fight began. At one point they almost broke through the perimeter. However, they were paying dearly, for trucks could be observed picking up the German dead at collection points. Our mortar fire was accurate. The mortar platoon leader, Lieutenant Farnham, was directing fire and doing a terrific job of it, too. I kept in touch with Captain Brummitt, who took over after Major Johnson was killed. He was on top of the situation.

The [German] artillery fire was very effective. They hit the church steeple, and Lieutenant Farnham and his assistant were killed. He was directing mortar fire from the steeple at that time. I was on the phone with him and the phone went dead when the shell hit.

Our interaction with the citizens had a calming effect as the French carried food, water, and ammunition. They were helping the wounded and sallying forth to get information. The mayor was there directing the French.

There was a short lull in the fighting. The lull was ominous. In the background we could hear the sound of heavy equipment. Then the Germans made their final assault. It was truly a coordinated attack, at least twice the size of the other attacks, and it was supported by mortar and 88-mm artillery fire. They had learned lessons from the prior attacks. We stayed and fought until there was very little ammunition left. We fired almost every round we had.

Like all the officers and senior NCOs on the line, I tried to be everywhere. My machine gunners were great. In one particular area, I had about twenty to thirty men behind an earth berm with a very good field of fire. It was dark, so I could not count how many casualties we inflicted. We poured almost every round we had into the advancing Germans. They picked the wrong place to mount their attack since we had an excellent line of fire, so they lost many men. We thought maybe five to six hundred casualties. Later we found their losses had been far greater.

During this time, many of the civilians moved into the church. Captain Sophian, the battalion surgeon, entered the church and told them we would have to stay and fight. But he advised the French civilians that they should leave, since our position was tenuous and they were in great danger. They didn't leave. They loved us for staying and also for advising them of the situation. I had one French lady tell me, many years after the war, that if the Germans held the town they would have used them as hostages, but I really doubt that. Captain Sophian, a fine officer, was killed shortly after this incident.

The Germans finally did break through. I guess you could say they ran over us. It seemed that every German who had a machine gun or pistol seemed to be firing indiscriminately. Then we could hear glass being broken and yelling. They were mopping up, and we knew it was the end. At the time we did not know the priest (Father Leblastier) and his assistant and his two housekeepers and three or four others were being murdered by the Germans. The Germans executed twelve paratroopers that were in the aid station. There could have been more, but I don't think so. Several men still can't be accounted for, as we had two men from the 29th Infantry Division, some German prisoners, and a few Spaniards that were on a work detail digging foxholes. How they got there, I'll never know. We also had an Air Corps flight officer who we weren't able to account for. Some of the men in the aid station escaped, but I know that twelve men were executed.

There was also Captain Bogard, in the 101st, who was carried into the town after breaking his leg in the jump. When he entered the town he asked [Major Johnson] for a job, and the major asked him if he would take over the switchboard, which he did and almost without relief, so short were we of men on the line. The French confirmed that he was one of the twelve executed.

With the perimeter pierced and the Germans around us in great force we had no place to fall back to, so we had to sneak back to the swamps. I had about two squads—twenty-three men, as I remember. As we went through the swamp, we had to cross several drainage ditches. We devised a system to help each other get across. Still, it was very time-consuming. Each time, I would work my way to the front again, and Sergeant Cannon would bring up the rear. We must have crossed five or six drainage ditches.

By dawn, we had worked our way around and could see the little town perched on a hill behind us. We could see the remnants of the church steeple. What bothered me enormously, even though we were a couple of miles from the town, was that we could be observed through binoculars. But that was the chance we had to take. By this time there was no safe place to go and no place to hide.

Then, it was reported back to me that a little girl had approached our lead scout. I had two or three men out in front acting as scouts. The water in the swamp was now less than knee deep. I remember my lead scout saying that there is a little girl here and she will lead us to a safe place. It turned out that she led us to a hayloft in a barn.

I thought to myself, is this where we are supposed to be? All it would take is one tracer round and the place would be up in flames. I thought I'd be court-martialed for sure if I lived. Fortunately, there was very little hay in the barn. However, I didn't have any options. This is a chance I had to take because the men were near the point of exhaustion. So was I.

I stayed below and was facing the door when somebody started opening the door. The person opening the door never realized how close he came to being killed. It was Mr. Rigault, the owner of the barn and the father of the little girl and the young lady who had been bringing supplies into town. He wanted to know how many men I had. There was something about him that made me trust him right away. He was very friendly, and he offered us food and water. He came back shortly with cheese, bread, and milk. I learned years later what a great French patriot he had been prior to and during the invasion. Then we waited till dusk. I figured we were about three miles from Carentan and under cover of semidarkness we could make it there. Suddenly, I saw something moving around in the bushes near the barn. It turned out to be a man of Captain Brummitt's group. Captain Brummitt had taken a larger group on a similar jaunt through the swamp.

Later that night a couple of young men from the Rigault family escorted the entire group, under the command of Captain Brummitt, to small river-boats. They took us through the swamp, via the drainage canals, to open land near Carentan where we eventually made contact with elements of the 101st.

STANLEY CLEVER

506th Parachute Infantry Regiment, 101st Airborne Division

After a massive naval and artillery bombardment that pulverized much of the city, the 101st Airborne Division encircled Carentan. The city was a vulnerable gap in the Allied lines that, if exploited, could allow the Germans to pierce the still-fragile Utah and Omaha beachheads that lay behind it. Starting with a bayonet charge led by Robert Cole on June 9, the 101st Airborne pushed the Germans from the city. Here, Stanley Clever describes his experiences during and after that action.

Our objective was to take the city of Carentan. As we were moving into the city, we were encountering quite a bit of resistance. The Germans were pretty dug in. That's when we called the captain of the HMS *Hawkins* for artillery. We had been briefed several times. The captain of the HMS *Hawkins* said he had the finest gunners in the British navy and they were trigger-happy. He said if we needed support, call them. My commanding officer did, and he laid it down. He put quite a few of them on target, probably saving us a bunch of casualties.

I got captured shortly after we took Carentan. [Headquarters] lost com-munication with an outpost, and they asked for volunteers to go on a night reconnaissance patrol to try and find this outpost. Three of us volunteered for it. It was night patrol, and we somehow got through the German line. We got to where the outpost was supposed to be, but evidently it was overrun, which was why we lost contact with it.

We got behind the damn line and we tried to get back once we realized what we had done, but we couldn't. The Germans popped flares and just riddled us with bullets. I tried to hide. I knew they captured one guy. The other guy got back but he got all shot to pieces. I figured I'd hide in this ditch because I knew the next day the Germans were supposed to make a push, so I hid in there and I just dozed off in that damn ditch.

I woke up and it was daylight. I heard someone yelling in German. I thought they were pretty close, so I looked up and there they were, looking at me. There were three of them; they had their damn guns on me. So they took me prisoner there. They took me back to what was probably their company headquarters or maybe battalion headquarters and interrogated me.

I couldn't understand what the damn interrogator was saying, but they kept pushing me on back, and I got into a higher echelon each time. Finally, I got back to their regimental headquarters and I was interrogated by a German officer then. I could understand what he was saying.

German Marder III self-propelled 75-mm gun knocked out in Carentan. (Photo courtesy Joe Pangerl)

I told him my name, rank, and serial number, and he said, "I don't care about that." He said, "How many tanks can you carry in those gliders?" and how many of this, how many of that? I kept giving him my name, rank, and serial number.

He told me, "Your name Clever. That's German." He said, "Your mother was German; your father was German. Why do you struggle against the Fatherland?" Oh, he was irate and hostile, jumping up and down. He told the guard, "Get him out!" The guard took me out. The guard seemed like a pretty nice guy. He was just a regular guy. The officer was quite a bit older than me, probably in his thirties, kind of heavyset, and he had kind of a balding hairline. He had a red face.

Before I went in there to be interrogated I heard him interrogating an Air Force pilot that they evidently shot down. Oh, he was jumping up and down, stomping up and down, and this guard told me (he spoke a little English), he told me, "You go in there and stand at attention." He said, "Salute him, give him all the military—because he's mean." So I did. I saluted him attention and he was reaming me out about my father and mother being German, and I must have relaxed a little bit, and, God, he blew his wick again.

Then he took us to a transit camp. There were hundreds of American prisoners at the camp. There were British prisoners. Hell, that was a regular transit camp. God, they starved us to death there.

The only way to get anything to eat was to volunteer for the damn work detail, then maybe the French civilians would throw you an apple or a biscuit or something. I was in occupied territory for sixty-three days. I didn't get food there in the transit camp, didn't get any food that was fit to eat the whole time I was there. I was probably there two weeks. But other than that, there was no mistreatment. They told us if you escape, ten of the prisoners would be executed. But I didn't believe that. I can't tell you if they did it when we escaped, but I don't believe they did.

We volunteered for a work detail. One particular detail there was about thirty of us, and it was at an airstrip where the Allies had bombed it. Our job was filling bomb craters. There were two guards and about thirty prisoners. We were working this airstrip filling the bomb craters and I saw these two guards, they didn't have their heart in it at all. Then two French civilian girls (maybe seventeen, eighteen, or twenty years old) go up there, playing up to the guards. They hauled out the wine and pretty soon they were partying. I worked up there and got fairly close. The girls looked at me and kind of gave me a mental picture, "Hey we're getting these guys drunk, giving you a chance to get out of here." That's what I interpreted.

In that camp we learned you can't trust anyone, not even prisoners. Being a paratrooper, I knew I could trust paratroopers, especially the ones I knew.

In this detail there was only one guy I knew from the 101st. But there was two from the 82nd that I got acquainted with and halfway trusted. We got together and I told them what the situation was, and we agreed the four of us would make a break for it one at a time.

You had to go to the guards and ask them if you could urinate or take a crap. This was in June, and there was a wheat field right by the airstrip, and the wheat was two feet high, almost ready to harvest. That's where we'd go to do our business. So one by one we went over there, and when we got over to the wheat field we got on our bellies and crawled. When we got far enough that they couldn't see us we got up and ran.

We knew by location where the front was; it was to the north. We knew we had to go north. We didn't have any compasses. We didn't have any maps. One of the guys had a newspaper he had gotten somewhere that showed the rough area there where the battle was and what was going on. We could see which way we had to go. I knew enough about navigation that I knew where the North Star was.

We had to travel by night; we couldn't travel by day. We'd hole up during the day. We traveled four or five nights. We traveled that first day in the woods and didn't look back until almost morning. We got to the point we'd raid gardens at nighttime; it was June, there were a lot of things—green beans, we'd eat them raw.

It got pretty tough, and about the fourth or fifth day we were getting pretty hungry and we were tired of eating the damn vegetables out of gardens raw. We got our heads together and decided to approach one of the farmhouses in this small village. A farmer came to the door and we, with our broken French, tried to explain that we were hungry and that we were from an American aviator that was shot down. We didn't want to tell him that we were escaped prisoners; we didn't want to spook him. There were two of us. The other two guys hid behind his house. I showed him my dog tag. I had my pay book in one of my pockets that had Washington, D.C. on it, and I showed him that, and I think he halfway believed us then.

He said, "*Entre.*" We said, "Wait a minute, we have two buddies out here." I thought we blew it. But he took all four of us in, and the people in the farm had plenty to eat. He had his daughter cook us up a couple dozen eggs. God damn, we devoured them! They hid us out.

We were getting close to the front, and the damn Germans were getting panicky. They'd break into houses almost any time, so it got pretty risky. We decided two of us better leave. We drew straws, and me and one of the guys from the 82nd drew the short straw, so we had to leave.

We moved up the valley, tried another place that happened to be a goddamn German collaborator! He was a big, rough-looking man. He was the only real farmer in this town; all the other farmers were tenant farmers. He took us in, but he didn't trust us. He didn't know if we were German plants or what we were.

The French Underground was very active there. They had a liaison officer from the RAF who was shot down in 1939 who was there working with the Underground. This collaborator was smart and he knew the tides of war were changing. So I think he saw a chance to maybe make things right and called this RAF pilot, Flight Lieutenant Norman Edwards. He didn't tell us he was an RAF man, he told us he was a Frenchman. We were waiting in his house for this Frenchman, and I saw him riding his bicycle, and when he walked in the damn door he took his hat off and I knew he was no Frenchman because Frenchmen do not take their hats off.

He came up and started speaking French at us, and we couldn't understand what he was saying. But what he did, he'd hear Mo and I talking back and forth. I'd say, "Mo, what the hell is he saying?" Mo would say, "God damn, I don't know!" Of course he knew that we were Yanks. Finally, after he was convinced, he pulled a dog tag out and handed it to me—a little round RAF dog tag. It said Flight Lieutenant Norman Edwards RAF. Boy, I jumped up and said, "Where can we see this man?" And in pure English he said, "That is me; I am Norman Edwards." He told us this old boy is a collaborationist. He said that he's had a change of heart. He was a big, rough-and-tough man, but he had a beautiful daughter. I met her last year, and she still remembered me.

We held up there after we got with the French Underground until the front passed through us, and we turned ourselves in to the MPs, and of course they sent us back to London to headquarters for debriefing. In the meantime our units had moved back to England to get ready for the Holland jump. We were interrogated by the FBI at headquarters. There were four of us, and they took us in one at a time. They wanted to get our stories straight. Of course, we all had the same story. They wanted to make sure we were who we said we were. They kept us in there until they were convinced.

There was another safety precaution: Our company commanders had to give positive identification. Our company commander came in and identified Nick and I, wrote us out ten-day passes on the spot and made sure we got some supplementary pay so we could enjoy ourselves in London. Then we rejoined our outfit.

They were getting ready for the Holland jump and they didn't know what to do with Nick and I, since we were escaped prisoners of war. At that point in time if we got captured again they could legally shoot us. We had the option to go home. We both opted to stay in.

JACK ISAACS

505th Parachute Infantry Regiment, 82nd Airborne Divsion

Once the 82nd broke through the main German line of resistance, the division advanced on St. Sauveur-le-Vicomte practically unopposed. The town was clogged with retreating Germans and recognizing an opportunity to deliver a crushing blow, the 82nd requested a massive "time on target" artillery barrage on the town. The 505th Parachute Infantry Regiment moved in to secure the town, still defended by its remaining Germans. When the town fell, a few hours later, the 9th U.S. Division quickly secured the last north-south highway, effectively severing the peninsula and, according to captured German reports, hastening the fall of Carentan by two weeks. Jack Isaacs, G Company commander, describes the assault on St. Sauveur.

Hardly anything was left of the town when we entered it. The battalion commander ordered us to move into the town and take the high ground that was occupied by the Germans. They were dug into a railroad embankment. We did not have any tanks supporting us.

You couldn't go over it [the railroad embankment] at all. The Germans were dug in on the other side. So we moved up to it and took up position on one side of the embankment while the Germans were on the other side. We were chucking grenades back and forth. The Germans of course were throwing their potato mashers, and we were throwing fragmentation grenades. There was no way that we could cross that railroad without being wiped out.

I Company was on our right, and I commanded G Company. So we went over across the embankment into I Company's area, since it wasn't under fire. We got across and had started back towards the area we originally were at. As we were moving back, a German jumped up from behind a hedgerow and fired a burst from a Schmeisser [MP-40 machine pistol], killing a very close friend of mine. I was talking to him when it happened, and it was a miracle that I wasn't hit. Your time on Earth is precious. I remember that on the way over to Europe I cut his hair. I wasn't very good at it. It is little things like that that I remember about people.

The Germans then hit the town with several tanks. The tanks were coming from the area near the underpass. I positioned my guys to deal with them.

Trooper from the 82ⁿᵈ Airborne Division tenderly removes the shell-torn body of a little Norman girl from the ruins of St. Sauveur. (Photo courtesy U.S. Army)

We had only three bazooka rounds left and scored direct hits on one of the tanks and we knocked the tread off the other. The other three withdrew.

A bit later, I walked into a German column. It was one of those dumb things you do in battle. We walked right in front of them; I thought it was H Company. I said to my radio operator in a perfectly normal voice, "These are Germans and we'd better get out of here." We just let the German column walk right by us. The only thing I can figure was the German column was asleep. I've seen it before where men were so exhausted that they would be asleep and keep walking. So we just let them go their way and we just backed off. We went on. The next day we continued the attack and cut the peninsula.

There was only seventeen of us left from the company. When the war ended, only three original members of G Company that started in Sicily with me were still standing.

FRANCIS LAMOUREUX

508th Parachute Infantry Regiment, 82nd Airborne Division

In the 508th Parachute Infantry Regiment's Normandy after-action report, the battle of Prétot is summed up in a single sentence: "Third Battalion attacks and captures Prétot after dawn on June 20th, casualties heavy." Attacks on Prétot were part the general expansion of the Normandy beachhead on the eastern side of the Douve River. Francis Lamoureux remembers a much deeper story in his e-history.

The morning of June 20, 1944, we were in a wooded area overlooking the village of Prétot. Low-lying wisps of steam rolled slowly over the fields between us and the shadowy outline of stone houses in the distance. I stood beside Lieutenant Woodrow Plunkett. The day before, he was told by Colonel Mendez to take over as CO for G Company. He replaced Captain Nowak, who had been G Company's commanding officer since the activation of the 508th at Camp Blanding, Florida, in October 1942. I had been his radio operator since joining the regiment at Camp Mackall, in April 1943. This would be my first day working with Plunkett.

All eyes were on Lieutenant Plunkett, waiting for his signal to move forward. He swung his right arm in an arc over his head and pointed toward our objective. We were off.

I was in a crouched position. I measured each step as I kept abreast of Plunkett. Straight ahead, we looked for any signs of movement. Occasionally I glanced left, then right, to see if our line was intact. I could see Kolterman and Hargrave and Campagna on my left. Vanmeter, Oley Majers, Sergeant Henning, and Lieutenant McDuffie were on my far right. We reached the village without firing a shot. Sergeant Sirovica's 2nd Platoon had cleared the buildings. There were no Frenchmen in sight. They had evacuated their homes and were hiding in underground shelters.

Lieutenant Plunkett pointed to a two-story stone house. He decided to set up his CP there. I followed him into the building. He wanted to survey the terrain from the second story. As we started to climb the stairs, the entire building shook; it had been hit by a German 88. Chunks of ceiling showered down on us. We all made a hasty retreat. The building was being shelled one round after another. We ran along the road away from the building and crossed over into an open field, where we took cover along what looked like a denuded hedgerow. The earthen wall resembled a New England stone wall but there were no trees growing from it. Plunkett gave us orders to dig in. It was hard digging. In minutes the shells were exploding along the wall. The Jerries had zeroed in on us. The shells came in succession, one—blast!—two—blast!—three—blast! I was really scared. I prayed to God to help us.

I cannot recall how long the barrage lasted. Fifty-five years later I do remember what I felt and the thoughts that ran through my mind: "Thy will be done," I prayed. "If I come out of this alive I will take it as a sign that I am destined to marry my fiancée, Hildegarde, and to raise a family." I vowed to marry her upon my safe return to the United States. From that moment on this vow was uppermost in my mind. I was driven to keep it.

Lieutenant Plunkett knew that we had to move to a new position. Colonel Mendez radioed orders for G Company to move forward. We headed through a rich green pasture which sloped down toward a wooded ravine. What a place for a picnic—we were sheltered from incoming freight and we were getting hungry. This was to be our new CP. We dropped down to catch our breath. Everyone felt secure. Time to eat. I stretched out on the ground, opened a K ration, and munched on some crackers. Hargrave hollered at me, "Lamoureux, do you have a stick of gum?" I was preoccupied with looking for the gum in my Cracker Jack–like box of K rations.

I found a stick of gum, and as I threw it over to him I rolled over face down and heard the familiar screaming sound of a mortar shell. I pressed my tensed body into the soil and waited. A loud boom, it hit between Lieutenant Plunkett and Lieutenant McDuffie. Another scream, another more deafening boom, it hit between Oley Majers and Sergeant Henning. A third shell hit about ten yards farther down the ravine. When the air cleared, I pushed up slowly on my elbows to look around. To my left I saw Plunkett and McDuffie both bloodied and writhing in pain. To the right were Majers and Henning.

Closest to me was Majers, who was moaning, his face buried in the ground. I was struck with horror as I watched Sergeant Henning pull himself up to a position kneeling on his haunches. His left hand covered the left side of his face. Bright red blood was dripping from his face and his hand. He tried to talk, but at first made only gurgling sounds. He made a sign as he looked over at the two stricken lieutenants and as he extended his hand I could see that his face was severely disfigured. He had only half a face. His left eyeball was suspended on a white cord to below his chin—I cringed. What was he feeling and thinking?

When I looked again at Majers, I did a double take. There was something strange and furry-looking on the back of his jump pants. A closer look revealed that the bristles from a shaving brush in his back pocket had been sheared off by shrapnel. More amazing still was the way in which the bristles were fanned out surrounding a gaping wound in his left buttock. It was as though someone had carefully laid each bristle side by side into the wound to form a perfect circle. I finally spoke to him. "Oley, you're going to be OK," I told him.

I looked back at Henning. His tongue and his lips were severed. He tried desperately to speak. "Kill me," he said. Lieutenant Plunkett heard him and with great effort he said, "Henning, don't you think about it. They'll fix you up."

Mercifully, medics arrived. With the help of G Company men, the wounded were evacuated to a holding area and given immediate aid by battalion surgeon Captain Brian Beaudin.

The news soon reached Colonel Mendez. He quickly assessed the situation and ordered Lieutenant Russell Wilde of H Company to take command of G Company. In less than twenty-four hours, G Company had gone through three company commanders.

I was dazed and numbed and did not know to whom to turn. I did not have a scratch on me, but the concussion of the shell bursts made it all seem dreamlike. I felt as though I had lost my anchor, but seeing Sergeant Risnes and Sergeant Sirovica taking charge reassured me. Word came that we were moving forward to take up defensive positions for the night, but the day was not over yet.

We started our march toward evening. The companies were staggered. We filtered through battalion headquarters CP. I learned that Oley Majers was killed by a shell burst an hour after he had been taken to the temporary field hospital. This was another blow to me.

We were marching silently up a dirt road in single file—one file on either side of the road. The men ahead of me turned their head down to look at something. As I got closer I saw the body of a paratrooper lying in the middle of the road. He was stretched out on his back, wearing his helmet. I looked back at his face. What I saw was seared into my memory as though by a branding iron. It was Lieutenant Gene Williams—not a mark on his body. He looked as though he had fallen asleep there. His face still had the color of life. To me it seemed as though he had been looking up to the sky and had fallen asleep. His lips were gently pursed into what I can only describe as an angelic smile. My surprise at finding him there turned quickly into shock and indignation. Someone had removed his paratrooper boots and had stripped him of his jump pants. He lay wearing his long johns and still had on his jump jacket. To me it was a desecration!

Lieutenant Williams was from Mobile, Alabama. He was twenty-one years old and he had a boyish look. He had been the officer in charge of the 3rd Battalion Pathfinder Team. I was one of his radar operators, and I had jumped with him into Normandy on D-Day. We had trained for nearly three months in England to prepare for our pathfinder mission, which was to jump in advance of the regiment on our assigned drop zone in Normandy. We were to set up lights which could be seen only from the air and to send the radar signal to the lead planes in the airborne armada which was to follow after us from England. All of us on the pathfinder team had worked closely with Lieutenant Williams and had learned to admire him.

As dusk set in that evening, Colonel Mendez received a communication for Lieutenant Williams to inform him that his wife, Mary, had given birth to twin boys in Mobile, Alabama, on June 8, 1944. Word spread quickly throughout the battalion, and there were many heavy hearts among the officers and the enlisted men who had known him.

We were getting ready to settle in for the night. There was a chill in the air. I was in no mood to talk to anyone. Someone came toward me. I motioned him away. I huddled on the ground in a fetal position to keep warm. As the events of the day reeled through my mind I started to cry, quietly at first, then I sobbed uncontrollably and I was close to hyperventilating. After a while I dropped off to sleep.

The next day the regiment was relieved, and we went into division reserve.

LOUIS MENDEZ

508th Parachute Infantry Regiment, 82nd Airborne Division

During the war, Colonel Louis Mendez was a battalion commander in the 508th Parachute Infantry Regiment. Typical of many airborne and Ranger officers, Mendez led by example, winning, among other commendations, the Distinguished Service Cross. Mendez personally directed a counter attack at Erria, Belgium, where they stopped a powerful SS thrust, and in the attack on Prétot. He was also one of the few Mexican-American officers to graduate from West Point before World War II. Here he recalls how, when pinned down in an open field, he was ordered to charge the German troops on a ridge-line outside La Haye-du-Puits on July 4, 1944, an attack that was part of Bradley's failed July third Normandy breakout.

Love and respect—if there is such a thing as success in combat, it is learn to love and respect your men. That's a hard word to use, love. I tried to instill this philosophy because in the final analysis that's what makes the men tick. It's not physical prowess. It was my men who inspired me more than my leaders. The way they worked, the way they spoke, the way they fought, the way they talked about their parents. It inspired me. You have to remember I'm a firm believer in love. I loved those men. I felt like they were my sons.

I remember one incident where I was taking care of one of my men. We got shelled. We were under cover in bushes so we couldn't be seen by the enemy. Pappy—we called him Pappy because he was practically baldheaded—had been wounded and I was trying to take care of him best I could when we got hit again and blew his head off, and his brains were all over me. It affected me terribly. How do you try and heal a man with his brains all over the place? I cried many times to do something for him as he died in my arms.

The day we charged the hill has affected me for fifty-five years. I received a call over the field radio from General Gavin to keep advancing on the hill. I knew it was suicide; we had hardly any men left. So I said to him, "You come down here and give me that order here, General!" The general responded, "You are a West Point officer. Do your duty and execute the attack." I slammed the phone down and swore for the first time in my life. I was very upset and knew many of my men would be killed.

Shortly after the charge, one of my best officers came over because the radios were not working too well. And telephones, of course, were pretty short-ranged at that time; we were pretty far apart. He came over personally to get me a special message. I don't recall what the message was about, but in the process he got wounded. He got in the line of enemy machine gun fire.

I picked him up on the battlefield and the enemy was firing at us. I was trying to weave back and forth so the machine gun would miss us. I was carrying him over my shoulders—he was a 195-pounder. I can still hear the thud and I thought I had been hit. It didn't hurt me though—it was Paul being hit again. So I was taking a dead man off of combat, and that was the biggest cry I'd ever had.

His mother wrote me a letter and accused me of killing him; she thought it wasn't the right thing to do. It wounded me. I dreamt about it several times.

[Crying.] I can still see myself carrying him, he was so big, I was a boxer at 165 pounds and he was 195 pounds. I thought I was doing the right thing, but in retrospect, I should have called for somebody else to help me—one carrying him by the feet and the other by his shoulders to get him out. I've often said to myself, "What did she want me to do? What did you want me to do, lady, leave him out in the field so he can be blown to bits?!"

ROBERT EDLIN

2ⁿᵈ Ranger Battalion

For several weeks, a German artillery battery known as the Graf Spee, for its four battleship-sized guns, was pounding the Rangers outside the port city of Brest, a large seaport that had the capability of supporting the continuing Allied invasion. The battery was encased in a massive concrete fortress that featured the four 280-mm guns and several 88-mm cannons, ringed by 20-mm cannons and machine guns. The fortress also contained a hospital and command center buried at least several stories below ground. In one of the most remarkable stories of the war, Robert Edlin, toting a live grenade, and less then a handful of men from 2ⁿᵈ Ranger Battalion forced the eight-hundred-man garrison of the fort to surrender, receiving the Distinguished Service Cross for his actions.[11]

[We had orders to] find and take out a big gun position that was pounding our positions. It was the size of a nine-story building, and most of it underground with a big dome thing on it. I have pictures of guns firing, I believe 280 millimeters, they looked like the biggest guns in the world, the rumor was they came off the battleship *Graf Spee*.* Colonel Rudder again sent me on a recon patrol to see if we could find any routes through the minefields.

We got down with my platoon close to a German pillbox, about two hundred yards. We could see the minefields six hundred yards out in front of the fort, and we were trying to figure out how to work through there, and that's

---

* It was only a rumor. The German pocket battleship *Graf Spee* sank in 1939 off South America.

when Ace Parker came along. (We called him Ace.) Ace came by, and he was company commander, he was a lieutenant but he was commanding A Company, 5th Rangers. He and I met there, and I told him I was going to take the fort. He thought I was joking. He said he was going to take it first. He had the same ambition I did, but we had to get through the minefields. So he and I parted our ways. I didn't talk to him until a year ago, fifty-five years later!

We got to the, there was kind of a thick hedgerow there, and Bill Courtney, who was an aggressive young fellow, said, "I believe I see a passage through that minefield." And I said, "Maybe we can work our way up to the pillbox." But I didn't want to risk the whole platoon, thirty-five men. I told the platoon sergeant to keep the rest of the platoon there and I'll take Courtney and Dreher and another man nicknamed Halftrack through the minefield.

Courtney was right: The German civilians had been delivering produce to a place up there, and we worked our way into the pillbox. There's been a lot of stories told about this, but the true story is there was no gunfight, there was nothing back in 1944 where we killed twenty Germans, but there is nothing to that whatsoever. When we got up to the pillbox door, we could hear them talking and laughing inside. We kicked the door open and jumped in. The three of us—we left Halftrack as a getaway man in case anything happened and he could go back and tell them what happened to us.

Courtney spoke pretty good high-school German and he yelled "Kamerad," and they all threw their hands up laughing and joking, and one lieutenant there spoke good English, and I started talking with him and I said, "You guys seem like you're glad this thing is over with." And he said, "Yeah we're glad it's over with, we've been bombarded by artillery, and the bombers been here, and the fighter planes, and we know we're going to get overrun. It's just a shame we're going to lose a lot of men. Of course, you're going to lose a lot of men, too."

I took into consideration the fact that they were so eager to surrender. I wondered if that ran through the whole fort, the same thoughts and feelings. So I asked him if he'd lead us up to the fort commander, a lieutenant colonel, and he said "jah."

I decided not to take Courtney and another one of my men with me because again it was a tremendous risk and I didn't see any point risking anybody other than myself, but I needed an interpreter in case they were lying to me.

[So] I took Courtney with me as an interpreter, and this lieutenant took us into ground floor, which was the hospital section, and immediately they were yelling at us and they sounded the alarm. Courtney was hollering something at them in German, and this lieutenant started talking, and they quieted down, and Courtney was interpreting to me and he was telling them that we were going to talk to the commandant trying to possibly end the situation.

He led me up to the commandant's office, and when we got to the commandant's office he started on the door and just went right in. I shoved the door open and walked in, and this lieutenant commander, a fellow was about fifty—I was twenty-two at the time—he was very alarmed, wanted to know what was going on. He spoke fluent English, so I told him that we'd taken the pillbox and that I wanted to discuss surrender terms with him about surrendering the fort and saving him a lot of casualties.

The first thing he did was to pick up his telephone. I told him to put the phone down, and he said he was just going to call to see how many Americans were already in the fort. In a minute or two he hung back up and said, "Well, there's only four of you, so you're my prisoners." Then the thing that happened, I have no explanation for it at all whatsoever, I had a tommy gun on one shoulder and a pistol on my hip and a knife in my boot, and I reached over and took a hand grenade from Courtney and pulled the pin on it and stuck it into his stomach and told him, "You either surrender right now or I'm going to release the pin and you'll be a dead man!" And why I used the grenade I don't know. (I was prepared to die.)

He said, "You know if a grenade goes off you die with me." And I recall saying, "Yeah but that would be worth it." And I did say I'll count to three, and I got to two and he said, "All right, all right, I'll surrender."

Now I'm seventy-seven years old and I know what I would do—I'd put the pin back in the grenade and surrender to him! But at that time I don't know. Nobody knows. No one will ever know. I think now over a cold beer that in my braver moments I would have released the pin, but I don't know if I would have or not. It is very likely we would have barricaded the office and I would have killed him and just stayed there and hoped that our guys got to us.

When he said he would surrender I told him to get on the PA system—he did.

The question came up—why didn't I tell Colonel Rudder what I was doing? Well, Colonel Rudder was a great leader and a great officer, probably one of the greatest, but I knew if I called Rudder, I was one of his favorite people, and I knew that if I called him and asked permission to go into the fort, he would say no. If I didn't call him, then I'm on my own. So I made the decision to do it, Courtney and the other guys with me.

When this man started the surrender process I looked out the window and I expected 100, maybe 125 people—there were 850 German soldiers stacking arms out in this kind of courtyard. I was overwhelmed. One of my men and Dreher came up saw them stacking arms, and I got word for them to get in touch with Colonel Rudder immediately and stop all artillery fire and stop all action completely, everywhere, until we sorted this thing out. Rudder got the

message by radio and he immediately contacted the 29th Division commander and the corps commander. But anyway, everything stopped. The air force
stopped, the artillery stopped, the tanks stopped, and over eight hundred guys
were standing out there with their weapons stacked like the old-fashioned
Revolutionary War surrender.

We got out there, and at that time Rudder was out in the courtyard. This
colonel told me, "I don't want to offend you or anything, but I would rather
surrender officially to a higher rank than lieutenant." Of course I told him, "I
don't give a rat's ass who you surrender to just so you stay surrendered." I had
his pistol that I had taken from him earlier. He said, "My God, I don't have
my pistol." He had to present it to Colonel Rudder. So I had to go dig the pistol out where I had hid it and give it back to the colonel so he could get it to
Colonel Rudder.

So that all took place, and years later Colonel Rudder kept the pistol—
but I didn't mind. It's in the Grandcamp Museum now. [I was] completely
flabbergasted [when I saw the Germans coming out]. It was probably one of
the greatest moments of my life. It didn't register until we got outside. And
Courtney and I and several of my buddies came out and we were hugging
each other. And the rest of A Company immediately came up.

We had a huge party that night when somebody found some liberated
wine, cognac, and beer. All of A was down there. Rudder got upset, came
down there and chewed me out for the party and asked me what he would
have done in my position. If I recall correctly, I think that he said something
like, "I hope to hell that I had the guts to do what you did. I'll be back to see
you all in a little while."

CHAPTER EIGHT

DRAGOON: The Invasion of Southern France

Hate-hardened heart, O heart of iron,

iron is rust.

There never was a war that was not inward.

—Marianne Moore, "In Distrust of Merits"

Rust-covered metal sticks out of the broken concrete that forms the base of a howitzer that fired its last shell fifty-five years ago. Gray with age and slowly crumbling with each passing year, the gun is in part of an old fort that watches over a valley in an eerie reminder of a forgotten campaign in southern France's Maritime Alps.

During the summer of 1944, the proposed invasion of southern France, code-named ANVIL and later DRAGOON, was nearly canceled due to disputes at the highest levels. Winston Churchill and the British high command wanted to scrap the entire operation and continue focusing Allied efforts on northern Italy with an eventual thrust into Central Europe and the Balkans, preempting Soviet control of the region. General Eisenhower, on the other hand, successfully argued that DRAGOON was necessary to support the main landings in Normandy.[1]

Several compelling factors influenced operation DRAGOON. Hitler had successfully bottled up most of the ports of northern France, forcing the Allies to obtain the bulk of their gasoline and other supplies through Normandy. The capture of the huge southern port of Marseilles would help solve this problem. The Allies also wanted to draw German divisions away from the main Allied push in northern France.

The southern invasion was scheduled to coincide with the invasion of Normandy, but delays caused by a lack of landing craft pushed the southern invasion back six weeks. On August 15, one of World War II's least-remembered D-Days began. The Allied assault force included the Seventh Army's VI Corps, which would arrive by sea, and an assortment of airborne units designated the 1st Airborne Task Force, which would drop in several miles behind the landing beaches in the early morning hours. French forces would start unloading on D plus one.

The German defenses in southern France were seven understrength infantry divisions along with a handful of naval and air force units operating in the area. The 11th Panzer Division was about four hundred miles away. German troop concentrations in the landing beaches, however, were extremely weak. Nevertheless, the Germans could muster about 285,000 men to the Allies' 151,000 troops.[2]

After a heavy shore and air bombardment, the U.S. VI Corps, led by three veteran U.S. divisions—the 3rd, 36th, and 45th—landed at St. Tropez, St. Raphaël, and Ste. Maxime respectively. The French II Corps would later join the landings. Overall German resistance was minimal along the thirty-seven-mile invasion area, and by the evening of D-Day the seaborne forces would link up with the airborne.

On the western end of the invasion beaches, the elite twenty-three-hundred-man 1st Special Service Force struck one of the first blows. The Force landed on two tiny islands, Île du Levant and Port-Cros, near Toulon. Allied intelligence had determined that the islands' defenses had long-range artillery that could devastate the proposed landing beaches. Once on shore, the Force discovered that the menacing guns were nothing more than drainpipes that the Germans had disguised as artillery pieces. The phony guns were quickly secured but the German garrison on Port-Cros fell back to prepared positions in old thick-walled forts and held out until August 17.

The airborne portion of the invasion was spearheaded by the provisional 1st Airborne Task Force. Led by General Robert Frederick, former commander of the 1st Special Service Force, the airborne unit was made up of a hodgepodge of independent units that never had fought together. The task force included the 517th Parachute Regimental Combat Team, 509th Parachute Infantry Battalion, 551st Parachute Infantry Battalion, and 463rd Parachute Field Artillery Battalion. The British contributed the Red Devils of the 2nd Independent Parachute Brigade. The glider units in the task force included the green 550th Infantry Airborne Battalion and an assortment of outfits that had hardly any glider training, including the Japanese-American 442nd

Airborne Operations in Southern France—Aug.–Nov. 1944

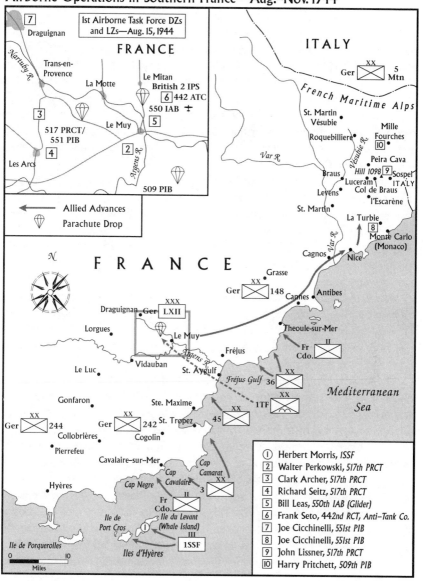

1st Airborne Task Force DZs and LZs—Aug. 15, 1944

FRANCE

7 Draguignan
Trans-en-Provence
La Motte
Le Mitan
British 2 IPS
6 442 ATC
550 IAB +
3
517 PRCT/
551 PIB
Le Muy
5
4
Les Arcs
2
Argens R.
509 PIB

Nartuby R.

←—— Allied Advances
⍟ Parachute Drop

N

ITALY

Ger XX 5 Mtn

French Maritime Alps

St. Martin Vésubie
Roquebillière
Mille Fourches 10
Var R.
Vésubie R.
Peira Cava
Braus Hill 1098 9 Sospel
Luceram ITALY
Levens Col de Braus
St. Martin l'Escarène
La Turbie
8
Monte Carlo (Monaco)
Cagnos Nice

F R A N C E

Grasse
Ger XX 148 Cannes Antibes

Draguignan Ger XXX LXII
Lorgues
Le Muy
Théoule-sur-Mer
Fréjus
Fr Cdo. II
Vidauban St. Aygulf
Le Luc
Argens R.
Fréjus Gulf 36 XX

Gonfaron
Ste. Maxime
1TF XX
Ger XX 244
Ger XX 242 St. Tropez
45 XX
Collobrières
Cogolin
Pierrefeu

Mediterranean Sea

Cavalaire-sur-Mer
Cap Camarat
Cap Cavalaire
Hyères
Cap Negre
3 XX
Fr Cdo. II
Ile de Port Cros
Ile du Levant
(Whale Island)
1SSF III
Ile de Porquerolles
Iles d'Hyères

0 ___ 10
Miles

1. Herbert Morris, ISSF
2. Walter Perkowski, 517th PRCT
3. Clark Archer, 517th PRCT
4. Richard Seitz, 517th PRCT
5. Bill Leas, 550th IAB (Glider)
6. Frank Seto, 442nd RCT, Anti–Tank Co.
7. Joe Cicchinelli, 551st PIB
8. Joe Cicchinelli, 551st PIB
9. John Lissner, 517th PRCT
10. Harry Pritchett, 509th PIB

Regimental Combat Team's Anti-Tank Company, a mortar battalion, and several service units.

Camouflaged and loaded down with more than 125 pounds of equipment apiece, the first airborne troops began landing in southern France around 3:00 A.M. on August 15. The airborne drops were scattered, despite claims by the Army Air Corps to the contrary.[3] The task force's mission was to secure several key towns and roads and prevent a German counterattack from hitting the beaches. As in Normandy, despite the misdrops, the paratroopers went about completing their objectives and creating a massive amount of confusion behind enemy lines by cutting communication wires and ambushing German columns.

The afternoon of D-Day included a parachute jump and a glider landing that brought in additional airborne reinforcements. Lieutenant Colonel Wood Joerg's paratroopers of the 551st were right on target, but the gliders again proved incredibly dangerous. The glider landing was also accurate but deadly. Of a total of 332 CG-4 gliders in the landing, only twenty-six could be reused for another mission, and scores of men were killed or wounded before the action began.[4]

Nevertheless, over the course of the next two days, road-junction towns such as Le Muy, La Motte, and Les Arcs were taken by the airborne forces. The 551st captured an entire German headquarters, bagging a German general and most of his staff, and leaving German command and control in southern France in a shambles.

By August 17, the airborne task force had achieved all of its objectives. Meanwhile, the seaborne forces had driven twenty miles inland and were preparing to move north up the Rhône Valley to link up with General George Patton's forces in central France. Two weeks after the start of the invasion, the French II Corps forced the surrender of both Toulon and Marseilles. The airborne was given a new mission of driving southeast to mop up German resistance in the posh resort towns of the Riviera, where the paratroopers were showered with flowers and the screams of newly liberated French citizens.

Meanwhile, the VI Corps rolled northward, its flank exposed to a possible German attack from Italy. In what has become known as the Champagne Campaign, most of the airborne task force was reassigned from the Riviera to positions in the crags of southern France's Maritime Alps, which make up the Franco-Italian border.

High mountains, deep gorges, hairpin turns on winding roads, and a series of well-positioned forts made the terrain ideal for the German defenders. From September to November, the mountain campaign became a stalemate and a deadly game of cat and mouse between Allied forces and the German defenders.

By the middle of November 1944, the last of the airborne units were pulled out of the Alps and sent to northern France for refitting. The Maritime Alps remained a static front for most of the war. The war as a whole was going well for the Allies, but the 1st Special Service Force would not be given a chance to see it through. The unit that conquered La Difensa and held the line at Anzio was unceremoniously disbanded and its personnel shifted to a variety of airborne and regular army units.

HERBERT MORRIS

1st Special Service Force

Before the main Allied landings took place, the predawn mission of the 1st Special Service Force was to destroy guns spotted on the tiny islands of Levant (Whale Island) and Port-Cros on the far left flank of the invasion force. To achieve complete surprise, the Force attacked the seaward side of Levant, a rocky cliff rising vertically for forty or fifty feet above the water. After overcoming part of Levant's German garrison, the Force discovered that the supposed artillery pieces that had been their targets were nothing more than disguised drainpipes. Herb Morris, an enlisted man in the Force, describes the rubber-boat attack on Levant in this e-history.

We were in the cargo hold of a destroyer that was really not made for troops, but the navy converted it. In the hold, we had hammocks hanging from the ceiling. They had them so close together you had to slide into them. There was somebody above you and below you.

We had blackened our faces, as was the normal routine for going out on missions. We packed the equipment we needed to take on the mission. What I had in my bag was this C-2 stuff we had for demolition. It comes in something that looks like a tube of long underwear. It was tied at the end and kind of looked like a stocking; I had several of those. I had a grenade launcher fitted at the end of my M-1 rifle. So here I am with this M-1 rifle. We had trained for this mission—we knew what we were supposed to do. The grenades that went on the end of the rifles kind of looked like little bombs. Each grenade slid into a circular cardboard tube; the tube itself was about three inches in diameter; they slide into there for safekeeping. I took them out, deciding that I wanted as many as possible. I also had grenades that were fitted to my sides and front. Now you should be getting the idea that I was a walking bomb—and that's about right! I also had some bandoliers of rifle ammunition. So I got all ready and I laid in my hammock.

In the hold of the ship packed with guys. I laid down on the bunk while the rest of the men were starting to get ready. I may have been more nervous than some of them or something. I got ready first. I always tried not to be the last. Ever since I was little, I never wanted to be the last one; that goes back to being from a family with nine children. I learned in those days that you are never the last one over the fence. So I was laying on my hammock and suddenly someone dropped a grenade. (I'm not going to give the name of the person.) And then someone else kicked it over into the corner and I'm just lying there; it's really too late to do anything. The grenade goes off in the corner of the hold (the hold was no more than fifty feet). Immediately there's this yelling and everybody dove to whatever corner they could get to, away from the grenade. The hold was filled with all these bunks and everything so there really wasn't too many places to go. I slipped out of my bunk, I was pretty fast in those days, and made it to the corner. In fact, I had several guys on top of me. Someone immediately yelled, "Medic!" The squad leader of my assault team was hit with shrapnel from the grenade. He had shrapnel in his buttocks, but he made the assault anyway. I did lose the platoon leader and the section leader. I know they were wounded and I think at least one person was killed, but I don't really remember.

To show you how fortunate we were, we had boxes of open grenades and C-2 laying all over and we also had some plain old dynamite, but fortunately, none of it went off. C-2 will go off by just talking to it! We had all sorts of things because you had all types of demolition jobs to do. My job was to stuff demolitions down barrels of the guns we were sent to destroy. That's why I was carrying all this stuff, to blow up the guns. The importance of this is that if it really had blown the rest of the stuff up, like they do in the movies, you would have had the entire ship go up. It could have destroyed the whole southern France invasion because we were coming in before the invasion was taking place. It would have alerted the Germans to where the invasion was taking place.

Anyway, we went ahead and got out of the hold. The wounded were moved elsewhere and we got up on the deck. They lowered us down to these launches and then we got into rubber boats. We were out past the horizon and the launches towed our rubber boats in; we couldn't see the land at this point. We were probably a little over a mile away from land. There were several launches that were towing the boats in. You could look out, and the sea of course was choppy enough that the boats would come up and then you'd see them and then you wouldn't. We had what was the equivalent to a petty officer running our launch. He decided that this was as far as he should go, according to his instruments or whatever. But it was still too far from the shoreline for the sergeant who was in charge of our boat and he said, "No, you are taking us in further!" He started to reach down for his pistol and the guy says, "OK, OK, I'll take you in farther." So we got in a little bit further and we started paddling. Several of our paddles hit together so our sergeant, who I mentioned had some shrapnel in his leg, was trying to lead us and make sure we are paddling all together. As I mentioned, our paddles were hitting together because I guess somebody was nervous. He said, "Hold it," in a whisper, and we all stopped paddling. Then he said, "All right you babies . . . now let's PADDLE!" Meanwhile, a German searchlight beamed from a beach about a half a mile from our position and passed over us several times (they kind of played it against the water) and we ducked down and stopped paddling.

We were able to paddle in and we made our way to the island. We paddled right up to the side of the cliff. Fortunately there was a small ledge that extended out from the cliff about three inches and was just about a foot below the lapping waves. With that foothold we were able with ropes to ascend the cliff.

It didn't take us more than a half hour to get up the cliff. One guy had tied machine gun ammunition boxes together and tied these boxes to his body. One of the boxes got away. It was before sunrise; there were no lights, just black, I was just a couple people behind this guy, and here comes this box of machine gun ammo; you hear it. It goes down a way and it hits the side of the cliff and then it goes down again and hits the side of the cliff and keeps going down and then it finally hits the water.

Once we were on top, we started to go through a meadow of tall grass and undergrowth that was chest-high. After we got out of the meadow, we had a few brief firefights. We had several casualties but instead of finding real artillery guns that we were supposed to knock out, we found dummy guns.

WALTER PERKOWSKI

517th Parachute Regimental Combat Team

In the early morning hours of August 15, paratroopers from the 509th Parachute Infantry Battalion and 517th Parachute Regimental Combat

Team started landing several miles behind the invasion beaches. The paratroopers' mission was to secure several key towns and roads and prevent a German counterattack from hitting the beaches. Walter Perkowski remembers the close calls of August 15.

From my platoon, I don't think that there are too many of us left. We started out with thirty-six, and I'd say at the end of the war there were about four or five of us left. I was a BAR [Browning Automatic Rifle] man. I jumped with that. I got airsick a lot. I heaved a lot, so they gave me a bucket. I think I was the only guy in the army that they issued a bucket! While in the plane I threw up in the bucket. Several other guys started heaving. The light came on and we got ready to jump. I dropped the bucket, and me and another guy were sliding all over the place, but we finally made it out the door.

We landed near Le Muy. When I hit the ground I could hear fighting all around me. I teamed up with four men, including a captain. We took this little house, and there were some old people in it, and we told them that they better get out. The captain set me up with the BAR, and I saw some movement behind the house in a vineyard. I said, "Captain, it looks like our men." As they got closer, we could see they were Germans. They surrounded the house and started firing. One of our guys got hit, and I took his rifle and started to run into one of the rooms. Before I got in there a grenade came through a window and blew up in front of me. It shocked me pretty bad. We were all wounded and out of ammunition, so the captain surrendered. He put out a white handkerchief and they stopped firing and took us out of the house.

A German had a machine gun, and they marched us down a street. I didn't know what was going on, I was still stunned from the grenade. We got into this little town and put us in a big yard. They had several English paratroopers there and they started to ask us questions. I had a phosphorous grenade in my pocket that I couldn't get rid of when I was captured. One of the Germans grabbed it and they took me in front of an officer. He was pissed off and started whupping my ass! He beat me up—blackened my eyes and broke my nose—but he couldn't get me on the ground. He kept asking me how many paratroopers dropped. I heard what the other guys were saying, so I said, "fifty thousand."

They threw me into a trench. Our shells started coming in, so they put us in a garage with more English paratroopers. There were about four or five of us in there along with some beat-up old cars and some other stuff. Then two Germans with machine guns appeared. They lined us all up and were going to let us have it. I heard the bolt go back on their guns. What came to my mind was the St. Valentine's Day Massacre in Chicago. All of a sudden an old

German on a bicycle came up and said something to these guys. So they grabbed their machine guns and took off. Mortars and shelling were coming in. The Germans left the town and things quieted down, and we moved from the garage, and I was sitting on a curb when our guys came into the town. My face was a mess, and this French girl felt sorry for me. She was wiping my face and gave me some wine. As I was sitting there I could hear hobnail boots coming up the street. It turned out to be a column of German prisoners. The German that worked me over was leading it. He faced me and was looking right at me. He was a high-ranking officer. It was kind of a natural thing for me to do. I was half-loaded and I pulled him out and took him in the alley and disposed of him.

CLARK ARCHER

517th Parachute Regimental Combat Team

The 517th Parachute Regimental Combat Team (PRCT) was the largest element of the 1st Airborne Task Force, with a little over twenty-six hundred men. The 517th's mission was to jump in an area outside Le Muy designated Drop Zone A and capture the high ground near Le Muy and the towns of La Motte and Les Arcs, thus blocking the main roads leading to the invasion beaches. Clark Archer describes one such roadblock on the Les Arcs–Trans road.

I arrived at the Château Ste. Roseline, the regimental CP [command post], at around 11:00 A.M. on D-Day with Private Kellogg. We located Private Sutton and Stephan Weirzba and were instructed to set up a roadblock. We moved down the slope from the CP and located the Les Arcs–Trans Road. Kellogg and Weirzba were in a ditch with Sutton to their rear on the higher ground as a lookout, and I took a position midway between them. At about 1:00 P.M., Sutton yelled, "One of ours. It's coming down Kellogg's side." Shortly thereafter, we could see the silhouette of a vehicle approaching. The car closed to within fifty yards of our position waving their arms as if to indicate a "friendly." There was considerable reluctance to commence firing; I did not see any visible weapons. All problems ceased as the convertible slowed down just past Kellogg's position and mine: They were Germans, there was no doubt about it. I stood up and started firing my grease gun into the driver's

Mercedes convertible ambush on the road from Trans-en-Provence to Les Arcs. (Photo courtesy Clark Archer)

side door until it jammed, after firing eight or nine rounds. Then Kellogg popped up and fired a full clip from his M-1 rifle. Next, Weirzba fired an AT grenade from his Springfield '03 rifle. The firing pin on the grenade had not been removed and subsequently did not detonate. It did, however, hit the driver's head, splitting his skull wide open. We cut the other Germans down with small-arms fire.

After going through the car, we discovered that the Germans were carrying a black canvas briefcase that contained maps. As I opened the case, I noticed that the top map was a German division's redeployment for the invasion of southern France. I put everything back in the case and we rushed everything back to headquarters. This intelligence later proved helpful in countering the German redeployment of some of their forces as the invasion was unfolding. Later, I read a book where an American OSS officer later tried to take credit for finding the briefcase and plans, even coming up with a story about capturing the car. Of course, that was all nonsense.

Not long after the battle, the car was put back into operational use. Blood was drained from the back by a few shots to the floorboards. John "Boom Boom" Alicki kept it hidden for several days and later made several excursions with it.

RICHARD SEITZ

517th Parachute Regimental Combat Team

Lieutenant Colonel Richard Seitz was a natural leader and a great tactician who later rose to the rank of three-star general. In the following interview, Seitz describes the attack on Les Arcs to relieve the 517th's trapped 1st Battalion.

I was only twenty-five at the time. I'm bragging at this time, but I was one of the youngest infantry battalion commanders of World War II. [Laughs.] When I took over the battalion, it was just three days before I turned twenty-five. It was a sobering effect. I don't think I was a wild officer, but I had a reputation for being cocky, capable of doing anything.

In the paratroopers I had some damn fine leaders. Gavin was my first company commander, in fact we went through jump school together, we were one of the earliest group to go through. We were just full of spirit. I think the whole bunch of us were cocky, with the attitude that, by damned, we could do anything—we were paratroopers. We were well-trained. I felt that way. I thought that was typical of the paratrooper officers and men.

My battalion had taken La Motte, one of the first towns to be liberated in southern France. We then moved near about three or four miles from Les Arcs. We were there on the night of D plus one in a very comfortable defensive position, getting some fire from the Germans. That's when the regimental commander told me that Bill Boyle and elements of the 1st Battalion were trapped in the town. They were surrounded by Germans and having a pretty difficult time. He ordered me to attack and relieve Bill Boyle. I moved the battalion down there and had E Company send out some patrols to feel out the enemy.

When we were in a defensive position, my soldiers were near a grape vineyard and would rush out seventy-five yards and pluck up a large bunch of grapes while the Germans were firing like crazy. It upset me when I saw them do this a few times, but the Germans exposed their positions and I was able to get mortar fire on them. That kind of showed you the spirit of these soldiers. Here they are in a defensive position getting some mortar fire, yet they'd rush out seventy-five yards to get a helmet full of grapes and run back.

Graves [the regimental commander] wanted me to attack that night. At the time Boyle, 1st Battalion commander, was holed up near the town's train station. There was too much confusion. The 3rd Battalion was closing in from their long march from their assembly area; they attacked that night but were halted on the outskirts of town. So we waited until the morning to do the job and had both battalions attack the town at the same time. I don't think we had any severe casualties.

When we first got into the town we didn't encounter much resistance, but when we got near the railroad station, the Germans counterattacked. The first time I drove them off with mortar fire, broke off their attack, and they reorganized and counterattacked again. This was August 17. Fortunately, there were some P-51s flying around and how we contacted them amazes me to this day, but we were able to bring the P-51s in. Finally, the Germans were driven off and we captured the town.

BILL LEAS

550th Infantry Airborne Battalion

On the afternoon of D-Day, a parachute and glider landing reinforced the paratroops from the 517th and 509th who had landed in the early morning. Some gliders came down on landing fields spiked with poles rigged with impact-sensitive explosives. Bill Leas describes his glider experience and the first two days of the invasion.

Once we cut loose from the towrope, we were conscious of gliders descending in all directions, but our attention was primarily focused on locating landmarks we had memorized from contour maps we had studied earlier. Just as it appeared our pilot was about to set down, another glider came in from our left and set down in front of us. The pilot pulled up over a clump of trees and set down on the other side in a patch of freshly plowed ground. We came quickly to a stop with the glider standing vertically on its nose. The dirt that was thrown into the air passed the windows and open panels under the wings, making it look for an instant as if we were on fire. When we finally fell back to the ground in an upright position, I was the first to exit my side of the glider.

As I exited, the dirt thrown up by our landing was still falling. Just in front of us was a vineyard, to which I immediately ran and hit the ground. I rose cautiously to look around. To my surprise, about two or three rows from where I was kneeling was a British soldier. He was down on his haunches in front of a small fire with long stick in his hand. He had a tin can fastened to the end of the stick. He turned to me and said, "There haven't been any Jerries around here. You want a spot of tea?" I declined his offer, and our squad headed for our assembly area.

Once on the ground, you had to stay alert for incoming gliders. You couldn't hear them coming until they were almost on you, and then the only noise was a whistling sound as the wind rushed by their wings. We were fortunate that we were not met by enemy fire when we landed. By the time we reached the ground, many of the gliders had already landed. Some were pretty damaged.

The most spectacular landing I witnessed was a glider that came in just over our heads and hit into the antiglider poles in the field next to the road we were on. The pilot did an excellent job. He went between the poles, clipped off both wings at the same time, dropped a few feet onto his wheels, and rolled to the end of the row. He did a ground loop at the end but didn't touch any of the poles.

I have many memories of the invasion, mostly related to the attacks on and liberation of Le Muy,[5] but the first thing that always comes to mind is that British soldier calmly making tea while gliders were landing all around him.

FRANK SETO

442nd Regimental Combat Team

One of America's most-decorated regiments in World War II was the 442nd Regimental Combat Team. Made up of Japanese-Americans, the 442nd's Anti-Tank Company was selected to land by glider in southern France to establish roadblocks on roads that led to the invasion beaches.

In 1939 I turned pro. I had my first pro fight in Hollywood Park, which was famous for having movie stars show up. When I got in the ring, people used to yell, "Kill that Jap! Kill that Jap!" So I embroidered "I am an American" on the back of my robe.

On the day the war began, I got in a couple of fights. I was in the toilet at a show and these two guys came in and said, "Hey, you goddamn Jap!" and a few other things, and the next thing I knew they attacked me while I was in the toilet. I smacked the one guy, and the other tried to hit me so I flipped him over. After that I went in the theater, and I was watching the show and somebody just slaps me in the face. I said to myself, "What's going on?" I was just sitting there watching the show and bam! This guy just slaps me in the face. So right away I swung back at the guy, and the ushers came and took both of us away. When we got outside I asked the guy if he wanted to finish it, and he took off and I went the other way.

Not long after that, they took my father to Manzanar, one of the camps. My dad signed me up to go, but I said I wasn't going to no camp! The whole thing upset me, but at least I knew he would be safe. When the war started, my father was scared because when he drove down the street people would come out and cuss him out and everything. We used to have a .22 rifle that we would go hunting with and a shortwave radio, but when the war started he was so scared that he threw everything out. Eventually I went to Santa Anita. It was an assembly center. I was in Santa Anita for several months.

Before the war, I volunteered for the army. When they found out that I had a perforated eardrum, they rejected me. When the war started, I volunteered again, but they wouldn't take me because they classified me 4C, which was classified as an enemy alien. Later in 1942 when I was in Glasgow, Montana, topping sugar beets, my foreman informed me that they were forming the 442nd. So I volunteered again at camp in Jerome, Arkansas, where they finally let me in and sent me to Camp Shelby, Mississippi. They put me in the antitank company.

It was early in the morning, after we ate breakfast, when we boarded the gliders. The 3rd Platoon was given the task of covering one of the main roads, since we destroyed two light tanks in Italy, in case the Germans tried to reach the beaches. The trip over was like riding an airplane. As you're looking down you see all the ships and everything. The C-47s were pulling us, and I was lying on top of the jeep that was inside of the glider. After we came over our landing area, the glider pilot said, "OK, we're going to cut you guys off now." Gliders were coming from all directions. I started praying. He said, "Hold on!" One glider cut right in front of us. So the pilot dropped a little bit. The wing hit a tree and hurled us right into the side of a hill. Both the glider pilots broke their legs, and our officer was strapped down, but he cut his face up real bad. I was on the jeep next to a water can and I hurt my knee. The radio operator was all right but he was knocked a little cuckoo.

When we took our training they showed us how to tie down the jeep in the glider. We had twenty-eight ropes and a cable that kept the jeep in place. The ropes were broken, but the cable was just a little shredded. If that broke, it would have killed both the pilots in the front. It would have gone right into them. The motor in the jeep even went through the radiator.

I heard an officer moaning, and I went up to him with my first-aid kit and wiped him off with bandages. The two glider pilots were moaning. I could see paratroopers coming up the side of the hill and I was hollering for medics. We took off for our objective, which was a road, and set up a roadblock with our guns, but it turned out the Germans didn't attack that day.

I think everybody set out to prove that we were good Americans and that we were going to show them. I think we all had that in mind because of everything we did. When we had to take a hill or something we were going to take it regardless of how many got killed. Our folks would always say, "Don't fail, since that would bring a bad name on the rest of the community." Everything we did we tried to do, we tried to do it right.

JOE CICCHINELLI

551ˢᵗ Parachute Infantry Battalion

On the evening of August 16, the 551ˢᵗ Parachute Infantry Battalion started to move on the strategic town of Draguignan. A and B companies of the battalion led the assault on the town. Joe Cicchinelli, a scout for A Company, and three other men picked their way through the streets of Draguignan, where they stumbled upon a German headquarters, capturing a general and his staff.

I went into the town of Draguignan and ran into a Frenchman and asked him where the Germans were. He pointed to a large building in town. At that time it was Sergeant Thompson, Schultz, Bud Hook, and myself. I was the scout and moved ahead of everybody.

We looked at the building, and there was hardly anyone around it, so we rushed the main door. Once inside there was door to the right of the entrance, so we crashed through that and charged into a room. There was a German officer that was sitting behind a desk with a monocle in his eye, and there were some other German officers in the room. I said something like, "Look at the Kraut with the monocle and all those decorations!" Then somebody said, "It must be a general."

The German officer was hollering at the other officers in German and we asked him if he could speak English and he said, "No." I searched him to see if he had any weapons and I found a hidden pistol in his boot. I took my bayonet and rifle and pointed it at the general and said to Thompson that I was going to "shoot this son-of-a-bitch!" The German officer then screamed in English, "Don't shoot me!" He pulled out of his wallet a million-mark note as a bribe; Thompson still has the note. Several other troopers entered the building and took the general back to battalion headquarters.

In a courtyard in front of the building there was a huge Nazi flag on a flagpole. I climbed up and took the flag and sent it home. I kept the flag until 1985 and I said, "Oh, hell, this flag doesn't belong to me." I went back to southern France and gave it to the mayor of Draguignan for the town museum.

Meanwhile, we searched the entire building. I got to the back of the building and found something that was kind of like a cave and I found five big burlap bags that were filled with German marks and French francs. The bags were about four feet high. We also found some beer and liquor and I told one of our guys to take the beer back to the officers and give the liquor to the men.

Thompson asked, "How much do you think is here?" And then somebody said, "This money is only good to the French and the Krauts." We took the money and found an old flatbed truck that backfired every so often. The headquarters was on a large hill, so we got on the truck and started going down the hill. I was throwing the money out the back of the truck to all the people and got rid of all the money! Everybody was yelling and screaming and excited to get the money; I felt like a hero.

As the 551st Parachute Infantry Battalion pushed southwest along the French coast, a small reconnaissance patrol led by Lieutenant George Luening and A Company scout Joe Cicchinelli came across one of the last pockets of German resistance in the French town of La Turbie, overlooking Monaco. Cicchinelli recalls the day at La Turbie when he confronted death on a personal level, and he has been struggling to live with it for most of his life.

As our reconnaissance patrol made our way down a road into La Turbie, on top of the mountain we could see a fortress manned by Germans. I remember we had several men in the patrol: Lieutenant Luening, Sergeant Anderson, Bud Hook, Virgil Dorr, and Lou Waters. I called back to Lieutenant Luening to use the binoculars to get a closer look at the fort, and I saw that a German soldier was also peering at me with binoculars. The German then started running along the side of the fort. I knew they would start shelling us. So I told everyone, "Get the hell off the road!" About a minute later, artillery fire started pouring in.

We sought cover and moved toward the hills west of the town to a large stucco house. I rapped on the door with my rifle and we were invited inside by a Frenchman named Charles Colari. Colari was a young, small man, wearing a plain white shirt, who told us the town was crawling with Krauts and the local citizens were warned to stay inside and out of sight. There were about four people in the house—mother and father and his two children. They offered us wine, and he took us outside and Colari started telling us about German gun positions and where the Germans set up a machine gun nest.

Luening wanted to return and report what we found out, but the rest of the patrol wanted to go, and we talked him into it. So Colari led the way to the nest, which was on the opposite side of the valley. You had to go down through La Turbie. As we were going through La Turbie, Colari's white shirt made him look like he was carrying a white flag.

We went through La Turbie and took a path up a hill. The nest was located inside of a flimsy wooden shack. The area around the shack was terraced and was typical of the terrain in La Turbie. I will never forget it—our first face-to-face encounter with the Germans.

Anderson yelled, "Here they are!" and started shooting. Next, I kicked the door open and we rolled the grenades into the shack. No sooner had we pulled the pins and rolled the grenades into the shack did Anderson try to barrel through the front door. Waters and I both yelled, "Grenades! Grenades! Get down!" and as a reflex I caught Anderson by his web belt and hauled him down on the ground, closed the door, and the grenades went off.

We entered the house, I shooting on one side and Lou shooting on the other side. I'm emptying my clip. I remember that after he fired a round or two, Lou's rifle jammed. On my side of the shack was a dead German soldier. He was a mess and looked like a bloody pile of old rags. Hook than yelled, "There's a couple of Germans on the ground back here." We went back behind the shack, and there were three Germans on the ground—two

German soldiers killed by Joe Cicchinelli's patrol at La Turbie. Photos retrieved by Cicchinelli from the soldiers' pay books. (Photo courtesy Joe Cicchinelli)

were dead and the other was barely alive. Bud Hook said to me, "Hey, Chic, this one is still alive," and I put my rifle to my hip and pulled the trigger and shot him in the head and blew his brains out the other side. It was something I did automatically.

They were eighteen or twenty years old. I took their wallets out and took the photos from their pay books. It's been with me for a long time and it still bothers me. I still wonder if I should have left him lie there. I've thought about that day a lot.

JOHN LISSNER

517th Parachute Regimental Combat Team

A small wooden plaque hangs in a restaurant in the tiny village of Col de Braus, the names of fifteen men etched into its wood. The men were from F Company, and most were killed on the top of Hill 1098, one of the seemingly endless mountains in the French Maritime Alps. John Lissner, then a lieutenant and commander of F Company, remembers the week his platoon spent on the hill.

There is a winding road, and you're exposed all of the time. We were so high up in the mountains that I remember we saw some Germans down in the valley and at the time all we had was a 60-mm mortar. So we fired, and it was like throwing snowballs into a furnace—they just disappeared. All we could see were small puffs of smoke. That's how impassable the terrain was.

It was maybe four in the afternoon. We were going around a bend in the road; it was closing in on darkness. There was a lot of fire and smoke coming in. We decided when we got around the bend to hold up there. This is where we were joined by a forward observer from the 460th. He got some mail and he showed me. He pulled it out and said, "Here, I just got this today, a picture of my newborn baby." I can remember it distinctly. He was maybe twenty-seven or twenty-eight. There were a lot of rounds coming in; some were ours, some were theirs. We bedded down on the reverse side of 1098 on a high point we called the Rock, which overlooked the hill. We radioed back to Dick Seitz [2nd Battalion commander] that we were on 1098. The next morning, after I sent some scouts forward, I realized that we were not on the hill.

I wanted to be true to my word, so that next morning we took the hill. As soon as we were up there, we started losing a lot of men. We had a clear view of the whole area and were able to see our battleships in the Tyrrhenian Sea. Before the war it was a park or something and people would go up there to admire the view. It was ideal for artillery observation, and we were able to put fire on some of the forts up there and in Sospel. We weren't up there long when the night artillery observer that showed me pictures of his newborn baby was hit by a piece of shrapnel that came through his shoulder blade and came down through his heart. I lost several other men up there.

Every day the Germans would shell us and kick us off the hill, and the next day we'd kick them off the hill. I told someone at battalion that if I had a bullhorn I would have said to the Germans, "Okay, now it's your turn to take the hill!" I was tired of getting our asses kicked.

I had one guy who couldn't take it anymore. If you don't want to be in the unit, you do something. You either shoot yourself in the foot, something that I never saw happen, or you can start berating a company commander or platoon leader and they will eventually get rid of you for court-martial reasons. As we were coming down off of 1098, this corporal started saying to me, "Lissner, you're yellow!" He kept saying, "You don't give a damn about the men!" This was in a truck as we were on our way down from the hill. There were over a half a dozen men looking at each other waiting to see what was going to happen. You could see by the look in their eyes they were asking what I was going to do with him. Shoot him, stab him, what was I going to do? I said nothing. I waited for the truck to stop and then he started again saying, "Lissner, you're yellow."

Everybody got out of the truck and I told him to "come here." I said, "Take your webbing off, we're going to fight this out right here."

What resistance he put up I don't remember. I jabbed him two or three times in the face. I hit him one more time and knocked him down. I said, "Get up, you sonofabitch, get up!" Then I said, "Now we can talk to one another." I said, "Why are you calling me all of these names? Do you want to get out of this outfit?" I said, "You can get out the way you should look!" When I got back to battalion I said, "I don't want this guy court-martialed, I want him returned." So he was gone.

HARRY PRITCHETT

509th Parachute Infantry Battalion

Fighting in the Maritime Alps deteriorated into a war of attrition, the constant patrolling and German artillery exacting a high toll. On the

night of November 8, as Harry Pritchett recalls, one of these patrols
was directed against German bunkers and barracks in what was
called Raid GERONIMO.

I was originally a platoon leader of the 509th Parachute Infantry Battalion on
the jump into southern France. It all changed when a classmate of mine from
the same company at West Point, Hubert Flander, who was the battalion intelligence officer, or S-2, came up in a jeep with the battalion executive officer. I envied him, his privilege of riding in a jeep. A day later his jeep ran
over a German Teller antitank mine buried in the shoulder of the road. The
mine blew up the jeep and killed the two officers and the driver. So I became
S-2. I was only about fifty yards away from him when this happened, and it
was my first experience in the war of seeing a friend killed. My mind still
flashes back to that scene and I reflect on the part that luck, good or bad,
plays in war. Lieutenant Flander went from being envied to being dead in a
matter of seconds.

We finally reached the Maritime Alps, and life was pretty quiet. We ran
routine patrols and so did the Germans. I felt that it was important that as the
officer planning and ordering these patrols to actually participate in this
deadly game that I was directing my men to do.

In November I ran a night patrol with one other soldier up to some old
Maginot Line forts on the ridge which formed the French-Italian border at a
place called Mille Fourches, which was occupied by the Germans. There
were some concrete bunkers and wooden barracks on the reverse slope of the
ridge. I did not use the route along the Turini–Mille Fourches road but approached up a steep, wooded slope to the west of the fort. I was able to get inside the German positions and get a general idea of their position, as I was
thinking about bringing back a raiding force to retaliate for their recent foray
against our outposts.

Upon returning I broached the idea to Major Tomasik, who, after coordi-
nating with higher headquarters, approved the plan, which was code-named
GERONIMO after the "stand in the door" symbol of the 509th. This plan included registering all of the artillery within range on the fort over a several-
day period so that all guns could fire a "time on target" to cover our
withdrawal and to add to the casualties that we intended to inflict. (Time on
target means that all guns would be fired so that the projectiles would all arrive on the target at the same instant regardless of the guns' distance from the
target.) This force was thoroughly briefed on the plan, and we set out after
dark on November 8.

We were in contact with base by radio so that I could notify them at the
time of our withdrawal and the artillery would come down fifteen minutes

Members of the 551ˢᵗ patrolling the French Alps. (Photo courtesy U.S. Army)

thereafter. I was in the lead as I had made this trip before and also needed to be able to make any decisions if the situation had changed.

On the way up I saw what I believed to be a crouching man who could only be a German. I could not shoot him as the shot would give away our situation. On the other hand, if the figure were a German, he would surely open fire and probably hit me and a couple of men behind me—he must be waiting to get a better shot at us or he was afraid to move. I froze, as did every man behind me, and I continued to stare into the darkness to verify what I thought I was seeing. This was probably the most uncertain that I would ever be during the war about what to do as the options raced through my mind. After more seconds' delay I finally moved forward and nothing happened! It was a bush—talk about imagination.

We continued up the slope and made an initial entry into the enemy position when a German cried out, "Halt!" We opened fire and according to plan, which was that once we were discovered each man would run to a predesignated area, open fire on any Germans and throw fragmentation and white phosphorous grenades into any opening. A machine gun opened fire from one of the bunkers near me, so I was able to move up and throw a white phosphorous explosive smoke grenade into the opening, and the gun stopped firing.

Shortly thereafter, I blew the whistle to withdraw and we reassembled along the route that we had climbed up and called in the artillery. A quick count showed that we were missing one man, but there was nothing that could be done to go back for him as the Germans were in a high state of alert. Besides, the artillery would be coming in a couple minutes. We continued back towards our positions when the sky lit up with the flashes of the artillery firing within a few seconds of each other, and true to plan the rounds landed almost simultaneously on Mille Fourches.

Shortly thereafter, when all was again quiet, we heard three pistol shots (on the raid, every paratrooper carried a .45 pistol in addition to his main weapon) from the direction that we had just come. We figured that they must have come from our missing man and that he was desperately signaling for help. I sent three men back to look for him, and sure enough they found him. He had suffered a grazing wound to the head which had knocked him unconscious. When he came to, the firing had stopped and we were gone, but he knew that he had to get out of there before the artillery came down, and he just made it. He later reported that as he was leaving the position a force of about thirty Germans was coming into the area deployed for a counterattack. They would have walked right under incoming artillery fire. I still continue to wonder how the Germans had been able to launch that counterattack in such a short time. It furthered my respect for the German army.

CHAPTER NINE

HOLLAND

It was only a small place and they cheered us too much,

A couple of allies, chance symbol of Freedom new-found.

They were eager to beckon, to back-slap, even to touch;

They put flowers in my helmet and corn-coloured wine in my hand.

—Paul Dehn, "St. Aubin D'Aubigné"

Each year on September 18, a runner brings a torch from Normandy to the Dutch city of Eindhoven to commemorate Liberation Day. Each year World War II veterans from the 101st Airborne had returned to the city to march in the vanguard of the parade. But in 1999, age prevented many veterans from marching, so they remained seated and quietly reflected on events that had occurred more than five decades earlier: Operation MARKET-GARDEN.

After being in the thick of the fighting during the battle of Normandy, the 101st and 82nd airborne divisions returned to their base camps in England in July for rest and a much-needed infusion of new troops. Midsummer 1944 also witnessed the expansion of the airborne into a true airborne army. Throughout World War II, airborne assaults were an evolving concept. Over the course of two short years, the Allies' airborne operations went from landing scattered parachute battalions in North Africa to a full-scale airborne army known as the First Allied Airborne Army, or FAAA.

Overall command of the FAAA went to an American Air Corps lieutenant general, Lewis Brereton. The FAAA was made up of the American

XVIII Corps and British I Airborne Corps. The XVIII Corps, commanded by the former 82nd commander, Matthew Ridgway, consisted of the 82nd and 101st airborne divisions and the soon-to-arrive 17th Airborne Division. The British I Airborne Corps, consisting of the British 1st and 6th airborne divisions and the Polish Airborne Brigade, was commanded by Lieutenant General Frederick "Boy" Browning. A transport arm, which included the U.S. IX Troop Carrier Command and the British Troop Carrier Command, rounded out the force.

After the successful breakout from Normandy, more than a dozen large-scale airborne plans were drawn up to aid Allied ground forces in trapping the German army. One, TRANSFIGURE, was a massive airborne operation to cut off the retreating German army south of Paris, but the operation was canceled when the Allied ground forces overran the proposed drop zones. Others, such as LINNET I and II, were similar in scope. LINNET I brought both the 82nd and 101st airborne divisions to the marshaling areas, but the operation was called off at the last minute at the behest of General Omar Bradley because it would have diverted C-47s from hauling gas to the Allied armies.[1] LINNET II, a parachute drop between the Belgian city of Liege and the Dutch city of Maastricht to support the American First Army, was canceled by Eisenhower to placate Britain's newly promoted Field Marshal Bernard Montgomery, who was angered that resources were being diverted from his northern thrust into Germany.[2]

In the early days of September 1944, the Allied armies were rolling through Belgium and entering Holland. The German army was on the run and in tatters. Montgomery saw an opportunity to charge into Germany's industrial heartland, the Ruhr, and proposed an audacious combined airborne-ground plan called MARKET-GARDEN, an attempt to punch through the remaining German defenses in Holland and cross the Lower Rhine River and enter northern Germany. The hope was to end the war by Christmas 1944.

The plan called for the airborne troops to drop from the sky and capture a fifty-three-mile corridor of highway and bridges that stretched north-south from the city of Eindhoven near the Dutch-Belgian border to the final bridge over the Lower Rhine River at Arnhem. Simultaneously striking from the Dutch-Belgian border along the Meuse-Escaut Canal, tanks from Britain's XXX Corps would push north about sixty-four miles to the last bridge at Arnhem within forty-eight hours.

The most daring aspect of the plan was MARKET—the largest airborne operation of all time. Three airborne divisions plus a British airlanding division, or about forty-five thousand men, were tasked with seizing seven major bridges and numerous smaller bridges and canals and securing the major road that would be used by the advancing ground forces.[3]

The 101st Airborne Division's objectives were spread over a fifteen-mile stretch of road that the paratroopers named Hell's Highway. They were to seize a bridge over the Wilhelmina Canal at the small town of Son, grab two shorter bridges over the Dommel River at St. Oedenrode, and then take four bridges over the Aa River at Veghel. The mission assigned to the 82nd Airborne was to first capture Europe's longest bridge at Grave, seize and hold the ground around Groesbeek against a German counterattack that would originate from the nearby Reichswald forest, grab at least one of four bridges over the Maas-Waal Canal, and finally take the main bridge over the Waal River in Nijmegen.

Once past Nijmegen, XXX Corps would proceed to Arnhem, the final bridge over the Lower Rhine and a gateway into northern Germany and the Ruhr. The bridge at Arnhem was assigned to the British 1st Airborne Division, which was reinforced later by the Polish Parachute Brigade.

MARKET-GARDEN began on the sunny Sunday afternoon of September 17. It was the Allies' most accurate major parachute assault of the war in Europe: The 82nd drops were 89 percent accurate, and the 101st dropped in parade-ground fashion, making it the division's best jump either in combat or in training. The British operation, too, was almost 100 percent accurate.[4]

Once on the ground, the 101st moved quickly on its objectives. The 501st Parachute Infantry Regiment (PIR) grabbed road bridges over the Willems Canal and the Aa River. The 502nd PIR seized a bridge over the Dommel River at St. Oedenrode. Farther south along Hell's Highway, the 506th Regiment was under direct fire from German artillery and was temporarily held up at Son. After clearing the town and knocking out its 88-mm artillery pieces, the paratroopers came within fifty yards of the Son bridge only to see it destroyed by the retreating Germans. Destruction of the bridge had little effect on XXX Corps, which arrived two days later and replaced the bridge with an Erector Set–looking temporary span known as a Bailey bridge. But when XXX Corps armor finally rumbled across on D plus two it was at least thirty-three hours behind schedule. Delays, largely due to the narrow two-lane road linking the airborne corridor, had pushed the timetable far behind schedule—and time in general was running out for the entire operation.

At the southern end of Hell's Highway was Eindhoven and the linkup point with British ground forces. On the morning of September 18, the 101st battled a garrison of German troops, and Eindhoven was in the Allies' hands around noon.[5]

To the north, the 82nd Airborne Division landed in a twenty-five-mile airhead between the Dutch cities of Nijmegen and Grave. The 82nd's 504th Parachute Regiment quickly seized the large bridge over the Maas River at Grave and captured another bridge at Heuman. The 82nd's next D-Day objective was to take at least one of the four principal bridges across the Maas-Waal Canal. After overcoming heavy German resistance, the Americans seized two bridges; the two others were destroyed by the Germans.[6] The bulk of the 82nd was taking up defensive positions along the high ground around Groesbeek to contain a German counterattack from the Reichswald. Specifically, the 505th captured Groesbeek and occupied defensive positions near Reithorst and Mook (towns a few miles west of Nijmegen) where the regiment encountered heavy resistance. The 508th occupied high ground around Berg en Dal. By the end of D-Day, the 82nd had captured all of its D-Day objectives.[7]

But for the next three days, both divisions had to fight for their lives, maintaining their ground to keep Hell's Highway and the bridges open for XXX Corps, still lagging behind schedule. Glider reinforcements started to trickle in, but weather delayed several glider landings. The 325th Regiment, for instance, landed on D plus six, five days behind schedule. German opposition at the landing zones was also a problem: The fields were cleared as the gliders were landing. The 101st's sector deteriorated into what Major General Maxwell Taylor called "Indian-style" fighting, with the 101st playing the role of the U.S. cavalry as they pushed westward into Indian country.[8] The 101st had to put together highly mobile task forces to deal with recurrent German thrusts on the highway. The 101st courageously held the road open, by means of highly mobile task forces that moved instantly on trouble spots, but over the course of the next week and a half the Germans were able to cut Hell's Highway in several places for short periods. The Screaming Eagles also achieved major victories near the Best St. Oedenrode area (west of Son), killing or capturing nineteen hundred German troops, and the 501st Parachute delivered a crushing defeat to the German paratroopers of the Jungwirth Battalion, massing to counterattack Veghel.[9]

Meanwhile, the British 1st Parachute Division at the final bridge at Arnhem ran into two understrength SS panzer divisions named Hohenstaufen (9th SS Panzer) and Frundsberg (10th SS Panzer). Both were top-notch units with combat experience in Normandy and on the Eastern Front. The British paratroopers could only manage to get one of three battalions across to secure the northern end of the bridge, and bitter street fighting ensued as the SS regained control of Arnhem.

The climax of the battle was on September 20. The long bridge at Nijmegen had to be seized by the 82nd or the offensive would fail. For the previous three days the 82nd had been trying to seize the highway and the less-remembered railroad bridge at Nijmegen while the Germans furiously resisted and continued to strengthen their defenses around the bridges. Moreover, starting on September 18 and continuing on September 20, the Germans

MARKET-GARDEN and Airborne Operations in Holland—Sept.–Nov. 1944

Oosterbeek

XX
Ger | 9 SS Pz
Hohenstaufen

Supplies

Arnhem

XX
Br. 1st Abn.
Urquhart

4th Para.
Bde.
Sept. 18

1st Air Landing Bde.
1st Para. Bde.
Sept. 17

GERMANY

9

Zetten

Ger | 10 SS Pz
Frundsberg

XX

Opheusden

Waal R.

Sept. 21
Pol. 1st Bde.

The Island

5

Reichswald

XX
U.S. 82nd Abn.
Gavin

Nijmegen

Wyler

508 PIR

4

504 PIR

Mook

505
PIR

8

Lower Rhine R.

Groesbeek

7

HOLLAND

3

Sept. 17

Grave

Heuman Reithorst

Maas R.

Waal R.

Maas R.

N

s' Hertogenbosch

501 PIR

"Hell's Highway"

XX
U.S. 101st Abn.
Taylor

Aa R.

Veghel

Sept. 17

6 Koevering

St. Oedenrode

Dommel R.

502
PIR

Son

Best

1 506 PIR

Sept. 17

2

Wilhelmina
Canal

Eindhoven

Willems Canal

⊘	British DZs and LZs
⬤	Polish DZs
⊜	U. S. 82nd DZs and LZs
⊕	U. S. 101st DZs and LZs
⍦	Parachute Drop
←	German Attacks
←	Allied Advances

1 | Don Burgett, *506th, 101st*
2 | Charles "Sandy" Santarsiero,
   506th PIR, 101st
3 | Joe Watts, *504th PIR, 82nd*
4 | John Hardie, *508th PIR, 82nd*
5 | Delbert Kuehl, *504th, 82nd*
6 | Don Burgett, *506th, 101st*
7 | Ray Gonzalez, *505th PIR, 82nd*
8 | Lee Travelstead, *325th GIR, 82nd*
9 | Glen Derber, *501st PIR, 101st*

Meuse-Escaut Canal

XXX
Br | **XXX**
Horrocks

BELGIUM

0 _____ 10
Miles

had launched their own large-scale attacks along Hell's Highway and were pouring out of the Reichswald forest and attacking the 82nd's thin defenses along the high ground around Groesbeek. Outnumbered, the 82nd was able to hold by counterattacking, shifting men around to plug holes in the line.[10]

The plan to take the bridges at Nijmegen was straightforward on paper: Attack the bridge from both sides. The hard part was getting to the other side. Using elements of the 504th's 3rd Battalion, the paratroopers crossed the Waal River in collapsible canvas British assault boats. With XXX Corps' ground attack creeping along at a snail's pace, the boats were launched at Nijmegen on the afternoon of September 20.

At midafternoon, what some have called the "second Omaha Beach" began, and twenty-six overloaded boats carrying hundreds of paratroopers crossed the Waal River under heavy fire. Artillery, 20-mm rounds, and machine gun bullets tore into the flimsy canvas boats, many capsizing or sinking in the Waal with scores of men wounded or killed. Only eleven of the twenty-six boats made it back to pick up another wave of paratroopers.[11]

Once on the other side of the Waal, the paratroopers surged forward, destroying machine gun nests and silencing Fort Hof van Holland, which was bristling with 20-mm antiaircraft and machine guns. The paratroopers then were able to capture the north end of the main highway bridge and converge on the north end of the railroad bridge.

The 505th Parachute, supported by British tanks, stormed the south side of the highway bridge until at approximately 7:00 P.M., the bridge, still crammed with high explosives, fell to the Allies. Not until the next day did the railroad bridge finally fall. The Allies counted 267 German soldiers dead on the railroad bridge, along with thirty-four machine guns, two 20-mm antiaircraft guns, and an 88-mm dual-purpose gun.[12]

After the highway bridge was captured, the British tanks halted. The men who risked their lives to capture the bridges were frustrated and infuriated by the order not to move forward after the tremendous sacrifices that were made to capture the bridges.[13] The British waited until September 22 (D plus five) to roll the final eleven miles to Arnhem and link up with the Polish Parachute Brigade, which was on the western side of the Lower Rhine, but it was too late. By the twentieth, D plus three, the SS units were in firm control of Arnhem, and by the twenty-first most of the 1st Airborne Division's three battalions in Arnhem were either killed or captured. All that remained of the 1st Airborne was a shrinking pocket around Oosterbeek, a suburb about a mile outside Arnhem.

On Monday, September 25, under the cover of darkness, several hundred British paratroopers were evacuated to the other side of the Rhine.

What was left of the 1st Airborne Division continued to trickle over to the Allied side of the Lower Rhine. The 1st Airborne Division's casualties were a staggering 79 percent.[14]

Around October 2, the 101st's portion of Hell's Highway was secure, but instead of returning to base camps, the division was moved up along a long, narrow stretch of land between the Lower Rhine and the Waal River that the troopers called the "Island." Meanwhile, the 82nd remained in its positions in front of the Reichswald. The static front deteriorated into trench warfare with trenchfoot caused by the cold and dampness and mounting casualties in both divisions. It wasn't until the middle of November that the final units in the 82nd departed from the area, on D plus fifty-seven, with most of the 101st leaving two weeks later.

MARKET-GARDEN was a defeat for the Allies, but it was one of the airborne's finest hours. The 82nd and 101st had achieved their objectives and won all of their battles and Germany's back was pressed ever more closely to the wall. In less than a month, however, the airborne would face its greatest challenge in the Battle of the Bulge.

DON BURGETT

506th Parachute Infantry Regiment, 101st Airborne Division

On the opening day of MARKET-GARDEN, the 101st's 506th Parachute Infantry Regiment tried to seize the main bridge at Son, as Don Burgett vividly remembers.

The Germans opened up on us with 88s; they wiped out about a third of my company. What made it so devastating was that the shells were hitting the trees and exploding. Shrapnel was coming down like a shotgun. One of our officers was killed instantly. When the shells hit we were all together. Men were falling all over the place. Dust was flying, limbs were flying, and bark was flying. You don't pick out individual faces when this is happening. Two men that I knew ran forward, they had a machine gun. They set it up and opened up. One of the 88s saw them and blew them apart. I don't think they found one of the men's heads until the second day. They were literally blown all to pieces.

One of my buddies, I didn't know that he was dead at first. I landed beside him and saw that he was dead. His head was split in half. The other half of his head was sticking up in a tree limb. The shells stopped exploding for a second and I rolled over and looked up into a tree and I saw part of his face and it still had his eye in it and he was staring down at me. I stood up and took my rifle and brought it down and put it inside his shirt and buttoned it up tight so that the graves registration that were taking care of the dead would find it.

We knew that we were in an outfit where we were all going to be killed. I felt that I couldn't get real close to anyone even though I considered many of these guys my brothers. If one of them got killed I went about my business. There's two things you have to do. You can't sit down and brood and cry when one of your closest buddies gets killed. Even though you think of him as a brother, when he gets killed, he's done and you move on.

I think you kind of bottle it up but you never forget it. I think about Bastogne where the dead were frozen on barbed wire and they stayed there for days and days. Someone asked me, "How can you remember all that?" I said, "How can you forget it?" I've talked to other combat men and they tell me that every night they see it, they remember it, and not an hour goes by that they don't remember it. You try to kind of deaden yourself to those things but it is always there. I remember the battles almost in great detail, for some reason. I may forget some people's names because we had so many replacements, but I remember what happened.

We organized and we began to charge the guns. The only way we were going to survive was to knock out the 88s even though a lot of us were going to die trying to do it. As we were running towards them they fired at us at point-blank range. We overran their positions. There were several 88s. They were sandbagged and dug in and used for antiaircraft. A trooper from D Company got in close enough and fired a bazooka and knocked out one of the guns. That left two 88s on the north side of the canal. There was another 88 on the south side of the canal but it was in an upward position; it had never been used against us.

We overran the 88s, took the German gunners prisoner, and someone said, "Let's take the bridge." We started to run towards the bridge. We were within yards of the bridge when the Germans blew it up. It went off with quite a force. I heard later that someone said two five-hundred-pound aerial bombs went off. We hit the ground. I rolled over on my back because everything got real quiet and I saw the debris in the air. I remember seeing this tiny straw that was turning so slowly way up in the air and as it hit its maximum trajectory and it started to come down, it became larger and larger. About halfway down we realized the size of this thing. It was probably about two feet wide and forty feet long. There was no place to run. When it hit the ground, the ground shook like Jell-O. It was one of the main wooden beams from the bridge. Both sides had stopped firing for a couple of seconds when the bridge blew up to take cover.

We then started firing again. At this time Major LaParade came up and I think he had his first sergeant with him. He didn't hesitate; he jumped into the water and started swimming to the other side. The first sergeant joined him and we gave them covering fire. Some of the Germans on the other side withdrew and some were still firing. We managed to get at least three ropes across and we built a little lattice that we could put our feet in to get across. We started going across one at a time while the Germans were firing on us. We created a bridgehead on the other side and the Germans slowly started pulling back.

CHARLES "SANDY" SANTARSIERO

506th Parachute Infantry Regiment, 101st Airborne Division

From overnight positions north of Eindhoven, Lieutenant Charles "Sandy" Santarsiero was to spearhead the 506th Regiment's attack on the city where the 101st would link up with British tanks from XXX Corps. In Normandy, Santarsiero had been recommended for the Medal of Honor, later downgraded to the Distinguished Service. Here he discusses his experiences in the attack on Eindhoven.

You bottle it all up and try to fight it. I fought it the hard way, believe me. I worked hard to try and get it out of my system. I was always active. If you took all that [death] in, you'd go nuts. What you did was close your eyes like it didn't happen. Believe it or not, this is the scary thing, you'd see somebody laying there in the mud, torn apart, and you'd look at him and you'd feel sorry for him but, "Thank God that isn't me." The selfish thing—"that isn't me." You washed it out. It was inside of you and it stayed inside you, and if you were able to cope with it, back then you were thrown right back into society, no counseling or anything.

The last time I got hit [wounded in combat], it laid me up for three years and two months in the army hospital, seventeen operations. The ten years after that, it was tough. I would walk down the street and I'd see a face there and say, "Jeez, that's one guy that I knifed or killed." That kind of stuff always stayed with you.

I took a job with a power company, and I used to work twelve, fifteen hours a day to try and tire myself out to get a good night's sleep but I slept very lightly. I'd wake up in the morning and have sheets ripped (my wife used to go nuts!). After about fifteen years of this I gradually got out of it and said, "To hell with this."

I talked to one of the officers who got out and went to Korea and shortly after that he ended up in the hospital in the nut ward. He told me, "Charlie, when they sent me to Korea, I was scared to death. I didn't think I could lead the men or anything because everything was happening so fast," and he cracked up. He then told me that the doctor said to him: "Look around. This hospital is filled with men from World War II. You're not alone." That was enough for him, and it snapped him out of it. When he told it to me it helped me also.

We were on the drop zone when someone was hollering, "Lieutenant!" When he came by, I tackled him. I said, "Jesus, when Germans are around you don't go hollering for a lieutenant." I said, "What do you want?" He said, "Colonel Sink wants to see you. He's up at the CP." I followed him and he went to the river, the first river of the canal where Captain Davis was supposed to take that bridge at Son before going into Eindhoven.

I went right into where the bridge was. It was nighttime, about ten o'clock. I went into the room, and there was Colonel Sink, General Taylor, a whole bunch of majors, all kinds of brass, and here I am a piss-ass first lieutenant coming in, and they're all looking at me wondering, "What does he want with him?" . . . No one said a word to me—I was dressed like a GI, no one could tell I was an officer. I carried an M-1, bandoliers of ammunition; my field glasses were hidden.

The colonel explained that Captain Davis, they [the Germans] blew the bridge on him and he sustained enough casualties in his company that it was ineffective as a fighting unit. Sink told me, "What I want you to do, I want you to go back and get your men." I had forty men, and he said, "You be the first to cross a wooden bridge. They tore a house down and put boards across the river, and you get your men on the other side." He said, "Tomorrow morning, at your discretion, when you think it's right, you lead the attack in Eindhoven." So I said, "Colonel, we have plans. Do you want plan A or plan B?" Colonel Sink said, "No, you punch the holes, Charlie, and I'll pour the men in."

At daybreak, when the mist was just rising, we headed towards the town. It must have been five hundred yards before we could get to a building where there was cover. We didn't have any artillery; we didn't use artillery on the town because it was a friendly town. I started the attack on the double, as much as we could go, and we'd pick up a German here and there, and I could see Germans getting out of their foxholes, running into the buildings. When I got close to a church I spotted a German in the church steeple and I waited for my men to catch up because I always lead from the front, I was old-fashioned. I was scout, and that's the way I lead my men, they followed me.

So I'm waiting for them to catch up to my flank, and Captain Kiley, a very close friend of mine, he just made captain, appears right on this corner where I'm standing. He's dressed in his uniform with his bars showing, binoculars, he was carrying map cases. Well I saw him, and being close friends, I started cursing at him: "What the hell are you doing up here. Go back where the hell you belong." "Sandy," he said, "There's not many of us old-timers left, and I worry about you because every time we start an attack and it bogs down, they bring you up to lead the attack for us." I stepped away from him, and he got one right in the neck where I was standing, killed.

If you think about something like this you'd go out of your mind. All you do is turn around and curse at him for doing such a thing to get it out of your system. I continued on through, and we went into the town. The Germans had two 88s in the town, and I went up the main street, and a pair of machine guns opened up on us. They were just spraying us. There was a foxhole right in the middle of the street, and a German ran out of there to go into a building. I jumped into the foxhole and I hollered back to my men, "Pass up the light machine gun." They passed up the light machine gun, and I started opening up on the Krauts, and where I was the corner of the building disintegrated. The bricks hit me and a guy behind me. I continued firing and they fired another [artillery shell], the same thing. I continued on up the road on a search; they fired another one and the projectile hit in front of me. It went over my head, whiz, whiz, whiz, and it hit the building and it was white phosphorus. Then I realized they were firing direct fire from an 88 at me, like a rifle. I looked around and spotted the 88 up the road and started coming up on them, and they left and ran into the buildings. Then I had one of my men set up the mortar because I knew there was another 88 around the corner and I had to drop a couple of mortar rounds in there.

About that time there was a battalion commander, he just made battalion commander, comes up to me and he's chewing my ass out something terrible that I'm blowing buildings up and they're on our side. I got so goddamn mad: "That building there [is] where the 88 tried to blow me the hell out of the way. If you've got something to say, say it to the dead trooper right in the street!" It was one of the men I couldn't save, he was in the doorway and the Kraut was on the other side, my side, and he was shooting at him and I hollered at him, "Get out of there, come over here!" When I said that he stood there and hesitated and got hit in the door. By the time he moved he got hit in the kidneys and fell right in the street; he was dead.

As we were going, Colonel Sink sent the 3rd Battalion, to make the flanking move. While he was making the flanking move, I held up my fire because I saw troopers coming in my line of fire. The Germans all started giving up. We started to move out, and there was about forty or fifty surrendering there. My men passed by the one German that I had shot in the stomach, he was hollering for help, and two of [the dead American soldier's] closest friends saw him laying in the street and they went over and gave him the bayonet, they just cracked up. They saw their friends killed and they didn't have any mercy.

We moved up to the defensive position. We got out of the town and we went to different defensive positions. That night the Germans came over and they bombed Eindhoven. That upset the people because they thought we pulled out because we knew the place was going to get bombed. The next morning you couldn't find an American flag. It was explained to them, and they [American flags] started coming back out.

JOE WATTS

504th Parachute Infantry Regiment, 82nd Airborne Division

One of the most significant D-Day objectives for the airborne units was the enormous Maas River bridge at Grave. The nine-span bridge, the largest in Europe at the time, fell quickly to the 504th because the drops had been so accurate. In his e-history, Joe Watts remembers the capture of the bridge.

As we closed on the northern end of the Maas River bridge, it was now a couple of hundred yards to our left front, we began to get incoming small-arms fire from just beyond the bridge structure near the river. We didn't get any mortar fire—we could hear mortars coming from someplace, but they weren't directed at us, evidently, but small-arms fire kept coming over. We would hear the crack and this stuff passed over us—none of it hit the ground, so evidently they were shooting too high. We may not have been the target, I don't know.

When we arrived at the north end of the bridge, we assisted clearing the flak tower; we found several dead Germans whose demise we attributed to aircraft strafing earlier in the day. Looking up, we could see B-24 Liberators passing overhead parachuting bundles from their bomb bays onto our DZ.

Across the river through the bridge girders we watched as at least one truckload of German soldiers and another vehicle came out of Grave and headed for the [southern approach to the] bridge. For the first time that day I was scared. Now all we needed were panzers, I thought. It seemed too far for us to take them under fire, but someone did because the truck swerved across the road and rolled off the east side, the Grave side, of the road. A few enemy soldiers scattered, running toward town. As we brought fire on them, enemy fire came out of the town toward us. We were taking fire from the town and initially from the bridge girders high up where at least two German snipers tied themselves to the girders. I kept firing my Thompson submachine gun into the girders at them as we made our way to the flak tower by running on the dike shoulders, then across the bridge, using girders as shelter.

I was following right behind Lieutenant Middleton for a while. Bullets and fragments were buzzing all around us—then I saw him get hit in the hand by a ricochet off a girder. We bandaged it. He said it hurt but he didn't need my help. The lieutenant already had been issued four Purple Hearts, the latest from Anzio. Therefore, I put more space between us; I ran ahead. If he was the target, I didn't want to be too close to him.

As we jogged and dodged across the last of the nine spans, we were running out of places to hide. Even though it was getting dark about now, we were still drawing fire from the direction of Grave. Fortunately, a friendly someone was standing at the base of the south flak tower warning us of mines off the dike shoulder to the west, at the base of the flak tower, right where I was headed. We then learned that John Thompson's [E Company] platoon had taken that tower and had taken out the north tower using the gun from the south tower.

An hour later it was dark, but by then the bridge was secured—we had the entire 2nd Battalion, about four hundred men, on the south side of the Maas River outposting the town of Grave and the bridge and patrolling to the east and west, awaiting the arrival of the British XXX Corps that was scheduled to relieve us two days later. Three of us patrolled into town to contact E Company. But they [E Company] weren't in the town. We later learned they were in a bistro down the main road about a hundred yards drinking and living it up with the locals. We found the people of Grave to be generous and kind.

That concluded our first day of Operation MARKET-GARDEN, with the Maas River bridge—the longest span bridge in Europe at that time, nine spans—in our hands.

JOHN HARDIE

508ᵗʰ Parachute Infantry Regiment, 82ⁿᵈ Airborne Division

On September 18, one day after the jump, B and C companies of the 508ᵗʰ Parachute Infantry Regiment were ordered to leave Nijmegen and proceed to glider landing zones outside the city to clear them of the Germans who would try to prevent the 82ⁿᵈ's reinforcements from landing. In one of the most remarkable small-unit actions of the war, Sergeant Leonard Funk, who would later become America's most decorated paratrooper, and three other paratroopers led a charge across that knocked out seven German 20-mm guns, killing their crews and taking several prisoners. John Hardie, a member of Funk's crew, recalls that day.[15]

We got hung up on a road; there was a lot of fire. Then, as often happens, one of the older men in our company, who we called Bones, got shot in the head and throat and died instantly. With that it triggered Funk [the squad leader] to stand up and shout, "Let's go!"

We started to cross the landing zone. We had four men: Funk, R. J. Smith, Bob Hupp, and myself. We took off across the open field. We swept across the landing zone and knocked out as many guns as we could, killing people and taking prisoners. People have asked me how many people were killed and how many guns we knocked out—I don't know. People that have studied this action say that there were about thirty people killed, forty prisoners taken, and seven or eight guns knocked down. I couldn't attest to that on my own. I just know that we kept moving fast and Funk was up front. We got out in front of C Company.

Within minutes the other companies starting sweeping across with us. Before we made our sweep across the field, the other companies were engaged in firefights across the landing zone. We swept through the field, aiming to get across it. There were guns positioned all around the field. The gliders were overhead.

We worked together well; we were all C Company men. C Company and B Company came up after us, and they really mopped up. The whole battalion could see us, because years later people would come up to us and ask if we were in C Company and ask if we were in that action. The guys from gliders came up to us and were cheering and said, "Thank you." We didn't think much of it; we were just doing our job. People ask me what did I do. And I just say, "I was doing what I was supposed to do." I was trained well and I was platoon sergeant. Actually, before that action I was busted back to private for something that I did. So I was acting platoon sergeant but actually only a buck private.

Leonard Funk was the most outstanding man that I ever met. People that don't know Funk but read his awards and citations would have a misinterpretation of what they would expect to meet. They would probably expect this huge ogre of a man, but he was about five foot five and a half and 130 pounds; he was a tremendous combat soldier. Anything that accosted him, he was going to go forward regardless.

Any discussions that I have had probably in the last year or so have only been with people that I served with. I generally wouldn't discuss it with anybody. I had two brothers in the service, and we all had our own individual experiences. We never talked about ourselves. Why? Because I thought there was an awful lot of skepticism: People wouldn't believe what you told them anyway. People would have no concept of the whole thing. I told somebody that my first sergeant was the most highly decorated paratrooper; people would just look at me with a blank stare. I bottled it up inside. It wasn't until many years later when I started to go to the 82nd Airborne reunions and we'd start to talk about it. I never dwelled on the heroics of one person or the horrors of war; I'd always try to pick out some hilarious moment and talk about that.

People don't understand the ugliness, the dirtiness of the war. I will tell you about the most devastating experience that I had. A guy that was right alongside of me, a very close friend of mine, had his head blown off. The ugliness that I felt was within me. [Chokes up.] I felt, "Better him than me." That's an awful, horrible feeling to have.

DELBERT KUEHL

504th Parachute Infantry Regiment, 82nd Airborne Division

On September 20, 1944, the fate of Operation MARKET-GARDEN rested on whether American paratroopers could seize the Nijmegen bridge before the Germans could destroy it. A daring daylight crossing of the Waal River was planned to capture the bridge, as Chaplain Delbert Kuehl relates.

I went to a wooded area in the evening and overheard several of our officers talking about how we were going to cross the river and take the bridges from the rear. While I overheard all of this they also mentioned that we were going to be using British boats. At the time I thought the boats would have to have some sort of armor and power since we had to cross a wide river with a strong current that was heavily defended on the other side.

I didn't have to go on the mission since I was the regimental chaplain, but I thought that this was going to be very difficult for our men, so I decided I was going to go. The colonel didn't know about it at the time. He found out about it when he went across (Colonel Tucker went across in the second wave), and he was really upset with me.

They decided to make the river crossing the next day. I thought we'd do it at night, under the cover of darkness, but they said we had to reach the 1st British Airborne troopers that were being decimated by armor in Arnhem.

We waited for the boats to come and I couldn't believe it when the British were unloading the boats off their trucks: They were canvas folding boats that you had to put pins in the sides to keep them up. I then asked how they were propelled; the response was "canoe paddles." On the opposite side of the river the Germans had dug in machine guns, mortars, and artillery support. I remember thinking to myself, How are we going to cross the river in canvas boats powered by canoe paddles?

So we sat near the riverbank. By that time we had been through a lot of combat: Sicily, the mountain fighting in Italy, and Anzio. We knew a little bit about war. I remember that we all looked at each other and said this was a suicide mission if we had ever seen one. I decided to go, thinking to myself that if there ever was a time that the men may need a chaplain it was now. One of the officers that I was with said, "I have no chance of getting across," so he threw away his pack of cigarettes and Zippo lighter.

When the boats came and we were ready to cross, we were supposed to have a smoke screen. The Air Corps came over and dropped some before we were ready to start. By the time we reached the riverbank with the boats, the smoke was gone. We were out there in broad daylight with no cover. We put the boats in the river. It was very muddy at the edge of the river, and the boats got stuck. Some of us had to jump out and push them out farther, and that delayed us.

Luckily we did surprise the Germans. We did have overhead fire from our second platoon from the bank on our side. There were also some British tanks that were providing some fire. While we crossed it looked like it was raining on the river, there was so much fire. The next thing I knew I heard a groan and glanced over and saw the man sitting shoulder to shoulder next to me had been hit by a 20-mm shell. The top of his head was sheared off and you could see inside his skull.

At this time Major Cook (the commander of the first wave of boats), whose boat I was in, was praying in a loud voice: "Hail, Mary, full of grace. Hail, Mary, full of grace. Hail, Mary, full of grace." He later told me that he was trying to say the rosary but that was all that came out.

I kept paddling until I was gasping for breath and kept praying: "Lord, thy will be done. Lord, thy will be done." It seemed like ages before we made it to the other side!

As I recall, of the twenty-six boats, only thirteen made it across. There were dead and wounded in each boat. I remember one boat that reached the bank had four dead troopers draped across each other. There were dead and wounded men all over the place.

I carried a first-aid kit and immediately began working on the wounded. While I was leaning over a trooper who had three bullet holes in his stomach, a mortar shell exploded behind me. I was hit by shrapnel, which hit my back, knocking me down. Despite being seriously wounded, the man cried out: "Chaplain, they got you, too?" That was the kind of men we had.

The men that made it bayoneted the machine gunners dug in all along the riverbank. They didn't pause; they bayoneted and bayoneted and took off for the bridge. I have never seen such bravery.

Many officers and men were killed. I Company lost about 50 percent of its men, and H Company lost about the same. They never hesitated for a

Nijmegen Bridge and the Waal River. (Photo courtesy Joe Pangerl)

minute. When they didn't have an officer, a noncom took over. Nobody ever stopped. They took the railroad and Nijmegen bridges.

DON BURGETT

506th Parachute Infantry Regiment, 101st Airborne Division

On the afternoon of September 24, the Germans cut Hell's Highway at Koevering, destroying a British convoy. Don Burgett describes the carnage and the 101st's efforts to drive back the Germans.

The trucks were all shot to pieces; they were all burning. Bodies were scattered around. The trucks had been looted; things were thrown out of them. Explosions had turned some of them over and they spilled out whatever they were carrying—ammunition, food. It was just like going back to the Indian

German paratroopers from the 6th Fallschirmjäger Regiment in Holland, September 1944. Throughout the war the elite 6th would be an archnemesis to both the airborne and Rangers. (Photo courtesy Heinrich Fugmann)

wars where the cavalry was coming up to the wagon train where it was just totally destroyed and the people were all murdered. You come up on this situation and the first thing that you see are the small green flies. Not black houseflies but small green flies. They come in right away and they are on the bodies laying eggs for maggots, laying them in the mouth and wounds. You notice the smell; I can still smell it to this day. The smell of fresh blood, the smell of iron. You can smell death. When you are in battle and even before you enter you can smell death.

The Germans kept cutting the highway. The last great cut was at Koevering. German paratroopers from the 6th Regiment attacked from both sides of the road. What we had to do was run back and be like a cavalry charge coming back down the road. We were on foot and we had to fight them, drive them back, and secure the area. By the time we got that secured they would cut it at another place three miles north of us and then we'd have to divide our forces and go back and forth. This is what you call Indian-style fighting.

We were on a full march going up to Nijmegen and we had passed through St. Oedenrode up through Koevering. We had just passed through the British convoy [at Koevering] and they were brewing tea. We got up to Veghel and we had to fight for that town. The Germans had cut that. So we fought and we were just clearing out the north end of that town and we made a big sweep around and we thought we had wiped out the last Germans that were in the area; we took a lot of prisoners. Then we got word that the Germans had cut the road again at Koevering.

Germans brought up some 40-mm cannons and they had some self-propelled guns and they shot the British who were lined up on the side of the road and they were brewing tea in these five-gallon tins and the Germans just opened up on them. They killed over three hundred.

When we got down to Koevering, the trucks were still burning. It had been raining most of the time and we had been fighting all this time, plus the march, and we had to almost double-time all the way back to Koevering. We went into the attack immediately. I remember we killed two Germans in a haystack. Then we made an attack west across the road to a farmhouse. The farmhouse was set on fire. We went into the German side and we drove them back.

We'd gone about two days with nothing to eat. I saw this British soldier laying there, of course there was a bunch of them, but this one soldier was laying on a bunch of Cadbury chocolate bars that had spilled out of one of the trucks and their tins of tea were knocked over and their rations were out; they were going to have dinner. I couldn't help myself—we were hungry—I grabbed this English soldier and rolled him off the candy bars and I started stuffing my jump jacket full of candy bars.

We went on across the road and fought through that night; there was no letup. The next day we went on the attack again. We finally got things settled and we were in the back of this farm and one of our men saw what looked like a round basketball up in the trees—by this time the trees were starting to lose their leaves. It turned out to be this big round of cheese that the Dutch had hidden up in the tops of the trees so the Germans wouldn't find it. We shot the branches out and the cheese came down. [laughs.]

[On the Island a week or so later] the battles went back and forth; the Germans were sending in troops from one side and we were holding the other side and it was just like a meat grinder. Men were going in and they were just getting butchered.

One of our guys who was brought in on a stretcher, they laid him down by a windmill and as they laid him down shells started coming in and he got hit and it just blew him away from the belly-button down; it was gone. He was conscious. He's your best buddy and you know he's not going to live but you can't shoot him, he's conscious. We always carried little syrettes of morphine; I had a whole pocket full. That's another thing where we differed; infantry wasn't allowed to carry that or maybe they had one of them. We took what we wanted. Anyways, the closest men to him, they all jabbed him, he must have been jabbed eleven times with the morphine. Right away he went under and died. That was the best you could do for him.

RAY GONZALEZ

505th Parachute Infantry Regiment, 82nd Airborne Division

On September 24, the Germans were once again mounting heavy attacks from the Reichswald near the small town of Reithorst, Holland.

I got about a dozen medals from France and Belgium and Holland, a Silver Star and Bronze Stars; I've got all these medals, and I put them in my trunk and I never did open it. One time in 1969, my daughters were down the basement and they opened this trunk up and they saw all these papers and medals and they said, "Dad, we didn't know you were in the army." I said, "I wasn't." I just didn't want to remember it. I try to forget it but I can't forget it. [Crying.]

It's something you try and forget, but every day, every night you think of it. You can never get it out of your mind. I go to sleep now and tears run down my eyes because I just didn't want to be in the war. I closed that trunk and tried to close a part of my life. Right now my face is full of tears talking about it because I never talk to anybody about it. I tell my boys, they say, "What did you do in the war, Dad?" I said I was a paratrooper. They said, "That was kind of a hardcore deal, wasn't it?" I said, "Yeah." They said, "Tell us, what did you do?" I said, "Well, I just didn't do nothing, I just fought. It was just kill or be killed, whatever."

You can't hardly describe the battles because you have to be there. You can't just say, "Oh, I killed that guy and I killed that guy," you have to be there to see what it's like. You just can't describe war. I guess one way to describe it is go get somebody, get a gun, and shoot them and watch them squirm. That's how horrible it was.

It was just a horrible, horrible sight to see thousands upon thousands upon thousands of soldiers stacked up like wood [in Normandy]. They were dead. Some of them were rolling in the water, coming in the beachhead. There were guys hollering for their mother, hollering for their father, hollering for their wives. You just couldn't hardly believe it. I think I was just so goddamn mad that I wanted to kill everything. They [paratroopers] would say, "Take this prisoner back to headquarters." But there was no headquar-

Ray Gonzalez in Normandy (Photo courtesy of Ray Gonzalez)

ters, I had to take care of them myself, I had to feed them and give them water. I said, "Bullshit, I'm not taking them back," so I just let them have it. I'm old and I just don't tolerate that stuff anymore. I still feel so bad because I remember a young soldier, he couldn't have been more than seventeen or eighteen, and he begged me not to shoot him but I shot him anyways. I still feel so bad about it.

[In Holland] we were getting attacked every day. On the twenty-fourth, we were being relieved by the 325th [Glider Infantry Regiment]. While we were pulling back we were getting a lot of machine gun and sniper fire. [Someone in the platoon] said Breyers got hit. I said, "Well I didn't see him." He said, "He's right up there by that hill." Everybody left because we were under heavy fire and weren't supposed to bring the wounded out; we left them there and the [medics] would take care of them. But I wasn't going to leave him behind, so I threw my knapsack down and I went over there and said, "How ya doing, Breyers?" He said, "Okay." I said, "I'm not leaving you. They told me to move out, but I'm not moving." He said, "Move out, soldier." I said, "I'm not moving."

In D-Day I had lost my toothbrush, and Breyers loaned me his toothbrush to brush my teeth, and that's how close we were. He was a kid that I used to hang around in camp with and go to town and drink a couple of beers, played baseball and football. He was just like a brother to me.

I stayed with him and he said, "Ray, you don't have to stay here." I said, "I'm staying."

I stayed there for about four hours with him and it was getting dusk and I told him, "I'm going back to camp and get some help." He was hit in the back. I went back and got some help and some men in a jeep to take care of Breyers.

As I was walking through fields to find my company and I found another kid from K Company that I knew and he was wounded, he had his knee knocked out, and he asked me not to leave him. I said I wouldn't leave him.

Eventually, I put one arm over my shoulder and I grabbed his belt and picked him up. I picked him up and put him over my shoulder, and his wounded knee was right by my face, and all he could do was squirt blood on me. I walked with him for about a half-hour; all I wanted to do was get away from that shell, they were shelling the shit out of us. Found another wounded man and tried to help him, also. I said, "Well, let's try and get out of here." I picked him up and I fell down with him and hurt his knee and said, "I don't think I can go any farther. I'm going to go over here to find some help." And he said, "Okay, Gonzalez." He thanked me, and I never did know what happened to him.

I stayed by the two men that got hit. I just forget it because it would wear you out to keep thinking of it. I live in a great country. I love my country. I hope we never have to have any more wars.

LEE TRAVELSTEAD

325th Glider Infantry Regiment, 82nd Airborne Division

On September 23, the 325th Glider Infantry Regiment finally landed in Holland. Weather had delayed the landing for five days, but once on the ground the regiment was quickly thrust into combat. The glidermen relieved the 505th in positions and an attack was drawn up to clear the Germans from the part of the Reichswald known as Kiekberg Woods. The first attack was launched on September 27 and was repelled by the Germans. At 8.00 A.M. on September 30 the 325th attacked again, and, as the Germans and Americans became entangled in the woods, one of the strangest incidents of the war occurred. Lee Travelstead remembers the incident.

We were attacking the Germans in woods. The whole scene was more like we read about combat in Vietnam, because you couldn't see anyone anywhere and all of the sudden they [Germans] all rose up around us. We were surrounded. We were all scattered like you would be in an attack; we weren't all bunched together. Where I was in the group there were maybe a half a dozen men. The woods were extremely dense with the undergrowth, the tree canopy, and the ground cover, all of it—the leaves had not fallen off. You couldn't see much of anything. There was a lot of excitement and noise going on. As I stepped over a ridge, a German sniper fired at me at and put a hole through the top of my helmet. I rubbed my head to see if I was hit; it didn't even graze my scalp.

I had been in since Normandy. But at this time we had a larger group of replacements than we ever had, so I would say offhand some had never been under fire before. It made it more confusing than ever, plus the fact that when we went into Normandy we'd been training together for a couple of years and everyone knew each other real well. But at this stage we had a lot of replacements. Outside of the few noncommissioned officers and a few of the officers that had returned from Normandy, some of them had just returned from the hospital even; we didn't know each other too well. It was a different kind of situation than it had been in Normandy, where it was almost like a family fighting. This was an army—people on the same mission but unknown to each other, our capabilities and so forth.

It was startling: We saw the Germans right in front of us. We had been in all kinds of attacks including fighting in the hedgerows and everything, but this was the first time we had been face to face with the enemy. It was something different and really something we had never trained for like we had for hedgerows, dropping by the gliders, and so forth and so on. It was just dense woods and all of a sudden there they were. I guess the Germans thought they were shooting at themselves and we thought we were shooting at ourselves, and all of a sudden everybody just stopped [shooting].

What I remember vaguely was that I was sort of in the middle of this and at that time I felt like I was one of the only people there. There were probably other people who were just as conscious as I was, but you were so concentrated on what you were doing that you think that you are the only one there even though there were people around. I was one of the ones who tried to converse with the Germans. I had a messenger with me who spoke some German; he was a German-American and we always used him for an interpreter. He was shouting at these guys and they were shouting back at us and finally he said, "You surrender!" And they said, "You surrender!" Vice versa. It was almost a comedy of errors: Nobody knew what to do, and all of the sudden you just stop fighting. It was very strange; it was such a commotion.

All of a sudden a youthful SS sergeant stood up and approached and repeated, "You have surrendered." A few seconds later a Hollywood version of an SS captain approached. He had the boots, medals, dress cap, and a saber scar on his face. Meanwhile we both sent word for our respective units to cease fire.

Attempting to bluff the SS captain, we told him he was surrounded. He seemed slightly amused and drew a "U" in the palm of his hand indicating our supply routes and that nobody was surrounded. He told me, "You must bring your battalion commander and I will get mine to a place in the woods so we can recognize our maps."

We were all standing around talking to each other. Everybody was being friendly. There was nothing going on, so I guess everybody hoped since they didn't shoot at us and we didn't shoot at them, things were safe. Meanwhile, a German rifleman approached me and pointed to a bullet hole in my helmet and grinned with satisfaction, indicating his marksmanship. In our unit they had this crazy idea that they didn't have in other places: We had to show our officer's insignia prominently on the front of our helmets for everybody to see it a mile away if you had a telescope, making officers easy targets.

A few minutes later, my battalion commander arrived and through an interpreter began to converse with the German commander. He urged him to surrender, but the German officer emphasized that SS men do not surrender. Nonchalantly, he looked down at his watch and announced, "There will be a one-hour truce in which you can prepare a new attack." Both commanders saluted, and the German officer wanted to shake hands, but our battalion commander refused.

Both battalion commanders went back to their units, and we fell back a little way in the woods. It was getting dark by then, and we laid out our perimeter. That night we were hit with a terrible attack, and a number of officers and other men who had been in Normandy were killed or wounded that night.

GLEN DERBER

501st Parachute Infantry Regiment, 101st Airborne Division

During the war, Glen Derber kept a small diary (forbidden in case of capture by the enemy) in a small calendar book about two inches square. There were only three lines for each day, so comments on the day's events were kept brief. A year after the war he got out the diary and found that some days were already difficult to remember, so he decided to sit down and enlarge upon the details still fresh in his mind. Years later, he passed along the following e-mail statement, which describes life on the "Island," a strip of land between the Lower Rhine and the Waal River, between Nijmegen and Arnhem, on which conditions resembled those of the previous world war as much as the current.

We drove up "Hell's Highway" and through Nijmegen and across the Lower Rhine onto what was termed the "Island." After crossing the Nijmegen bridge, which had become a constant target for German artillery, we dismounted and dispersed in an orchard to await our march to the front, where we were to relieve the Limeys. They were glad to see us because the Germans had given them a pretty bad time of it. We started our march to the front late in the afternoon, and it was dark by the time we got there to move into our positions.

The Limeys had already pulled out before we got there, so had the Krauts known they could have walked right through us! I didn't get on the MLR [main line of resistance] that night but stayed back near the CP to furnish the "brass" some protection.

The next day I moved up to the MLR, which was on the reverse slope of a dike. The dike was anywhere from fifteen to twenty feet high with a macadam road on the top of it. I had to work my way through lulls in a mortar barrage to get to the dike, for this was indeed a hot spot. Our platoon suffered several casualties the very first morning. There was a continual exchange of artillery barrages on this front. We had lots of Limey artillery to back us up, and this was strictly a defensive position, so we felt pretty secure.

The next day we were back at the CP again for a couple days' rest. Our platoon had dwindled from eight gun crews down to five gun crews, and only four were used at once on the MLR, which left one extra which stayed at the CP to pull guard. They changed about so each crew got a chance for some rest. I didn't like the boredom back there, though, so I would go up to the dike when I got a chance and do a little sniping. I just loved to fire my rifle.

Well, it seems the Germans had caught on to this sniping, too, and they had a well-concealed sniper at work on a certain section of our lines. . . . Two men had been hit in the head when they stuck their head up over the dike to look around. I was itching for a rifle fight this day, so I thought I'd try and find him and have a little duel. I tried all the tricks I knew. I'd push my helmet up one place and then sneak up near a place where I had a background against which I wouldn't be easily seen. Then I'd poke the glasses through grass and look around the landscape trying to locate that sniper. He must have had a powerful telescope, or something, because he never would shoot at just a helmet stuck up in view. I can thank my lucky stars that he wasn't too good a marksman because here I was looking around through the glasses when, all of a sudden, a bullet hit the sod directly across the road from me. Six inches higher would have put it right through my head! I figured maybe I'd forget about sniping for a while, and especially so on my own time, when I didn't even have to be on the line. . . .

Next day, my twenty-third day of this mission, turned out to be my twenty-second birthday. It was a terribly dull day. It rained, and there wasn't any excitement to speak of, so I just sat in my foxhole and wrote letters home. The following couple of days were very quiet, so one evening I headed for the dike again to find some excitement. Visited some buddies and fired some tracers at the tail of a Limey plane which had been shot down and landed in the river in front of our lines.

Then we found some grenades, which the Limeys had left. One of them said "White Phosphorous," so we said: "Let's toss it over the dike and watch the pretty sparks fly." So we tossed it over, and the sparks flew all right, but they left a great big white cloud of smoke! Right on the front lines! Well, we got out of there in a hurry, just in case the Krauts got suspicious, and fired a few mortar rounds or artillery shells at it.

Finally our turn came to go into division reserve, so we were relieved and marched away from the front about seven miles, to an orphanage, where we billeted. We stayed back there for five days, during which time we had to work like mad cleaning our guns and equipment for inspection. But we did get a truck ride to Nijmegen to take a shower. Then some more inspections and a little visit from General Taylor, the division commander, and we were ready to go back up on the lines again. I never liked being in reserve because it was too much like garrison life: reveille every morning, chow lines, details, formations and all that. At the front you could do, within limits, more or less as you pleased. There were usually four men in one gun crew, whose duty it was to man the gun and keep it in working order.

So, I felt better when on the thirty-first day in Holland our period of acting as division reserve was over and we moved up to the front again. It was a quiet night with a steady, light rain falling. We moved to different positions from those previously held. The outfit we were relieving had all the positions and foxholes dug in for us, so we simply took their positions, crawled into their holes, and settled down to guard our LMG. As soon as it was light the following morning we came out and took stock of our surroundings.

It was usually quite a surprise to find that the real situation was entirely different from what you had conceived it to be in the darkness. This day we had our first American ten in one rations, and they were a wonderful treat after a month of nothing but Limey chow. The stew, and haricot, oxtail, and kidney pudding got pretty sickening, but what really hurt was when we'd see some of our Limey friends eating American Lend-Lease food. Even the chocolate candy in their rations finally became so sickening that I couldn't eat it. But I really couldn't complain. Perhaps I was just getting too choosy, because, after all, I was taking on considerable weight. Of course, we just lay around all day, so who wouldn't take on weight?

For lack of excitement I would think up all sorts of things to do. Someone picked up a tommy gun, and having never fired one, I had to try it out. Then everyone else along the line would raise a fuss because they were afraid it would draw enemy fire, so I'd have to quit.

I was continually thinking up crazy things to do and stunts to pull. One stunt was to get some "increments" from mortar shells and when everyone was sitting around the fire eating or, better yet, while they were reading mail just after a mail call, one of us (the one who didn't get any mail) would slip an increment into the fire unnoticed. When they burned there was a big flash and a whishing sound like a shell coming in, and everyone, being on edge anyhow, would scatter like mad! Big joke!

We liked to experiment with demolitions, too. We'd get hold of some "Prima-cord," which is an explosive that looks like a piece of fuse. We'd tie it around a fence post, unscrew the cap from a grenade to set it off, and then what results it would have on the post! Another good stunt with a hand grenade which some of the men in our platoon pulled on each other was to unscrew the fuse and dump out all the powder. Then they'd have the pin come out "accidentally" and the grenade would start sputtering and smoking while everyone ran for their lives. There'd be a harmless little pop, after which everyone would look around sheepishly at one another.

Our ten-day stay at the front went by in a hurry. The weather was pretty favorable, we were getting enough to eat, the mail came regularly, and the enemy wasn't causing any trouble anymore. We seldom saw any infantry anymore, just mortar and artillery fire on our positions occasionally to keep us on our toes. There were orchards all around and there was a good crop of apples, so we never had to worry about getting enough fresh fruit to eat.

On the forty-first day we were relieved and had to march back to the orphans' home again for some more garrison life. The enemy tossed some shells over while we were making the march back and causing some tense moments, but no one was hurt. Again there were the inspections and details, and the usual garrison routine, which became worse the longer we stayed on the lines. Halloween night found me pulling CQ duty. All next day I was running errands for the first sergeant, which was especially distasteful duty because everyone hated the first sergeant, probably because he was the one who had to issue all the orders to us.

Next day they showed us a movie, and I don't think I will ever quite appreciate another movie as well as I did that one. As I sat there, fresh off the lines with my rifle between my knees, watching the scenes that were so much like home, it suddenly dawned on me what a huge gap there was between my two lives. Looking at that show was like looking back into another world!

That night we again moved to positions on the front. This time we went up in trucks instead of marching, which was a great relief because after lying around without exercise on the lines all the time we were getting pretty soft. We had calisthenics every day while in reserve, but they didn't help too much.

We were amazed one night to see, on the German side, what appeared to be a meteorite going the wrong way. We thought they might be buzz bombs. Next day we were amazed again when we saw a missile of some sort rise high in the sky leaving a trail of white smoke in its wake. They turned out to be the new German V-2 bombs that were being aimed at Amsterdam.

The next day was November 11, Armistice Day, and to celebrate we had a big surprise for the Germans. At 1100 hours everything we had was going to open up on the Germans. Artillery, 81-mm mortars, bazookas, machine guns, grenades—everything on the line opened up. I was at the CP on some errand when it started, so I rushed up to the dike and began target practice with my '03 rifle, and to see what was going on. It certainly was an impressive array of firepower and must have made the Krauts wonder what was coming off. But they were right there, and about five minutes later answered with a barrage of their own. It wasn't much in comparison with ours, only I just happened to get caught out in the open with only a shallow ditch for cover. As I lay there listening to the shells whistling down at me I had visions of myself flying in all directions as one landed in with me. And what scared me even more than that was the fear of having one land just close enough to badly mangle me. There is a sudden feeling of smallness at times like that and you wish you could crawl right up into your helmet and hide. I had the presence of mind to roll over on my back to put my spine, the most vulnerable part of one's body, down in the lowest part of the ditch.

I could then also observe the closer mortar shells as they whistled down out of the sky and the thought crossed my mind, "I wonder if there would be time to roll out of the ditch and far enough away to save myself if I saw a direct hit coming?"

Then one night we had a wonderful detail bestowed upon us. It seems there were some forty-odd Limey paratroopers and escaped flyers who were across the river from our positions and we were going to cross over at night and pick them up. We were in reserve and got to help in the operation. We went up to the front after dark, and after waiting around for the proper time we had to carry two large rubber boats over the top of the dike and out to the river in front of our positions. It was an exciting job because, had the Krauts become suspicious, we all would have been caught in the wide open. We must have had the Krauts scared back a good distance because no shells ever came, not even when they started the motors on the boats to make the crossing.

The sixty-fourth day we had to move up into positions on the lines again. No one seemed happy about going this time, for by now we had all become pretty much sick of the whole thing. We knew winter would be setting in and we wanted action. The positions at the dike were a mess now. The rain had leaked into the poorly constructed foxholes and even caused some to cave in. Most of the foxholes on the dike were soaked and it was impossible to keep dry. All the foxholes on level ground were filled with water to within eight inches of the surface. The only dry places left to stay were the basements of demolished houses along the front. There was no such shelter near enough to my LMG position to be made use of because we had to stay on the gun, especially at night. During the day all but one of us would go to an old barn for shelter.

We cooked meals in there and built a fire to dry out. I used an old raincoat over my LMG to try keeping it dry but to no avail. It was just mud and water everywhere. The side of the dike got so greasy with mud that we could hardly crawl up and down it to our gun position and steps had to be cut in. One poor chap got caught in a mortar barrage while traveling on level ground to the barn. He jumped into a foxhole and was soaked to the armpits.

The nights were getting longer now and the cloudy weather lengthened them still more. It took four turns at watch now and to get out of your hole once you were settled down was especially hard to get used to. Sleeping with my shoes on didn't work so well anymore since they were always wet and muddy and they'd get cold at night.

Thanksgiving came and, as a special treat, we were to get a day's supply of American ten in one rations. Everyone was so eager to get some good food that they even took our platoon's rations so we had the prospect of no food at all for Thanksgiving. No problem, though, because someone came to the rescue with some fresh liver from a cow which had "accidentally" been killed by enemy fire. So we had fried potatoes and liver for Thanksgiving. That tasted even better than the ten in one rations would have! We weren't worrying about food anymore, for the rumor was flying around that we were finally to be relieved. It seemed too good to be true!

Sure enough, the next day we were kept busy policing the whole line in preparation for our leaving. A Canadian unit was going to take our place. We worked hard carrying all our extra ammo together to be hauled away. All the loose hand grenades we found we'd toss into the water-filled foxholes and watch the geyser of water that would fly into the air. At 2200 hours that evening of the sixty-eighth day the Canadians finally came to take over our positions after what seemed an eternity of waiting, and we marched off to the rear and safety. It had been a long, hard campaign, and our plan to outflank the Siegfried Line had failed. Eighty-five percent successful, they told us, so we shouldn't feel too badly about it.

Of the men in the platoon who flew into Holland with me two months ago, only a little better than half marched away that night. I recall how the men who were assigned to my crew after Normandy jokingly called me a jinx and didn't want to be in my crew because it had sustained the highest rate of casualties in the Normandy campaign (one killed and two wounded out of four). Now I would surely be called a jinx, for I had gone through three gun crews during this campaign! Of the eight corporals trained as machine gunners, only three of us remained to make the march back that night. And, of the new replacements used to fill our ranks, depleted from the Normandy fight, one lone survivor marched with us that night (only to be killed in Bastogne)!

We stayed at some civilian residence that night and after everyone was settled down they came around with a double ration of rum, which is issued regularly in the Limey army. I never would touch the stuff while on the front (in fact we never saw any of it!) because I believed that the best way to stay alive was to always have a clear and alert mind. But now we were in safety and I could relax. There wasn't much for each one of us so someone suggested that we draw cards and then one of us would have enough to do some good. I collected two gun crews' rations; that made two-thirds of a canteen cup full. (I drank less than half and gave the rest away.)

I was in a pretty jovial mood for the remainder of the evening, but was finally convinced to go to bed so I could march in the morning. In order to leave the "Island" we had to be ferried across the Lower Rhine in boats, since the Germans had finally put the Nijmegen bridge out of commission with their shelling. On the other side in the city of Nijmegen a Limey convoy of trucks waited for us. We got aboard and at 1135 hours began the long trip back to a new base in France. We rode all afternoon and all night, arriving in camp at 0930 hours the following morning. It was a cold, miserable ride and no one got much sleep. The only excitement was watching the buzz bombs fly over on their way to England and the streams of tracers reaching up for them. Every now and then a flash on the horizon or in the sky would give proof that their efforts were not in vain. The other bit of excitement would occur whenever we passed through a large city, whereupon all on board would hang their heads out to admire and yell at the girls, and make caustic remarks to the rear-echelon soldiers who had them in tow.

Back in garrison, we settled down to getting used to sleeping in bunks again and enjoying the warmth of a red-hot stove. Training soon started and we got in new replacements, who had to be trained, so there was no rest for us as yet. In fact, they began to get stricter than ever with us; why, I don't know, but it made life very miserable. It made us feel pretty bitter to think that after seventy-two days of combat we were to receive no reward whatsoever. All we could do is shrug our shoulders and say it was just another one of the aspects of belonging to the paratroopers. The first men out on pass raised so much hell in Rheims that they restricted the whole regiment to camp! They finally started letting some officers out and worked down through the ranks. Two other LMG corporals and myself finally got to go to Paris but were called back when the Germans broke through [at the Bulge].

CHAPTER TEN

WINTER HELL: The Battle of the Bulge

Nor any voice of mourning save the choirs,—

The shrill, demented choirs of wailing shells;

And bugles calling for them from sad shires.

—Wilfred Owen, "Anthem for Doomed Youth"

Eerie reminders remain for those who survived one of the greatest battles of World War II. The sight of snow-covered pine trees or the tingle they get in their once blackened and frozen feet as they walk down a snow-covered driveway takes them back to the Bulge.

Six months after D-Day, the war in Europe seemed to be nearing its end. A series of victories had brought Allied forces onto German soil west of the Rhine River, and the Allies believed the German army was on the verge of collapse.

Hitler, however, was determined to gamble one last time to reverse the Allied advance and force the Allies into a negotiated settlement. On December 16, 1944, he struck back in an effort to split the Allied forces, cross the Meuse River, and retake the critical Belgian port of Antwerp that he had lost just three months earlier to the British. The result was the Battle of the Bulge, the largest and one of the bloodiest battles ever to include U.S. soldiers. More than one million men fought on both sides. Casualties were enormous; the United States alone suffered more than eighty thousand troops killed, maimed, captured, or missing in action.[1]

The bulge of Hitler's desperate final assault that ripped through American lines extended from the German town of Monschau in the north to Echternach, Luxembourg, in the south. The offensive, roughly in the shape of an arrowhead, sprawled across several rivers and cut through dense pine forests until the tip extended sixty-five miles to the Belgian town of Celles. Then the Allies started pushing back.

U.S. airborne troops played a key role in stemming the German attack and a leading role in the counteroffensive. For three days the Germans poured divisions into the Ardennes, advancing along a sixty-five-mile front, while initially, winter weather prevented the Allies from enjoying their overwhelming superiority in the air. The Allies had few units in reserve to reinforce the area under attack. The 82nd Airborne Division and the 101st Airborne Division began to arrive on the third day of the German offensive; the 17th Airborne Division came later.

Because the airborne units were among the few reserves available during the early stages of the German attack, they were deployed in some of the most strategically important areas. The 82nd Airborne Division and several independent units, for example, the 517th Parachute Regimental Combat Team, were deployed in the northern portion of the Bulge in towns near the Salm River, close to the strategic crossroads city of St. Vith. It was this portion of the Bulge that initially bore the brunt of the German attack, since it lay in the path to Antwerp. Towns such as Trois-Ponts, Cheneux, Soy, and Hotton would become synonymous with the airborne units that held off some of the most powerful divisions of the German military.[2]

The 101st Airborne Division was deployed in the south at the crucial crossroads town of Bastogne, the hub for most of the road network that fed the southern portion of the Ardennes. Surrounded, the Bastogne garrison, which consisted primarily of the 101st Airborne Division and an assortment of artillery and armored units, held off determined attacks from numerous German tank and infantry divisions, the commanding general, Tony McAuliffe, delivering the famous "Nuts!" in response to the German demand for surrender. For these heroics, they later received the honor of becoming the first full army division to receive a Presidential Unit Citation. The battle was fought in the small farming villages that ring Bastogne—Wardin, Hemroulle, Flamierge, Noville, and others. Like the 82nd in the north, the 101st Airborne in the south was able to stop the German advance for a few precious, precarious days.

On December 26, 1944, elements of General Patton's U.S. Third Army linked up with the 101st fighting in Bastogne, exposing the Germans' southern flank and ending the Germans' drive for the Meuse River bridges and Antwerp. But rather than retreat or concede defeat, Hitler shifted the focus of his offensive to eliminating Bastogne. Three SS panzer divisions, two panzer grenadier divisions, one parachute division, three volksgrenadier divisions, and two panzer brigades, along with elements of the Panzer Lehr Division, squared off against the American units in and around Bastogne.[3]

Meanwhile, the Allies were planning their own counteroffensive to clear the Germans out of the Bulge. Eisenhower favored a broad front that would push the Bulge back at all points.

The Allied counteroffensive began January 3, 1945, and it proved one of the most costly and horrendous offensives of the war. The terrain and the snow made maneuvering all but impossible, so the Allies used brutal head-on attacks to clear the Germans out of well-prepared defensive positions and push the Bulge back to the German border. British forces were responsible for pushing back the western tip of the Bulge arrowhead, but the primary focus of the counteroffensive was a massive two-pronged attack by U.S. forces: the First Army from the north and the Third Army from the south. About twenty-five miles of difficult terrain and tens of thousands of Germans separated the two armies, which eventually would link up in the Belgian town of Houffalize.

Spearheading the First Army's attack in the northern portion of the Bulge was the XVIII Airborne Corps (82nd Airborne Division and attached units), which went about driving the Germans back from positions near the Salm River towns of Fosse, Bergeval, Dairomont, and Rochelinval, to name a few. The attack developed slowly, the Germans bitterly contesting every inch of ground in the worst weather in fifty years. Knee- to waist-high snow and wind chills of fifty below zero at night froze arms and legs and killed wounded men left untended. But the men pushed on, the fan-shaped attack stretching twenty-three miles wide and ultimately recapturing the strategic town of St. Vith and pushing the Germans back to the positions they held before their offensive.

On the first and second days of the southern counteroffensive, the Third Army collided head-on with an all-out German assault to capture Bastogne. After stopping the German attacks, units from the Third Army along with the depleted 101st Airborne Division and 17th Airborne Division went on with the difficult task of clearing the towns around Bastogne and driving through dug-in German positions reinforced by tank units to link up with the U.S. First Army at Houffalize. The 17th Airborne Division attacked on the second day of the counteroffensive, moving into position approximately twelve miles west of Bastogne where the green unit sustained appalling losses along a heavily defended ridgeline known as Dead Man's Ridge.[4]

Eventually, after a high cost on both sides in men and equipment, the southern counteroffensive was successful and the Germans were cleared out

The Battle of the Bulge

1. Robert Bowen, 327th GIR (401), 101st
2. William McMahon, 501st PIR, 101st
3. Robert Kinney, 504th, 82nd
4. Bill Meddaugh, 505th PIR, 82nd
5. Mel Biddle, 517th PRCT, Attached 82nd
6. Robert Piper, 505th PIR, 82nd
7. Harry W. O. Kinnard, Div. HQ, 101st
8. Joseph Lyons, 463rd Parachute
   Field Artillery Btn., 101st
9. Joe Tallett, 505th PIR, 82nd
10. Ernest Machamer, 550th IAB, Attached 17th
11. Doug Dillard, 551st PIB, Attached 82nd
12. Richard Durkee, 551st PIB, Attached 82nd
13. Alex Andros, 506th PIR, 101st
14. Ken Shaker, 509th PIB, Attached 82nd

BELGIUM

Liège
Eupen
Verviers
Spa
Monschau
Elsenborn
Malmédy
La Gleize
Stavelot
Cheneux
Trois Ponts
Basse-Bodeux
Werbomont
Dairomont
Rochelinval
Losheim
Manhay
St. Vith
Hotton
Soy
Marche
Celles
Rochefort
Prüm
Houffalize
SCHNEE EIFEL
Flamierge
Noville
Deadman's Ridge
Clervaux
Renaumont
Bastogne
Wiltz
Bitburg
Neufchâteau
Echternach
Arlon
Trier

GERMANY

ARDENNES

Meuse R.
Amblève R.
Ourthe R.
Salm R.
Clerf R.
Wiltz R.
Sure R.
Our R.
Sauer R.
Semois R.

XXXX 1
XXX XVIII
XX 82
XXXX 6 Pz
XXXX 5 Pz
XX 101
XX 17 (Jan. 3)
XXXX 3
XXXX 7
XXXX Ger 5 Pz
Ger 6
Ger 7

LUXEMBOURG

→ German Attacks
← Allied Advances
.... Farthest German Advance,
          Dec. 25, 1944
▬ Siegfried Line

N

0   20
Miles

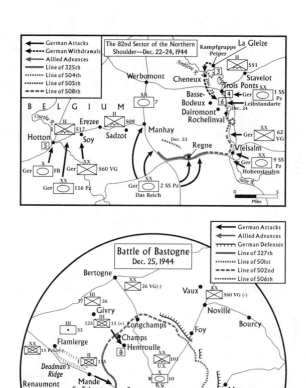

The 82nd Sector of the Northern Shoulder—Dec. 22–24, 1944

⬅ German Attacks
⬅⋯ German Withdrawals
⬅ Allied Advances
〰 Line of 325th
⋯ Line of 504th
⋯ Line of 505th
– – – Line of 508th

La Gleize

Kampfgruppe Peiper

|II| 551

Werbomont

Cheneux |3|

Amblève R.

Stavelot

Trois Ponts |XX|

|4| Ger

|1 SS Pz|

BELGIUM

Ourthe R.

|XX| 7

Basse-Bodeux

|6| ← Leibstandarte Dec. 24

Erezee

|II| 509

Dairomont

Rochelinval

Hotton

|II| 517

Soy

Sadzot

Manhay

Dec. 23

Regne

Vielsalm

Ger |XX| 62 VG

|5|

Ger |X| FB

Ger |XX| 560 VG

Ger |XX| 2 SS Pz Das Reich

Ger |XX| 9 SS Pz Hohenstaufen

Salm R.

Ger |XX| 116 Pz

0 ⸻ 5
Miles

Battle of Bastogne Dec. 25, 1944

⬅ German Attacks
⬅ Allied Advances
⊤⊤⊤ German Defenses
〰 Line of 327th
⋯ Line of 501st
– – – Line of 502nd
⋯ Line of 506th

Bertogne

|XX| 26 VG(-)

Vaux

|XX| 560 VG (-)

|III| 77 | 26

Givry

Noville

Bourcy

|III| 125 | 15 (+)

|III| 33

Longchamps

Foy

Flamierge

Champs

|XX| 15 PzG (-)

|II| 115

|8| Hemroulle

|XX| 101 U.S.

Deadman's Ridge

Renaumont

Mande St. Etienne

|B| |X| 10 U.S.

Bastogne |7|

Mageret

Neffe

Chenogne

|III| 39

|2| (Dec. 19) Wardin

(Dec. 19)

|1|

Sibret

Marvie

|III| 902 PGR

Remoifosse

|III| 901 PGR

|XX| 130 Pz Lehr

|XX| 5

|XX| 4 U.S.

0 ⸻ 1000
Yards

of the area around Bastogne. The Third Army, including the 17th Airborne Division, linked up with First Army forces from the north in Houffalize.

For many men and their units, the Battle of the Bulge was the defining moment. Infantry companies and battalions that came into the battle at full strength were reduced to a handful of men. For most individual soldiers, the battle was the ultimate test of mental and physical endurance. The price they paid was immense, but worth it nonetheless. The Bulge broke the back of the German army, taking from it some of Hitler's most dedicated troops, whose transfer from the east to the Ardennes had weakened German positions on the Eastern Front, allowing for a massive Russian breakthrough. For the rest of the war America—often led by her elite troops—would push inexorably east.

ROBERT BOWEN

327th Glider Infantry Regiment, 101st Airborne Division

When the Germans attacked, numerous American units made heroic stands, but the sheer size of the German counteroffensive created holes in the Allied lines. On December 18, the 82nd and 101st airborne divisions, recovering from more than fifty days in combat in Holland, were directed to the Ardennes to plug those holes. The 82nd Airborne arrived first, moving to the northern shoulder of the Bulge, in the town of Werbomont. Following closely behind was the 101st Airborne, which moved into Bastogne, in the south, as Robert Bowen remembers in this e-history.

"All platoon leaders report to the orderly room immediately. That means now!" Matt Pass sang out as he went through the barracks right after morning chow on that fateful morning. Red Adkins had one of the few radios in the company. All morning it had been blaring out about a German offensive in the Ardennes, a place along the Belgium frontier; it was a hundred miles north of us and I couldn't imagine how it could involve the 101st. In the orderly room I soon found out.

We weren't a very happy group. Instead of the passes to Rheims and Paris I expected, it meant another trip to the front. With memories of all those we had lost in Normandy and Holland fresh in my mind and with a body run down from too many sleepless nights, improper nutrition from the greasy British rations, and the stress of performing in a job which I had little training for, I certainly wasn't looking forward to more of the same.

Besides, the company was much understrength, with three of the four platoons being led by NCOs. First Lieutenant Robert Wagner still led first platoon, but First Lieutenant Martinson had moved up to executive officer, with senior Sergeant Cecil Caraker taking over the platoon. No replacements had come from the repo depot aside from the few with minor wounds like Andy Mitchell. There should have been forty-five men in my platoon, with a platoon leader and platoon sergeant. Instead we had twenty-eight with no officer to lead us. Some of the other platoons were worse off.

Captain Towns's face was abnormally grim as he began telling about the situation in the Ardennes, so sketchy and convoluted that even he was puzzled by it. There had been a breakthrough by the Germans but troops were being rushed up to counter it; those included the 82nd and 101st. He asked for questions and got plenty, most of which he had no answers for. He concluded by saying, "That's as much as I know, or anyone else here, for that matter. I do know we'll go in corps reserve to be used only in the event of an emergency." He paused thoughtfully, actually, I believe, thinking that was true. Then, as an afterthought, he said, "I know you've got men in your platoons that are beat. I don't think we should take them. Give me their names and we'll leave them behind."

"What'll happen to them, Captain?" Claude Breeding said.

"It's my understanding that they'll go to the rear-echelon outfit. You know, the quartermasters or something similar. Anyway, they won't see any more combat. You can draw ammo and rations from supply. Instruct your men to take overcoats and overshoes. There could be snow where we're going. Trucks are supposed to pick us up at 1800. If there're no more questions, I suggest you get cracking. We've got a helluva lot to do and no time to do it in."

I assembled my platoon and told them the unwelcome news. They took it a lot better than I imagined. However, when men are programmed to follow orders and accept the inevitable, in most cases they'll do what is asked of them provided they have faith in their leaders. At least that was my experience in situations where normal people would say "No way." Being trained to be a warrior is not what most Americans look forward to. Men get killed and maimed in wars, especially in the infantry, where about 80 percent of the casualties occur. My thoughts drifted to John Aspinwall, Howard Kohl, and Howard Hill, now dead, leaving children which they had never seen. And there was Frankie Demarco with two children. Ted Feldman in my first squad had four children and another on the way, and the odds against him escaping death or wounds were about one hundred to one. Sentimental notions about war are for the writer who can work plots to suit his fancy. In reality, war is much different.

I asked the squad leaders to pick men who they thought should be left behind. It was a hard choice to make. The platoon was only half-strength to begin with. Three men were obvious picks. Private Morris Zion, a vet and an old friend, was an older man from Chicago who had pushed his body to the limit to keep up with the younger ones. When I hear antisemitic jokes, I think of Pop Zion, the Jew who gave everything because he was willing. George Damato, another older man who should have been in the kitchen instead of rifle platoon, a clown whose humor kept sanity in insane situations. The last was Ken Schenese, an outstanding high-school athlete whose nerves had reached the breaking point. Later I called the three to my room and told them their new assignments.

While all were sorry to be left behind, I could detect relief on their faces. However, Utopia wasn't to come that easy for them. Because of the horrendous casualties in the Bulge, nineteen thousand KIA, more than fifteen thousand MIA and over forty thousand wounded or disabled by the bitter weather, all three men were pulled from the repo depot and sent to the front as replacements; Zion and Damato died among strangers.

We packed everything, as if we would never return to Mourmelon. I insisted that every man take an overcoat and overshoes. Most men detested both and would discard them at the first opportunity. The overcoat seemed to weigh a ton after being soaked by rain, and the overshoes were like anchors, especially in deep snow. I insisted on taking an extra blanket in the bedrolls. We left behind two platoon sergeants, Irving Turvey and Cecil Caraker. Turvey had reported to the aid station with a pulmonary infection. A spot was found on his lung. Caraker was in jail in Rheims, a victim of a con game by a civilian.

Latrine rumors were circulating like water in a whirlpool. Radio reports from the fighting front were grim and confusing. There was talk of a massive breakthrough by the enemy, a monumental Allied defeat. We formed on the company streets, where Turvey said goodbye, tears flowing on his cheeks. I envied him. We marched to a waiting convoy of open-bodied trucks as darkness fell. Jammed aboard like olives in a jar, we left for Belgium.

It was a long, cold ride with a biting wind chilling us to the bone. The headlights of the trucks were on despite being in a combat zone, blackout regulations be damned. We raced through small towns as we headed northeast, civilians with anxious faces cheering and waving to us. Were we to be their saviors again? After two wars, I was sure they had had enough.

Bastogne was our destination—inadvertently. Actually, we were supposed to defend Werbomont, twenty miles north of Bastogne. It was cold, rainy, and foggy when we passed through the town near daybreak. We took a main road to the west, over rolling hills, through sleeping hamlets and patches of woodland and farms. The trucks pulled on a side road just west of the hamlet of Mande St. Etienne. Cold, hungry, and stiff from hours of cramped riding, we unloaded silently, moving off the road to await orders. In the distance I could hear the boom of artillery, really not that far away. Corps reserve? Hell, that wasn't more than a few miles to the north, I thought. It was. No sooner had the 501st unloaded than it was engaged in a firefight with an enemy column.

WILLIAM McMAHON

501st Parachute Infantry Regiment, 101st Airborne Division

The 501st Parachute Infantry Regiment was the 101st Airborne Division's first unit to arrive in Bastogne, and it was sent immediately to find and link up with friendly forces east of Bastogne. I Company was dispatched to a friendly roadblock at the small farming town of Wardin. Instead it ran into a reinforced battalion of the German 901st Panzer Regiment and several German tanks, as William McMahon reports.

I'd been in Normandy and Holland, where everybody is talking about going home, and here we are in the midst of another battle. As we were coming into Bastogne, all these tanks and troops [were] leaving. I thought to myself, "What the hell was going on here?" If you've never seen a retreat, you can't imagine what it is like; it is kind of wild. All the tanks were leaving, all the infantry were leaving, even the support troops were leaving.

As we started into Bastogne and these troops were leaving, some of our guys were running over to them and they were giving our guys some of their weapons and ammo because they had no use for them. A lot of the guys got their helmets, weapons, and ammo from them.

We had one-track minds: We were going in and staying. We had just come back from Holland a few weeks before, we weren't re-equipped yet, but I was one of the lucky ones—I had an overcoat, a rifle, and galoshes.

As we went into Bastogne and started down the main street, God knows where we were going, I think it was towards the direction of Foy, but some-

Troopers from the 502nd PIR wearing bed sheets and pillow covers used for camouflage, donated by the citizens of Hemroulle. Shortly after the war, the citizens received repayment in the form of new linens, as promised. (Photo courtesy Ed Benecke)

thing must have happened because they held us up. All of a sudden we came to a halt and they turned us around, making us the lead company. They paired us off and gave orders to check these wood lots [pine forests] out in front of us. We got in there and it was very exhausting carrying all your ammo, and galoshes, and overcoat, and everything, and going through forests like that.

Well, we searched and searched and didn't find anything, so we kept on going. We came out to a road and this little town, that turned out to be Wardin, was in front of us. As we came into Wardin, there were two American tanks [Task Force O'Hara] sitting there, and we didn't pay any attention to them; we went on by them. We went across a little bridge and got into town and they hollered "break," so we took a break, when all of a sudden at the end of the village we heard firing. Our lead platoon was out front, then 1st Platoon, 2nd Platoon, and then my platoon, 3rd Platoon, was in the rear.

The order came down and they told me to take the machine gun section up on the top of the hill because the Germans were trying to flank us. This put us further away from our lines. We got up on top of the hill and we saw some heads pop up. We opened up on them and they disappeared. We heard cannon fire in town.

Suddenly, tanks started firing and we heard the bogeys—you know how the tank makes that certain noise, it is unmistakable. One of the guys said, "That's our tanks, that's our tanks." And I said that our tanks wouldn't be coming down the street blowing the hell out of the buildings where our guys were hiding in. But that's what they were doing, they were coming down the middle of the street. At this point, we realized we were on the wrong side of the action. We were on the side towards the German line.

One of the guys said we got to go down and help, and I said we can't go down, we are ordered to stay here or they'll try to flank us. We stayed there about a half-hour and the lieutenant came up and said, "If you guys want to live, follow me now!" We picked up the machine gun and pulled back.

Smoke was pouring out of houses that were burning, and a couple of the guys had knocked out the first two tanks and that blocked the road. The German tanks were right out in the road. They looked like Tigers or Panthers. They were coming down the street just firing at everything. In fact that's where most of my friends were killed, out in the street. If I Company hadn't gotten to that village, in ten minutes they'd have been in Bastogne. We were the only thing between the Germans and Bastogne, and I think that they thought there were more of us than there were.

Before we went up on the hill, when the bullets started to fly, I ran into this yard. I took my pack, gun, overcoat, and galoshes off and left them in the yard. I figured I would get them on my way back. But, unfortunately, during war you don't always come back the same way you went. Men with rifles and machine guns can't do much against tanks.

The order came to pull out and, hell, there was hardly anyone left. We ran between the houses down towards a stream that goes by a little bridge. There were a couple of strands of barbed wire to keep the cattle from straying, and I ripped the ass out of my pants as I crossed the stream. That was the coldest goddamn water I had ever felt in my life.

We made it to the top of the next ridge and we started to dig in. There were only about ten of us left. I said to the guys with me, "Jesus Christ, this can't be all that is left of my company." We started to dig in and for some reason they didn't pursue us. I don't know if they thought we were stronger than we were or what.

We couldn't figure out why those American tanks didn't come to our aid, but they didn't, they just sat. After we got out of there, they asked for volunteers to go back down and withdraw those guys, so I volunteered to go back down the hill. They, of course, were all buttoned up, so I got a rock and started pounding on the side of the tank. A guy stuck his head out and I said, "I got an order to pull you guys out of here."

We stayed on the hill until dark because we thought they were going to attack us, but they didn't. Then they pulled us back into Bastogne. We got there, and I think we had fifty or sixty men left, and they took us to this school. I'll never forget it. There was a church where the 101st Airborne had set up a kitchen. Actually, it was a Catholic school, and there was a big statue of Christ in the middle of the hall there, and we had just candles for light. We started counting the men who started filtering in, and then we realized how many men were gone. Some drifted in during the night, but that was practically the end of my company.

ROBERT KINNEY

504th Parachute Infantry Regiment, 82nd Airborne Division

"Only four more shopping days until Christmas," one trooper joked as he passed the 504th's regimental headquarters in Rahier, Belgium, as the 1st and 3rd battalions of the 504th moved toward the town of Cheneux on the north side of the Bulge.[5] On December 20, the 504th's two battalions launched an attack on Cheneux, which held a crucial bridge spanning the Ambleve River. Cheneux was defended by elements of Kampfgruppe Peiper (1st SS Panzer Grenadier Regiment), which was assigned to spearhead the German attack through the Ardennes, but leaving the bridge in German hands would have given the Germans an opportunity to attack the 82nd Airborne Division's base at Werbomont. The 504th's mission was to destroy the SS garrison and capture the bridge. Bob Kinney, a machine gunner, describes the attack.

We were called out at dusk and we lined up in the road. Word came in that we were going to attack lead elements of the 1st SS Panzer Division that had killed those [captured American] soldiers at Malmédy. Word came down from upstairs that we don't want any prisoners from that outfit. We were all pretty fired up and ready to exact revenge.

I was a member of a machine gun squad and ammo carrier. I never made corporal, though I acted as a corporal. Pauley, our squad leader, had been wounded in Holland, and he had not been out of the hospital long when we began this mission.

We started toward Cheneux on a pretty good road, well built with gravel. We were going up the road and [Pauley] said, "Man I can't go, I'm hurting so bad." I said, "I'll take the gun and you drop out." He did, and I had a couple of guys [Emmons and Zogelman] left with me and I said, "You guys have a new squad leader." We all laughed about it because I was more of a funny guy than leader.

We headed up the hill and had a burst of phosphorous mortar shells. There were some brand-new troops with us and they were screaming, "Gas!" and running. We were saying, "No, no, no! It's phosphorus, come on!" So we were going up the hill, and I went to the left of the road with my squad, and as we got to the top of the hill we met the German armor. I can't tell you how much armor, but there was at least one or two tanks, at least three half-tracks, flak wagons with a 20-mm weapon on them. The fire got heavy then. It was blistering. I was with B Company and I didn't dare shoot that machine gun because I knew I'd shoot some of our own people. The rest of our machine gun platoon got off to the right side of the road, and they were in a wooded area, and I could hear a lot of fire over there.

I went down to go across the road and I said, "Zogelman and Emmons, are you guys with me? We're going across that road." They said, "Sure." We ran down and jumped in a ditch and one of our corporals, one of our newer men, came down and said, "You guys can't go across that road, you'll all be killed." I said, "We are going across that road because we got guys in trouble down there!" So we took a sudden lunge across that road, jumped over a barbed-wire fence, and we got down into where that shooting was going on. The firing was coming from behind an old farmhouse built up on the bank of the road.

A half-track [flak wagon] had our guys pinned down there and they were just laying it in heavy. One of our boys was shooting a .30-caliber machine gun at that half-track and I could see the tracer hit it and go towards the sky. I hollered, "Stop shooting! Whoever is shooting over there, stop! You can't hurt that half-track!" About that time, somebody said Haden got it. I hollered and said, "Everybody here throw me an extra hand grenade." I took four or five and stuffed them in my jacket. I was wearing one of those tanker jackets, the zipper type.

I had a pistol and I ran up by the house. I knew I had to go by the door and I didn't know if there was anybody in there, so I stopped and put three or four shots into the door and went around the house. I was right on the road and that half-track was on the [opposite] side of that house from where I was. I went around there and the guys just kept shooting. I threw hand grenades in that thing. It started booming and banging as their ammunition blew up and they were yelling. Some of the Germans started moving back down the road. I ran back and hollered, "Somebody bring a machine gun up here, let's get the son-of-a-guns as they are going down the road!" Lopez brought the machine gun up and we just covered that road with fire.

Later, these 90-mm tank destroyers had pulled up late in the night and Lopez and I decided we'd have a cigarette. We got down to the bottom by the house, got down by the ground and pulled an overcoat over our heads. We lit the cigarettes, and about that time that doggone antitank thing let go of the 90-mm and shot through the house above us and scared us to death! I thought the Germans had seen us and fired on our position. I think I swallowed the cigarette!

The night got quiet. At dawn, the Germans had moved back up in front of our position and they started shooting 88s [artillery] from the trees above us. My buddy Zogelman and I took a machine gun and dug in on the side of the road. Somebody came by and threw some K rations. I sat there opening K rations and I heard that 88 screaming. I yelled, "Get down!" It hit a tree right above us, and we both were hit. A lot of our guys were hit. The medics set up an aid station down over the hill in an old barn, and we went back there.

I helped Higgins; he got hit in the back of the neck, he was all bloody and came crawling in on his hands and knees. I said, "Higgins, are you all right?" He said, "Man, just wipe the damn blood out of my eyes so I can see where I'm going."

I got hit in the ribs but I didn't realize it. Zogelman jumped right in the air and screamed and I thought he got it in the stomach the way he doubled over. I picked him right up and took him down through the woods to the aid station. There were a lot of guys at the medic station; we had several men killed.

I got back up to the top of the hill and it was daylight by then. As I said, many of us got hit and we were streaming back to the aid station. On our way down, I saw our colonel, Willard Harrison, and I said, "Colonel, get on those damn antitank buggers out there, they don't know what the hell they're doing. They're shooting at us down there!" He said, "Never mind, you guys go back up there and get bandaged up and we'll take care of this end of the war." We went back to the aid station and I saw the big lieutenant of ours, Kimbell, and he was digging a hole, and I said, "Dig it deep, Lieutenant!" He said, "Yes, sir! You boys go on there and take care of yourselves now."

BILL MEDDAUGH

505th Parachute Infantry Regiment, 82nd Airborne Division

On December 21, 1944, E Company of the 505th held a bridgehead at Trois-Ponts, on the east bank of the Salm River, against a fierce attack, led by armored elements of the 1st SS Panzer Division, that hit E Company at dawn. Greatly outnumbered and outgunned, E Company fought skillfully and held its ground until overwhelming numbers of Germans forced it to withdraw across the Salm, losing many men in the crossing. Further German assaults to cross the Salm failed, dooming any chances of a German linkup with SS Colonel Peiper's *kampfgruppe* trapped in La Gleize. Bill Meddaugh, the captain of E Company, describes in his e-history the efforts to slow down the 1st SS.

During the morning of December 20, 1944, we pulled out of a bivouac area and began an approach march along a narrow mountain road leading to Trois-Ponts. I was in command of E Company 505th. No maps were available, and I wasn't sure where we were headed. I was asked to send one platoon forward by truck as an advance force to occupy the town and reconnoiter the immediate area around the town. I selected the second platoon under Lieutenant John Walas, who boarded the trucks and headed for Trois-Ponts. The rest of the company [and battalion] continued the march. As the column approached the town, I went forward to meet with Lieutenant Colonel Ben Vandervoort, 2nd Battalion CO [commanding officer].

Lieutenant Walas had set up the platoon as a base of fire along the Salm River, on both sides of the damaged bridge, to cover the area across the river directly opposite the town. The terrain rose sharply across the river, giving the appearance of a cliff or bluff. A narrow road wound up the side of the cliff and disappeared in the woods to the left of the top of the mountain. A patrol under the command of Corporal Putnam had reconnoitered and waved that all was clear.

Colonel Vandervoort ordered me to move E Company across the river to the high ground and to establish a defensive position denying enemy troops and vehicles the use of the road. I sent for the rest of the company and ordered Lieutenant Walas to move the 2nd Platoon across quickly and set up a defensive position straddling the road, inside the woods, just over the crest of the mountain. When the balance of the company arrived, we moved across the bridge and up the winding road to get into position. I then ordered Lieutenant Jack Bailey's 1st Platoon to move into the woods and dig in on the right flank of the 2nd Platoon. Lieutenant Howard Jensen's 3rd Platoon was kept in reserve and located in the immediate vicinity of the Company CP [command post], which I established in a small home located on the road about a hundred yards from the 2nd Platoon positions.

At 2000 hours, the 2nd Platoon reported mechanized activity to their front. Bazookas were dug in, covering the road, and at this point several land mines were placed on the road. Shortly after that, two armored half-tracks approached the 2nd Platoon positions. The Germans were noisy and shouting back and forth, apparently unaware of our presence. The first vehicle struck a mine and was disabled. Almost immediately, the second half-track was hit by bazooka fire and was destroyed. A brief firefight developed, and several enemy soldiers were killed. We had no casualties. There was no further activity that night.

It was obvious we were facing some sort of mechanized unit. At dawn, the Germans attacked straight down the road into the 2nd Platoon's positions. Their infantry was accompanied by armored vehicles.

Walas called me at the CP and said, "The Krauts are all around us." The 2nd held their positions and the 1st Platoon began to fire at the flanks of the enemy force. I was able to get immediate 81-mm mortar support from the battalion in front of the 2nd Platoon area, which was getting the most pressure. The mortar platoon did a tremendous job and was mainly responsible for slowing down the attack.

I went forward to check on the situation in both the 1st and 2nd platoon areas and realized the attack was on a wide front. I went back to the company command post and committed the 3rd Platoon. The terrain wouldn't allow direct reinforcement of the 2nd Platoon, so I put the 3rd on the right flank of the 1st to get more enfilade fire on the enemy forces.

As the morning wore on, the situation was becoming more serious. Second Platoon was suffering heavy casualties, and it appeared [it was] not going to be able to hold on much longer. The 1st and 3rd platoons were also being pressured badly, and casualties were mounting. Part of our 2nd Platoon area was overrun, and Germans were occupying foxholes dug by our men. They had captured two or three men in the process. They were last seen being moved to the rear of the enemy lines.

About the time it looked like we would literally be pushed off of the hill, I received orders to withdraw back across the river. I got the word to my platoon leaders to bring their units out independently and as orderly as possible. F Company was moved up on my right flank, and [its] support enabled us to break contact and covered our withdrawal.

The withdrawal was disorganized as men formed small groups in the attempt to get out. I had the company headquarters group and some stragglers from 3rd Platoon who had become separated and drifted back. As we started down the winding road, we came under automatic weapons fire. The Germans had been able to break through at some point and put fire on the road. We considered dropping down the side of the cliff to avoid the fire on the road, but the 20- to 30-foot drop discouraged us from that. By moving single file and staying close to the bank on the side of the road, we managed to work our way down the road to the bridge. Due to the small-arms fire directed at the bridge, we were forced to run across one at a time to the other side.

The rest of the company made [its] way back by similar means and drifted in over the next hour or two. In spite of our traumatic experience, we quickly reorganized and moved into defensive positions along the Salm River with the rest of the battalion.

We suffered heavier-than-usual casualties in this action, but our stubborn stand forced the German forces to back off from Trois-Ponts and try to find another place to cross the river. E Company fought well under extremely tough circumstances. We learned later that we had faced a German armored battalion, and my guys fought them to a standstill with bazookas, mortars, and small-arms fire.

MEL BIDDLE

*517th Parachute Regimental Combat Team,
Attached to the 82nd Airborne Division*

After arriving in the Ardennes on December 22, the 517th Parachute Regimental Combat Team was rushed to the northern part of the Bulge to join the 82nd Airborne and the rest of the XVIII Corps. The 517th's 1st Battalion joined the line at a break between the Belgian towns of Soy and Hotton where the Germans were readying themselves to exploit the gap and envelop the 82nd Airborne dug in along the Salm River. The 517th also was trying to open an escape route for four hundred GIs surrounded by the Germans. For his actions that day, Melvin Biddle, then a private, won the Congressional Medal of Honor.

We started up to the Bulge on December 21, 1944, and got to Soy the night of the twenty-second and pulled up right outside of town on trucks. As soon as we got off the trucks, the Germans started throwing artillery at us; they could have caught us on the trucks, which would have been a bad situation.

The captain came around and said: "I want you to come with me to headquarters." There was an officer at the headquarters in the basement, and the captain apparently told him we'd have to take the area between Soy and Hotton at any cost. They gave us seven tanks in the morning, and around 1000 hours we started out, and I was the lead. In about ten minutes, two tanks were hit. There was a German antitank gun down in the valley, and they were able to zero in on our tanks.

We had a fellow who'd just come into the outfit from the 82nd Airborne. When one of these tanks caught on fire, he went over and pulled the boys out. Shortly after he pulled the last man out, the 82nd guy got hit with a piece of shrapnel and killed. We felt so bad because he went through four combat jumps already and he didn't even have to come up here. We told him he could stay at the barracks as a baggage guard, but he insisted on coming with us.

We started out, and a rabbit jumped out in front of me. I followed that rabbit with my rifle, just like hunting, knocked the safety off my gun and followed it. I didn't fire, but I came dang near it. I turned around to the guy in back of me, who was so scared he couldn't laugh, he couldn't even smile, and I thought, "He is worse than I am."

Troopers from the 517th PRCT, 1st Battalion, outside Soy, Belgium, December 1944. (Photo courtesy U.S. Military History Institute)

We just went on and didn't see much for a while. We came up to a railroad track and three Germans by the brush adjacent to the railroad track, and they seemed to be looking down the track. I came up to them at an angle. The first guy never saw me and I stood there for a second and thought, "Should I shoot him or not shoot him?" I decided I better shoot him. My shot knocked him down, and he said *Kamerad*, which is their way of giving up. I felt kind of bad about shooting him; he was an older guy, probably thirty-five or forty-five years old, which was old to us nineteen-year-old guys. We sent him on back as a prisoner.

Just a few feet there was another [German]. I thought I shouldn't have shot the first guy so I won't shoot this one, but he tried to shoot me. He tried to get his rifle off. As he was trying to get his rifle off to fire at me, I shot him twice. He laid on the ground holding his stomach like it hurt, so a few minutes later I loosened his belt for him and he died. About another five to ten feet there was heavy underbrush and another German. He ran from me and I fired and hit him in the shoulder. He kept going, so I fired again, but he still kept going. I thought, "Boy, those other two just dropped, but this guy didn't."

A minute or so later everything broke loose—machine gun fire and mortar fire. The lieutenant was laying next to me and he started to light a cigarette. There was a branch right next to his nose and a bullet clipped it off and he about fainted! He put his cigarette away.

As I moved forward, we were pinned down by machine gun and rifle fire. I saw a nest and pitched a few grenades in it, killing the crew. About twenty yards forward I ran into another nest and I threw a grenade at it and charged it, firing my rifle. Then the rest of the fire just seemed to stop. I don't know if they withdrew to another line or what, but they quit shooting at us.

I told the captain that it seemed like they quit firing, and he told me to go out there and see if I could see what outfit it was and what's out there. I went over to the road, it was the main road between Soy and Hotton, and we were coming from the north, I think. There was an intersection where I was going out to the road and I saw a vehicle or two that had some stars on it. I thought it was an American outfit, but I couldn't see how it could be with the Germans out there, but I could see the white stars. I got out near the road and three Germans came along; they were walking parallel to each other. One of them said "Ja," so I knew they were German. I went back and told the company commander that there were German troops even though I had seen a white star on a vehicle. He told me to take a couple of guys and capture a prisoner if we could.

Donald Haney was made second scout. He was an expert with a rifle and was an expert with a .45 pistol, also. He was real good. They told him to go with me to capture prisoners. A friend of mine, Bloom, who later got killed, said he'd go too; he just volunteered. He was a dedicated person, a dedicated soldier. He and I were friends, and he just kept telling me, "Take it easy, this war is going to last a long time and I want you to live through it."

We went up this road between Soy and Hotton, and there were [German] tanks, half-tracks and vehicles running up and down that road. The fellow who volunteered to go with me said, "I'll capture one of those fellows going up and down that road." He got to the road and said "Halt" so low I could hardly hear him. I don't think the German did either. He said "Halt!" again just like it was a police action or something. He fired at him and missed, and the German officer turned around and took out his pistol.

At this time it was getting dark and he couldn't see us, but I could see him. He had one of those pistols that had a bolt on it. He reached across with his left hand to cock that thing and put a round in the chamber. I stood there, looked at him, and I was so dumbfounded that Bloom had missed him. He turned around and fired at us a couple of times and missed us. He said, "Hey, Johnny!" He couldn't see us but he was trying to get us to say something so he could shoot at us. It was so crazy that I didn't shoot him. I'd been shooting people all day and here I am only ten or twelve feet from him and I know I can get him. He had on a coat that came all the way down to his ankles, one of those beautiful German coats, and a fancy officer's cap—he was probably a general. I never found out who it was.

We started back to our outfit. I went the wrong way and ended up amongst the German line alone. I laid out there until about three or four in the morning. The Germans were walking past me. One would say *Alt* and another would say *Acht*—that was their password for that night. I didn't think I could say *Acht* like they did, but I was going to say *Acht* if I had to confront them.

My hands were so cold I wasn't sure I would be able to fire my rifle. I determined I was going to put a finger through and pull on the thing if I had to. I laid out there, and all of a sudden they withdrew and went back towards Hotton. I lay there a little bit longer and heard our machine gun firing. It would go "burp—burp—burp" and theirs would fire back and go "unk." I could tell which was which, so I went over towards my outfit, and somebody over there said, "Is that you, Biddle?" And I said, "Yes," and they said, "Come on in." Most of them would have fired and wondered what that noise was. It was just amazing somebody called out.

We spent the rest of the night there, and one of our planes came over and shot down a German bomber, a JU-88. It burst in flames right across the road. The next morning the pilot and copilot were laying out there, deader than dead. They had black aviator clothes on, real nice, and each of them had a pistol.

We moved out again and I thought that would be the end of that [being in the lead] and they said, "Biddle, out front again." I was kind of shocked that they put me out front again. But that's the way it worked. We went just a little ways and there was a young German, about fourteen or fifteen years old, chained to a tree with a machine gun and a bunch of grenades. Everyone in back of me said, "Shoot him," and I said, "I don't think we need to, he's so scared he can't fire." We cut him loose and sent him back as a prisoner; he was so happy.

The captain said we need this platoon to move over there, to protect our left flank. I kind of edged to the left a little bit and went a few yards and saw a whole string of German soldiers coming across in front of me. I motioned everybody down and I started firing. They didn't come back up—I thought they would. I told them to. I started shooting. I was about 100, 150 yards from the Germans. I fired at their helmets and I fired a couple clips at their rifles. When the first clip ejected it kind of scared me.

I was in a sitting position and just tall enough over the grass and underbrush to see the Germans clearly, so I just sat there shooting at them until they ran out of people. There was a squad or so that just marched across; they never fired. I could hear one popgun and I wondered if it was a soldier putting another out of his misery. I didn't go up and look at them; the other guys did. I was grateful because I would always have that on my mind. They said there were fourteen of them. I had gotten every one of them in the head, which was amazing to me.

We moved into Hotton, and the only other German I saw going in there was running. He had given up—he had his hands up. I just walked up to him, didn't say anything, and he took his watch off and handed it to me. The guy who was guarding him said, "Why didn't you give that to me?"

That night we went to a little town that was four or five houses and we were put up in a farmer's house. The Belgian farmer cooked supper for us. There was roasted chicken cooked in butter and this dark Belgian bread—it was terrific. While we were talking around the stove, the farmer looked at my pipe. I had a pipe that I'd chewed the wooden stem and it was coming apart. The farmer threw it in the fire and went over to his pipe case and gave me one of his. I wanted to keep it as a souvenir so bad and I lost the darn thing.

ROBERT PIPER

505th Parachute Infantry Regiment, 82nd Airborne Division

On Christmas Eve 1944, the 82nd Airborne Division and 7th Armored Division were directed to withdraw from their positions in front of the Salm River and pull back to high ground between Trois-Ponts and

Hotton. At the time, the airborne had been fending off three-plus SS panzer divisions. The order to "tidy up" the lines was issued by British Field Marshal Montgomery, who feared that the Germans could outflank the Allied lines and reach their objective of the Meuse River. The withdrawal was very difficult since it was at night and in woods that were swarming with eight hundred SS troops from *Kampfgruppe* Peiper, the same unit that had perpetrated the Malmédy massacre on U.S. troops. The SS troops were, ironically, also withdrawing. The 82nd was also facing the full weight of the powerful 1st SS Panzer Division. Robert Piper, in command of the 505th Regimental Intelligence Section (S-2) described the withdrawal, and witnessed an incident overlooked by history.

We went through a series there, on the way along the Salm River line, where you're in the woods and you move for twenty-four hours [and] then a regiment would pass through you that night. One regiment would come through us; then we'd go through them twenty-four hours later. But during that twenty-four hours you were there [in place], you had to be up and you had to walk around a tree. That's what you did because if you sat down, your tail was going to be frozen, your feet were going to be frozen, your butt was going to be frozen. (After the Bulge, I was evacuated to Liege and I was debating whether to cut my toes off because they had been so badly frostbitten.) It is pretty hard to describe. I think the average guy got pretty toughened, impersonal. After a while, I think, in retrospect, they were torn up pretty well when they really got to think about what they'd seen or done and experienced.

Combat is difficult to describe to someone that wasn't there. A man was alive today but, if he caught one, he was a vegetable the next day whether you liked it or not. It might have been your good friend. I had a very good friend standing next to me in Normandy, and a mortar round came in and capped him—just took the front half of his head [off] and sent me flying. I was bleeding in both ears because I'd been knocked on my tail from a concussion, but I didn't get a scratch; I don't know why. This is fate, you see. If it's your time, it's your time. You have to become very fatalistic; you can't worry about yourself. The fact that somebody is shooting at you is not the point. The name of the game is, if you are an infantryman, you find the enemy, you close with them, and you destroy them. You don't sit back and debate what about this, what about that, what about something else. People don't understand that. After a while you just have to accept the fact that people get hit and people get hit badly. But a month later the medics put people back together, and I've seen this several times. In my thirty one years [of service] I've seen a lot of people badly shot up but the medics put them back together.

People don't realize it's not a matter of worrying about anything. You don't worry about anything. If it's your time it's your time. You don't even think about if it's your time. You don't think about it ever being your time, especially if you're a hard-charging guy, and you got no immediate family.

I think one of the most memorable things [in Belgium] was Christmas Eve along the Salm River line. We had twenty-some-odd German prisoners that we'd taken, and on Christmas Eve, the 505th, in their deployment, stuck out in the overall [line] of the German advance. So the name of the game was to withdraw. You cannot make a night withdrawal with enemies in a bitter-cold snow and bring these people back; I won't go on record and say it was another Malmédy massacre. But it was in fact another massacre that took place that you can't read about, you won't hear about.

It was a matter of not being able to comply with the order to withdraw and do it without losing your own people and bring back a bunch of enemy people. You can't do that; it is impossible to bring these people back in the dark, cold as it was, and the snow. No roads to speak of and you're coming back through the damn woods, so the name of the game was, you don't bring prisoners back. It's a sad commentary, and this was Christmas Eve, and we had to withdraw, and we had twenty-two to twenty-three [SS] prisoners. One of the German prisoners who was very well educated—an officer that went to school in the United States and spoke English very well—couldn't understand what was going on, he didn't understand the rationale. If the shoe had been on the other foot, you'd have said the same thing. To be just a statistic, that's just some of the fate of being in a wartime situation. It was right there and then, a matter of elimination. There were about eight or ten [American soldiers]. It was just doing a job and it was over.[6]*

There are very few of the people alive that are involved in the operation. I don't think there's many who ever talked about it. I don't talk about it lightly. I just think it's sort of a sad commentary, really. But, at the time, it was not a sad commentary. It was a matter of either you take some steps against the enemy or he was going to shoot you in the back. So you have a job to do and you can't afford to be a "jolly good fellow." Like a lot of American attitudes like being hale and hearty, chin up, school colors, and all the rest of this crap people put out, or about being cold-blooded; you just think about getting the job done. You got to go from A to B and, if there's something between A and B, you got to get rid of it. So the name of the game is, you go from A to B and you get very impersonal.

I think, in retrospect, you get very cold. I don't think cold-hearted is the right term. But you get impersonal. I think that is the best term to use. It doesn't mean a helluva whole lot. But to see some of your own people, good people—zap, bang, and then they are gone. Good people you've trained with in the United States, you've gone to Africa and Sicily and Italy and England and Normandy and back to England and Holland and back to France, and you get committed to the Bulge in short notice—I mean these are people you've known for, Christ, one and a half, two years. I'm talking about soldiers—privates, and sergeants.

---

*Col Robert Piper (Ret.) made it clear to the author that he only witnessed the incident.

HARRY W. O. KINNARD

Division Headquarters, 101ˢᵗ Airborne Division

The town of Bastogne is strategically located at the center of the road network of the Ardennes and was referred to by the Germans as a "road octopus." The Allies recognized Bastogne's importance, and General Eisenhower dispatched the 101ˢᵗ Airborne Division to hold the town at all costs. Their ability to do so earned them the first-ever Presidential Unit Citation awarded to an entire U.S. Army division. Harry Kinnard, then a lieutenant colonel and Division G-3 (planning officer), remembers here the German demand for surrender.

We got into Bastogne late on the night of December 18, 1944. We were not well-equipped, having just gotten out of combat in Holland. We were particularly short of winter clothing and footwear. On the twenty-first of December, we became completely surrounded by Germans and our field hospital was overrun by a German attack. We had put the hospital in what would normally have been a safe place, but no place is safe when you are completely surrounded. At this time, we were not able to receive air resupply because the weather was absolutely frightful. It was very, very cold and snowy. Visibility was often measured in yards. The citizens of Bastogne who gave us blankets and white linens that we used for camouflage offset our lack of winter gear.

While we were still surrounded, on the morning of December twenty-second, a German surrender party, consisting of two officers and two NCOs, and carrying a white flag, approached our perimeter in the area of our glider regiment, the 327th. The party was taken to a nearby platoon command post. While the enlisted men were detained, the officers were blindfolded and taken to the command post of the 327th, where they presented their surrender ultimatum. The ultimatum in essence said the 101st's position was hopeless, and that if we elected not to surrender, a lot of bad things would happen.

The following ultimatum was delivered on December 22, 1944:

> The fortune of war is changing. This time the U.S.A. forces in and near Bastogne have been encircled by strong German armored units. More German armored units have crossed the river Our near the Ortheuville, have taken Marche and reached St. Hubert by passing through Hompré-Sibret-Tillet. Libramont is in German hands.
>
> There is only one possibility to save the encircled U.S.A. troops from total annihilation: the honorable surrender of the encircled town. In order to think it over, a term of two hours will be granted beginning with the presentation of this note.
>
> If the proposal should be rejected, one German artillery corps and six heavy A.A. Battalions are ready to annihilate the U.S.A. troops in and near Bastogne. The order for firing will be given immediately after the two-hour term. All the serious civilian losses caused by this artillery fire would not correspond with the well-known American humanity.
>
> Signed: The German Commander.

Major Alvin Jones, the S-3, and Colonel Harper, the regimental commander, brought in the message to the division headquarters. They brought the message to Paul Danahy, the G-2, and me. My first reaction was that this was a German ruse designed to get our men out of their foxholes. But be that as it might, we agreed that we needed to take the message up the line.

We took it first to the acting chief of staff of the division, Lieutenant Colonel Ned Moore. With him, we took the message to the acting division commander, General Tony McAuliffe. Moore told General McAuliffe that we had a German surrender ultimatum. The general's first reaction was that the Germans wanted to surrender to us. Colonel Moore quickly disabused him of that notion and explained that the Germans demanded our surrender. When McAuliffe heard that he laughed and said: "Us surrender? Awe, nuts!"

McAuliffe realized that some sort of reply was in order. He pondered for a few minutes and then told the staff, "Well, I don't know what to tell them." He then asked the staff what they thought, and I spoke up, saying, "That first remark of yours would be hard to beat." McAuliffe said, "What do you mean?" I answered, "Sir, you said 'Nuts.'" All members of the staff enthusiastically agreed, and McAuliffe decided to send that one word, "Nuts!," back to the Germans. McAuliffe then wrote down: "To the German Commander, 'Nuts!' The American Commander."

McAuliffe then asked Colonel Harper to deliver the message to the Germans. Harper took the typed message back to the company command post where the two German officers were detained. He told the Germans that he had the American commander's reply. The German captain then asked, "Is it written or verbal?" Harper responded that it was written and added, "I will place it in your hand."

The German major then asked, "Is the reply negative or affirmative? If it is the latter, I will negotiate further."

At this time the Germans were acting in an arrogant and patronizing manner, and Harper, who was starting to lose his temper, responded, "The reply is decidedly not affirmative." He then added, "If you continue your foolish attack, your losses will be tremendous." Harper then put the German officers in a jeep and took them back to where the German enlisted men were detained. He said to the German captain, "If you don't know what 'Nuts' means, in plain English it is the same as 'Go to Hell.' I'll tell you something else: If you continue to attack, we will kill every goddamn German that tries to break into this city."

The German major and captain saluted very stiffly. The captain said, "We will kill many Americans. This is war." Harper then responded, "On your way, bud." He then said, "And good luck to you." Harper later told me he always regretted wishing them good luck.

JOSEPH LYONS

*463rd Parachute Field Artillery Battalion, Attached
to the 101st Airborne Division*

On Christmas Day, 1944, eighteen German tanks camouflaged with white paint followed by grenadiers clad in white ponchos penetrated the American line held by the 2nd Platoon of A Company of the 327th Glider Infantry Regiment,[7] their pincer-shaped attack falling on the small towns of Champs and Hemroulle. After several German tanks were knocked out by tank destroyers (TDs) and infantry wielding bazookas, the remaining tanks charged a position near the town of Hemroulle occupied by the 463rd Parachute Field Artillery Battalion, nearly breaking into Bastogne. Joe Lyons, executive officer of B, or Baker Battery, recalls how the 463rd used pack howitzers—weapons not designed for close-in fighting—by bore-sighting their muzzles on the tanks.

A little after dawn on Christmas morning, we got a call from the officer of number-one gun in Baker Battery. He reported that tanks were visible about six hundred yards from his position. Baker Battery was equipped with six guns; however, we had only three guns that could shoot in that sector. The guns were numbered one through six, and guns numbered one through three were pointed towards the enemy tanks. According to the orders from headquarters, we had to have the guns shoot 360 degrees; just in case the Germans did break through, we could have guns covering any field of fire. On number-one gun was Sergeant D. B. Nickols, and the gunner was Joe Hibble. Hibble was a fine gunner. Sergeant Smith, or Smitty, as we called him, was over on number-two gun, and number-three gun was manned by Keller, one of our best gunners.

I was the executive officer of Baker Battery. At this point we didn't have much ammunition remaining. Our supply of shells consisted of a few armor-piercing, smoke, and phosphorous shells. Once the tanks came into view, we paused a bit to make absolutely sure they were German tanks. We waited for the sight of muzzle breaks and low silhouettes, both distinct features of German tanks. But once we saw the muzzle breaks there was no question about it, we knew we were facing German tanks.

Once the tanks were in range, I said to Joe Hibble, our gunner, "Joe, when you start firing, for God's sakes don't fire over." If you fire short, at least you get a ricochet shot. I was really wasting my time telling him that because he was such a good gunner; I knew he would instinctively do it. We waited maybe three or four minutes and then started to fire.

From my vantage point, I saw about four tanks. Some of the men who were in the other gun positions said there were a total of eight tanks. The first shots fired by Keller and Hibble got a direct hit on one tank, forcing the German crew to bail out of the turret of the burning tank. The second tank was hit with a phosphorous shell, and they were forced to bail out of that tank. The third tank was hit, but the motor was still running. The machine gun section that was guarding our flanks was able to capture the running tank. They also picked up about twenty or thirty prisoners.

Our machine gun section drove the captured tank near our positions. Meanwhile, the German prisoners were disarmed and marching behind the tank toward number-one gun. Sergeant Childress and Gus Hazard of the machine gun section were riding the tank and stopped in front of my position. At that point I said to them, "Get that tank out of our area, because if the skies ever clear they'll see the German tank and we'll catch hell from our own airplanes." I said, "Why don't you take them up to battalion." So they took the German prisoners and operational German tank up to battalion.

I remember the one German officer we captured, who spoke English, said to me, "Lieutenant, you're wasting your time all around the perimeter," and I said, "You're the prisoner, I'm not." So they took them all up to battalion. I would say the whole thing lasted fifteen or twenty minutes. This was the second time in the war that a pack howitzer knocked out tanks. The first time was at Biazza Ridge in Sicily.

JOSEPH TALLETT

505th Parachute Infantry Regiment, 82nd Airborne Division

The Allied counteroffensive to push the Germans back into Germany began on January 3, 1945, and involved some of the most costly fighting of the war, conducted during the worst winter in fifty years. Leading the First Army's attack in the northern portion of the Bulge was the lightly armed 1st Battalion of the 505th.[8] Joseph Tallett of C Company describes the first few days of the attack.

January 3 was the day we started our counterattack. We launched the attack near a wooden bridge that crossed a creek or river. I think it was some sort of creek that sprung off from the Salm River.

As we crossed the creek, there was a hill that stretched seventy yards to a wooded area, and it continued sloping up. The Germans started shelling us as we approached the bridge. I remember Gus Sanders got hit. That was his fourth Purple Heart. It was a leg wound, so we weren't that concerned.

As we went up this hill we came upon a crossroad. The Germans had four 88s [field artillery] that were zeroed in on the road. We subsequently captured the 88s; they were brand-new. They were firing at the crossroad in sequence, so what you did was wait for a pause in the sequence and you would dash across the crossroad up into the woods. When we moved forward in the woods we lost some people; we lost our assistant platoon leader, Robbins. He had been captured in Normandy and escaped. He could have gone home, since theoretically he had been a POW. He opted to stay with the regiment, and of course he died with the regiment. Two other men in my platoon charged the emplacement but were killed by a burst of machine gun bullets.

This wooded area was large and full of dense pine trees. Three or four hours later, when we finally got out of there, it looked like someone had taken a lawn mower and just mowed the trees down. All that was left were tree stumps. About another three hundred yards farther there was an open space, maybe one hundred yards long. That was the problem, the open space. The Germans had laced it with machine guns. [Our commanders] decided to wait before another assault on the machine guns. They decided to wait for the tanks to cross the river.

From where I was on the hill, I could see combat engineers working feverishly near the damaged bridge to repair it so the tanks could cross the river. It was really a hot area. The Germans were concentrating their artillery fire on the bridge. I was pinned down on the side of the hill but could see what was going on down by the bridge. General James M. Gavin, commander of the 82nd Airborne, was in water up to his chest assisting the combat engineers to get that bridge back together so the tanks could cross. That was a sight as far as leadership goes. You had to say this was a good place to be with men like Gavin. In any event, they did get the bridge back.

Meanwhile, A Company was flanking around the left, and tanks rolled across the repaired bridge.

I never harbored any hate for the Germans, but there were men in the platoon that did. This happened when we were on the side of the hill near the crossroads and prisoners were coming in. They [the Germans] were saying, "Me Polish." One of the troopers who spoke Polish, along with another man, would take them down lower on the hill, strip them of anything of value and then shoot them. I don't know how many they had done this to, it wasn't many, but it was enough. Ironically, one of these men was killed that day and the other was killed later in Germany. There was too much going on, and most people thought that they were taking them back to our lines. But how do you send people back when you're getting your tail shot off in the middle of a firefight?

In Holland I was in an outpost with one of these people, and oh, what a maniac! He was screaming at the Germans to attack so he could get some watches! He was kind of an outcast in the platoon. They wouldn't let him jump in Normandy. He came in by boat and I believe knocked out several machine gun nests. He killed Germans. I understand that he lost a brother in the Philippines, I don't know the time frame. We would have been better off if we kicked him out of the outfit.

The next day we pushed about half a mile and were on high ground. We came upon a valley that had two German tanks refueling. One of the tanks was on one end of the field and the other tank was on the other end of the field. They were pouring gas into their tanks from jerry cans. The tank destroyers [TDs] were right next to us and the lieutenant who commanded them said, "One HE [high-explosive shell] and one AP [armor-piercing shell]." Each TD picked a tank and fired two rounds and knocked them out. The HE got a few of the Germans that were standing outside.

About the same time B Company caught a German battalion in the woods. On either side of this pine woods were firebreaks [a clear path through a wooded area]. A and B companies moved men down either side of these firebreaks, squeezing the Germans in the middle. TDs moved along with them, using their .50s [.50-caliber machine guns mounted on the tanks]. It was a turkey shoot; the Germans didn't have a chance. We [C Company] were strung out in a moving skirmish line picking off anything that came out. Dozens of Germans came out of the woods and into our skirmish line. There was quite a bit a firing. I don't like to use this analogy, but it was like crushing roaches.

A group of four or five Germans came out and they were shot to hell. One of the Jewish guys in the platoon went out from the skirmish line and attacked the German wounded men. I couldn't believe it when I saw it happen. He went out with a trench knife and he tried to pick the eyes out of one of the Germans. Our sergeant saw what was going on and he ran out and I ran out behind him and disarmed the guy. This stuff kind of just happens in war.

Surprisingly, the Germans looked like they were on parade compared to us. Many of them had brand-new uniforms and black boots. If you had to decide who was winning the war by how you looked, we were losing because they looked like a million bucks; they really did. Many of the Germans in the woods survived, and that's why there was so many damn prisoners around that night. You could believe it if you saw it. At the time there had to be fifty Germans around trying to surrender. The wounded Germans were screaming and crying.

The next day as we were moving forward, I saw this trooper; I really can't describe it to you. His one side was bloody and his one arm was bandaged. His rifle was at the ready. As we came up and went by, he gave us a smile and I thought to myself, "If you could ever catch that picture." He looked so placid even under the dire situation. He wasn't wearing an overcoat, just a jump suit. Who would ever think that this guy was winning the war?

Wounded paratrooper heading back to the aid station. (Photo courtesy U.S. Army)

ERNEST MACHAMER

550th Infantry Airborne Battalion, Attached
to the 17th Airborne Division

On the morning of January 4, 1945, the second day of the Allied counteroffensive in the southern part of the Bulge, the 550th Infantry Airborne Battalion, America's second airborne battalion, formed during the summer of 1941 in Panama, was attached to the 17th Airborne Division. The battalion, along with most of the 17th, was tasked with capturing and holding positions along the Bastogne-Marche highway known as Dead Man's Ridge, about twelve miles west of Bastogne itself. That night the Germans counter attacked in force along the ridge. Most of the 550th was in or around the small town of Renaumont, but poor communication with the 17th and a lack of flank protection by neighboring units doomed the independent battalion. Elements of the Führer Begleit Brigade, an indepen-

dent German unit roughly half the size of a panzer division, surrounded Renaumont and hundreds of troops supported by assault
guns overran the 550th defensive perimeter, killing or capturing most
of the battalion. Ernest Machamer recalls that night.

The morning of the attack was bitter cold and the snow was nearly knee
deep. As we neared Renaumont, we crossed an open field and were shelled by
German artillery. While passing a rural home, we saw a family. I vividly remember it—a man, his wife, and one or two children had been tied to a fence
and shot by the Germans. The bodies were frozen stiff. Off to the side, two
dead German soldiers were laying face down in the snow and several hogs
were gnawing on their legs. Before we moved forward, we chased the hogs
away from the bodies.

As we approached Renaumont, we were fired upon by snipers and my
platoon leader was wounded and evacuated. I was placed in command of the
platoon and moved the men into a gully to avoid the sniper fire. In order to establish exactly where sniper fire was coming from, I sent a volunteer about
twenty-five yards behind a haystack. As he was about to reach the haystack,
he took a bullet between the knee and hip, tearing the bone and muscle away.
I took a medic with me and we ran to his aid dragging him behind the stack,
where the medic applied a tourniquet. The sniper fired two or three more
shots near us. The wounded man told me where the sniper was so I directed
some of the men to lay a volley of fire into the top window of a house and that
put an end to the sniper fire.

We moved through the town cautiously. A command post was established
and we set up position between Renaumont and the road leading into the
town. Not long after we set up, the Germans counterattacked. Germans
dressed in American uniforms led the attack. When they started to fire, we reacted and fought them back across the road into the woods. The Germans
mounted a second counterattack but we fought it off.

It was getting late in the day and we had several wounded men. Captain
Morton took it upon himself to evacuate the wounded. Not being a line officer [having direct combat command], he volunteered for the job jokingly saying, "Only the good die young." So the wounded were lifted onto a jeep and
taken to battalion aid station. On a return trip, Morton's jeep hit a Teller mine
and he was killed. The jeep looked like a pretzel since the front and back
wheels were practically joined together. Everybody loved this officer and
morale sank like a rock among the men when we saw what happened.

By late afternoon B and C companies were repositioned to get ready for
night perimeter defense around the town. My platoon was assigned the left

flank of the perimeter. After digging in, a jeep drove up and stopped about twenty-five yards from my position. An officer and two men approached one of my men and ordered him out of his foxhole. He came to attention and words were exchanged. The officers then left. I went down to question the man about what had went on. He said that it was General Patton who chewed him out because he was unshaven, didn't know how to come to attention, his clothing was dirty, and about ten more things he found fault with.

Not long after nightfall, we could hear German tanks moving around the town. We knew that a night attack was imminent. Shortly afterward, the town was surrounded and German infantry started to move into the town. I had a runner named Roy Seltzer, who kept running messages from me to the command post in the center of the town. Gunfire and explosions echoed throughout the night. Finally the tanks broke through our defensive perimeter. We knew things were getting desperate.

I tried to contact the 194th Glider Infantry Regiment, which was supposed to be on our left flank, but got no response. By this time German machine gun fire was all around us. Seltzer came back for the last time and told me that some men were surrendering. I decided to get out of there with as many of my men as I could.

We went back along the edge of town and came upon a small group of men who I thought might be Germans, so I challenged them. One man said, "We're Americans with an engineering group." They had no weapons. I couldn't determine if they were our men or if they were Germans so I said, "Walk in front of us." As we left the town we moved over a hill and approached a fence. Someone about a hundred yards to our left was hollering, "A Company assemble over here!" Knowing that to be unlike any order previously issued by our officers, we continued on and attempted to get over the fence but several men were cut by machine gun fire.

About a mile from the town, we were challenged around daybreak. We were told to advance one at a time and be recognized. It was the 194th. We were fed and the walking wounded cared for. What was left of the 550th was formed into a company, ninety-seven men at first count that morning and more dribbled in later in the day. The final count was about two hundred men. We entered the Bulge with over six hundred men.

A few days passed and I was sent with a group to identify those who had given their lives. The town was filled with the battalion's dead and scores of frozen German corpses. The cellar of one of the buildings contained about twenty dead men from the 550th. None of them were carrying weapons. Some people speculated that they were the battalion's critically wounded that had been thrown in there by the Germans. One GI did not have his dog tags and nobody could identify him. I thought it looked like Roy Seltzer so I recorded it that way. Later during the Korean War, someone knocked on my door at home wearing a GI uniform. When I opened the door, it was Roy Seltzer—not a ghost or an apparition but the real thing. He had been captured in the CP on the morning of January 5, 1945. He told me how his family received his insurance check and how elated they were when they discovered that he was still alive.

In retrospect, we did what was asked of us, while enduring long stretches on the fighting line, bitter cold, and frostbitten feet and fingers. Practically every day I remember the many who were captured and those who were wounded and killed. The most saddening part of reflecting upon this is that the 550th died at the end of that night.

DOUG DILLARD

551st Parachute Infantry Battalion,
Attached to the 82nd Airborne Division

Before the beginning of the twentieth century, machine guns and re-peating rifles made bayonet attacks an obsolete tactic, but extraordi-nary circumstances such as lack of ammunition or fear of hitting friendly forces at times justified the bayonet's resurrection. On Janu-ary 4, 1945, Lieutenant Dick Durkee ordered his men to "fix bayo-nets" and led one of the few bayonet charges in the European Theater of Operations in a field outside the small town of Dairomont. Doug Dillard, a communications sergeant with the 551st Parachute Infantry Battalion, describes the charge.

"Fix bayonets and charge!" That was the order that Lieutenant Durkee gave us as we charged across this field and wooded area into the German positions. It was a surprise to me, since we had never heard that order before. In retrospect, I can understand why he did it and can see the advantage in it. He did it in Ko-rea, also. I'm sure it occurred to him that, "Hey, we can scare the hell out of these guys by fixing bayonets!" It may also boost the morale of our own troops. It had been a hell of a day. There was lots of activity and we lost a lot of men. People were pretty mad and fired up. You wanted to accomplish something.

When we heard him say, "Fix bayonets!" everybody charged like crazy. People were yelling and screaming as we moved toward the German positions. We could see the Germans' breath in the cold air and flashes from their two machine guns. As we approached the German positions, Durkee damn near knocked the head off the first German with the butt of his carbine. I can very clearly remember the first row of Germans that we encountered. There were seven or eight of them in a row in their foxholes and they'd been firing in another direction. I remember the Germans turning around, wearing their gray greatcoats and their helmets, trying to get out of their foxholes. As we came around, they didn't have time to get us in their sights; we were on top of them. [Durkee] went from one to the other, running up through that wooded area using the butt of his carbine and, of course, shooting, too.

It was kind of like a scene from a movie. People don't realize some of the scenes that really do happen. At the time, I was right behind Durkee when this happened, and I tried to fire my Thompson submachine gun, but the receiver and barrel was frozen so I couldn't fire it. As Durkee moved from one position to another, it was like he was going down a row of corn, eliminating it. There were six or eight Germans in those foxholes that he alone killed.

I remember looking at this surreal scene with these guys lying back in their foxholes; their breath was going back up in the air, vaporizing as the heat and warmth of their bodies evaporated. I can remember this as clear as [if] it happened yesterday. I helped him round up some of the men and got them under control. Everybody sort of came unglued and were bayoneting the dead German bodies. They just wanted to kill the Germans. The men just unleashed all of this fury that was pent-up inside. It was like the last thirty seconds of a basketball game. It lasted for about ten minutes.

RICHARD DURKEE

551st Parachute Infantry Battalion,
Attached to the 82nd Airborne Division

On the morning of January 7, 1945, the 551st Parachute Infantry Battalion was sent to take the small, fortified Belgian town of Rochelinval. The town was bristling with German machine gun nests and was defended by approximately five hundred Germans from the 183rd Regiment. Before the attack, the 551st had sustained a large number of combat casualties. The cold weather caused "trench foot." Minimal artillery support, a lack of armor (only one tank arrived after the attack started), and poor communication with supporting units made the attack tragically bloody. (The day before the battalion commander supposedly had tried to persuade higher-ups to call it off—to no avail.)[9]

A Company, led by Dick Durkee, consisted of fewer than fifty men and was assigned to make a diversionary attack on the town while B and C companies moved around the flank. Durkee was the only surviving officer—and one of only seven surviving men—from A Company. Miraculously, B and C companies took the town, though with heavy casualties.

Just before we launched the attack, Sergeant Hill told me that the attack was going to be a bloody fight and that a lot of men would never get out alive. I reconnoitered the area prior to the attack and realized how impossible the task would be. I expressed this to Lieutenant Booth, A Company commander, who agreed. However, we had our orders—take the town. Our route of attack was a small country lane that had brush on both sides. Our jumping-off point was about 250 yards from the town.

When Lieutenant Booth gave the nod, we moved out. We had one squad, led by Sergeant Hill, go down the left side of the lane and one squad, led by Sergeant Courtney, go down on the right side of the lane. Lieutenant Dahl and I were in the lane behind the two scouts. Private Mowery was the first scout; he was hit in the stomach and once through the head. I immediately put my machine gun into action behind a tree stump. No sooner had we set up the machine gun than the Germans started firing on our left flank.

We were caught in crossfire. Sergeant Hill, seeing Mowery die, picked up his BAR [Browning Automatic Rifle] and stood there firing two magazines at the Germans. He was wounded several times and finally killed. Following Hill's example, Lieutenant Booth tried to take out the machine gun that killed Hill but was cut down. Meanwhile, I became second scout and Dahl first scout and we continued moving toward the town. A bazooka man followed me.

Halfway up the slope of the hill, which was close to the outskirts of town, I fired the bazooka (the other man loaded), obliterating a machine gun nest. Meanwhile, a sniper was firing on us behind the corner of one of the buildings in town. I knew that I could lob a grenade at him if I had covering fire. So I told Dahl to fire on the sniper while I tossed the grenade. It came up short. Again, I asked Dahl to continue firing, but he was kneeling there with his eyes closed—dead.

I still had the bazooka man with me and saw another man running up the hill. I recognized him as my runner, Pat Casanova. I yelled at him to bring up the rest of the men in a hurry. His answer is something I'll never forget: "Sir, they're all dead." I knew that this was it. After breaking off the attack I ordered the bazooka man to crawl back while I covered him. He started crawling back and then he got up and began to run for the woods. He got about three feet and was cut down by a hail of machine gun bullets.

I started crawling back and found the reason for Casanova's response. The bodies of the men were all over the place, in all kinds of positions. Some of the men were lying face up with sightless eyes, others face down, faces submerged in the snow. From my position, I could not be seen by the Germans, so I said a prayer to myself and got up and ran for the woods. I still don't understand how I survived that day.

ALEX ANDROS

506th Parachute Infantry Regiment, 101st Airborne Division

By the middle of January, the Battle of the Bulge was winding down. The Allies' strategy was to pinch the Germans off from the north and south and link up in the middle of the Bulge at Houffalize. The companies that pursued the retreating Germans were decimated but expected to perform as full-strength units despite their casualties. Alex Andros describes his last day at the Battle of the Bulge near Houffalize.

On January 16, the battalion was ready to launch one of our last attacks. At the time we [H Company] had twenty-four men, I Company had fewer men than we did, and G Company was stronger, with about thirty men. So that's fifty-four, and I think I Company was less than twenty, and this was supposed to be a battalion [750 men]; hell, it didn't even make a company. When we first started out in Bastogne, we had ten officers and, I would say, about 130 enlisted. That last day, there were just two officers left and we had about twenty-four men. The battalion commander at the time was Major Patch. He said to me, "Hey, Andy, how do you think we ought to start out?" I said, "Major, let's just go single file and spread out and if they start getting fire then we can spread out," and that's how we went. It was sort of dumb. The idea was to try and form an attack with fifty men. Here are these troops, down to 20 percent of full strength, and you're attacking. It doesn't make sense. We were too dumb to protest—we didn't know any better! When you think back on it as a mature person, it's hard to believe some of the things we did. That's the way it was—unbelievable people—no one questioned and no one bugged out.

By that time, the Allies' strategy was to pinch the Germans off so they couldn't get back into Germany. I remember we crossed a main highway. We went north of Noville to a little town of Wicourt, near Houffalize. We went across this open field to the east of Noville. The Germans had pretty good positions on a wooded hill. One of my guys was killed going through the field. We went up there and overran the German positions in the woods. There were a few German wounded, quite a few dead, not by our fire but American artillery. It was getting late in the afternoon by the time we got there. We found this neat German dugout which we made our company command post. At that time I was company commander.

Willie Miller, my assistant, was in the CP with my platoon sergeant so I went out to the exit. Looking to the east, there was a valley between us and another wooded area, I'd say about five hundred yards. You could see the Germans retreating—the tanks and self-propelled guns were moving. I was at the exit looking with my binoculars when all of a sudden I saw this blast. Maybe the binoculars had glinted in the sun (I don't know what drew their attention), but man they fired at me, they put three rounds in our position. I was hit by some tree-burst shrapnel.

Elements of 4th Armored Division rolling north during the U.S. counteroffensive. (Photo courtesy Ed Benecke)

That was the third time I got hit during the war. It was a tree burst, it went right through the top of my helmet and just slammed me to the ground. I was stunned, of course, and when I came to, I reached up and was bleeding pretty badly. I was scared as hell and I started yelling, "Medic! Medic!"—but, hell, there was no medic around there. I finally got my senses back and I groped and found my way back to my CP. Old Willie Miller says, "Oh, Jesus, Andy, you're bleeding!" I said, "Yeah." But I had no pain, it was a head wound. He bandaged me up and some medics actually picked me up and took me down to a farmhouse that was turned into an aid station. It was a pretty big house. It was just loaded with smoke; guys were smoking. There were wounded Germans and wounded Americans. One thing I'll say, the medics treated everyone equally, be they Germans or be they Americans. What they did was look for the guys who were in really bad shape. They came and they checked me and said, "Lieutenant, you're okay. You'll be all right." They finally got me in an ambulance; it was dawn the next day and I went back to a hospital in France.

Willie later told me that the battalion commander got them together and, at the time he was the company commander, and he said, "How many men do you have? We're going to continue the attack." Old Willie chirped up and said, "Attack? Hell, I only got seventeen men left!" The next day the 101st was pulled out of Bastogne.

KEN SHAKER

509th Parachute Infantry Battalion,
Attached to the 82nd Airborne Division

By January 28, 1945, time had run out for the men in the 509th Parachute Infantry Battalion—the battle-hardened unit that first saw action in North Africa. During the battle, no airborne unit had suffered more casualties than the 509th. Arriving in the Bulge as a full-strength battalion of about seven hundred men, the 509th was reduced to only fifty-five men.[10] Nevertheless, the order came down to attack and secure the high ground near St. Vith. The day after the final attack, as described below, the 509th, the unit that made America's first combat jump, was disbanded, and the survivors were sent to other units as replacements. Ken Shaker was the ranking officer who led the attack.

I would like to tell you about the last day of the 509th Parachute Infantry Battalion. Of the original seven hundred soldiers there was only about forty of us left. Battalion headquarters consisted of about ten or so men and was located in a house in a wooded area. I was in command of the men and Major Thomasik was the battalion commander. Major Thomasik and I reviewed a map, which showed the location of a hill down the road that our battalion was supposed to attack. After reviewing the map I told the major we would see what we could do (while thinking to myself that I did not want to go).

I moved the battalion down a narrow road that was wooded on both sides. I decided that there might be Germans out ahead of us so we would have to get off this road. I took the men off the road to the right in the woods. I decided to make a left turn and parallel the direction the road was going. This road contained a fire path where the woods were cut down.

My lead scout was in front and I was behind him about three or four yards. We started going across the fire path and a shell went over our heads and blew up right between the two of us. We dropped and the rest of the men followed us crawled on their bellies across the path. We turned left and stopped short of a clearing in the woods. In front of us was the hill we were to attack. It was clear of all vegetation and covered with snow up to the top, where it was wooded. To go up that hill under those circumstances would have been suicide; we would all be killed. Not only did we have to get up the hill, which had no cover, we had to go through snow that was maybe a foot or so deep. I was undecided on exactly how to organize an attack on this hill. I decided I would take one man with me, go off to the right, and see if there was a covered approach to the top of the hill. If a covered approach were found I would take the men up that way.

We were moving parallel to the edge of the clearing and had gone four hundred to six hundred yards when I saw a valley off to the right. There were four or five American tanks in that valley with a large group of American soldiers around them. The men, some infantry and some tankers, appeared to be fresh troops. I had fully intended to attack the hill until I saw these troops. When there are fresh troops available I was not going to attack that goddamn hill. I went a little bit further and saw a covered approach and decided to go back to the men.

Of the forty men we had left, four were replacements and one was a sergeant who looked very competent. I decided I would have the sergeant take a four-man patrol up the covered approach just to see if there was anything at the top of this hill. Up to this time we were not faced with any enemy fire. I went back to the men and told them about the patrol. Then I did something that I always regretted. I asked my radioman, Ed Wojick, if he would be willing to go along with the patrol. (I hated myself for making this decision because in hindsight I know that it was not that necessary.) I wanted to have radio contact with the patrol in case they ran into a problem. He said he would go, but his heart was not in it. I have always regretted that I did not change my mind.

Evidently, the patrol used the covered approach that I had found at the top of the hill. When they got into the woods they encountered a German machine gun position. They received some fire and they returned the fire. After this exchange some of the German soldiers in the machine gun position ran away and one surrendered and was taken prisoner by the patrol. Unfortunately, Wojick had been killed during the fire exchange. I spoke a few words of German to the prisoner, saying "How many men are on the hill?" and pointed to the top of the hill. He gritted his teeth and would not tell me. I took my pistol out and put it at his forehead and I asked him again. He was clenching his teeth but he still would not tell me anything. I told two of my men to take him back to battalion headquarters.

Meanwhile, from headquarters, Major Thomasik asked me if I was going to make the attack. I told him that I was getting into position and suggested that he come up here and see the position for himself. He did not come up and continued to ask me when I was going to attack. I continued to tell him I was getting into position. After seeing all those fresh troops and tanks I was never going to make an attack on that damn hill.

When the two men brought the prisoner back to battalion headquarters there happened to be an interrogation team there. They asked him the same question I had and he still refused to answer. They had him take his shoes and socks off and stand out in the cold; it was a bitter cold day. After about half an hour he decided to talk. He told them that there was a company of 160 Germans somewhere up in the hill. Finally around three or four in the afternoon we got word to go back to battalion headquarters because the attack had been called off.

Subsequently, I learned that this had been a departure point for a new attack and those fresh troops I had seen were in preparation for that attack. The reason we had been told to take the hill was that it was a line of departure for the new attack.

My battalion got on trucks and we went to a place called Trois-Ponts. On our third night there we were told that the 509th had been deactivated.

CHAPTER ELEVEN

DARK FOREST: Battle for the Hürtgen

You smug-faced crowds with kindling eye

Who cheer when soldier lads march by,

Sneak home and pray you'll never know

The hell where youth and laughter go.

—Siegfried Sassoon, "Suicide in the Trenches"

Today a thick green canopy still covers many of the trails winding through Germany's Hürtgen Forest, shielding the forest floor from sunlight. Even in summer the forest is a damp, gloomy place. Once-deep craters and foxholes are now indiscernible depressions. Rain drips down a gray tree trunk into scars created by shrapnel more than five decades ago. They are the legacy of one of the deadliest battles of World War II.

The forest covers a roughly rectangular area, with each side about twenty miles long. On the top right-hand corner of the rectangle is the German town of Düren, and anchoring the top left is the town of Aachen. Nestled in the bottom left lies the German town of Monschau, and on the bottom right are seven hydroelectric dams that control the Roer River, which snakes its way through the forest.

During the heady days of September 1944, the Allies' northern armies were attacking east, trying to punch through Aachen. They had to contend with the nearby Hürtgen Forest, and the Roer and Rhine rivers that guard the German border. Among their obstacles were the huge hydroelectric dams on the Roer. As long as the Germans controlled the dams, they could open the floodgates and sweep away the advancing Allied units or trap them on the east side of the Roer.

For most of the battle, American commanders did not recognize the importance of taking the dams. For nearly three months, the U.S. Army would focus on clearing the villages and road junctions in the forest without plans to seize the dams.

But the rugged terrain allowed the Germans to exact a high toll in lives and time for a few miles gained in the Allied drive into Germany. Camouflaged bunkers that contained machine guns with interlocking fields of fire and mortars and artillery that were ready to fire on set map coordinates at a moment's notice were all part of the Germans' deadly defense. Thousands of mines, too, complicated the Allies' every movement.

Fighting in the forest negated the Allies' armor, because there was not enough room for heavy vehicles to maneuver on the narrow roads and trails. (There was barely enough room for two regiments to operate effectively.)[1] The forest also blocked Allied air support, and artillery was hampered because the Germans held most of the high ground during the battle. Ultimately, the five-month campaign in the forest cost the Allies about forty thousand casualties.

The Rangers arrived in the Hürtgen Forest on November 14, 1944. With the exception of B Company, which sustained heavy casualties in and around the small forest towns of Germeter and Vossenack, most of the 2nd Ranger Battalion was placed in reserve. Their time was not wasted, however, and the Rangers went through another period of intensive training, ending late on the evening of December 6, when they boarded trucks on a mission that would be the defining moment for the unit.

The assault and capture of Hill 400 was one of the Rangers' most impressive yet least remembered actions of the war. Hill 400, also known as Castle Hill, was heavily defended because it offered artillery observers a commanding view of the forest. Rangers were called upon to charge across an open field that was laced with a deadly mixture of interlocking machine gun, mortar, and artillery fire. After about an hour of intense combat, the Rangers captured the hill.

For the next two days, the Germans threw everything they had against the Rangers. The top of the hill offered hardly any protection, and by noon on December 7, the two Ranger companies were badly depleted. D Company, for instance, had seventeen men left from an initial assault force of about sixty-five men. Yet these seventeen and men from F Company held the hill against hundreds of German troops from the crack 6th Parachute Regiment.[2] The hill was so important that Field Marshal Walter Model offered Iron Crosses and a two-week furlough to any Germans who could recapture

Ranger and Airborne Operations in the Hürtgen Forest—Nov. 1944–Feb. 1945

HOLLAND

Aachen •   Düren •

Bergstein •

Hürtgen Forest

Schmidt •

BELGIUM

Schwammenauel Dam

Monschau •

GERMANY

Röer R.

Ranger Actions on Hill 400—Dec. 7–9, 1944

2nd Ranger Btn.

Bergstein

E Company

D Company

400

⟨4⟩

⟨3⟩

⟨2⟩

Ger   ⊠ III 6

Zerkall

Röer R.

Kall R.

← German Attacks

⊐ Bunker

Note: On December 8 elements of E Company reinforce Hill 400

Brandenburg

Germeter •

⟨1⟩ (Thanksgiving Day, 1944)

505   ⊠ III   82 (Feb. 8)

517   ⊠ III (Feb. 6-8)

Röer R.

Hill 400 ▲ ⟨6⟩

Bergstein   Zerkall

Nideggen

Vossenack

Death Valley

Kall R.

⟨5⟩

Kommerscheidt

Harscheidt

Röer R.

9 ⊠ XX

78 ⊠ XX

Schmidt

(Feb. 9)

Schwammenauel Dam

N

⟨1⟩ Sid Salomon, *2nd Ranger Btn.*

⟨2⟩ Bud Potratz, *2nd Ranger Btn.*

⟨3⟩ L-Rod Petty, *2nd Ranger Btn.*

⟨4⟩ Herman Stein, *2nd Ranger Btn.*

⟨5⟩ Duaine Pinkston, *505th PIR, 82nd*

⟨6⟩ Carl Kiefer, *517th PRCT*

0   1

Miles

it.[3] After sustaining a large number of casualties, the Rangers were relieved by the 8th Division's 13th Regiment on December 9, 1944, and placed in defensive positions in a relatively quiet sector of Belgium during the Battle of the Bulge.

By the first week of January, the Battle of the Bulge had practically been decided and the Allies were turning their attention to seizing Germany. The combined Allied Chiefs of Staff determined that the main Allied thrust into Germany would come from the north near the Ruhr, the industrial heartland of Germany. This would be led by the Twenty-first Army Group, supported by the U.S. Ninth Army. The Ninth had to cross the Roer to reach the Rhine River, but could not do so until the Roer's dams were under Allied control.[4]

The dams were made the highest priority, and, after fighting its way to the Siegfried Line and the German border in February 1945, the 82nd Airborne Division was dispatched to the forest to help the 78th Division to capture them. Spearheading the effort of the 82nd was the seasoned 505th Parachute Infantry Regiment, and on its left flank was the 508th Parachute Infantry Regiment. As the 505th surged forward, they saw the human wreckage of the men who came before them: Hundreds of dead GIs were frozen there, along with their tanks and other equipment, trapped during the 28th Division's doomed attack in the fall.

Using Hill 400 and Bergstein as launching pads, the 517th Parachute Regimental Combat Team mounted an important diversionary attack on the German 6th Parachute Regiment. The Germans fell for the diversion, believing that the 517th attack was a main thrust on the dams, and the action kept the bulk of the German forces away from the main Allied thrust at Schmidt.[5]

That thrust succeeded, and the 78th took the dams, but not before the Germans blew the discharge valves, flooding the Roer Valley and delaying the Allied offensive for two weeks.

The effectiveness of the Rangers and airborne notwithstanding, the battle for the Hürtgen Forest was a disaster for the U.S. Army. Failure on the part of the American high command to realize the importance of the Roer dams delayed the drive on Germany and cost a large number of men their lives.

SID SALOMON

2nd Ranger Battalion

On the night of November 21, under cover of darkness, B Company of the 2nd Ranger Battalion made its way through the gloomy bowels of the Hürtgen Forest. Its objective was to provide flank protection for the 12th Infantry Regiment. Sid Salomon's vignette is typical of fighting in the Hürtgen.

We went in there the night before Thanksgiving, and it was pitch dark, so it must have been pretty late at night; my guess would be probably eleven at night. If you put your hand in front of your face you couldn't see it. The forest in general was so dark that even in the daytime you had a hard time seeing. When I say it was a forest, those trees weren't just scattered around, they were densely packed together. You had to put your hand on the shoulder of the man in front of you, it was so dark and thickly wooded.

As we moved toward our objective, we ran into K Company of the 12th Regiment. We were supposed to go in there and protect their flank. We went in there and found the 12th Regiment sergeant hiding in a dugout. He was supposed to guide us in, but he wouldn't get out of the dugout. My first sergeant, Ed Andrusz, told him to get out, and when he didn't, he just yanked that sergeant by the collar and gave him a bash in the jaw! He just sat there cringed down in the dugout. So I led the company in there.

Unfortunately we went pretty far and we walked into a minefield. Mines went off one after the other. A couple of people were killed, and a lot of people lost part of their legs. I had the one platoon dig in right there, and the other platoon came in and joined them. I figured we'd just wait until dawn. I took what had been a German headquarters, it was a good-sized hole that was half-covered with fallen trees purposely used as a protection from shell tree bursts [artillery that exploded around the tops of trees and scattered deadly shell fragments].

I grabbed this dugout and made it my CP [command post], and the first sergeant and the company runner and one platoon sergeant, J. J. Young, they came in there. Well, a shell landed directly on top. With the trees across it (it was put up like a log cabin except it was in the ground), my first sergeant, platoon sergeant, and company runner were all wounded. (The runner got his leg amputated, he was wounded so badly.) It got me too, lightly, and I'm knocking wood now.

When dawn came, we pretty much looked to find out where we were. We grabbed a couple of prisoners who came walking through; they were scared to death, but I was pretty rough with them because I was absolutely livid that so many of my men had been hit. I did not treat them with kid gloves. I put one on a stump and I said, "Start calling names." I had German in high school, and some of it came back to me, and I said, "Call Fritz and Johann and everybody else!" The guy was almost in tears. I had two of them on the tree stumps, and shells were coming in, and I just made them stand up there. We started to evacuate some of the wounded guys and we made the prisoners help carry the guys back.

A Company came into what was left of my company. I would say that's the first time I was truly thankful on Thanksgiving night, when A Company came to relieve us. When we came back, the rest of the battalion was in the reserve area, and when we came back, all the other men from other companies had dug foxholes for the men of B Company. Boy, that was really comradeship within the battalion; they had heard what we were undergoing up there and we didn't have to dig a foxhole; the foxholes had already been dug by the battalion [2nd Ranger Battalion].

When we got back, we all got a good night's sleep that night. The mess sergeant had saved a hot turkey dinner for us. We didn't eat anything while we were up there, so of course we all ate it ravenously, and wouldn't you know, the next day we all had the GIs [the runs].

BUD POTRATZ

2nd Ranger Battalion

In the cold morning hours of December 7, 1944, D and F companies of the 2nd Ranger Battalion attacked the most important hill of the Hürtgen Forest. Crossing an open field, the Rangers stormed the heavily defended Hill 400. Bud Potratz of D Company offers his recollections of that day in this e-history.

I was just talking with my wife this evening, we had just gotten back from church, and we were talking about different things. I don't know how we got on the subject of the war, but I said, "It's surprising that now that I am retired how all these memories keep coming back." Seeing certain faces during the day also reminds you of someone that you fought with. Last night on our local TV station they had something on the Battle of the Bulge, and seeing that brings it back, looking at the empty eyes of the fellows in combat, the blank stare. They come back in the day, at night—they just never leave.

The call came down from the Company CP to rack it up and be ready in twelve minutes. We gathered our personal belongings and placed them in our duffel bag, and we had to carry a bedroll made up of an OD blanket, raincoat, pair of socks, and a cartridge belt of .30-caliber bullets, bandoliers, our shovel, two fragment grenades, and our M-l rifle. I wore two pairs of trousers, shirts over long-john underwear, wool knit cap under my helmet, sweater, jacket, overcoat, wool knit finger gloves and combat boots, but no overshoes as my size was not available.

At darkness, the noncoms returned to their sections and prepared their men. We were told the objective would be a high hill called Sugerloaf (per Mike Sharik at the time). We later found the hill was called Castle Hill 400 in the Hürtgen Forest and that we were the farthest troops penetrated on German soil.

We boarded the trucks and rumbled in darkness into the dark Hürtgen Forest toward a small hamlet called Klienhau. The town was leveled and burning. Curtains flapped in the wind, casting errant shadows. We dashed past the burning buildings into the darkness.

The weather was wet, with stinging sleet in our faces. Our overcoats became heavy with moisture, and our packs dug deeply into our shoulders. When the column stopped briefly, we would bend over to relieve the pressure on our backs. It was stop and go all the way to Bergstein, where our objective, Hill 400, was located.

The road to Bergstein was ankle deep with mud. It was a hard trudge and very tiring. The most shocking thing we saw on our march to Bergstein was

The front side of Hill 400, which D and F companies of the 2nd Ranger Battalion assaulted on December 7, 1944. Many of the survivors of Pointe-du-Hoc were involved in the assault and valiant defense of the hill. (Author's photo)

the eerie silhouettes of knocked-out American tanks occupied by dead GIs blackened by the cold. It was real spooky, very haunting. We were annoyed by the delays, and some of us climbed the tanks searching for bedrolls for protection from the sleeting winds. We did not know that there was a reconnaissance patrol from D and F companies' platoon leaders searching the base of the hill for the best advance and to determine the strength of the enemy.

We finally got into Bergstein and entered the cellars of the gutted buildings. I remember sitting on a coal pile. We readied our weapons and smoked and tried to dry out and get warm. It was cold and miserable. I smoked several cigarettes recently received from my aunt for Christmas (a whole carton of Luckys). I assumed this was the jump-off spot for the attack.

Mike Sharik, our section leader, said, "Let's move out." I got to the top of the stairs, and Captain McBride was standing at the doorway and yelling to us, "There she is!" I just looked at the hill through the misty dawn, and the hill looked like a cookie cone upside-down; it came to a point.

When we hit the streets, all hell broke loose! Shells fell all around us. The Jerries were hitting us from three sides, the east, north, and south.

Easy Company was first through the town and flushed out the enemy still occupying the east end of the town. I saw the enemy running down the street toward us with helmets off and hands in the air. I couldn't believe that they were not getting hit by shrapnel. We moved on down the street past a cobblestone small bridge of only fifteen yards or so. We then advanced on the run through the shrapnel adjacent to the large stone church and into a cemetery. The tombstones had fallen over and some of the graves ripped open. On our advance we used the stones for protection. We finally made it to the sunken road that ran like a half-moon from the south and bending in a curve to the north.

Fox Company led the way followed by the 1st and 2nd sections of the 1st Platoon of Dog Company. We fell on the ground at the sunken road and began firing our rifles toward the two burned-out buildings in front of the D Company attack. Mortar shells fell all around us, and our guys were getting hit. We lost several men in the advance through the cemetery. The company aid man was patching up the wounded throughout all the shelling. We called him Doc Kildare (from the B movies of our time and played by Lew Ayres). Mike and I were the farthest on the south side of the line. Sharik knew some of our guys who stayed in the cellars and ran back to get them. During that time we continued to fire over the terrain at the buildings and at the machine gun nests at the base of the hill. Mike returned with Lieutenant Lomell, Sergeant Floyd Webb (1st section), Levering, and Greenwood (recent replacements in my section from the Headquarters Company). One was a cook and the other a truck driver in the motor pool.

Captain Masny gave the order to fix bayonets, and suddenly Mike Sharik stood up and said, "C'mon, you unholy bastards!" and off we went. A few men did not get up for the charge. I remember firing at the hip and hollering "Hi-Ho Silver!" as we trotted across the open field toward the base of the hill. I slammed against one of the buildings, and Mike and Lomell were at my right side.

All of a sudden, our bazooka man, Karr, came around the building screaming, he was hit. I grabbed him by the cartridge belt and roared at him to get down. I could not attend to him. I had to move on. Mike, Lomell, and I ran past several Jerries who raised their arms to surrender at the machine gun nests. I heard later that [one man] following the 1st Platoon cut them down in the haste of battle. I used my M-1 rifle as a staff in the steep climb of the hill. At one point I turned my head to see who was behind us and I only saw John Riley about twenty yards behind me.

I turned from looking down the hill at Rip Riley and looked to all sides looking for Jerries. I remember that my mouth was dry as cotton and [I was] perspiring profusely. At times I would use my rifle as a staff to give me more strength and push.

As we got to the top of the hill, a large concrete bunker and observation tower loomed before us. Captain Masny was already at the top with several of his F Company men. Masny placed his large foot (with overshoes on) against the cast-iron door. He hollered for a bazooka, but there was none around. Karr, our bazooka man, and perhaps F Company's man were already casualties.

Upon arriving at the very top, Masny looked at Lomell, Sharik, and I along with two other men from F Company to go forward over the top of the hill to the east and go down the other side and set up a line of fire to ward off a counterattack. I recall sliding down on my butt down the steep hill. My shovel fell out of my cartridge belt that was anchored on the belt in the rear. I saw the shovel slide down the hill rapidly. I had no time to retrieve it as we had our eyes glued on the terrain looking for Jerries. Upon hitting the base of the hill, we could see the river in the distance. On the other side of the river there was another hill where the Jerries had dug in some artillery. We knew the Jerries were looking down our throats.

Mike and I lay together (bad thing to do, but there is always the feeling of security being close to someone). Lomell was to our right and the guys from F Company to our left. Suddenly, a shell came in and took out the large tree to our right. The tree fell in front of our view and we had to move to establish a clearer line of fire. The tree saved our lives! As we lay on the ground looking east and south and north, we began to shiver from the cold. We both smoked cigarettes. Chain-smoked. I even gave Mike two packs of Luckys!

Then without warning shells hit the hill from three sides. We could hear our comrades trying to dig in above. There were screams of dying men. The smoke burned our eyes and nostrils. It was horrific, and the voices of the wounded tore out our hearts. Within about fifteen minutes all was quiet. After a spell, I don't recall the time, but it was a long period, Lomell stated he was going to the top and see who was left of the companies and seek reinforcements for us.

An hour passed, and with no additional help, Sharik pondered our withdrawal. I told Mike that if the Jerries do counterattack, we would be in a better position to fight in a higher position and have a better advantage. Mike then stated to the two men from F Company to go northeast and up to where we thought F Company may be dug in. The center of the hill on the east was sheer rock and had a very sharp dropoff. Mike and I then went to the southeast of the hill toward the D Company sector (we hoped). We came upon Secor and Lawson dug in under a huge rock and very much alive. At that moment, I wondered if we were the only survivors of D Company. We continued up higher among dead Rangers, further to the south. Then we came upon Dick Martin (1st Section) and further to the south and a bit higher ran into Staff Sergeant Lester Arthur. (Arthur was wounded at Hill 63 in late August/September and just came back to the outfit just before departure from the rest area.) Alongside of Arthur was Robinson (our company barber) dug in together. They were digging a deep foxhole!

Next to them was Sergeant Leroy "Pop" Adams with the 1st Platoon mortar, who was used as an assault troop in the charge up the hill. Pop was hit badly in the neck and it appeared a main artery was nicked. He was bleeding steadily. Arthur said he stuffed a bandage on his neck and gave him a morphine shot. I looked at Pop and tried to console him but I could see he was dying. Pop did bleed to death that night of the seventh as the aid personnel of C Company came up to get him. I hardly knew Pop.

Mike then started to dig in what was Robinson's foxhole. I saw three dead Rangers to my right. One was Pat McCrone, still on his knees, shovel in hand, helmet blown off and his brains were exposed. Next to Pat were Frank Lewis and Staff Sergeant Michael Branley, also of the second platoon. One could only ID them by their dog tags.

I grabbed Pop's shovel and began to dig in near McCrone, Lewis, and Branley. By early afternoon, Tech Sergeant Joe Stevens, his runner PFC Sam O'Neal, and Lomell came above our position and had little to say other than we had taken severe losses. We had Jerries on all three sides.

I had just about finished digging my foxhole at dusk when a guy from the 2nd Platoon jumped into my foxhole. His name was Brown. He had been in the bunker and was told to get outside and help ward off an impending attack. We had repulsed two counterattacks on the seventh, about late morning and in the middle of the afternoon. There was a large enemy tank parked on the east side of a building in the near distance. We could see the burst of fire as the tank zeroed in our position. We were helpless as there were no artillery observers available. By early afternoon we were told that D Company had but thirteen men and F Company had eleven or twelve men. Our hopes began to fade.

That night the Jerries sent out a recon patrol on our side of the hill (and probably on F Company side, too). Later in the evening, Brown got straight up and stretched in the darkness. I pulled on his leg to get him down. Just plain stupid! Within seconds a grenade bounced off the top of our foxhole, and the impact was to the front of the hole. We were lucky! We were on the double alert from then on in. Later that night, a three-man machine gun crew come up on our side. They were from the 8th Division. We told them to pipe down and be careful where they walked. I told them to be careful as there were three dead Rangers next to us. These guys became stone quiet. They moved to our right and dug in about thirty yards to our right.

At dawn, all hell broke loose! The Jerries hit us with everything they had, artillery, mortars, and tank fire. I had never experienced such a long and hard barrage [as that] laid down on us that morning of the eighth. Mike Sharik hollered out that he was hit in the leg. Then he hollered again that he was hit again in the leg. Tree bursts. Suddenly, Brown started to scream and holding his hand. His thumb had been sheared off, and only a bloody stump remained. Both Mike and Brown bolted from the foxhole and made their way to the top of the hill to the bunker, which was the aid station for the wounded.

I then felt a sickening burning on my left upper hip. I knew I was hit, but not the extent of the wound. The shelling stopped and I tried to help myself, but all the clothes I had on made the effort all but impossible. Suddenly, an aid man came to my foxhole and jumped and cut away the clothing and dumped sulfa on the wound. I could see the mangled flesh. He stuffed a bandage into the wound and he disappeared.

I braced myself in my foxhole so as I could stand. The guys in the machine gun squad were all killed. That left only Secor, Lawson, Martin, Arthur, Robertson, myself, and two guys that came up the hill on our side in the very late afternoon of the seventh. Eight men on our side. There was a big gap now to our right. We had no idea the number of men left on the morning of the eighth in F Company.

Then the counterattacks started in earnest. The Jerries hit F Company side and then to the southwest on our side. The hill was too steep for them in the east (center) of the hill to advance. I would hazard a guess that the attack on each side was made up of a platoon or better. We just kept on firing at the black helmets, and I thought I'd burn out my M-l [rifle]. But I had a reserve, and so did the rest of us. We took guns, grenades, and ammo from our fallen comrades. We repulsed the first attack of the morning.

I was shaking and almost exhausted after the first attack. I drank water and readied my weapons for the next attack. I remember praying to God to be gentle with my parents when they learned of my death.

After the first attack, we got help from the 8th Division. A lieutenant (forward observer) came to our position and laid in artillery support on the tank to our south. I'm sure he got the tank, as we never had any more problems from it later. Then we had the Air Corps with P-47s dive-bombing the enemy to the north of the hill near the F Company sector. God, what an uplifting sight it was.

Lawson and Secor took a prisoner in the first counterattack the morning of the eighth. He appeared to be regular German army. Then there was a lull, and about noon it started again. The Jerries just kept coming and coming. We fired at will and took our toll. We didn't lose a man! Again the enemy retreated down the hill (what was left of them). We then had some recon action but nothing compelling as the earlier attacks. Guess the Jerries wanted to find out what our strength was after the attacks.

Joe Stevens came around to our positions in the A.M. and later in the late afternoon. Captain McBride came up part of the way of the hill to where the three infantrymen lay dead. He looked our way and then went down the hill. Later, near dusk, Tex Lawson and Arthur took the light machine gun to Secor and Lawson's position. Sure as heck, the Jerries made one last attempt at dusk, but the machine gun ended their hopes for good.

Just before total darkness, a runner came to our position and told us we were going to be relieved later that night. I know I was exhausted and stiff but thanked the good Lord for the protection.

BILL "L-ROD" PETTY

2nd Ranger Battalion

Bill Petty is an old soldier fading away in a nursing home, just one of many treated by a staff that barely knows him.* But Petty isn't forgotten by his fellow Rangers or his family, and they scrounged up this let-

---

* Sadly, Mr. Petty passed away in the spring of 2000.

ter he had written to Ranger Sid Salomon in the 1980s about Hill 400.
For his actions as a staff sergeant, Petty received two Silver Stars.

During the wait for the jump-off [from Bergstein], Otto was very much his usual self—moving up and down the line checking the men. Roland had become extremely agitated. Most of the men near me seemed to be calm at this point. A few minutes after we were in place, a German at the edge of the woods jumped up, put up a flare and made a dash to the left toward a pillbox. Most of us took a shot at him, but all missed. Almost immediately there were a few pot shots exchanged across the field but this petered out as we began to get mortar fire to our rear.

The first mortar bursts exploded about 75 or 100 yards behind us and seemed to be coming from our left front. In establishing their range and lateral adjustments the bursts began to creep nearer. You could feel the tension building up in the line and voices grumbling about why we didn't charge. Of course we could not because almost simultaneous with the mortar fire our own artillery commenced to shell the hill.

I think that every man on the line was convinced that the mortars would reach us before our artillery lifted. I know I was. Caught in a space of less than 200 yards between two barrages, tension was building up to the exploding point. Incongruously, [a new officer] squatted beside me and yelled, "Send out a scout." My response was, "Fuck you—no way!" After repeating the order to me a couple of times and getting the same response, he switched to McHugh with the same order and received the same response. He then yelled the same order to Private Bouchard screaming that it was an **order!** Here, he got results against both McHugh and I both telling him not to go. Bouchard stood and started walking across the field. At no more than four steps he was shot in the belly. This shot was the fuse that ignited the explosion of the Ranger charge.

I was crawling out to pull Bouchard back by his feet and was just reaching for them when I heard McHugh yell, "Let's go get the bastards!" Waving his Tommy gun over his head, he broke across the field. The fuse had reached the powder!

As one man, D and F [companies] with bayonets shining, hip firing, and yelling a battle cry that probably goes back into the eons of time charged into the jaws of death. I know that I will never see a more brave and glorious sight. It was for me indeed a moment of being proud to be a Ranger.

But as with all things of glory there is always a price to be paid. Halfway across the field the line began to become staggered as some were faster runners than others. It became a disarrayed assault with no one in command. It would have been impossible to do so. As we entered the forest at the foot of the hill the force of the charge carried us into our own shelling that was still in full barrage. We had temporarily escaped the enemy but were being slaughtered by our friends.

The result for F Company was costly. Three dead and several seriously wounded. Here is where I lost both section leaders from my platoon. McHugh, my right hand and brother, wounded, and Winch killed. What had started as a grand and glorious charge had turned into pandemonium.

Jumping the gun by several minutes, although costly, was probably a bargain. Had this not occurred, the mortars would have chewed us to pieces. Had we lasted through that, the pillbox's machine guns would have mowed us down. It is doubtful that any, or very few, would have reached the woods.

Having been caught off guard when the charge surged forward, I arrived about a couple of minutes late, which probably saved me from injury. As previously stated I was in the process of trying to reach Bouchard when the jump came; consequently I had difficulty catching up. However, from behind position, I was able to see it all unfold.

When I reached the area just inside the woods where F Company had run into our artillery and experienced its first major casualties, I found a situation of turmoil. There were people trying to help the wounded, others hesitant to move forward, and one man doing his usual—shooting prisoners.

From this confusion, individuals began to separate and continue toward the top. No organization, platoon personnel becoming intermixed, each man on his own. I might add at this point that these were the same 12 or 15 men who had carried the company in combat since we landed D-Day. Along the way we had lost some of these men, but there always seemed to be a couple of replacements who filled the gap in this group—Moss, Hanahan, etc.

I am ashamed to admit that I paused in this confusion only momentarily, which was the wrong move for a platoon sergeant. I should have tried to get them organized. I didn't. I guess my adrenaline was pumping to the extent that I reacted as an individual. Whatever—my drive was to reach the top, which I was able to do in six or eight minutes along with Manning and Anderson from the 1st Platoon. This was because we had passed through and out of the barrage and met no small arms fire on the way up.

On the F Company side of the hill we were the first three up. Manning was about 30 yards ahead and just kept running right over the top. Anderson and I saw the bunker and went for it. We received no fire as we moved in. We ran into the main entrance and encountered a steel door to our left along a hallway about eight feet. We could hear the enemy inside. In the door was a small flap (somewhat like a mail flap) that opened in. I got my BAR [Browning Automatic Rifle] into it, got off a magazine and held it open for him to drop in both our grenades.

In anticipation of the explosion we both started to break for the outside. The sight of my BAR got caught in the slot when the flap closed. I left it hung up and was right on his heels as we reached the main entrance. A shell burst within 10 feet and blew him backwards into me. As I clutched him to hold him up with my hands across his chest, the force of the blood from his heart (direct fragment) blew my hand about a foot away. He never knew what hit him and I let him down. The enemy's short-range shelling had begun.

I was momentarily alone and somewhat shaken. Very shortly, maybe a couple of minutes, Rat Top and Pannes arrived and I put them to digging in. Impossible. Right on their heels came Masny and the usual F Company contingent of front men. He immediately took over and began to clean out the bunker. I remember some of D Company men being involved, but can't remember who they were. In the meanwhile there was a temporary lull in the shelling. As F Company people arrived, I tried to get them under some sort of shelter as Masny was busy cleaning out the bunker.

After the bunker was cleared, Otto, Roland, Ryan and I were standing in front of it evaluating the situation when four shells hit the face of it, knocking us helter-skelter. Amazingly none of us were hit, but the fragments gave several others serious wounds. [One man] was in stunned hysteria so I slapped

The main observation bunker on top of Hill 400 as it appears today. (Author's photo)

his face sharply a few times to get him out of it—I couldn't—so I put him in the bunker.

The shelling began again and we were receiving heavy casualties. Otto made the decision to go for reinforcements himself as he felt he wouldn't get them unless he did it himself. He was probably right; because I sent requests for it several times during the day and received none. He had not gone far on his mission when he was captured. He was close enough for me to hear it happen. And suddenly after less than an hour at the top I found that I had a company on my hands—or what was left of it.

It was not a position I wanted to be in but [I had no choice]. We had turned the bunker into an aid station before Otto left. It rapidly became a refuge for many trying to stay out of battle. It was very tempting when you carried someone in to stay. Anyway, I couldn't keep Roland out of it, so I gave it up and assumed command. On the D Company side of the hill, Len Lomell was in charge and we were in touch occasionally throughout the rest of the day.

For the remainder of the day I tried to keep F Company in some sort of organization and to set up defenses for the enemy attacks that I knew were bound to come. Herm Stein had already taken on part of this responsibility. He had positioned himself with mostly 1st Platoon men and a couple from the 2nd near the bottom of the hill toward the river—where we all should have been. From the F Company side I am convinced that these six or eight men were the vital factor that kept F from being overrun.

My efforts to organize were hampered by another heavy barrage that began shortly after Masny left. What had been thick forest when we took the top was rapidly being blown apart. Actually, I spent most of my time for the next 30–50 minutes getting wounded people disentangled from downed trees and carrying them into the bunker. Screams for L-Rod seemed never to stop. The few of us able to function were eventually able to get the live wounded under cover. It was during this barrage that I carried Anderson's brother Jack into the bunker, and as I did so I knew that he was dying. Thus I had the dubious distinction of having held both brothers while they were in the process of dying within an hour's time. When this barrage ended most of the 2nd Platoon were out of action.

Some time after the barrage ended (I don't know how long) an enemy probe was made in our sector from the direction of what I later found out was the pillbox area. They didn't show much determination and were repulsed with no casualties for us. Sometime shortly thereafter there was another probe from somewhat the same direction. They showed less determination and withdrew.

After this withdrawal Whitey Barowski and I did a recon in the direction from which they had come. We got close enough to their position that I could see they were preparing to attack. They seemed to be organizing into five- or six-men squads. We retreated back up the hill and I began the not too easy task of getting all able bodies out of the bunker to fight off the attack.

Roland helped me with this and we were the last two out. By this time Barowski and several others had engaged the enemy and were involved in a brisk firefight at fairly short range. Roland charged immediately into the midst of the fray. The Germans were either prone or kneeling but all of the Rangers were standing and moving to meet them. I began trying to get people down but to no avail. All their combat training had gone to hell in the excitement.

I don't know how many got hit—if any except Roland. There seemed to be a lull on both sides and Barowski got Roland on his back piggyback style (he was bleeding from the chest) and started back up the hill with him. Roland was then fatally shot in the head and Barowski began shouting, "They're firing from the top of the trees!"

As I looked up at the few trees left standing I picked up a group of the enemy moving even with us to our left as we faced down hill. Reading it as a flanking movement to get above us, I grabbed a new kid named Shannon and moved across and up to cut them off.

In my opinion some were already above us and had shot Roland; hence, Barowski's feeling of being shot at from above. My reasoning on this is as Shannon and I were running to the left on an upward slant I saw some at least even with us.

Whatever the facts of that, I was running at full speed with Shannon only a couple of steps behind. We came upon a German about 20 feet away in a prone position and a rifle aimed dead center on me. I saw him too late. I fired, but a second too late. He must have flinched because the bullet passed through my right shoulder and into Shannon's chest. He lived. After emptying my BAR [Browning Automatic Rifle] into the German, I found that I could not lift it to reload.

That was the beginning of the end for me. As neither Shannon nor I could fire a weapon, we retreated towards the bunker. I don't know what happened to the enemy that we were after. My guess is that D Company took care of them, or they retreated as their main thrust in the middle had been stopped.

While moving back towards the bunker I felt completely naked and helpless. Many people have never believed this, but as long as I had that BAR in my hand, combat didn't bother me that much. It was never pleasant, but I always had felt that I could handle anything I encountered. I guess it was my security blanket.

Herm Stein, hearing the attack, had come up the hill to help. I met him near the bunker and I was crying with frustration. I still had the BAR but couldn't use it. I think I was about as near flipping out as one can get without going over. Perhaps had I not met Stein at that moment I would have. He took the BAR off me and pushed me into the bunker. I had started off the day at 7 o'clock, as a platoon sergeant, confident, and had thought competent, with a full platoon. By 4 o'clock, four men were left of this platoon, and during my brief stint as acting company leader had had almost an entire company wiped out. So much for L-Rod's leadership.

I remained in the bunker for two to three hours and helped the medic get the walking wounded on their way. We sent them out in groups of one and two accompanied by one able-bodied man who was armed. There were two or three of these men who made several round trips. The only one that I remember was Ferry.

I would like to interject here that the young medic up there should have received some sort of high decoration. He kept his cool all day, and believe me that had to be difficult considering the seriousness of some of the wounds he had to handle. The hell of it is I can't remember his name or if he lived through it. The only small error I saw him pull all day was giving me another shot of morphine whenever I asked. By the time Ferry took me down the hill I was feeling no pain, I was high as a kite.

As Ferry and I arrived in Bergstein they were shelling the streets so we ducked into the church basement. The first thing I saw when I went in was a first sergeant sitting comfortably against the wall smoking. I don't know why it infuriated me so much, for the entire company had known he was yellow since D-Day; but I went nuts and began kicking the hell out of him. By the time they got me under control I had had the satisfaction of giving several other officers my opinion of them. I can assure you it was not complimentary.

Apropos comparison between D-Day and The Hill: My feelings are that A, B and C had a similar tough job. However, Pointe-du-Hoc, in my opinion, received (and still does) credit out of proportion to what really happened there. Hell, after the initial assault and the counterattacks across the road, all we did was hide for the next couple of days. I personally would take my three days there as an annual holiday when compared to my one day on The Hill.

The trauma to me was deep and lasting, and the battle will always be yesterday. Please keep in mind that in this account I intend no criticism of anyone who actually participated. I felt then, and still do, each man performed to his best ability under very trying circumstances. Sound bitter? You can bet your ass—unforgivingly so, even after 43 years.

HERMAN STEIN

2nd Ranger Battalion

Herm Stein describes the crack German 6th Parachute Regiment's numerous attempts to retake Hill 400.

There is a camaraderie that just grabs you. You just can't let the guy that you are with down, that's all. The guys that you fight with, you feel for, that's the patriotism. You are not even thinking of surviving. You are thinking of the best way to get by and do your job; the easiest and best way you can do it.

[On December 7] we moved up in the churchyard and we came along a long bank that was two and a half, maybe three foot high, and you sort of crouched along there. We were on the forward side, the left side. As you face the hill we were on the left side, and we went all the way down. The Germans started throwing artillery at us seventy-five yards in front of us, pounding away, creeping closer to our positions each minute. The Germans were in a wooded area, and they had a couple of machine guns.

The field we had to cross was completely bald. It was in the wintertime, so there was nothing growing there. Before we went, the German artillery was coming up behind us, and our artillery was in front of us. We were supposed to move at 7:30, but we felt if we didn't make a move beforehand we'd get slaughtered by the German mortars. Then McHugh stood up, had his gun over his head and said, "OK, let's get the bastards!" And we stood up just like in a movie. It was also like seeing a wave in the football field. It started all with us and moved across into D Company—we were F Company. We went over as one. I wasn't thinking about a goddamn thing. You're thinking, "Let me get the hell across this field into some woods over there." I got about halfway across and a German was coming with his hands on his head to the right of me and he just came down on his knees when he saw one of our guys. He had a wild look in his eyes, and one of our guys just shot him right in the head for no reason. I figured, "Shit, how could any asshole do that?"

Half of the enemy gave up and were waving their hands, and the other half were running up the hill. In the midst of artillery shells landing all over the place, a German prisoner was being waved back to our lines. Until he met up with one of our men, who was cussing him out and hollering at him. The German promptly got on his knees, pleading for his life, but this Ranger with a wild gleam in his eyes shot him through the head. You think in your head, "What the hell are you going to do?" but you can't do anything about it. You can't shoot the guy—shit, maybe he'll do something good next time. You just go on.

The guys in the front took off or ran up the hill or the other guys gave up; half of them gave up and half of them ran. I guess if you see 120 men acting like a bunch of Indians coming at you, you think these guys are nuts! We were yelling like crazy—rebel yells.

The goddamn shells were bombing away in front of me. I figured we'd go around [the hill] because I didn't know if they were our shells or the German shells—it really was our own shells, we figured out later, 'cause it was supposed to go up with the walking artillery group but we got started ahead of them. I just went off to the left side and the rest of the guys followed me. My ten guys, we sort of circled to the left, hoping we'd be out of that mad shelling. I didn't realize I went around and saw a German troop shelter [pillbox].

Once I got up the other side, I started to dig in, and the rest of the guys one by one were getting wounded. I guess one of them [shells] didn't have my number on it—I lost my whole section; all of them were walking wounded, they just got fragmentation wounds and they were able to walk. We were already at the German troop shelter (it was made from cement, similar to a pillbox). L-Rod and Andy took that thing.

L-Rod had the 2nd Platoon; as I came up on the hill I took on the right side as I was in the 1st Platoon and L-Rod was in the 2nd Platoon. His platoon stayed on the left.

Most of the attacks on the first day were directed at the 2nd Platoon. Each side wanted that pillbox, since you were being shelled on the outside. The [pillbox] walls were two foot thick with concrete; it could take any hit. We kept the troops in there and then they'd bombard the hell out of the mortars and artillery. Once they stopped one of their attacks, they attacked with small portions of men where the first two finally realized that we weren't going to give up so they'd come up with a bigger attack. That night we had maybe a dozen guys holding the hill from F Company.

Ninety percent of your wounds and stuff come from artillery and mortars. Everybody thinks that you get shot; very rarely were we only bothered with the shooting! The shooting didn't bother us, it was the other stuff that would wear you down. And as soon as they stopped one goddamn thing, they'd start firing on us again.

During the attack, Lomell came over from D Company, he wanted to check and see what's going on with us guys, and I intercepted him and said, "Jesus, where are the guys from D Company?" He said, "Well, they're right down the hill there." And he pointed down the hill, and Christ sake, his hand was all bloody and his finger was half dropping off and he pointed down the hill. So down the hill I went with Moss, and then we picked up a stray guy from D Company. We dug in there and we said, "Jesus, we might as well just dig in here for a little while and then we'll have to face reality again, but let's just dig in." What a relief that was.

Meanwhile, the three of us were in that foxhole, and along comes a German patrol, and they were paratroopers. (You could tell by the camouflage ponchos they had on.) We figured, "Shit, should we bother? Should we take them on?" We said, "Hell, no." They got about a dozen guys and they looked pretty sharp and they were well spread out. We said, "Jesus, we ain't got no support at all, let them go on by." So they went right past us, but they were on a hiking path or something about fifty yards from us. We spotted them a long ways off and were figuring out what we should do with them, but when we saw more than two and three and four we said, "Uh oh . . . let these guys go by."

After about a half an hour we kind of looked at each other and looked a little guilty and said, "We'd better get our asses back up the hill." So that's what we did. We no sooner got about halfway up and they spotted us and they opened up, and I guess it was a self-propelled gun, and we got some fast-needed energy then, and up the hill we went double-time!

After the third attack, we went back up the hill. Me and Moss and another Ranger heard the self-propelled gun. The Germans were making a flank move, and L-Rod picked up these two guys, and he got shot in the shoulder, and he came back trudging up the hill and shouted, "Who's going to take my BAR [Browning automatic rifle]? Who's going to take my BAR?" We were sergeants, but we both carried a BAR all the way through the war. The BAR to us was the best gun you could get. So here I have a BAR and I have to intercept L-Rod and I said, "I'll take his BAR, but what am I going to do with two BARs?" I knew I better take it 'cause he was kind of a mess then. He was shot up and we just kind of stood him in the pillbox and gave him morphine and so forth.

We stayed out all night and there was sort of a drizzle. At that point we only had about six guys from F Company left. One of these men included a replacement, Julian Hanahan, who fought like a veteran. We had a few guys down below. In fact the mortar sections didn't come up and the headquarters didn't come up.

The captain came up but he got captured. He was going down about nine that morning to get reinforcements, but he got a little too close and he got captured, so that's when L-Rod took over. They had a lieutenant there, but he was a new guy and he wasn't worth much.

The next morning the Germans attacked again. It was a half-hearted [attack] and wasn't a sustained one. And then we went all day and then we got a good one that night. They were paratroopers. They come out in full force. I don't know how we ever stayed with it. We had about ten guys from E Company come up, and they were between us and a couple of guys from the 2nd Platoon, and me and two guys from the 1st Platoon. One of our officers had come up by that time with an artillery observer [Lieutenant Kettlehut], and at one point they went out and tried to call us in, but we never heard the guys. They wanted to shoot at our own position because they were all infiltrated between us and to the side of us.

We were a holding force at this time and the Germans were attacking. I was in a foxhole. We all had our own foxholes. I had two BARs, an M-1, a pistol, and grenades. One of my men who we called the Mad Russian got wounded and he had to go back into the pillbox, but Moss stayed out with us all night, about three hours. Once that observer called our artillery in on our own positions they got slaughtered—the Germans just were slaughtered. Of course we were under cover and they weren't.

Another German attack started right at sundown. As soon as they stopped with their own artillery, I looked out of my foxhole and there were a couple of guys [Germans] not too far in front of me, maybe fifty feet in front of me, walking up the hill. They didn't know I was there. They looked like they were kidding with each other. Naturally, they did not kid much longer after I got them with the BAR.

The Germans would try and keep contact with each other with whistles and sheep calls—"baah, baah"—and they were whistling with each other. By this time it was pitch black, and this was going on for two and a half, three hours. We just held our positions. Of course we didn't shoot constantly, we'd just give it a spurt and a burp and throw a couple of grenades now and then because we piled up a whole bunch of ammunition. As far as I know I didn't have anybody closer to me than those two guys. They were trying to come up in between us to try and get to the pillbox because once they get to the pillbox they figured they're home.

Once our own barrage stopped—Christ, they must have thrown that barrage a good twenty minutes, a half-hour—once that stopped you could hear them with their whistles and their "baaaaaahs" going back down the hill. They had had it. I didn't hear any screaming; they kept pretty good control, they were good soldiers.

That morning the 8th Division sent up a heavy weapons company. I didn't realize what it was at first. I told Winston I'd stay there and show him our positions.

When they got up there they kept piling into the pillbox. I got hold of the platoon sergeant and I told him, "I'll take you guys down there and show you our positions." He said, "No, I got to wait for the lieutenant." I said, "Where the hell is he?" "Well, he's in the back there, the back part of the pillbox." I waited for the sergeant to find him. When I finally find the guy he gives me the same shit: "The sergeant's in the front hill and he'll take you out." I said, "Christ, I just talked with the sergeant and he said I got to see you." He said, "Well, you see him and tell him I told you to go out." By that time I could hardly get through back out there because they were piled in there like sardines. I couldn't even find him. So I said, "Fuck this, if this is the way they want to play, let them stay here!" So I just left. I was with another sergeant from E Company and we were the last two guys off the hill around 10:30.

Pointe-du-Hoc was like going out to a picnic compared to this. On that hill they [Germans] gave us round-the-clock bombardment and attacked for two days.

DUAINE PINKSTON

505th Parachute Infantry Regiment, 82nd Airborne Division

On February 8, the 505th Parachute Infantry Regiment relieved the 8th Infantry Division in the towns of Vossenack and Hürtgen, clearing, in conjunction with the 78th Division, a path to the Roer River. As they pushed toward the Schwammenauel Dam, the regiment passed through the Kall River Valley, dubbed "Death Valley" because a battalion from the 28th Division had been annihilated there by a German attack in the fall. Duaine Pinkston, a combat medic, recalls his day and night in Death Valley.

C Company was up on the line around the town of Schmidt near the Roer River. On our way into the forest we went through what we called Death Valley. It was kind of spooky. You didn't feel right. Tanks, jeeps, and half-tracks were all over the place. The broken bodies of American soldiers were rotting away in the melting snow.

That day we received five replacement troops. Usually in the paratroops you didn't get replacements on the front line. We got them in a rear area. These guys were green. Seeing all of this didn't help these guys. They had a rude awakening in a big hurry. They were asking me, "When do you know when to hit the ground when the shells come in?" I couldn't take them up to the line till just about dark. I said, "You just watch me. If I hit the ground, you hit ground." That's what you do, you watch the guy in front of you.

As we were making our way down this trail to C Company's positions, we were shelled by some 88s [German artillery]. I hit the ground, but two of the new men were killed. It shook all of us up. It stays with you. You never get over it when it's that close. But there's nothing you can do.

When you're in combat it seems like the new guys always get it the first day. If you survive after a few days on the line you're generally all right. It's because they don't know what to do. When we got new guys we never put them together. We put them with the old guys. None of us were old; we were all just kids. If you had experience you were considered an old guy.

I took them [replacements] up and I came back alone. I followed my tracks, since I was afraid of mines.

That night we got a call, it was two or three in the morning. One of the men I took up had a breakdown. He was a machine gunner. So that morning I went back up to where C Company was at on the line. He wasn't any better. He was crying. He was all shook up. He didn't even know what his name was. I took him back to the aid station. He wasn't any good to have him around the other guys.

Going back down the trail we walked by the two dead guys. We left them there as a rule. Medics don't move the dead. That was left to the graves registration teams. You're so busy with your job, if they are wounded, that was my job. When we went by their bodies he went berserk. Seeing those two dead men completely touched him off. He went running and bawling into the forest. Everything was mined up there. I ran in his tracks. I caught up to him and to tackle him and bring him down on the ground. I finally got him walking again in the right direction.

We made it back to the aid station and I pulled out his dog tags. I saw that the numbers on his tag started out as 36. I know that that meant he was from Michigan, Illinois, or Indiana. I started naming towns in those areas. I said, "Chicago." He kind of snapped out of it and said, "My mother is from Chicago." We tried to take his helmet off to help relax him, but he wouldn't let us take it off. We had another group of guys that were wounded, so we sent them all back to the regimental aid station. We wrote up the prognosis; we called it combat fatigue.

I was in combat for a long time in even tougher situations, and this hardly ever happened with our people. I think it boils down to the type of person you are, how your nerves are. After a while you're going on your nerves. A lot of people learned how to pray up there, a lot of young guys. We lost a lot of the old guys getting hit, and you start to think, hey, we can still lose this war.

Those guys that were killed couldn't have been in Europe more then a week. I kept thinking their parents wouldn't even believe it. They were killed and never saw a German. It was one of those oddities of war.

At one of the reunions, I was in the hospitality room and about five or six guys came up to me. They all said in a very sincere voice, "If it hadn't have been for you, there wouldn't have been a C Company." I didn't know what to say for a minute. I said, "If it wouldn't have been for you guys, I wouldn't be here either."

As I thought about it later, it was one of the best compliments that I ever had. Not because of what they said, it was the type of men that they were. I said I really appreciate that because of the type of men you guys are. I still do. To me it was the best thing that I could ever hear.

I was always trying to do a good job. You saw them taking chances, some of them getting blown up. I had quite a few of them die in my arms. When a guy got hit he wanted a cigarette, he wanted water. It was just about the only thing that the movies got right. He also wanted you to stay with him; that was hard with so many other people getting wounded.

You could tell if they were going to die. The first thing you did was see where they were hit and how bad it was. After a while I could tell by experience just how much the human body could stand.

After the war you'd think about this stuff. For three months it seemed like I had to put a big bath towel near the bed. I'd wake up in the middle of the night shaking and sweating. I would be soaked with sweat. It seemed to be way down inside of me and I couldn't make it stop. I'd wipe the sweat off and change the sheets and finally go back to bed.

I went to the doctor, got some medicine for my stomach. I'd be so hungry but I couldn't eat. I'd take three bites and throw it up. I lost a lot of weight. If I heard an explosion, that also set me off and brought me back to the war.

I had another buddy who was all shot up during the war. He had the same problems. I'd help him and he helped me. We had a boat and we'd go up to a lake. We'd get on the lake and we'd fish. It seemed so good. Everything was quiet and peaceful. It put me at peace. It was my way of letting the war go.

CARL KIEFER

517th Parachute Regimental Combat Team

Using Hill 400 and Bergstein as launching pads, the 517th PRCT mounted an important diversionary attack on the elite German 6th Parachute Regiment on February 6 through 8. The Germans fell for the diversion, believing that the 517th attack was a main thrust on the dams; meanwhile, the real main Allied thrust was at Schmidt. As Carl Kiefer recalls, however, no one informed the 517th that their attack was a diversion, and they made every effort to take impossible objectives.[6]

It was the night of February 7 and we came from Bergstein. Our instructions were to take off from the very top of Hill 400 and take the town at the bottom of the hill—Zerkall.

We had lost a lot of people, but I don't know if our morale was down at all. I heard that later on a lot of the brass had argued about whether we, since the war was going our way, whether we really should have pushed down there. We were obviously very tired. We were getting pretty tired of the war, but again, I don't know what there is about the 517th, but boy, it's got spirit to this day.

We kicked off at midnight at the very top of Hill 400. It split into two paths that went through the forest, and I took the one on the south with I think I had twenty-nine guys left in the platoon, and I was platoon sergeant. Another officer had the other section that went to the north. Again, this is dark at night and we are in the forest and we hadn't gone more than a hundred yards down, and the incline started getting terribly, terribly steep, and we suddenly walked into a minefield. As it turns out it was an enormous minefield.

One of our guys tripped a mine, and when he did that, the Germans obviously knew exactly where we were at because they zeroed in on the position. They knew exactly where to set their mortars. They started getting mortar, a lot of machine gun and rifle fire. Some shelling, but it was mostly big guns because they wouldn't have been able to shoot that close. We simply were stopped dead. They fired flares up in the sky every once in a while, and it felt like you were playing night football, it was so damn bright, and you just didn't move, and there wasn't any protection there except the trees.

We quickly set up a machine gun that was manned by Pappy Anderson, one of my good friends. I told him to set it up, and he did, and he started shooting, and he didn't shoot twenty, thirty seconds and he was hit. And his assistant gunner, Jack Dallas, who had just returned from the hospital, we didn't expect him back, just went AWOL from the hospital. He had his back really torn up in southern France when a big shell hit. He took over as second gunner, and he wasn't on it ten, fifteen, twenty seconds and he was killed. So every time we tried to move, they were just so zeroed in on us, they had the flares, and we had just passed by a pillbox, and I am convinced still to this day that there was a German in there, we went by him and he was radioing directions back to their headquarters. I went back there years later and I found German wire all around the pillbox that led to Zerkall.

We really got hit bad. One of the things I always remember is one of my guys was hit pretty bad and started crying. We lost six men there and more wounded. Only six of us went back up the hill from the twenty-nine. This was the worst day of combat I ever saw, and it was the last day. We simply walked into it. We walked into that minefield. After we walked into it, they were zeroed in and we got the hell beaten out of us.

I kept reaching around me—I was on the ground—I kept reaching out and speaking very softly, looking for mines and trip wires. I knew the

Members of the 517th take the wounded to an aid station. (Photo courtesy U.S. Army through Clark Archer)

weather was just starting to thaw, so it was part mud and part snow. Most of the mines had been set in when it was firm, so with the mud you could touch the wires and you had a little leeway because the wire wouldn't be taut and you wouldn't trip them, and I felt these wires all around me. At about that time we tried setting up the guns, and we tried everything that is normal military practice. And you never knew when a flare was bursting—if you were moving and that flare went off, they nailed you. Most of us were behind trees because that was the only thing that was there.

This one guy was crying, he got hit pretty bad, I tried to calm him down because of the noise, and he crawled over on my lap and I just said, "Glen Mizner, knock it off if you can, knock it off." Of course, he was hurting pretty bad. I think he got hit in the hip and upper leg. Even in the dark I could see the blood all over him. He kind of crawled up on my lap and I kind of consoled him a little bit. About that time I heard a thud and one or two machine gun bullets hit Glen. He was laying across my lap; he protected my stomach. That would have been my bullet. It went into him and killed him.

The only thing we could hope for was to stay calm, stay hidden as best we could, and don't move until we saw some sign of them, and we couldn't until daytime, and by that time they pulled back. We went back up to the hill, back up to where we started, and there were six of us left. I think we had six killed there and about sixteen wounded. Only six of us came out unscathed.

It really hit me when we struggled up the hill at daybreak. I turned around and tried to assess the situation. I sat there in the damn mud for a while and tried to assess who was left, and when I realized who was gone it really hit me. I knew they were laying down there, and I knew that all of us were thinking that it wasn't long until the war was over, and yet these guys went from start to finish and got it on the last day. I just felt so bad because the guys I had been training with back in the States, obviously I got to know families and they had visitors and so forth, so I knew Anderson's family and Jack Dallas's family, and I knew Glen Mizner's brothers and sisters, and it really hurt, it really hurt. And when it set in that that was the last combat we were probably going to see, we just had hell beat on us—it really hit me. Why the last day, God? Why did these guys have to suffer all through the goddamn Bulge, so miserable, so cold, just to die on the last day of combat?"

I have thought about it quite a bit since the war. I'm not one of those guys to sit here and stare at the wall like I'm transfixed, but when I'm thinking of it, I'm really thinking and can still see a lot of it happening, still remember a lot of it, still can remember their pain, their shouting and crying.

It just comes back now and then. I've got a lot of mementos and I have pictures at home, years ago we circulated pictures around, and you open a drawer and there's a picture and you go through that same agony again. You just miss the hell out of those guys, it's amazing. I still feel that they're alive and just around the corner somewhere. We were a close-knit group. We went through all of this stuff as a small little group as a regiment and not a division, so we went through it all together, and I think that has a lot to do [with] why we were so close—even today.

CHAPTER TWELVE

GERMANY

Calm fell. From Heaven distilled a clemency;

There was peace on earth, and silence in the sky;

Some could, some could not, shake off misery.

—Thomas Hardy, "And There Was a Great Calm"

By the middle of February 1945, the Allies were advancing into Germany along a broad front that stretched 450 miles from the North Sea to the Swiss border. The main Allied thrusts would be made by British Field Marshal Bernard Law Montgomery's Twenty-first Army Group, into northern Germany, and by General Omar Bradley's Twelfth Army Group and Lieutenant General Jacob Devers's Sixth Army Group, into southern Germany. A series of pillboxes, mine fields, and concrete "dragon's teeth" antitank obstacles, known as the Siegfried Line, along with Germany's greatest natural barrier, the Rhine River, lay in their path.

After maintaining defensive blocking positions near Simmerath, Germany, during the opening days of the Battle of the Bulge, the 5th and 2nd Ranger battalions entered a relatively quiet period that streched to late January 1945. Then, after additional training and an infusion of replacement troops, the 2nd Ranger Battalion moved back to the Hürtgen, where it was attached to the 9th Infantry Division. There the unit performed reconnaissance patrols and was scheduled for an assault crossing of the Roer River. The initial crossing was delayed, and on February 23, 1945, the Rangers were placed in V Corps reserve.

To the south, the 5th Rangers were attached to the 94th Infantry Division, part of General Walton Walker's XX Corps. Walker was to smash through part of an uncleared portion of the Siegfried Line known as the "Saar-Moselle triangle," a gateway to the Rhine. It measured about sixteen and a half miles from its apex at the Saar and Moselle rivers in the north to a thirteen-mile east-west base along the southern border of Luxembourg. Fortifications and mines two miles deep, known as the Orscholz Switch, ran across the base of the triangle.

After several attacks on the triangle, the Allies had achieved minimal gains, and Walker decided to launch a larger attack on February 19, 1945. The 94th Division would punch a hole through German defenses at the Orscholz Switch, and tanks from the 10th Armored Division would roll through the gap. The 5th Ranger Battalion, attached to the 94th Division, attacked the Orscholz Switch near the German town of Oberleuken. The attack ground to a halt as the Rangers became hung up in mine fields and pillboxes. On February 21, the 10th Armored Division and 94th Division began crossing the Saar River, and by the night of the twenty-second the bridgeheads across the Saar were secure.[1]

Walker was eager to exploit his success and called upon the 5th Ranger Battalion to conduct the unit's first and only raid by advancing three miles behind German lines and establishing a roadblock on the Irsch-Zerf road. The roadblock would not only speed up Walker's advance but would prevent the Germans from flanking the American units crossing the Saar River.

At midnight on February 23, the Rangers began infiltrating three miles behind German lines. By early morning, the Rangers had set up defensive positions and started to run into opposition from small groups of Germans. After wheeling several hundred yards right to better defensive positions, the Rangers encountered more Germans holed up in pillboxes and houses and overran their positions, taking prisoners.

The following day, the Rangers were again on the march, and at 8:30 A.M. February 25 they established their roadblock on the Irsch-Zerf road. Starting in the afternoon and continuing the next two days, the Rangers repelled several large German attacks (four hundred to six hundred men). The situation was critical on several occasions, and Allied artillery was called nearly on top of the Ranger positions to wipe out the German attacks. By the twenty-sixth, elements of the 10th Armored Division finally broke through to the Rangers, and for the next five days the battalion was on the offensive, taking several critical positions. By March 3 the Rangers' mission was finally over. The cost was high: 186 total casualties, practically half the battalion.[2]

By the end of February, all three active airborne divisions in the XVIII Airborne Corps were taken off the line for rest and refitting to base camps near Rheims and held in reserve for several large airborne operations. The 82nd Airborne Division was removed from the Roer River dams area to Sissone, France; the 101st from the relatively quiet six-mile area along the Moder River in Alsace to Mourmelon; and the 17th Airborne Division, which was about four thousand men, understrength from losses in the Bulge, moved from a bridgehead along the Our River to Châlons, France.[3] The veteran divisions were joined by the newly arrived 13th Airborne Division, the only division in Europe that never entered combat.

Plans for a slew of airborne operations were drawn up during the closing stages of the war, but most did not get beyond the planning stages. The largest and most extravagant operation was called ARENA: It called for use of all six Allied airborne divisions and the airlifting of four regular divisions into an airhead about two hundred miles east of the Rhine between Paterborn and Kassel.[4] CHOKER II, another airborne operation, designated the 13th Airborne Division and its recently attached veteran 517th Parachute Regimental Combat Team to jump on Worms, Germany, to help secure the Rhine crossing area for General Bradley's advancing American armies. Plans were even drawn up for a jump on Berlin, code-named ECLIPSE. The capture of the Remagen Bridge over the Rhine and the swift advance into Germany of Bradley's Twelfth Army Group (Hodges's First Army and Patton's Third Army) caused the cancellation of CHOKER II and ARENA. ECLIPSE was scrubbed to leave Berlin as a target for the advancing Soviet army.[5]

The one airborne operation not scrubbed was VARSITY, a massive parachute and glider attack supporting General Montgomery's push into Germany at Wesel, on the Rhine. Two airborne divisions were earmarked for the operation: the 17th Airborne, which was making its first combat jump, and the British 6th Airborne Division.

D-Day was the night of March 23–24. After one of the largest artillery barrages of the war, the ground forces began crossing the Rhine at 9:00 P.M. and had firmly established beachheads on the east bank of the Rhine when the airborne assault was launched at 6:00 A.M. About 17,000 men—8,801 paratroopers and 8,196 gliderists—were involved in the operation.[6] The 17th Airborne's mission was to clear the high ground east of the dense Dieresfordter Forest and secure the bridges over the Issel River.

Paratroopers were the first to land, clearing the way for the gliders that would land fifteen minutes later. Heavy antiaircraft fire took its toll, and several C-46 Commando transport planes, used in combat for the first time, burst into flames when hit by enemy fire: They lacked self-sealing fuel tanks. Making matters worse, the Air Corps mistakenly dropped many units of the 17th right onto German positions. Casualties were high, exceeding the first day's airborne losses in Normandy.[7]

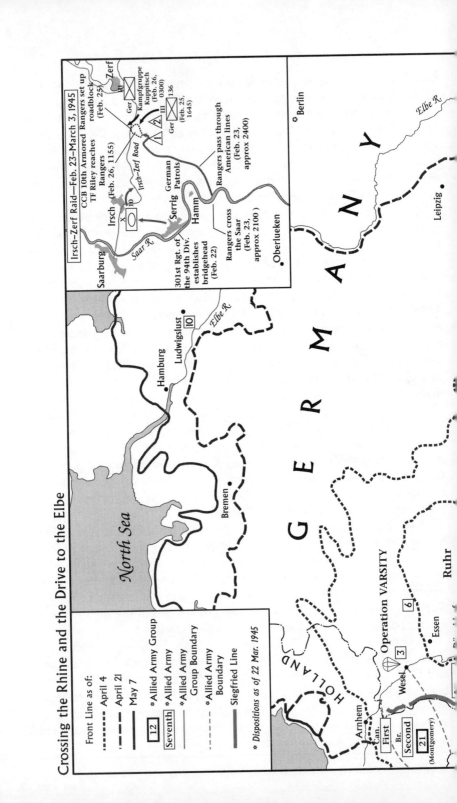

Crossing the Rhine and the Drive to the Elbe

Front Line as of:
- ········· April 4
- – – – – April 21
- —— May 7

12 *Allied Army Group
Seventh *Allied Army
—— *Allied Army Group Boundary
– – – *Allied Army Boundary
———— Siegfried Line

* Dispositions as of 22 Mar. 1945

Irsch-Zerf Raid—Feb. 23–March 3, 1945

CCB 10th Armored Rangers set up roadblock (Feb. 25)
TF Riley reaches Rangers (Feb. 26, 1155)
Kampfgruppe Kuppitsch (Feb. 26, 0300)
Ger III 136 (Feb. 25, 1645)
Irsch-Zerf Road
Rangers pass through American lines (Feb. 23, approx 2400)
German Patrols
Serrig
Hamm
301st Rgt. of the 94th Div. establishes bridgehead (Feb. 22)
Rangers cross the Saar (Feb. 23, approx 2100)
Oberlueken
Saarburg
Saar R.
Irsch
Zerf

G E R M A N Y

North Sea
Hamburg
Bremen
Ludwigslust 10
Elbe R.
Berlin
Leipzig
Elbe R.

HOLLAND
Arnhem
Can. First
Br. Second
21 (Montgomery)
Wesel
Operation VARSITY
3
6
Essen
Ruhr

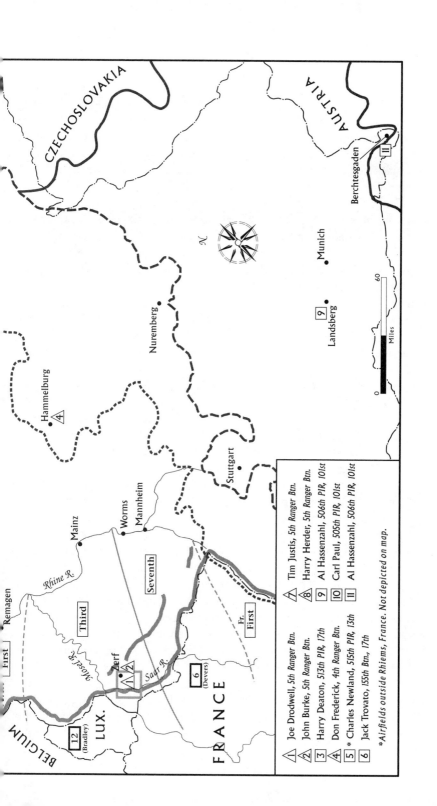

CZECHOSLOVAKIA

AUSTRIA

☲ Berchtesgaden

N

Munich ●

⑨ Landsberg ●

Nuremberg ●

Hammelburg ● ④

0 ____ 60
Miles

Stuttgart ●

Mainz ●
Worms ●
Mannheim ●

Rhine R.

Remagen

First

Third

Moselle R.

Zerf ① ②

Saar R.

⑥ (Devers)

Seventh

Fr. First

⑫ (Bradley)

LUX.

BELGIUM

FRANCE

△ Joe Drodwell, 5th Ranger Btn.
△ John Burke, 5th Ranger Btn.
③ Harry Deaton, 513th PIR, 17th
④ Don Frederick, 4th Ranger Btn.
⑤ *Charles Newland, 515th PIR, 13th
⑥ Jack Trovato, 155th Btn., 17th
△ Tim Justis, 5th Ranger Btn.
△ Harry Herder, 5th Ranger Btn.
⑨ Al Hassenzahl, 506th PIR, 101st
⑩ Carl Paul, 505th PIR, 101st
☲ Al Hassenzahl, 506th PIR, 101st

*Airfields outside Rhiems, France. Not depicted on map.

The first on the D2 was Colonel Edson Raff's 507th Parachute Infantry. The 1st Battalion landed about two miles from its drop zone and quickly eliminated several machine gun nests and a battery of artillery. The other two battalions landed near their drop zones and wiped out a German strongpoint in a castle. By nightfall, the 507th was in positions along the Diersfordter Forest and made contact with the British 1st Commando Brigade, which had made an amphibious assault across the Rhine.[8]

Coming down shortly after the 507th was the 17th Airborne's other parachute infantry regiment, the 513th. All three battalions were dropped about two or three miles from their designated drop zone, landing near the town of Hamminkeln. Pinned down for hours, scores died before the unit organized and moved toward its objective.[9]

Just behind the paratroopers came hundreds of American and British gliders. The 194th Glider Infantry Regiment landed in the correct landing zone and encountered the same chaos as the other regiments in the 17th Airborne Division, their landing zone on fire and filled with German flak units. After about two hours of intense combat, repulsing German counterattacks and knocking out several tanks, the 194th secured its landing zone and moved toward its objective: a bridge over the Issel River from which they could protect the division's right flank.[10]

By the end of D-Day, the 17th Airborne had accomplished all of its assigned objectives, and VARSITY appeared to be a huge success. Airborne units had smashed the German 84th Infantry Division and its supporting artillery and aided British troops crossing the Rhine. But historians compare the airborne's high casualties with those of the amphibious landing by the 30th and 79th Divisions—only forty-one killed[11]—and question whether the airborne operation was worth the cost.

By March 28, Montgomery had started to push into Germany in the north, and Ridgway's XVIII Airborne Corps spearheaded the attack, making strong headway. But the British army did not keep up with the airborne, and the operation slipped behind schedule. Frustrated, Ridgway requested to be transferred to the U.S. Ninth Army, and Montgomery agreed.[12] On the afternoon of March 28, paratroopers from the 17th Airborne Division (513th Parachute Infantry Regiment) raced seventeen miles, riding on top of tanks toward Münster. A large arc was being formed by Montgomery's Allied armies around the industrial heartland of Germany known as the Ruhr.

To the south, the First Army, which crossed at the Remagen bridgehead, was forming a second large arc around the Ruhr. On April 1, the First Army linked up with the Ninth Army, and the Ruhr was surrounded. Hundreds of thousands of German troops were trapped inside what would become known as the Ruhr Pocket.

For the first two weeks of April, the Allies squeezed the pocket. The 17th remained in the middle of the fighting, taking Münster and moving into Essen and Duisburg. The 82nd and 101st airborne divisions were held in reserve as occupation troops. Their only combat was several company-size raids across the Rhine.[13] By April 18, a staggering 317,000 prisoners had been bagged from the Ruhr Pocket.[14]

In late March, the 2nd Ranger Battalion crossed the Rhine with the Ninth Army. Several days later, the 5th Rangers followed suit, and both units were slicing into Germany, at times at the van of the advancing Allied armies. Riding in half-tracks and trucks, often working in conjunction with mechanized cavalry units, the Ranger battalions attacked dozens of German towns. Both units also performed security duties, guarding prisoners and policing captured towns.

As the war drew to a close, the 82nd and 101st were pulled out of their defensive positions on the western edge of the Ruhr Pocket. The 82nd would help Montgomery's drive to the Baltic by making an assault crossing of the Elbe River on April 30 at Bleckede. Using the same canvas-style boats as in the Waal crossing in Holland, the 82nd's 505th Regiment crossed the Elbe and quickly routed the German defenders on the other side. Combat engineers followed the paratroopers and constructed pontoon bridges for the advancing Allied troops to cross.

To the south, the 101st Airborne Division was trucked 250 miles and attached to the Seventh Army to mop up German troops in Bavaria. Allied intelligence reports and Nazi propaganda declared that hundreds of thousands of diehard German troops would attempt to hole up in the Bavarian Alps and form a "National Redoubt." It was propaganda only. The 13th Airborne and its attached 517th Parachute Regimental Combat Team were activated for a jump into the Alps known as Operation EFFECTIVE, but the jump was canceled when the Third, Seventh, and First French armies mopped up the area without assistance.[15]

As both the Rangers and the airborne led the advance into Germany, they stumbled across the horror of Germany's death and slave labor camps. Elements of the 5th Ranger Battalion were among the first units to enter Buchenwald, on April 15, and the 101st's 506th Regiment moved into the Landsberg concentration camp on April 28. After crossing the Elbe, the 82nd liberated Wobelein concentration camp near the city of Ludwigslust.

The final days of the war had American elite infantry units spread out all over what was left of the Third Reich. The 82nd, stationed near Ludwigslust, accepted the surrender of a German army group of 150,000 men and linked up with Russian forces near the Baltic.[16] To the south, in Bavaria, the 101st captured the ultimate war prize: Hitler's famed Alpine retreat at Berchtesgaden—the Eagle's Nest. The 5th Ranger Battalion, attached to the 3rd Cavalry Group, captured several lightly defended bridges across the Danube River and closed the war out in Austria.

At 2301 hours on May 8, 1945, the war in Europe was officially over. Over the next several months, America's elite troops, which had so altered the course of the war, began their journey home.

JOE DRODWELL

5th Ranger Battalion

On the night of February 23, the 5th Ranger Battalion began infiltrating through German lines to establish a roadblock three miles into enemy territory. The mission, which was supposed to last forty-eight hours, after which the Rangers would be relieved, turned into a nine-day nightmare. The Rangers secured all their objectives, but lost half the battalion to German counterattacks and artillery fire. Their stand contributed directly to the collapse of German defenses in the area and the XX Corps' drive on the Rhine. Joe Drodwell, a platoon sergeant, remembers the mission.

I remember I started to like it. I mean I started to like the war; the raid changed that.

We moved into position on the opposite side of the Saar River. We started across this field which was a minefield, and one of the boys stepped on a bouncing betty mine; they bounce up about three or four feet, and then they spray. One fellow got hit in the canteen and he yelled, "I'm hit." Of course water was running down his leg; it was kind of funny (well, it wasn't funny). He was all right. One of the BBs went through the collar of my jacket, just grazed my neck; I was lucky. The other guy, who stepped on the mine, lost his leg.

Just about then, 88s started to shell us. I think we lost several men with the 88s shelling us. That is just before we crossed the Saar. It was just another day. I had been in combat since the Normandy beachhead.

We crossed the river at dark, and one of the sections of B Company got lost and fought somewhere else. We advanced at night and could see our initial objective in the morning. Coming down the road in the morning, I remember this [German] officer was coming down with his jeep or car. We stopped him. He couldn't believe his eyes. "You're not supposed to be here"—in perfect English. "You're not supposed to be here, it's four thousand yards behind the lines. You're not supposed to be here." After capturing him, we moved into positions that we were supposed to be [in]. Colonel Sullivan moved up about three hundred yards; it was a better terrain position as far as he was concerned. That's what I remember going in. I remember we got in our foxholes, and that night they didn't even know we were there, I think, because it took the next day before we drew any fire.

The next night [about 3:00 A.M. February 26] they really started to shell us with 88s. During that night I think a force of about six hundred Germans hit us and overran Easy Company and A Company. We went over to help out Easy Company.

We went over and battled the Germans and drove them back with Easy Company's help. They were still fighting. We lost a few men in my section. When the Germans counterattacked, I had never seen anything like it in my life. We dug as deep as we could in our foxholes and laid down, covered ourselves with sticks and anything we could find, and the colonel called 155 [artillery] on our position; that's how bad it was getting. We called for artillery on our position because we knew the Germans were counterattacking and would overrun us.

When we got out and looked around after the artillery lifted, you wouldn't believe it. I never saw so many dead Germans in my life. The area was just literally covered with bodies. Some of our guys got killed, too, but nothing like the Germans: They were really slaughtered. When artillery gets you with a direct hit, forget it, there's nothing left of you, just body parts all over the place.

After a few days of combat, we were running low on ammunition so they made us a drop. We never got any of it; the Germans got it all. The Germans picked up some of our weapons because one of my men got killed with a tommy gun.

That was about the fifth day—nothing to eat. All we could get to eat was what we could scrounge up. I scrounged up some black-green German bread. We scraped off the green, soaked it in water, and ate it. We only took two days' rations. If you brought some gum or something like that, you sucked on it for the sugar and threw it out. Some of us had some candy bars and some chocolate. We drank what water we had from our canteens. We learned to preserve water. (You never drank it like you drink water here.)

I think around the fifth day I went back to the CP, and as I left my foxhole, I went about ten feet and my sergeant, Ted Walters, and some mortar men covered my foxhole. I said, "I'm going to get a cup of coffee, will you watch it for a while?" He said, "Okay." He was in my foxhole, I went ten feet and an 88 made a direct hit on my foxhole and killed him instantly. Ted and I were pretty good friends, and this kind of shook me up. I had my rifle, and I was going to go to the front lines to do somebody in! I was never so upset in my life. I don't remember much after that because they must have shot me with morphine or something like that. My company commander said they had two guys grab me and take my rifle away and hold me down. For three days after that I don't remember a thing.

JOHN BURKE

5th Ranger Battalion

John Burke, a medic, recalls the Irsch-Zerf raid.

I was a medic and I was attached to A Company from D-Day all the way through. When we got the word to attack a place called Zerf and they started shelling us and I said, "I don't think this is going to be a good deal." They said it was going to be a forty-eight-hour mission and they gave us two K rations, two or three D bars, a canteen of water, and the guys got ammo.

We left about eleven o'clock at night. We went across the river and we got up in the hills, and everything was small-arms fire. It was the first time we ever encountered just small-arms fire; it was rifles against rifles and machine guns against machine guns without any mortars. It was a different thing.

Our mission was to go and cut off the road so the tanks couldn't get through. I think it took something like nine days. My recollection of it was just pure, absolute murder.

The adrenaline flows beyond belief every second you were in combat. You just said you're not going to get out of it. Our squad and the guys I was with, even though I was a medic, I stayed with the squad, only two of us came out walking. We went in with four hundred guys and we came out with two hundred and something.

I was thinking [on my way to a Ranger reunion at Fort Benning, Georgia] that I dismissed all this after I got out of the service; I didn't tell anybody what I did. I went back to college, got my degree, went on with my life. My brother was killed during the war, and I used to say to myself, "Why didn't I mourn?" My brother was a terrific guy: He was a big athlete, All-Southern Conference football player, everything. I cried a couple days when I found out he was killed; I found it out before we crossed the river [Saar] in February.

I was driving down here and I thought there was something wrong with me. I've got to psychoanalyze myself. What the hell was it that I was so hard that I didn't mourn when my best buddy Ted Walters was killed at Zerf, John Jagosh, all these guys—killed. When they said Ted got it, I was in a pillbox getting some supplies, and they said, "Ted Walters just got it." I remember my reaction was, "Jeez, that's bad." And I just kept going on. He was my best buddy. Every time I go to church, every Sunday I go to church, I talk about Ted Walters in my prayers. But I keep saying to myself: "Why didn't I mourn then, why didn't I mourn later, for Ted, my brother, all my buddies that were killed? Why didn't I mourn?"

I think something happened to us. We saw so much. I saw a lot at D-Day, but that was all new; I was just a kid. D-Day to me was an adventure. That sounds weird. I remember running across the beach and bullets hitting the water and I wasn't scared: I was too dumb, too young. But as time took place after that, we got up to Pointe-du-Hoc, clearing that place out and going on to Grandcamp and on to Brest, and it all wears on you.

After Zerf, Colonel Sullivan came up to me and he said, "You're gonna go home. I'm going to send you home on rotation because we just got relieved. Our armor came through." I got on a jeep with two other guys, and I'd gotten hit in the hip but I wouldn't tell anybody. He told me to go home, and I figured that since I got hit they'll put me in the hospital and I'll never get home! We were in this jeep and we had to go across a river, and there was an 88 sitting up in the hills that nobody could find. That son of a bitch would just shoot right down on that river. When we went across the top of the river, up on the other side, the shrapnel came across the top of the jeep and I said, "Jesus, wouldn't this be a hell of a time to get it?"

To make a long story short, I got home. I got home, and it was a hero's welcome.

When I got back to work, I never thought about being in the Rangers. I never talked about it; I never said anything about it. Every once in a while somebody would say, "Oh, I understand that . . ." I'd say, "Yeah." And they'd say, "Oh, tell me about it."

Maybe eight, ten months ago, the local historical society took a trip to Normandy. A lot of people who are in the historical society go to the fitness center at my club, and a couple of doctors came up to me and they said, "We just came back from Normandy. I understand that you went over on D-Day." I said, "Yeah." All of a sudden they made me a hero. It was weird. They said, "How'd you do it?" I said, "It was quite simple. They told me to go. I was trained to do it." They said, "How'd you do it?" I said, "I just put one foot in front of the other, that's all. We trained to do it."

Of course, when you are in the Rangers and the paratroopers or whatever, they kick out the weaklings before you get there. We had a few we had to kick out when we got into combat, but that was the exception. You could always depend on the guy next to you. I didn't want to let down the guy next to me. That was the first thing that went through my mind. It was above survival. I'm going to protect my buddy. I wouldn't dare let him down—no!

When we were going up the hill on D-Day, that was the first thing that went through my mind—"I'm going to protect my buddy." And when we were going up there I'd always turn around and see the guy behind me to make sure he knew what we were going to do. I'd yell to the guy in front of me, and he'd yell back to me.

You fought then because you knew your country was behind you. When you got home you were proud of what you did; I was proud. When it was all over and you go back to school and 90 percent of the guys in your class were there too, and they did their jobs, nobody talks about it—no one!

These people over at the historical society want me to talk about it; what am I going to tell them? I can't give you a Hollywood answer about what war is all about. I wish there was a cliché about it. It was horrible and I hope it never happens again. God forbid that any of my children or your children will have to go through it.

I took a lot of history, and there's nothing but wars throughout history, and you stop and think of the number of wars we had, whether you call them wars or skirmishes, whatever you want to call them, they kept going on day after day, month after month. It keeps going on. What the hell do you prove by killing each other, blowing buildings up? I wish I knew.

HARRY DEATON

513th Parachute Infantry Regiment, 17th Airborne Division

On March 24, the Allies launched the last major airborne drop in Europe—Operation VARSITY. During the operation, all three battalions of the 17th Airborne's 513th Parachute Infantry Regiment were dropped about two or three miles from their designated drop zone, directly onto German positions. Many men were pinned down on the drop zone for hours; scores died trying to organize and move toward their objective. Sergeant Harry Deaton remembers the jump.

I was just a kid. As soon as we got into position, as we crossed the Rhine, we got ready for the drop, and then the flak started flying and my goodness, you could almost walk down on the flak. The sky was filled with planes and gliders on fire. I had a problem jumping out of the wrong side of the plane, which I had never jumped out of before. [The new C-46 transports had two doors, unlike the C-47, which had one.]

It didn't seem that we were in the sky long when we were given the green light to jump. One of the company clerks, who jumped just in front of me, was wearing a phosphorus grenade, and the flak hit the grenade and burned him up on the way down. He was just a sheet of flames, screaming and trying to get out of the harness, and the phosphorus burned him up. It was horrible, and I'm sure he was dead by the time he hit the ground.

On the drop zone, things were pretty hectic. We had men hanging in trees, we had cattle killed all around us, we had men killed all around us, and I was hit on the drop. It seems like after that I grew up pretty quick.

A lot of German soldiers were scurrying around, and in fact, the Germans ran right on top of us. We laid still, played dead, until they thought they cleared the area by a farmhouse that was their shelter. We saw a lot of smoke and a lot of flames from burning gliders. People were yelling for help and medics and that sort of thing, and I remember one of my fellow troopers in a

A dead paratrooper hangs from a tree on one of VARSITY's drop zones near Wesel, Germany. (Photo courtesy U.S. Army)

tree. Several German women dressed in military uniforms came out of the farmhouse cellar, went over to the tree, and one of them actually slashed the trooper in the tree with a bayonet and then one of them shot him.

I was filled with rage but continued to play dead until they went back inside. The next thing I remember was one of my close friends yelled at me. He wanted to know if I was hit, and I said, "Yeah." I was bleeding pretty bad in the head. I got hit in the back of my head, and the bullet cut off my ear and then went out the back of the helmet. In fact, I wore that helmet until the war was over. My friend took me over to the first-aid station, where they bandaged my head, and then I got right on into the attack all day long and all night.

DON FREDERICK

1st and 4th Ranger Battalions

At the end of March, south of Montgomery's push at Wesel, the American First Army was streaming across the Rhine River at Remagen. Meanwhile, after smashing through the Siegfried Line at the Saar River, Patton's Third Army had crossed the Rhine farther south at Oppenheim. Once across the Rhine, General Patton saw an opportunity to make a deep foray into German territory and liberate the Hammelburg POW camp, which happened to hold his son-in-law, Colonel John Waters. A small force under Captain Abraham Baum, which included ten Sherman tanks, six light tanks, twenty-seven half-tracks, and three self-propelled 105-mm guns was assembled for the mission.[17] Advancing more than forty miles behind German lines, Task Force Baum made it to the camp and, as Don Frederick recalls in this e-history, tried to shoot its way out back to the American lines.

It was on a Sunday evening that I heard gunfire to the west of camp. I could see some American tanks engaging several German tank destroyers not far from the camp. Around five or six o'clock, the first American tanks busted through the gate. Everybody was cheering. It was a joyous occasion. Then reality set in and I remember standing around and one of the officers who was there said, "Well, where is everybody? There is only a handful of tanks and infantry here."

Only a few tanks came through; the rest of them stayed outside the camp and they formed a perimeter. They still had a lot of German infantry around that they were engaging at that point. During the firefight the camp guards took off.

After the tanks came through the front gate, Captain Baum appeared. He looked around to see what he had left. I think he was discouraged—there were so many people there—and disappointed that there wasn't enough vehicles to carry everyone out. I would guess there were about fifteen hundred American officers there, and a lot of them had been old-timers, and some of them were captured in North Africa, some of them in the Battle of the Bulge, along with a large group of Serbian soldiers who had also been captured.

He got on top of a jeep and said we might be able take out a couple hundred. I knew when I saw the half-tracks and tanks that we had left, we could not possibly take that many out [the task force did not have enough vehicles to take all the prisoners back]. Anyway, he told these people that if they wanted to get out on their own the best thing they could do was go across country in pairs of twos or threes. Meanwhile, the guys [POWs] were all asking for rations. Because we hadn't been eating much, the tankers gratefully gave what rations they had.

As we were pulling out, a wounded POW was laying on the ground behind one of the tanks. He was wounded and just laying on the ground. A couple of POW officers were hollering at him to get away from a tank. Well he either didn't hear them or he didn't understand, I don't know, but the tank backed over his head and all that was left were his torso and legs. There was a tank tread where his head used to be.

It was horrible.

I elected to go out with the tank column. I figured, "Boy I can get out of here a lot quicker on that tank than by walking." My friend Jack and I got on the tank. We didn't leave until about one in the morning. We had to do a lot of switching gasoline around because the only extra gas we had was on the half-tracks. We figured that they had enough gas left for the vehicles we had left; they could go at least thirty-five, forty miles, which would be pretty close to the American line; the line was moving fast towards us, too.

We got on the tank. Before Baum came into camp there was a German truck that came into camp that was loaded with butter and bread. My friend Jack took the butter, all he could carry, and I took the bread. So we took off, and things seemed like they were going very smoothly. We were going across country trying to find the road that went into a little town called Höllrich.

I was on the second tank from the front and we got into town. It was a very quiet evening. There were about twelve, fifteen guys on the tank. We approached Höllrich, and the lead tank came up against a roadblock made of telephone poles; the streets were very narrow. The tank that I was on pulled up behind the lead tank, and I saw somebody behind one of the buildings and I saw a flash, and boy, we got hit by a bazooka.

It went between my friend Jack and another man, who was killed. The blast blew us right off the tank. Luckily there was a ditch there. Jack was badly wounded and had about twenty pieces of shrapnel in him. So I helped Jack get back up the ditch and then loaded him in the first half-track. I didn't see him again until we got into Moosburg [POW camp].

Not long after we were hit, the column reversed itself and went back to Hill 427. It was actually not too far from Hammelburg camp. We got back up on the hill, and of course there was a good defensive position up there. I could hear firing to the north of us and to the east of us. We knew at that point they were closing in. I didn't know whether I should take off cross-country or what to do. They came in from three different directions with infantry and dogs. I could hear the dogs barking as they closed in on the hill.

They came closing in on us; they had us completely surrounded with tanks and infantry. I didn't see any armor, but they had a lot of bazooka men among the infantry, and, God, they were firing those bazookas fifty yards away from us. There were about two companies of German infantry; these guys looked like young kids to me, sixteen, seventeen years old! They rounded us up and ordered us to get on the road and march back to Hammelburg. They were very well-dressed, and boy they were trigger-happy. They were going to shoot if you made a wrong move.

We got back to Hammelburg about five, six in the morning. Soon afterward they shipped some of us to Moosburg [POW camp], and some of the men were shipped to a camp called Luckenwalde.

CHARLES NEWLAND

515ᵗʰ Parachute Infantry Regiment, 13ᵗʰ Airborne Division

General Alexander Patch's Seventh Army crossed the Rhine at Worms, Germany, on March 26, with the 13ᵗʰ Airborne Division in tow. The 13ᵗʰ, which had been scheduled for an operation code-named CHOKER II, which was canceled, was now gearing up for Operation EFFECTIVE, which would provide support for the Seventh Army in eliminating the National Redoubt in the Bavarian Alps. But the Seventh Army and French First Army overran the area, and the mission was canceled on April 19, while the 13th was loading into planes. The 13th was destined to be the only U.S. division in the European Theater never to see combat, despite more than three years of training for it. Private Charles Newland describes the 13th's canceled jump.

I was in the marshaling area, and this was in a sense a splendid time because we didn't have to pull duty, we were given relatively speaking marvelous food—cake and soda in the evening while we were attending movies. I tended to be really athletic then and took every chance to play volleyball and baseball and softball. We were playing cards, pinochle, bridge, whatever.

It was really quite nice, looking back on it now. It was kind of like a last supper kind of thing. People were sharpening their knives and getting equipment ready. In the 81-mm mortar group, we were getting all that gear fully prepared as well as making sure we had all the shells that were necessary because you have little explosive charges that go on the tails of those things. We were issued carbines, so all these things were generally being prepared.

I don't remember any speeches, but there were sessions around sand tables [sand mockups of the DZ], which at that time I really didn't understand, but I was there and I paid attention and I was pretty gung-ho when everything was going on. I wasn't really frightened or scared, but I was apprehensive of the unknown. In a real sense I was looking forward to it, but I was smart enough to know that this was serious business.

We were all packed, all the supply planes were packed, all the supply chutes, and we were in full gear. We were in the plane, I'm guessing, for one to two hours—it was a very long time. It was really quiet, quiet in the cabin; everybody was "in himself." There was very little bantering; it was very serious business. We just waited, and the thing got canceled.

I somehow thought that this was just a temporary relief and ultimately we were going to be committed in it and this was just a temporary exoneration. I remember taking the flag off my jacket and later sewing it back on before each mission. I did this two or three times.

I am continually impressed at the luck of the draw or toss of the dice. For instance, the best friend I ever had was my roommate at Syracuse, where I was the quarterback and he was my receiver; we were a great team. We went through jump school at the same time, and he gets assigned to the 101st. He gets machine gunned at Bastogne. I get shipped to the 13th and nothing happens; there's no rationale for it.

Irrationally, I know there exists a void within most of the men I served with. I guess, paradoxically, because of our good fortune, there's a sense of worthlessness that we were the only combat division in the ETO not to be committed [to combat]. After all the years of training and sacrifice of the other units, I think that still haunts some of us.

JACK TROVATO

155th Battalion, 17th Airborne Division

On March 27, Field Marshal Montgomery began to break out of his successful crossing of the Rhine. For the next two weeks, the 17th Airborne Division and XVIII Airborne Corps spearheaded the drive to encircle and squeeze the Ruhr Pocket, the 17th remaining in the middle of the fighting, taking Münster and moving into Essen and Duisburg. Here Jack Trovato looks back at the combat in northern Germany.

I put the war completely behind me until I got this call to go to a reunion about ten years ago; with that, everything came back. I started having nightmares. I went to the reunion and we talked about things, but in a joking way, even about guys getting killed—that's the way we discussed it. After I got active, I started having nightmares, so I quit going to reunions. I just about quit writing to a bunch of guys. [But] there is something you have to get out, like me sitting here with you today. It never leaves you.

There is no movie that really explains combat. I mean, how are you going to get into a guy's mind? I can't explain combat to you. I can't get close to it; I can't even draw an analogy for you. There's pain and suffering, there's hunger, but even that's hard to explain unless you've been through it—but then you don't have to explain it! The only thing I can tell you is that you are still a young man, and there will be some time in your life where you almost wish you were dead. There were times when things were so bad that I wanted to be dead.

You really get hardened in combat. I'm not saying these guys were cut-throats, but the atrocities I've seen and some I almost participated in—like killing a [German] guy just to get his rations. You're hungry. We had our C and our K rations, but they carried in this little tin can jerky beef, meat that was seasoned, biscuits, and you'd almost shoot a guy so you'd get his damn rations. [Chokes up and cries.] And also you almost ended up like dogs trying to claim that you shot the guy and the rations are yours. That's how bad it got. You didn't give a shit about any arms that he had, any money, any watches that he had. You were going for the food.

Let me give you an example of combat. You're taking a position, basically it's a defensive position, and you're getting into, in my case, a German-made foxhole that they'd left and I filled it. So it starts raining, it starts getting cold as hell, and the artillery starts coming in, it starts coming in heavy, so you know when the artillery starts coming in heavy on your position, the next thing that's going to happen, there's going to be German infantry that's close behind it. If they're truly effective, the artillery is so close it is almost hitting the German troops. As soon as that artillery stops, in they come, fast and fu-

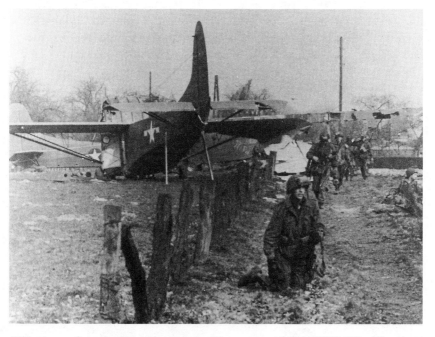

Glider troops from the 17th Airborne exit gliders on one of VARSITY's LZs. (Photo courtesy U.S. Army)

rious. So you know that's coming. You don't know how fast and furious it's going to come—but you know it's coming. You're in that friggin' hole for twelve hours and they're shelling and shelling and shelling. You've got to relieve yourself, but you don't want to get out of that friggin' hole. You shit in your pants—it's diarrhea from all the crap you've been eating. So here you are with shitty pants, freezing cold. You almost feel like coming out of the foxhole. All kinds of thoughts go through your mind. And the next thing you know, the shelling stops, and sure as shit here they come, and sure as shit you've got pants filled with shit, and you're not really sure if your rifle is going to fire. So you're clearing the son of a bitch for the first shot, and you take a shot even before you see a German because you want to be sure the son of a bitch is going to work.

Revenge enough was to shoot at a tree line or to shoot at a guy who was shooting at me. In one particular case I got into hand-to-hand combat and I knifed the guy to death. This was about three weeks later [after VARSITY]. We were on patrol at night. It was a German outpost, because there were only four guys there, and we just came up on them. They popped up, nobody had a chance—we were twelve guys, they were four—no chance to even fix bayonets, no chance to fire rifles. Now we're right in the middle of it. It ended up mayhem. Everything was done with what you had at hand. You didn't want to even fire your rifle, so I reached down and pulled my knife from my boot. I had this guy—he had his back to me and he was working on one of our guys. I got him in the back, turned him around and hit him in the belly a couple of times. It was almost joy doing it. Just about this time, after finishing with this guy, I turned around and all I could see was this butt of a rifle coming at me. I jerked my head back, and it knocked out two teeth and cut my lip. Behind him, one of my buddies put a knife into him and we finished him off. When we got back, one of the officers said, "I guess you want a Purple Heart?" I said, "No, I just want my teeth back!"

BILL JUSTIS

5th Ranger Battalion

At the end of March the 5th Ranger Battalion was crossing the Rhine and slicing through Germany. On April 15, lead elements of the 5th crashed through the gates of the Buchenwald concentration camp, as Sergeant Bill Justis recalls.

I was astonished at what we were seeing. It was hard to believe the human beings, the survivors that we saw. These emaciated people, there were literally hundreds of them, and I remember it was in April and still cold. There were stacks and stacks and rows and rows of human bodies stacked like cordwood, and this was absolutely incomprehensible.

After the sight of the human beings was the smell. It is one of those things that is just real difficult to describe, but it was a stench. You wonder for a moment: Where in the world are we? Did we come through the gates of Hell? It absolutely rendered you speechless. You wonder what in the world this could possibly be.

Some of them could speak English rather fluently, and this is where we found out what it was and why they were there and how long they had been there and this kind of thing. A lot of those folks had been there for quite a time, and you had absolute compassion for what you'd been seeing. There was a huge vat that had some sort of broth or gruel or soup in it; it wasn't real appetizing. They had a horrible time with diarrhea and this type of thing and the filthy living conditions.

There was this one fellow, he was darker-haired than a lot of them and he had more hair than most of them. He couldn't speak very good English and he was interested to know if we had any food. All of us had rations. Then he wanted to know if I had a cigarette. I told him I did and I gave him a cigarette. I remember when he lit it, it almost strangled him. He turned around and told me that it was strong.

It [the crematorium] was absolutely incomprehensible. It was hard to realize that human beings had been there and the way that they had been disposed of. It was a big room, brick, and they had the furnaces along one wall, and leading into the furnace was a concrete trough, and I reckon they laid the bodies on that and scooted them into the furnace. Inside the furnace you could see the bones and ash. Some of the bodies and bones were partially burned. The thing about it is there is no way that you could imagine what you were seeing, what the real impact was and what the reality of it was. It was the most horrible thing that a person could ever imagine.

HARRY HERDER

5th Ranger Battalion

A day after Buchenwald was liberated, privates Harry Herder and Bill Justis and another Ranger stumbled into a cell that contained a

small crowd of prisoners who were interrogating a camp guard that
they had found in nearby Weimar and dragged back to the camp.
Herder captures what transpired in this e-history.

We walked through the gate to the door that opened to the cell area. It was
crowded and the onlookers parted to let the three of us through, and we went
to the door of the cell. The German was standing at attention in the middle of
the room and was being peppered with questions that we did not understand.
Tears were coming down his cheeks. One of the Buchenwald prisoners
seemed to be in charge, but a group of them were participating in the interrogation. The one who appeared to be in charge also appeared to be the one calm
individual. The three of us watched, but we couldn't understand what was being said, so we turned and left. The crowd parted again to let us through.

We eventually rose and wandered back to the barracks. A half-dozen or
more of us sat on the front steps and enjoyed the early evening as the sun was
getting ready to set. I remember that I had found a pretty good cigar in the PX
ration box, and I was enjoying the cigar. The talk shifted around to the German
guard the prisoners had found. There were a couple of people who hadn't heard
the story yet, so Bill, Tim, and I became the authorities for a moment, telling
the story as we knew it. The others listened, and they wanted to see, so we led
them back to the prison cell. (We still had our rifles. We were trained to go
nowhere without them, ever.) The bunch of us walked over to the gate, through
it, and toward the door to the cells. The crowd of people were still there and
seemed to have grown, but it parted to let us through. Inside the cell the
Buchenwald prisoners and their prisoner presented a riveting scene: The hands
of the German were untied and in them he held a stout piece of rope. He was
being given instructions and as we watched it wasn't long before myself, and
the people who had come with me, realized he was being told how to tie a
noose in the rope. The German guard was corrected three or four times, and
had to undo some of his work to redo it correctly. When he was finished he had
a very proper hangman's noose, thirteen turns of the rope and all. A table was
brought to the center of the room and placed under a very strong-looking elec-
trical fixture. The guard was assisted onto the table and instructed to fix the
rope to the light fixture. Finishing that, he was told to put all of his weight on
the rope and lift his feet. The fixture held. (One had to wonder why the Germans had made the fixture so strong in the first place.) The guard was told to
place the noose over his head, around his neck, and to draw the noose fairly
snug. Then he was told to place his hands behind his back, and his wrists were
tied together. The table was moved until he barely stood on its edge. He
couldn't see that—his eyes were unhooded and open, but the noose kept him

from looking down. He was talked to some more and then he jumped. He was caught before all of his weight was on the rope, and they set him back on the table. The next time he stepped gently off the end, and the table was quickly slid away from him and out of his reach, and he dangled there. He slowly strangled. His face went through a variety of colors before he hung still. My stomach did not want to hold food any longer. I turned and walked away, the rest of our guys following me. The Buchenwald prisoners stayed on to view their handiwork.

I walked through the crowd and out the door, through the gate, and on up to the barracks, and I didn't say a word. The others with me didn't speak either. Here we were—five or six of us—fully armed with semiautomatic rifles, and we did not make the Buchenwald prisoners stop. We let them continue. In one way, we sanctioned the event. It was murder; there can be no doubt of that. The Buchenwald prisoners never touched the rope after it was placed in the German's hands unfashioned. They did not tie the noose, nor did they fix it to the ceiling. They did not place the rope around the man's neck. They did not pull the table out from under him. In one sense, they had not committed murder; rather, the German had committed suicide. A sophist could rationalize that one, I suspect. That was not what was bothering me, however. I had the ability and the means to stop the whole thing, and I did not. Neither did my companions. Ever since that day I have been convincing myself that I understood why the Buchenwald prisoners did what they did.

I had witnessed their agonies. I had wondered how human beings could treat other human beings as the prisoners at Buchenwald had been treated. I felt I knew why the prisoners of Buchenwald did what they did—so I did not stop them. I have become some kind of a sophist for myself now. I could have stopped the whole action, and I did not. I have had that under my hat for the past forty-six years. Now I have written it. I have acknowledged it. Maybe it will go away. There are so many things from that week I wish would go away, things I wish could be scrubbed from my memory. When we returned to the barracks we did not tell anyone what we had witnessed. I didn't. I don't think the others did either.

I was not about to sleep, however. I flopped on my bunk without a thought of my tiny bunkmates, the bugs—I merely lay there. My eyes were closed, but my mind wasn't. I tried to think of other things, but it was impossible. I reviewed in my mind the multiple things the Buchenwald prisoners had gone through, the length of time they had been living through them, and I didn't have to rationalize their actions. Hell, I knew why they were doing what they did. That train of thought took me further and further from my own guilt and, in a little while, I was absolved. At least, as absolved as I was ever going to be. Absolved enough to be a little more comfortable with myself. That was enough for then.

AL HASSENZAHL

506th Parachute Infantry Regiment, 101st Airborne Division

On April 20, the trucks carrying the 101st Airborne Division began a 250-mile trip southeast to join the Seventh Army and mop up the so-called National Redoubt. Once Allied troops such as the 101st rolled into the area, however, it became clear that there was little in the way of preparation for a redoubt. On April 28, the 506th Parachute Infantry Regiment was tasked with mopping up Landsberg, which had fallen to the 10th Armored Division the day before. Instead, as Al Hassenzahl remembers, the 506th discovered the Landsberg concentration camp.

We came into the area in the spring of 1945. The war, of course, was winding down. As I have said so many times, when you are a platoon commander, a company commander, especially when you are in combat, you see a very small area that is right in front of you. You don't see a big picture; you are not privy to that.

We went into various places in Germany by truck, and one mission that we had, our battalion was assigned to flush out any Krauts in this small town of Landsberg; that's the place that had the prison as well, the place where Hitler wrote his book *Mein Kampf.* So we went in there and got off the trucks and deployed several of the companies. We deployed and entered the outskirts of the town, and then we happened on this, we didn't know it was there until we encountered it, and that was the concentration camp.

We smelled it before we got to it. There was a terrible stench in the air. We got into it, and I personally, and I think many of my compadres, had a certain "tongue in cheek" when we heard about the atrocities and so on. You just kind of dismissed it because you can't visualize anyone doing the things we heard about.

Well, when we got into Landsberg, there was no doubt in anybody's mind that those atrocities were taking place, because when we got in there, those poor God-forsaken human beings were walking skeletons. They had striped suits on, and some of them could walk. A lot of them were lying in bunks in these stifling barracks that stank. They probably had done their business in their clothes, didn't have the strength to get up and wash; they probably didn't have facilities to wash, as I recall.

There were lots of them, and it was embarrassing to some extent because these poor human beings realized we were American soldiers, they dropped down on their knees and more than one tried to grab my hands and kiss my hands. Of course I wouldn't let them do it. They were so filled with gratitude. We made the mistake of trying to give them food, rations, K rations, chocolate bars that everybody carried at that time. Our rations had caught up with us, and everybody had something in their pockets. We caused a lot of illness, if not deaths, among them, by giving them food until the medics got to us and said, "Don't give these people food because their systems are so parched for energy, for food, and so on that they have an adverse reaction, sometimes even death." But we did that not knowing, of course.

The other thing I remember was stacks of bodies. Some were naked, some were partially clothed, and they were stacked like cordwood. That's something you'll never forget. It always stays with you.

A quick decision was made—our battalion commander was there, it was a unanimous decision with the company commanders and myself—to roust out the civilians in the little town and bury the bodies. We had to do something with them: They were decaying. We rousted the women and the kids and the old men out of their homes, formed them up into a column, and brought them into this camp. Some of them were porky as hell, and some of them were belligerent; they didn't stay belligerent very long, they were kicked into submission in a hurry. One kid, he was probably fifteen years old or something, he was a fairly good-size kid, he gave the Hitler salute to one of my sergeants, it was right at the side of a pit that the civilians were digging. My sergeant hauled off with the mightiest kick in the ass that you've ever seen and kicked him right into that pit. The look on that kid's face changed. I think as he tried to crawl out of the pit he was kicked in the face back into the pit again. So he lost his cockiness in a hurry. A few civilians were cocky— not many, but a few were. They got whipped into submission, they got cracked across the head or across the face, and then they minded what they were supposed to do. We didn't take any bullshit—we didn't have to!

When the pits were dug and they put the bodies in, we covered them up and that was that. Then we got orders to move on shortly after that.

CARL PAUL

505th Parachute Infantry Regiment, 82nd Airborne Division

Spearheading Montgomery's drive to the Baltic, the 82nd Airborne Division's 505th Parachute Infantry Regiment made an assault crossing of the Elbe River on April 30. The paratroopers quickly routed the German defenders. A day after the crossing, as Carl Paul remembers, the 82nd liberated the Wobelein concentration camp near the city of Ludwigslust.

They shelled the hell out of us after we got across the river. As soon as the engineers got the bridge built, they [Germans] ran from their foxholes and surrendered. They were sad: They had nothing. They had no food. They had no fuel for the vehicles. They had a lot of horse-drawn equipment. They were whipped. We just told them to get the hell off the road so we could get ahead.

The next day we got into Ludwigslust. It was the first time I was in the concentration camp. I looked around and could see that there was about a thousand dead bodies, and the living were starving to death. One guy gave one of them a candy bar, and he went into convulsions and died right in front of us. Another one gave one some milk and the same thing happened: His stomach couldn't even take a can of milk. [Sobs and chokes up.]

We went over to the barracks. The bunks were three high, and there were holes and barbed wire stretched across these things for beds. There was nothing on the barbed wire. These men were laying all along the wall, just as close as they could sit together. Some of them never got up. One Dutchman spoke English, and some of them wanted to throw their arms around us, and so he told them "not to give our lice to our liberators."

I never smoked or drank, but I had a cigarette ration like everybody else. I had a carton of cigarettes and walked up and started to give each man a cigarette. I didn't have enough, and it was the most pitiful thing to see. Those men wanted a cigarette so badly. In those days everybody smoked, and there were at least twenty that I didn't have cigarettes for, and needless to say they were just begging for a cigarette, but I couldn't give it to them because I didn't have any left. It was the saddest day of my life.

I went back fifty years later with one of the men in our unit, and we were joined by several of the people we liberated. We were accepting thanks from those people for their lives. One really got to me. He just hugged me and hugged me and hugged me just like he was a child. His wife, his son, and his daughter were there, and they of course would have never been born if we were arrived a few days later. Another girl came up and said: "We're Jewish. My father doesn't speak English . . ." She broke down.

It is hard to visualize if you weren't there. They all knew if we were a few days late, they would all have been dead.

AL HASSENZAHL

506th Parachute Infantry Regiment, 101st Airborne Division

The last combat mission assigned to the 101st Airborne was to capture Berchtesgaden, the town containing Hitler's home and the mountain retreat known as the Eagle's Nest. On the afternoon of May 5, the 506th Parachute Infantry rolled into Berchtesgaden. Captain Al Hassenzahl, then a company commander, remembers the Nest.

We were probably one of the first troops up there. There was a bronze door, as I remember it, at the bottom of the shaft. It wasn't working, so we had to climb up to the bird's nest, and surprisingly there were no sleeping facilities there, it was just a meeting place. It was top flight. They had a huge round table in a circular room with stone walls with windows looking out over the mountains and the beautiful countryside. They had the very best of china and silverware. This was before the division or corps people got up and supposedly catalogued. There was a lot of stuff taken for souvenirs. As a matter of fact, I sent my mother home some Nazi cups and saucers, egg cups, very fine china. Some of the guys got a hold of pieces of silverware with the initials on them: *AH.* I still treasure a couple of books that I picked up in the great room. One was a beautiful volume, obviously a fine paper, high rag count, that never deteriorated over the years, and it shows the rise of the Third Reich from Hindenburg's gesture of surrendering the reins to Hitler, the shovels brigades and uniforms, the German youth movement—it's all pictorially there, in German.

I had a beautiful four-door Mercedes convertible. I had it for three or four days in a little town in Austria. One of my guys found this, and we appropriated it for a company car, and we all took rides around the countryside. The

Wartime photo of the Eagle's Nest a month after its capture by the 101st Airborne Division. (Photo courtesy of Leonard Rapport.)

war was over. Finally I got ranked out of it: The battalion commander took it. He was ranked out of it by the regimental commander, and finally it ended up at division. I think it was the very same vehicle that went back to the States and was shown across the country. I think that it is still in existence; it was the Hitler car.

We also found, buried in a haystack—how my guys found it I don't know—a 1940 Buick Roadmaster, a black one. I have a picture of it in my den wall. It was almost brand new, and we had that for about a week. I appropriated it as the command car for Company C.

We had a gun-happy crew. I had a few guys that were excellent combat men, but when they got back to garrison they were a real pain in the ass and real hard to control! We found a stash of SS liquor, top-grade whiskey, Scotch, wine, liquor, beer, you name it; it was stashed in a cave. Somebody got the bright idea, I think it was one of my officers, "Why don't we make a company club here?" I thought that was a pretty good idea: Give the guys a place to go and relax and have fun, have a couple of drinks.

The first night we had it open, I told my first sergeant, Sam Smith, "Sam, we got to work out some sort of system so these guys don't go nuts on this booze, because you know how they are." He agreed. It was hard to control. Some of the guys got too much to drink and they started to shoot up the place, and it got a little hairy at times. Some guys can control their booze and some can't. This went on for about three nights, and I was really getting worried that somebody was going to get shot or killed. It would be my ass as company commander. I took a truck that we had and loaded all that booze on a truck and drove up where we knew there was a cliff and I dumped it all over the cliff, and it all smashed to smithereens. I was not very popular!

My state of mind was relieved. I was glad it was all over. I was very happy it was over, very happy that we were in the victor's seat, which we were. I didn't intend to stay in the service, so I was looking forward to going back to college, where I left off.

CHAPTER THIRTEEN

HOME

They returned to their hometowns wearing the diamond-shaped golden eagle discharge patch known as the "Ruptured Duck," and behind the badge, each veteran coped in his own private way. Most were too eager to forget mankind's worst war.

Once home, the citizen soldiers melted back into American society. The qualities they had learned as members of an elite team—high standards, self-discipline, determination, and hard work—gave them an edge in civilian life. Many men used the GI Bill to help pay for college or home mortgages, helping to make the World War II generation the best-educated and best-housed generation in U.S. history. Families were begun and careers built. Some men remained in the military and fought in Korea and Vietnam.

Most men chose to forget about the war as best they could, but very few of the men elected to sever all wartime ties. Combat created bonds of friendship that have withstood the passage of time. Many World War II veterans still remain close to the men they served with. On fishing trips, the telephone, and at regimental or battalion reunions they talk, sometimes about the present, sometimes about the past. The men are as different from each other as are the members of any other generation, but there is a universal pride in their service and their units and a sense of bittersweetness that dominates them all. Many still ask themselves why they survived. Cemeteries around the world are filled with World War II's legions: the Henrys, Loustalots, and Ted Walters who gave up their futures for our future. They are honored, and rightly so.

JACK TROVATO

155th Battalion, 17th Airborne Division

World War II ended in Europe at 2301 hours on May 8, 1945. Here Jack Trovato remembers his emotions at war's end.

A slew of eighteen-year-old kids dying, some of them for glory, some for the adventure of it, but the reality is that they were sacrificial lambs. It's war: Somebody has to die. [Chokes up, sobs.] I believed in what we were doing, and the reward is what we have now.

At the end of the war we had this chaplain, he was giving a service, he was a Jewish chaplain giving a service to everybody. He said something then, and I guess it was after that I started thinking, "Does anybody care?" He told us that "nobody is going to care when you get back except for your buddies here. They are going to care. They are going to know." He asked us, "How do you feel about the men of World War I?" My father was there, so I had an understanding, but I didn't give a shit about the guys who died in World War I. I didn't give a shit for them, so why should I think anybody is going to give a shit for all these young kids who gave their lives?

JOHN BURKE

5th Ranger Battalion

John Burke recalls his homecoming.

I can remember a sense of joy when I came home. Oh, God, I can put my head down, the sheets on the bed, there're no bugs on them, there's no rain falling on you, your feet are warm, your hands are warm, you're gonna get a hot meal, there's nobody shooting at you, there's no artillery coming in, there's no mortars, no snipers, nothing. You can just lie in bed and be comfortable. That meant so much to me—so much.

I can remember the first day I got home. I came into Union Station [in Washington, D.C.], got into a cab, the cabdriver says, "Where've you been, soldier?" I said, "I just got back from overseas, in Europe." At that time my mother was living in the Washington area and he dropped me off at her apartment and he wouldn't even charge me.

I walked in, and my mother (this was April and my brother was killed in January—I had a guilt complex here since I didn't think of my brother when I came home, I only thought about myself) was glad to see me. My girlfriend was there, and my sister.

I look back on it and I'm really critical of myself. I'd become so hardened; I didn't show any remorse about my brother, when I look back on it. I cry now. I look back on it and say, "Was I an egomaniac? Was I so happy to be home?" I think it is a combination of things—being away from all the fear, killing, kill or be killed, the total discomfort—you live a dog's life, mud, slime, filth, rotten socks, dirty clothes—you just learn to accept it—and you get home and you're so happy. Maybe I was just overpowered by that.

I make excuses for it. I hope it was the war that did it: that death was so commonplace and then when we went back up on the line again, we were in such a critical situation there wasn't anything to think about except your own salvation and the guys around you.

JOE CICCHINELLI

551ˢᵗ Parachute Infantry Battalion

For more than fifty-five years Joe Cicchinelli has been battling post-traumatic stress disorder (PTSD).

A week after I got home I started working part-time at the Post Office. I had this one route known as the Wells Road Route. On one side were houses, and on the other side was a large farm. There was a great big open field and a farmhouse. When it snowed, Jesus Christ, I couldn't even look at it. I tried changing my route and coming back an opposite way. But I saw the guys lying on the snow with their bright red blood running all over the white snow. I could see the tanks. It was horrible. This open field brought me back to Belgium, when we were caught in a field and lost a lot of men. I feel so guilty about leading that attack.

Not long after the war I started getting seizures. My seizures started from a death odor. It's a real foul odor, the smell of rotting flesh. I get disoriented and I don't want anyone touching me or anything like that. It only lasts a few minutes. It comes and goes.

The war never leaves my mind. I don't watch war movies or anything. Sometimes I'll talk about it and I'll have flashbacks all day or be up all night thinking about it.

MORRIS WEBB

2nd Ranger Battalion

When writing this e-history, Morris Webb journeyed back to his homecoming from the war and the results of the worst days of his life: on Hill 400 in the Hürtgen Forest.

I arrived at Camp Atterbury around the middle of October 1945 where I was to be discharged back into civilian life. As I was standing in line to be discharged, we were being given our final medical checkups when I fainted and fell to the floor. An ambulance was called and I was taken to the hospital. I spent about a week in the hospital going through a series of tests and examinations, after which I was sent back to the barracks to await my second go-around with the discharge process.

I was lying there in bed when I woke up. As I lay there I felt my heart stop! I knew that that couldn't be, but I jumped out of bed, dressed, and went to the Charge of Quarters office. I told him what had happened and asked him if there was any transportation to the hospital. He said there wasn't any at night, but the hospital was near and he gave me instructions on how to get there. I took off on foot. When I got there I explained to the duty nurse what had happened. She saw my hands and wrists—they had drawn up like claws and turned purple. She felt my hands and immediately called for the duty doctor. He came and examined me and gave me a shot of something and had me taken to a ward. The shot the doctor had given me allowed me to sleep the rest of the night.

Early the next morning an army psychiatrist came and examined me further and had me sent to another ward. Thus began three months of treatment and counseling.

My father came up from southern Kentucky to see me and talk to the doctor. The doctor talked to him at length explaining my problem to him and also told him that they had been thinking of sending me to Cleveland where they had a facility there that could deal with my problem better than they could there. Later I learned that treatment may have included shock therapy.

My father was against the shock treatment and convinced the psychiatrist that I would be better off if I was discharged and allowed to return home.

In hindsight, coming home may have been the wrong move. My father meant well, but the doctor should have overruled that move. Anyway, it was done, and that was water over the dam. Before my father had come for the visit, the doctor had told me a little bit about nerves and how they react under stress and what normally happens when the stress is relieved. He likened nerves to a rubber band. He said that normally they returned to normal, but like a rubber band that has been wound as tight as you can wind it, when you turned it loose it would snap back to normal, but on rare occasions they would break. He said nerves react the same way. When the nerves break, we call it a nervous breakdown, shell shock, combat fatigue, etc. That is what happened to me.

After I had graduated from college, I had a few mild setbacks. It was a terrible feeling, and there was nothing you could do. Going back to my army psychiatrist, he said, "You had been under extreme duress for so long and you were able to cope with it, but when you returned home you realized that there was nothing to be stressful any longer. Instead of the nerves returning to normalcy, they snapped." I experienced trauma for many years; my poor wife can vouch for it. I am so happy for her understanding and her ability to put up with my trying times. We have been married for fifty-three years, and without her I don't know if I would have made it this far; she has been my medicine.

WARREN "BING" EVANS

1ˢᵗ and 3ʳᵈ Ranger Battalions

Warren "Bing" Evans reluctantly spoke about his return to civilian life.

After the war, I started working for a Fortune 100 firm. I was probably one of their fastest-rising stars. I lived in nine different states and eleven different cities. Most of them were promotions; some of them were sideways moves. On one of those moves, when I became division sales manager, I found that I was beginning to withdraw from people and I had trouble putting one foot in front of the other. I found I was making excuses for not doing what the company expected of me. Knowing this, I put myself in a psychiatric hospital.

They gave me electric shock treatment and so forth and so on. It didn't do any good. For two or three years, the company was very good to me. I had to resign from the company, but they were still very good to me, very patient. They knew something was wrong, but they knew nothing of the post-trauma syndrome, which is what I had.

Once I got over that, the healing process was slow. I suspect my faith in God snapped me out of it, and my wife. She stuck with me at a time when it was very difficult. When I resigned I even went into work. I went into accounting, where I could be in the background, where I could work by myself, and I became very successful at it. I probably didn't make quite as much money as when I resigned from Ralston Purina Company, but I probably accumulated a lot more satisfaction.

[Dealing with the post-traumatic stress disorder is] a part of your life that you don't tell people about. It's personal, or they wouldn't understand it, or they'd think you were weak, which wasn't the case at all.

It was very hard. For forty years I didn't even tell my family. My wife knew because I had so many nightmares and I tried to explain them to her, and she began to learn what went on. They were black periods. They would come in the middle of the night when I was sound asleep and all of the sudden I'd relive a moment. Actually, there were four that I relived.

One of them was Anzio when the shell exploded, or whatever it was. I could remember the ground coming up and hitting me but I could never remember hitting the ground. That's one of them, and I'm still falling, but I haven't hit the ground after all these years.

Another time was with a soldier at Sened Station in [North Africa]. I look into his eyes, and I still haven't been able to pull the trigger to this day. There were several like that.

One of them is in retrospect. I was the tailing company going into Anzio. We had two experienced officers in—I was one of them and Joe Larkin was the other one—so for every action one of our companies would be at the point and the other would bring up the rear. This was the day I was in the rear and Joe called me: "Bing, we're in trouble, we need your help." I thought then, knowing what I knew about what was there, that if I had taken my company around I could have probably gotten most of them out of there alive. But I didn't because you don't leave a fallen man in combat. So we negotiated the whole column, got up there. So to this day I wake up yelling in bed to hold the company back.

Now there are a couple of things I don't talk about to this day. After my second escape [from a POW camp] they put me in solitary confinement because they figured I'd do something. I was thrown in a heat cell in solitary confinement with heat radiators all along one wall, and I had no clothes on. Every now and then [Germans would] come in and offer me a cigarette and turn the heat off and give me a good beating, and by the time I got sick they'd leave. They finally decided that that was worthless. By this time they tried me and I was sentenced and was supposed to be shot as a spy. So they put me out into a Russian compound, and they [captured Russian soldiers] were really starving to death. I remember they brought the bones of an old dead horse by and tossed those bones over to us, and I remember we fought like cats and dogs to get a bone. I got a big bone so you could eat the marrow out of it.

Then I sat back and looked at myself and thought, "What kind of a human be-ing am I who can stand here and fight like an animal for the bones of an old dead horse?" I began crying, and still wake up crying.

SID SALOMON

2nd Ranger Battalion

At age eighty-six Sid Salomon continues to compete in international rowing competitions—and he typically wins. When Sid Salomon re-turned home, he just picked up his life where he had left it.

We came into a temporary camp, Camp Patrick Henry, in Norfolk, Virginia. Our battalion commander wanted us to return to the United States as a unit, so consequently we had to stay in Czechoslovakia for a few extra months be-fore we returned home. Once home, we were separated into groups. For in-stance, I entered the army at Fort Dix. All the guys that came into the army from New Jersey and Pennsylvania went by train to Dix, and everybody who came in from the Chicago area went to Fort Sheridan. There wasn't even time to shake hands and say goodbye, so waiting the extra months to return home as a unit didn't make any difference.

I only lived about sixty miles from Dix. We had to be processed at Dix, and they said, "It will be another three days, so just relax." I figured the heck with the army, and I got on the train to see my mother and father. [Laughs.] It was over three years since I had last seen them. I got home and spent the night at my parents' house. The next day I went over to Dix and processed out. Nobody knew I stayed the night with my family. They tried to talk me into staying in the army. I went in the reserves, but that was it.

It was great to have my own room. None of my friends were home. I had only two that were home, since they had jobs that were essential to the war ef-fort. So not long after I got home, I went back to Wisconsin, where I had a sales job with a paper mill before the war. I got my job back and I got right back into the routine of things, and that was it. I was not interested in loafing around and not doing anything. I just wanted to get on with life.

METHODOLOGY

In the summer of 1992, I began interviewing World War II airborne veterans and researching the original source documentation surrounding airborne units and, later, the Rangers. I mined the National Archives, the United States Army Library at Carlisle Barracks, and other repositories for practically every after-action report, unit journal, and correspondence for these units. Overall, I found the official documents and secondary sources hollow, revealing only the high-level details, telling only a tiny fragment of this epic story. So I went on a crusade to interview the participants with only the vague goal of preserving their history and no real plans beyond that.

The project started to jell in 1995 when I created The Drop Zone Virtual Museum World War II Oral History Project at www.thedropzone.org. The Drop Zone is the first online oral history project. It is maintained by volunteers, and we never have accepted any funding for our efforts. Our goal remains to preserve and share these experiences.

Around The Drop Zone we created a virtual community of hundreds of World War II veterans. It became one way of interacting with the men who fought the war. While these men are in their seventies and eighties (or older), the same pioneering spirit that propelled them into combat nearly six decades ago compels many of them to embrace technology today. The veterans and the volunteers at The Drop Zone created a new paradigm on gathering personal accounts: interactive e-mail personal interviews, called e-histories. The Drop Zone's Virtual Reunion and one-on-one e-mail interviews became forums for veterans to share and gather their recollections interactively. The methodology was described in numerous leading newspapers.

At the urging of several veterans, I took the next step and began to amass the oral histories that constitute the bulk of this book. I did this not only to tell their story but also as an extension of my initial crusade. That crusade even led me to propose a Virtual Monument (to complement the stone memorial that the World War II Monument Association is constructing on the Mall in Washington, D.C.), using e-histories to capture the memories of all World War II veterans.

The interview process has been an amazing journey. I'm honored to have been trusted as a messenger of the veterans' stories. Over the past nine years I've interviewed at least six hundred World War II veterans in their homes, at reunions, and abroad in areas where they fought. Numerous trips to Europe both with these men and with my family provided an invaluable window, letting me see where these men fought and where their fellow soldiers died. Scores of their former enemies, from Germany's toughest units, were also interviewed to get the "other side" of the story.

Most of the men I interviewed were privates, corporals, sergeants, lieutenants, a few captains—the men who fought the war from the foxhole level. My interviewees were at first reticent about their war experiences. It is a testament to their humble nature that they were so reluctant to speak of their own heroism.

My experience has led me to believe that written accounts that are not interactively obtained generally do not go beyond the basic facts and tend to offer a résumé of those individuals' war experiences. After seeing many previously written accounts (noninteractive) from the men I interviewed, I have come to appreciate how far below the surface oral history can go to uncover a part of the war that has been rarely reported.

In each interview, I tried to pull out the veteran's strongest memories. I never used a set of prepared questions. I'd like to think they were conversations rather than interviews. As a result, these oral histories are more vivid and candid than they would otherwise be.

Nevertheless, faulty memories, skewed perspectives, and the tendency for self-serving are all inherent dangers with oral history. At times individual memories do not jibe with the collective memory. But these same flaws are also found in the documentary record. The eyewitness combat accounts in this book have been verified to the best of my ability. First, all of the veterans interviewed have been referred to me by several other veterans and often through the appropriate veterans associations and their designated historians. In a sense, this peer review helped me to screen many of my interview candidates. Additional verification was obtained by interviewing men they served with who may have gone through the events they describe. The most provocative accounts in this book have been corroborated by several sources.

Documentation in the form of unit journals, after-action reports, and award citations also corroborates the accounts of the veterans. I remember the eerie feeling I got pulling apart the original onion-skin map overlays marking the position of the 508th Parachute Infantry Regiment's fatal July attacks in Normandy and the message center commands in faded yellow trip-licate calling for stretchers to pick up the scores of dead and wounded men. Many of these men are decorated heroes, and I've had a chance to review the written citations behind their Silver Stars, Distinguished Service Crosses, and the one Medal of Honor awarded to a soldier included in this book. As you would expect, the paperwork does not do justice to their bravery and sacrifices.

One of the most difficult aspects of preparing this book was choosing which stories to include, since there is so much wonderful material, easily enough for three thousand or four thousand pages. I chose to limit this book's scope to the European Theater only, not because the contribution of the elite troops of the Pacific was any less, but because it seemed to make sense that these two sagas be told separately. This limitation aside, I have tried to provide a fair sampling from each of the elite groups. Furthermore, the focus of this book is the voices of the men, and therefore historical back-ground on the units was kept to a minimum.

While some people may disagree with an individual's recollection of events, I think the accounts collectively tell an important story. As Ronald Grele states in his classic oral history work, *Envelopes of Sound,* oral history "is a way to get a better history, a more critical history, a more conscious his-tory which involves members of the public in the creation of their own his-tory."[1] I believe their voices should be heard.

APPENDIX

WWII Order of Battle: U.S. Airborne & Ranger Units

Airborne and 1st SSF
European Theater

DIVISION	Infantry Regiments/BNs; Parachute/Glider	Artillery Parachute/Glider BNs
13th	517[1] PIR / 190 GIR / 326 GIR 88 GIR; 515 PIR / 189[10] GIR	458 / 676; 460 / 677
17th	507 PIR / 193 GIR (550) 513 PIR / 194 GIR	464 / 680; 466 / 681
82nd	504 PIR / 325 GIR 505, (507)[2], 508[2] PIRs	376 / 319; 456 / 320
101st	502 PIR / 327 GIR 506 PIR / 401 GIR[9] 501[3] PIR	377; 463[8] / 321; 907
1st Airborne Task Force *(created for invasion of southern France)*	517 PRCT; 550[4] IAB 551 PIB[5]; 509 PIB	460 / 602; 463
Independent	509 PIB; 517 PRCT; 1st SSF[6] 550 IAB; 551 PIB[5]; 555 PIB	

Pacific Theater/CBI

DIVISION	Infantry Regiments/BNs; Parachute/Glider	Artillery Parachute/Glider BNs
11th	511 PIR; 187 GIR / PIR; 188 GIR / PIR	457 / 472; 674 / 674
Independent	542 PIB 503 RCT; 1st SSF[6]; 541 PIR[7]	462

The Rangers

EUROPEAN THEATER OF OPERATIONS	
Darby's Ranger's 1st, 3rd, and 4th Ranger Battalions	*Ranger Battalions:* 2nd and 5th

[1] The 517th PRCT entered the division in 1945.

[2] The 508th was officially listed as an attached unit to the 82nd Airborne. The 507th was attached to the 82nd in Normandy and became part of the 17th Airborne Division after *Market-Garden*.

[3] The 501st was officially listed as an attached unit to the 101st Airborne.

[4] The 550th Infantry Airborne Bat. was attached to the 1st ATF in southern France. The unit was the second airborne unit formed and trained initially in air-landing operations. Before southern France, about a hundred members were parachute-qualified. The unit fought with the 17th Airborne in Belgium and was nearly destroyed on January 4. Inactivated in March '45 and used to form the 3/194 GIR.

[5] Officially designated 1/551 PIR, but never received two additional round-out Bns.

[6] Most members of the 1st Special Service Force were airborne-qualified. The unit landed in the Aleutian Islands and was then transferred to the ETO.

AA BNs Cos	Eng BNs Cos	Sig Co	Ord Co	QM Co	Med Co	Prcht Maint Co
153	129	513	713	409	222	13
155	139	517	717	411	224	17
80	307	82	782	407	307	82
81	326	101	801	426	326	101
AT Co, 442 RCT	596; 887	512		334	676	D Co., 83d Chem BN A Co. 2nd Chem BN

AA BNs Cos	Eng BNs Cos	Sig Co	Ord Co	QM Co	Med Co	Prcht Maint Co
152; 675	127	511	711	408	221	11
	879; 161					

PACIFIC THEATER OF OPERATIONS / CIB
6th Ranger Battalion
5307 (Provisional)

[7] The 541st remained Stateside for most of the war. Arrived in the Philippines in June '45. Inactivated August 10, '45, in Lipa, Luzon, Philippines. Assets used to form the 3rd Bns of the 187th and 188th GIR, which were subsequently redesignated "ParaGlider."

[8] The 463rd was originally the 456th. The unit was practically independent and only officially became part of the 101st Airborne at the end of the war.

[9] The 401st, like the 327th, was a two-battalion regiment. In March 1944 the 2nd Battalion of the 401st was sent to the 82nd Airborne. The 1st Bat, while officially remaining the 1st Bat of the 401st during the first months of combat, actually functioned as the 3rd Bat of the 327th, 101st Airborne Division. The unit was not officially the 3rd Bat 327th until spring 1945.

[10] The 189th and 190th were inactivated and their men transferred to the 88th and 190th respectively. The 513th was also initially part of the 13th but was transferred to the 17th Airborne Division on March 10, 1944.

NOTES

Introduction

1. Geoffrey Perret, *There's a War to Be Won: The United States Army in World War II* (New York: Random House, 1990), p. 167.

2. After seeing a Western movie featuring the famous Apache chief Geronimo, members in the Test Platoon bet Eberhardt that he would pass out while he stood in the door of the airplane before a parachute jump. Eberhardt retorted that he would yell "Geronimo!" when he left the plane his voice was so loud that even men on the ground could hear him as he made the jump. True to his word, Eberhardt successfully made the jump and "Geronimo" was said to have been heard by the men on the ground.

3. Harris Mitchell, *The First Airborne Battalion: As Told by Its First Sergeant Major* (Rockville, MD: Twinbrook Communications, 1996), p. 72.

4. James Huston, *Out of the Blue: U.S. Army Operations in World War II* (West Lafayette, IN: Purdue University Press), p. 118.

5. Lucian K. Truscott, *Command Missions: A Personal Story* (New York: E.P. Dutton, 1954), p. 40.

6. Robert Burhans, *The First Special Service Force: A History of the North Americans, 1942–1944* (Washington DC: Infantry Journal Press, 1947), p. 60.

Chapter 1: Dieppe

1. "The Dieppe Raid Combined Report," 10/42, produced by Combined Operations HQ Whitehall.

2. "Commando Organization to HQ USA in Britain," 6/1/42; General Orders No. 7 to HQ USANIF and V Army Corps "Activation of 1st Ranger Battalion" "Report on Dieppe Operations," 8/31/42. Total strength of the battalion was 473 personnel plus a 10% overage for projected losses in training.

3. "Report on Dieppe Operations," 8/31/42.

4. "The Dieppe Raid Combined Report." 10/42. 2/503's planned participation confirmed through the author's interview with 2/503 (509 PIB) Commander Col. Edson Raff. "SHAEF G-2, Captured German analysis of the Dieppe Raid," 2/26/44, cites the lack of an airborne drop as one of the reasons the raid failed. The document provides an enlightening view of the German side of the Dieppe raid minus the British spin.

5. "The Dieppe Raid Combined Report," 10/42 produced by Combined Operations HQ Whitehall.

6. Ibid. "Operation Order No. 1, CAULDRON," provides a detailed operation plan for No. 4 Commando.

7. "The Dieppe Raid and Combined Report." Howard Henry's death is described in "Doomed Strike Force," by James Altieri, p. 32.

8. Before TORCH began there was a crisis concerning the use of elite troops, ignited by the departure of the 1st Ranger Battalion. Some within the U.S. Army—including Lieutenant General Lesley McNair—recommended dissolving elite units; George Marshall and others, on the other hand, favored their use and sought the creation of a second Ranger battalion. The pro-Ranger camp won and the 29th Ranger battalion was formed. Some of its men went on to participate in the early raids in Nazi-occupied Norway, and the 29th's final mission was in September 1943, when they knocked out a German radar station on the Ille d'Ouessant. That raid is described in the 29th Division's official history, *29 Let's Go! A History of the 29th Infantry Division in World War II* (Washington DC: Infantry Journal Press, 1948).

Chapter 2: TORCH

1. As quoted in the historical novel *The Killer Angels* by Michael Shaara (New York: Random House, 1974).

2. George Howe, *Northwest Africa: Seizing the Initiative in the West* (Washington DC: Center of Military History United States Army, 1991), p. 12. Resources are outlined in: Mark Clark, *Calculated Risk* (New York: Harper, 1950), p. 34.

3. America's glider program did not get underway until 1942.

4. The battalion was first renamed the 2/509 or second battalion of the 509th Parachute Infantry Regiment on 11/2/42. The 509th never received the extra battalions needed for a regiment; therefore it remained the 509th Parachute Infantry Battalion. For the purposes of the chapter it will be called the 509th Parachute Infantry Battalion.

5. Little official documentation exists on the original jumps. Foreign Observer Reports by Lt. Col. Harris and Higgins, 2/19/43, offer a fairly detailed description of three jumps and the forays into Tunisia. Interviews by the author with the principal officers, Raff and Yarborough, filled in the gaps.

6. Howe, *Northwest Africa: Seizing the Initiative in the West,* p. 193. A Ranger company consisted of 65 men, less than half the size of a normal infantry company. There were six companies in the battalion designated A to F. Detailed description of the landing is found in Darby, "1st Ranger Battalion Report of Action," 1/1/1943.

7. Foreign Observer Reports by Lt. Col. Harris and Higgins, 2/19/43, p. 6.

8. Letter: Eisenhower to Marshall, 12/30/42.

9. Foreign Observer Reports by Lt. Col. Harris and Higgins, 2/19/43, p. 7; Edson Raff, *We Jumped to Fight* (New York: Eagle Books, 1944), pp. 182–184; "Report of Visit to North Africa," Dexter, 6/11/43, G-3.

10. William O. Darby and William Baumer, *Darby's Rangers: We Lead the Way* (Novato, CA: Presidio, 1980); Darby, "1st Ranger Battalion Report of Action," 3/5/1943.

11. Darby, "1st Ranger Battalion Report of Action," 4/9/43.

12. Howe, *Northwest Africa: Seizing the Initiative in the West,* p. 666.

13. Foreign Observer Reports by Lt. Col. Harris and Higgins, 2/19/43, p. 8; Charles Doyle and Terrell Stewart, *Stand in The Door! The Wartime History of the 509th Parachute Infantry* (Williamstown, NJ: Phillips Publications, 1988), p. 87.

Chapter 3: Sicily

1. Minutes from Casablanca Conference "60th Meeting CCS," January 18, 1943.

2. Albert Garland and Howard Smyth, *Sicily and the Surrender of Italy* (Washington, DC: Center of Military History United States Army, 1991), pp. 80–84.

3. Dammer, "Report of Action 3rd Ranger Battalion," 7/31/43.

4. Darby, "Report of Action, 1st Ranger Battalion," 8/5/43.

5. Ibid.

6. James Gavin, *On to Berlin* (New York: Viking Press, 1978), p. 41. While the 505th's 1st and 3rd battalions along with scattered elements of Tucker's 3rd Battalion of the 504th engaged the HG Division, the 505th's 2nd Battalion landed in a two-mile area near Marina di Ragusa that was several miles from their designated drop zone. After first knocking out several large pillboxes, the battalion would continue to eliminate enemy resistance on the 45th Infantry Division's right flank, assisting their movement inland. One 505th group commanded by Lt. Col. Gorham killed or captured 200 German infantry and destroyed two tanks and damaged two others, forcing the German battle group to retire that day and preventing it from hitting the fragile Allied landings: "505th Report of Action Sicily,"; Allen Langdon, *Ready: History of the 505th Parachute Infantry* (privately published), p. 24

7. Ibid, p. 38; Carlo D'Este, *World War II in the Mediterranean* (Chapel Hill, NC: Algonquin Books), p. 59.

8. Ridgway, "Casualties in the Sicilian Campaign," 5/19/43.

9. *The Papers of Dwight D. Eisenhower* (Baltimore, MD: The Johns Hopkins Press, 1970), p. 1269; Eisenhower to Marshall, 7/20/43; Lucas, "Observers Report on Sicilian Campaign," 9/8/43.

10. Colonel Darby was the only other member in the 1st, 3rd and 4th Ranger battalions to receive the DSC.

Chapter 4: Tough Old Boot

1. Martin Blumenson, *Salerno to Cassino* (Washington DC: Center of Military History United States Army, 1968), pp. 4–7.

2. Initially, an airborne operation known as GIANT I was drawn up to seize the mountain passes at Sorrento and drop a combat team along the Volturno River. The paratroopers were to create a diversion and block reinforcements from hitting the beachhead. The operation was later canceled since sandbars were found at the mouth of the river, making it hard to stop German reinforcements from coming across in multiple areas. This plan was considered too risky.

3. Matthew Ridgway, *Soldier: The Memoirs of Matthew B. Ridgway* (New York: Harper & Brothers, 1956), pp. 84–90; Clay Blair, *Ridgway's Paratroopers* (New York: Doubleday, 1985), p. 139.

4. James Altieri, *The Spearheaders* (New York: Popular Library, 1960), p. 258; Darby, "Report of Action," 9/9/43–9/29/43, pp. 1–3, 11/15/43 and 11/25/43.

5. Ibid, p. 259. Fifth Army records indicate that the Rangers were outnumbered by nine to one.

6. Clark, *Calculated Risk,* p. 198.

7. Tucker, "504 Action in Italy," p. 1.

8. The drop was considered one of the 505th's best. Gavin, "505 After Action Report," 10/43, p. 3; Allen Langdon, *Ready: History of the 505th Parachute Infantry* (privately published), p. 31.

9. Yarborough, "Citation of Unit," 5/2/44, pp. 1–6.

10. The Germans had several defensive lines. The Germans' first line of defense was behind the Volturno River. Next, a hastily constructed and ill-defined set of fortifications called the Barbara Line stood in the way. The next belt was the Winter Line, also called the Bernhardt Line. Finally came Kesselring's masterpiece, the Gustav Line.

11. The 504th Regimental Combat Team included engineer support troops and a battalion of parachute field artillery. The 456th Parachute Field Artillery Battalion, later part of the battalion was renamed the (463rd) also was in Italy.

12. S.E. Morrison, *Strategy & Compromise* (Boston, MA: Little, Brown, 1958), pp. 40–47.

13. Refer to the introduction of this book for a detailed overview of the Plough Project.

14. The cliff was not entirely sheer; the Force also inched its way up several ledges and goat-sized trails.

15. Robert Adleman and George Walton, *The Devil's Brigade* (Philadelphia: Chilton Books, 1966), p. 19.

16. Burhans, *The First Special Service Force*, p. 124; Frederick, "After Action Report," 1/44.

17. Truscott, *Command Missions,* p. 252.

18. This action is referenced in the 509th's "After Action Report," 9/43. The road was cut for at least one day.

19. The Force had a service unit and three small regiments of 600 men each.

Chapter 5: Anzio

1. Churchill tended to dismiss the dangers as just negative thinking of generals he liked to refer to as "masters of negation." Carlo D'Este, *Fatal Decision: Anzio and the Battle for Rome* (New York: HarperCollins, 1991), p. 93.

2. Ibid, p. 7.

3. D'Este, *World War II in the Mediterranean,* p. 142. The doomed attack had the ultimate aim of capturing the Alban Hills.

4. The Rangers were probably outnumbered even more than ten to one. Around Cisterna were the battle-tested Hermann Göring and 4th Parachute divisions and elements of the

29th Panzer Division. With the overwhelming firepower and numbers the outcome of the battle was practically preordained. The destruction of seventeen tanks and flak wagons is referenced in Altieri, *The Spearheaders*, p. 265.

5. Several accounts back up this statement. Such as After Action Report by Shunstrom to Darby on Cisterna 6/44 and numerous interviews by the author to principal Rangers in the attack, such as Major Dobson and Warren Evans.

6. Darby and Baumer, *Darby's Rangers: We Lead the Way*, p. 167.

7. D'Este, *Fatal Decision*, p. 167. Major Dobson, 1st Battalion Commander, estimates the number of prisoners taken. Based on the author's research and interviews, this number seems more accurate than the number provided by the Germans, which probably includes a combination of 7th Infantry and the 504th that were also involved in the operation.

8. Burhans, *The First Special Service Force*, p. 166. The Force took up a 13-kilometer (8-mile) front of a beachhead that stretched 52 kilometers.

9. Graves, "504 S-2 Narrative of Events at Anzio," 4/44.

10. Blumenson, *Salerno to Cassino*, p. 431. Large attacks were also made on the 3rd Division, 504th, and FSSF.

11. The number of artillery rounds fired is referenced in D'Este, *Fatal Decision*, p. 293. A complete overview of the attack can be found in the 509th's After Action Report by Yarborough, 5/44.

12. Burhans, *The First Special Service Force*, p. 194.

13. Accounts vary slightly and some individuals state that the Germans used two armored cars and one tank.

Chapter 6: The War from Within

1. Bradley Biggs, *The Triple Nickles* (North Haven, CT: Archon, 1986).

2. From 11/4/44 to 8/8/45 285 incidents were reported. The Japanese released more than 9,000 balloons, and 1,000 are estimated to have reached North America. A balloon bomb was also responsible for the temporary loss of power at the Hanford, Washington atomic energy plant. J. Mikish, "Bomb Attack on North America" (Washington DC: Smithsonian Journal), p. 38.

3. Postwar discussion between Biggs and General Davis, who was on the McCloy committee remembers Marshall making the change from battalion to company.

Chapter 7: Invasion: Normandy

1. German strength: George Harrison, *Cross-Channel Attack* (Washington, D.C.: Center of Military History United States Army, 1951), p. 243. Hitler had placed fatal constraints on German panzer divisions. The mobile panzer reserve was not placed near the coastline but inland, with the argument that it would prevent their destruction and that they could quickly be moved to the invasion area. The panzer reserve could only be deployed by direct order from Hitler and did not move until the afternoon of D-Day—too late to repel the invasion. Rommel, on the other hand, correctly argued that the tanks should be placed on or near the coastline. He argued that Allied air power would inhibit their movement to the beaches and the tanks would best be deployed by repelling the in-

vaders at the beachhead. Had his request for another panzer division at St. Lô been granted, the results could have been decisive in favor of the German forces.

2. A rough breakdown of the major D-Day objectives for each airborne division and parachute regiment is listed below.

Planned Drop Zone	Regiment	Mission
A	502 PIR, 101st	Causeway Exits 3 and 4.
	377 PFA, 101st	Destroy the coastal battery at St. Martin-de-Varreville.
C	506 PIR, 101st	Causeway Exits 1 and 2.
	326 AEB, 101st*	Capture the Douve River bridges.
D	501 PIR, 101st	Capture the La Barquette lock.
	326 AEB, 101st	Establish defensive positions along the Douve; demolish several bridges over the Douve.
N	508 PIR, 82nd	Defensive positions west of the Merderet.
T	507 PIR, 82nd	Capture several bridges over the Merderet.
O	505 PIR, 82nd	Seize the bridges at la Fière and Chef-du-Pont and capture Ste. Mère-Église.

* Platoons of the 326th were divided between the regiments.

3. The bulk of the 101st's glider units would arrive by sea with the 4th Division at Utah Beach. The 82nd also had a special task force made up of 90 glidermen from the 325th Glider Infantry Regiment, elements of a glider field artillery battalion, and a company of tanks from the 746th Tank Battalion, commanded by Edson Raff. Raff Force was to land on Utah Beach on D-Day and quickly move inland, linking up with the 82nd around Ste. Mère-Église.

4. The first to land, at about 12:15 A.M., were the pathfinders. They attempted to guide the main airborne assault by marking the drop zones with special radar equipment.

5. Only about a dozen E Company men made the initial attack; they were joined later by a handful of men from D Company of the 506 PIR.

6. "2nd Ranger Battalion Report of Action," 6/44 and 7/22/44.

7. Sergeants Len Lomell and Jack Kuhn were credited with finding and destroying the guns. Men from E Company may have also had a hand in their destruction. The five 155-mm guns were pointed at Utah, yet they could easily have been rotated to fire on Omaha.

8. "2nd Ranger Battalion Report of Action," 6/44 and 7/22/44. "5th Ranger Battalion Report of Action," 6–10 June 1944 and 7/22/44.

9. 508th and 507th S2 and S3 Journals, July 1944.

10. For 101st Airborne casualty figures: Leonard Rapport and Arthur Northwood, *Rendezvous With Destiny* (Greenville, TX: 101st Airborne Association, 1948). For 82nd casualty figures: Gavin, *On to Berlin*.

11. The story of Edlin and the other three men who captured the Lochrist Battery (Graf Spee) is recorded in the 2nd Ranger Battalion's after action report and S-2 journal.

Chapter 8: DRAGOON

1. Jeffrey Clark and Robert Smith, *Riviera to the Rhine* (Washington, DC: Center of Military History United States Army, 1993), p. 19–20; William Goddard, "Seventh Army Historical Section Report of Operations," p. 32.

2. Clark and Smith, *Riviera to the Rhine,* pp. 70, 91.

3. Wesley Craven and James Cate, *The Army Air Force in World War II* (Chicago: University of Chicago Press). Only four of ten serials landed near their designated drop zone, according to research conducted by historian Clark Archer, *Paratroopers' Odyssey: A History of the 517th Parachute Combat Team* (Hudson, FL: 517th Association), p. 44.

4. September—Allied Force Headquarters G-3 Section Subject: "Airborne Operation *Dragoon*." A total of 332 American gliders made the assault; six were lost in the Mediterranean. Official records of the 1st ATF.

5. Interestingly, it is worth mentioning that the British 2nd Independent Parachute Brigade was tasked with taking Le Muy but failed to move on the objective. Accordingly, the town was captured by the 550th and elements of the 509th.

Chapter 9: Holland

1. "HQS FAAA Outline of Plan for LINNET," 8/29/44; F. Parks diary, several references. "CG FAAA Outline of Plan," amended, 8/30/44.

2. LINNET I: Dwight Eisenhower, *Crusade in Europe* (New York: Doubleday, 1948), p. 303; LINNET II: Bradley and Blair, *A General's Life,* pp. 321–324.

3. Ultimately, about 35,000 airborne troops were deployed in the MARKET-GARDEN operation, 20,190 by parachute and 13,781 by glider. The full 45,000 were not used because the British 52nd Airlanding Division was not deployed. "FAAA Narrative on MARKET," p. 26. In contrast, only about 17,000 men were used in Operation VARSITY for the crossing of the Rhine.

4. 82nd drops: "Operation MARKET: Report of Operations 82nd A/B," p. 7; 101st: Rapport and Northwood, *Rendezvous with Destiny,* p. 267; Charles MacDonald, *The Siegfried Line Campaign* (Washington, DC: Center of Military History, 1963), p. 139.

5. "After Action Report For MARKET 506th PIR," 12/4/44.

6. "Operation MARKET: Summary of Operations 82nd Airborne Division," 11/44; "Invasion of Holland 505 Operations Report," 10/27, pp. 1–4; "504 Operations Report"; "508 Operations Report Holland."

7. "Operation MARKET: Summary of Operations 82nd Airborne Division," 11/44, p. 2.

8. Maxwell Taylor, *Swords to Plowshares* (New York, Norton, 1972), p. 91.

9. Rapport & Northwood, *Rendezvous with Destiny,* pp. 307, 336.

10. "Operation MARKET: Summary of Operations 82nd Airborne Division," 11/44; "Invasion of Holland 505," p. 6; "Operations Report," 10/27, pp. 1–4; "504 Synopsis of MARKET," 11/4, p. 2; "508 Operations Report," 10/44, pp. 1–11.

11. "504 Synopsis of MARKET," 11/4, p. 2.

12. "504 Synopsis of MARKET," 11/4, p. 2; MacDonald, *The Siegfried Line Campaign,* p. 181.

13. *Gavin, On To Berlin,* p. 181. Gavin remembers: "Tucker [commander of the 504th] was livid. I had never seen him so angry. He had expected that when he seized his end of the bridge, the British armor would race on to Arnhem and link up with Urquhart [commander of the besieged 1st Airborne Division]. His first question to me was, 'What in the hell are they doing? We have been in this position for over twelve hours, and all they seem to be doing is brewing tea.'"

14. Out of a total of 11,920 men in the British 1st Airborne, Polish Brigade, and glider pilots, only 3,910 were safely evacuated: Martin Middlebrook, *Arnhem 1944: The Airborne Battle,* (New York, Viking, 1994), p. 439. "Allied Airborne Operations in Holland," September-October 1944, p. 5, states that since 9/25/44 the 1st Airborne sustained 6,462 causalities.

15. The exact number of men and guns destroyed is difficult to determine. "508 Operations Report: 57 Days in Holland and Germany with the 508" 10/44, p. 3, states that the battalion neutralized sixteen 20-mm guns, killed fifty Germans, and captured 149. Eyewitnesses state that Funk's team did a lot of the damage. Funk would receive the DSC for the charge. He would later receive the Medal of Honor for his actions in the Bulge. John Hardie received the Bronze Star for the action.

Chapter 10: Winter Hell

1. Charles MacDonald, *The Last Offensive* (Washington DC: Center of Military History United States Army, 1973), p. 53.

2. Surprisingly, considering their remarkable performance in stopping the German attack and playing a key role in the counterattack, only two units attached to the 82nd Airborne Division received the Presidential Unit Citation, the nation's highest honor for a military unit. These units were the 509th Parachute Battalion and the 1st Battalion of the 517th Parachute Infantry Regiment. In 2000, 56 years after the battle, President Clinton also awarded the 551st Parachute Infantry Battalion the Presidential Unit Citation.

3. As of January 2, 1945, three German corps were positioned around Bastogne.

4. Based on 17th Airborne unit journals and after action reports, casualties were very high. On January 4 General Miley, commander of the 17th, reported to Patton that some of his battalions had reported losses of 40 percent. Martin Blumenson, *The Patton Papers* (New York: Houghton Miffin, 1974), p. 615.

5. In an interview with 504th veteran Louis Hauptfleisch, he remembers a trooper making this statement before the 504th's attack on Cheneux.

6. Colonel Piper's testimony was corroborated by my interviews with several veterans that have personal knowledge of the events described by Colonel Piper.

7. The 327th was formally the 401st Glider Infantry Regiment but was renamed prior to the Bulge.

8. The 505th had the farthest advance of any unit in the First Army. Gavin, *On to Berlin,* p. 277; Blair, *Ridgway's Paratroopers,* p. 420.

9. Based on interviews with several officers of the 551st.

10. Doyle, *Stand in the Door,* p. 338.

Chapter 11: Dark Forest

1. Edward Miller, *A Dark and Bloody Ground* (Houston: Texas A&M Press, 1995), p. 2. Casualties were estimated by Edward Miller.

2. "2nd Ranger Battalion Report of Action December," 1944, p. 3. The remaining companies of the 2nd Ranger Battalion not on Hill 400 were defending against counter attacks on Bergstein. The battalion cleared the remaining pockets of resistance in the town on 12/6/44.

3. Salomon, *2nd Ranger Battalion—Germeter-Vossenach-Hurtgen-Bergstein-Hill 400* (privately published), p. 72. Based on intelligence obtained from 8th Division Commander, General Weaver.

4. Not until November, 1944 did the Allied Generals recognize the importance of the dams.

5. The author conducted extensive interviews with members of the German 6th Parachute Regiment who participated in assaults against Rangers on the hill. They confirmed that the hill never fell after it was captured by the Rangers. This fact is also confirmed by 517th and 508th after action reports.

6. Archer, *Paratrooper's Odyssey: A History of the 517 PCT,* p. 167; and interviews conducted by the author with former 517th battalion commanders.

Chapter 12: Germany

1. Dimensions of the Saar-Moselle triangle were referenced from MacDonald, *The Last Offensive,* pp. 117, 130.

2. "Report of Operations, 5th Ranger Battalion," 3/10/45.

3. 17th Airborne Division Summary of Operation VARSITY, p. 1.

4. "Operation ARENA: Headquarters XVIII Airborne Corps to CG FAA," 3/7/45; "SHAEF FWD," 3/12/45; "3/8/45 HQS FAAA Memo re: Airfields in Kassel Area."

5. "FAAA Operation ECLIPSE," 12/31/45; "SHAEF Outline of Airborne Plan," 1/9/45; "EFFECTIVE Memo to IX Troop Carrier Command," 4/20/45. Various references in F. Parks (Deputy Commander of FAAA) diary.

6. Blair, *Ridgway's Paratroopers,* p. 456, and calculation by the author. Several publications, including the official *U.S. Army History, The Last Offensive,* are incorrect and may be including troops in both airborne units that crossed the river a few days after the initial operation. In reference to the largest aerial and artillery bombardments: "FAAA Operation VARSITY," p. 13, 5/19/45, and MacDonald, *The Last Offensive,* p. 297.

7. The 17th Airborne alone lost 393 KIAs (Summary of Operation VARSITY, p. 8). (Breuer, in *Storming Hitler's Rhine,* lists losses in Normandy at 182 KIAs for the 101st

and 158 KIAs for 82nd). British airborne losses at VARSITY also exceeded their Normandy losses for the first day.

8. "17th Airborne Division, Summary of Operation VARSITY: Appendix: Drop Patterns 507"; "507 PIR Report of Operations," 4/45.

9. "17th Airborne Division Summary of Operation VARSITY: Appendix: Drop Patterns 513."

10. "17th Airborne Division, Summary of Operation VARSITY," p. 4

11. William Thompson and Theodore W. Parker, Jr., *Conquer: The Story of the Ninth Army* (Washington DC: Infantry Journal Press, 1947), p. 247.

12. Ibid, pp. 260–261; Blair, *Ridgway's Paratroopers,* p. 473.

13. It is worth noting that the 501st Parachute Infantry Regiment, attached for most of the war to the 101st Airborne Division, and the 508th, also technically only attached to the 82nd, were detached from the referenced divisions and began training for Operation JUBILANT to jump on POW camps. The operation never was executed.

14. MacDonald, *The Last Offensive,* p. 372.

15. F. Parks diary, several references; "FAAA Operation EFFECTIVE," 4/19; Bradley and Blair, *A General's Life,* pp. 430–431.

16. Gavin, *On To Berlin,* p. 288.

17. Blumenson, *The Patton Papers,* p. 669; Waters's letter to OCMH. It is worth noting that the first ambush occurred at Höllrich and not Hessdorf as reported in some accounts.

Methodology

1. Grele, *Envelopes of Sound: The Art of Oral History* (Chicago: Precedent Publishing Chicago, 1975), p. 3.

ACKNOWLEDGMENTS

I have many people to thank. I am deeply indebted to every veteran that took the time to share his experiences with me, including the hundreds of veterans that I was not able to include in this book.

I'd like to thank the following veterans as they appear in Beyond Valor: Bob Slaughter, Alex Szima, Lester Kness, Ed Furru, Bing Evans, Col. Edson Raff, Lieutenant General William Yarborough, Roland Rondeau, Robert Reed, Randall Harris, Col. Edwin Sayre, Al Ireland, Delbert Kuehl, Joe Watts, William Sullivan, Justin McCarthy, Don MacKinnon, Robert Kinney, Ken Markham, Carl Lehmann, Frank Mattivi, Charles Shunstrom, John Martin, Charles McKinney, John Schuetz, Walter Morris, Bradley Biggs, Carstell Stewart, Ted Lowry, Melvin Lester, Al Hassenzahl, Dutch Schultz, Judge Lynn Compton, Lieutenant General Julian Ewell, Sid Salomon, Ray and Audrey Alm, Dr. Frank South, Len Lomell, Major General John Raaen, Bill Reed, Reverend Clinton Riddle, Ed Jeziorski, Judge Francis Naughton, Stanley Clever, Jack Isaacs, Francis Lamoureux, Col. Louis Mendez, Robert Edlin, Reverend Herbert Morris, Walter Perkowski, Clark Archer, Lieutenant General Richard Seitz, Bill Leas, Frank Seto, Joe Cicchinelli, John Lissner, Harry Pritchett, Don Burgett, Sandy Santarsiero, Dr. John Hardie, Ray Gonzalez, Lee Travelstead, Glen Derber, Robert Bowen, William McMahon, Bill Meddaugh, Mel Biddle, Col. Robert Piper, Lieutenant General Harry Kinnard, Joe Lyons, Joe Tallett, Ernest Machamer, Col. Doug Dillard, Richard Durkee, Alex Andros, Ken Shaker, Bud Potratz, Bill and Rodney Petty, Herman Stein, Duaine Pinkston, Carl Kiefer, Joe Drodwell, John Burke, Harry Deaton, Don Frederick, Charles Newland, Jack Trovato, Bill Justis, Harry Herder, Carl Paul, Morris Webb. Special thanks needs to go to Dutch Schultz, John Burke, Joe Cicchinelli, Bing Evans, Reverend Delbert Kuehl, Lester Kness, and Sid Salomon, who aided me throughout this process.

Nearly every Veteran Association has an individual designated as the unit historian or officer; I relied on them heavily. They provided me invaluable references and often furnished me rare nuggets of information that are not found in official documents. I'd like to thank Charles Newland and Col. Jim Mrazek from the 13th Airborne, Joe Qaude, Bill Tom and Bart Hagerman from the 17th Airborne Division, Joe Tallett and Al Ireland of the 505th, Frank Varelli from the 504th , Clarence Hughart of the 507th, George Stoeckert of the 508th, Bill Ausenbaum of the 325th, Joe Murchison of the 555th and Jean Foster from the 907th. Charlie Doyle from the 509 was also a big help as was Gene Tennison of the 550th. 101st Historian George Koskimaki provided several key references. I'd also like to acknowledge former 101st Secretary, the late, Bill Carrington, one of the first to recognize the value of on-line oral history. Brigadier General Edward Thomas and John Dawson furnished leads and information on the 1st Special Service Force. From the Rangers, historian James Altieri provided several important references as did Len Lomell and Ranger Secretary Tom Herring. Jack Herzig from the 503rd provided editorial comments. Don Lassen, "Mr. Airborne" and the editor of the Static Line airborne newspaper, has done so much for the airborne community and also supported the Drop Zone www.thedropzone.org over the years. I'd like to acknowledge Gordon Sumner, National Director of the 82nd Airborne Division, a true leader and supporter of the Drop Zone. I'd also like to thank Clark Archer, unit historian for the 517th and a fountain of knowledge who graciously gave a paratrooper's eye to many of my chapter introductions.

I'm indebted to my close friend Carl Fornaris who was incredibly helpful throughout the entire process of putting together this book. His advice and keen historical insight led to important improvements to the text and the accompanying maps. I'm also indebted to my editors Bruce Nichols and Dan Freedberg for their vision and editorial excellence.

While the heart of this book is it's oral histories, a significant amount of time was spent reviewing the official documents and other primary source material. Therefore, I would like to extend my thanks to the archivists at the National Archives, in particular Wil Mahoney. The staff at the U.S. Army Military History institute also went above and beyond the call of duty. I specifically like to thank Dr. David Keogh.

Several folks also graciously furnished photos for this book: Joe Pangerl, Ed Benecke, Leslie Cruise, Don Frederick, E.W. Jones, Jon Gawne, Bradley Biggs, Hienrich Fugmann of the 6th Parachute Regiment. I'm also grateful to the staff at the National Archives and U.S. Military History Institute.

Finally, I'd also like to acknowledge the folks that over the years provided their time and assistance to the Drop Zone or helped this book along in various other important capacities: Gant Asbury, Peter Bostrom, Shawn Faherty, Tom Lombardo, Eric Minkoff, Dave Prim, Chris Robinson, Peter Sheingold, Mike Horn, Dave Campbell and Jeff Baron who helped me throughout course of this book. I'd like to thank Linda Zweibel and Therese Morin from PricewaterhouseCoopers. I am grateful to my agent Andy Zack at The Zack Company, Inc.

Finally, I'm indebted to my loving wife, Robyn, who was extremely helpful and supportive throughout this entire process, as was my beautiful daughter, Lily.

INDEX